The CISO's Next Frontier

Raj Badhwar

The CISO's Next Frontier

AI, Post-Quantum Cryptography
and Advanced Security Paradigms

 Springer

Raj Badhwar
Ashburn, VA, USA

ISBN 978-3-030-75356-6   ISBN 978-3-030-75354-2   (eBook)
https://doi.org/10.1007/978-3-030-75354-2

This Springer imprint is published by the registered company Springer Nature Switzerland AG
The registered company address is: Gewerbestrasse 11, 6330 Cham, Switzerland

This book is dedicated to the women in my life – to my deceased paternal grandmother, Agyawati Badhwar (Biji) for always being there for me; to my deceased mother, Saroj Badhwar (Mummy), who overcame a lot of personal and family strife while raising me (and my brother); to my deceased Aunt, Reeta Badhwar (Bua), who was instrumental in educating me and giving a professional purpose and direction to my life, my mother-in-law Jackie Meade who has accepted me into the family in spite of my many flaws; and to my multi-lingual wife, Michelle Badhwar, who helped edit most of the content for this book and has provided a lot of general guidance and support during the process of writing.

I would be remiss if I don't thank my daughter Noelle Badhwar and my son Neil Badhwar for providing me a bouncing off board into the Gen Z mindset and giving me a vision into how teenagers think about technology and security at the current time, and my (younger) brother Kanishka Badhwar (Monu) for all the support and encouragement he has given me all my life.

–Raj

Foreword

Enterprise agility has become the new operational ambition, the new IT mandate, and the new competitive differentiator. Technology, and specifically, the management and subsequent security of enterprise technology, is evolving to support that agility ideal. Nowhere is this more apparent than in the massive acceleration and adoption of cloud technology. The cloud has enabled a new way of work, one where employees enjoy direct connectivity, short-lived connections, and work-from-anywhere flexibility.

The cloud has fundamentally shifted how businesses drive initiatives and pursue goals. Moving applications, infrastructure, and assets to the cloud has allowed businesses to become more agile and more resilient in the face of market pressures and disruptions.

Cloud technology used to improve user experience, respond quickly to business needs, and "fail fast" has enabled progressive enterprises to employ the internet as the new corporate network and the cloud as the new corporate data center.

But how do you secure users, devices, and data in a cloud-first, device-agnostic, work-from-anywhere environment? Traditionally, company data was kept safe in the castle, behind a perimeter moat, protected by a complex boundary secured with expensive stacks of hardware appliances. But now data and connected users moves everywhere all the time, outside of the corporate castle, and onto the internet. Employees don't just access information and applications inside the perimeter—they work remotely and on the road. Applications sit in the cloud and communicate between public clouds. Digital workloads move between IoT sensors and operational systems. People now use devices other than corporate-issued desktops and laptops everywhere—at home, at hotels, on the road, in the air.

The new reality of work has stretched legacy security models past their breaking point, opening new doors for threat adversaries. The attacks have grown more frequent, more complex, and more targeted. As a result, today's CISOs must understand how cloud technology is changing the nature of enterprise security, and—just as importantly—how security must become an enabler of business development. For many years, these two goals seemed at odds. But they can (and must) come into alignment in progressive enterprises that prioritize agility.

Raj Badhwar's new book *The CISO's Next Frontier* offers a constructive blueprint for enterprise security transformation, giving progressive CISOs a roadmap for aligning security, IT, and business objectives. And ultimately, that's what's required to make a global enterprise successful.

Zscaler CEO, Chairman, and Founder   Jay Chaudhry
San Jose, CA, USA

Preface

Cyber risk has skyrocketed in the past decade. Every information technology-dependent business entity has become susceptible to a litany of attacks and breaches. Sophisticated malware attacks, threat actors with access to advanced hacking tools, insider threats, and persistent threats from nation states and other local and global criminal elements can all upend the operations and profits and services of a business and its clients. The Chief Information Security Officer (CISO), responsible for remediating, mitigating, or transferring the risk from these threats, must spearhead the implementation of the needed security controls, incident response, and business continuity and disaster recovery capabilities, with the foresight to plan for future security issues.

Let's discuss the title first – CISO's Next Frontier. Where anyone stands in relation to the "frontier" depends on both the moment in time as well as the geographical location and technological sophistication of their organization. In one sense, the frontier can be defined by future technologies which have not yet come into fruition, such as those related to quantum computing, advanced encryption or and unsupervised machine learning. With the uncertainty of when technology advancements may develop into immediate cyber threats, the future state of cybertechnologies is also highly relevant to the present work of the CISO. In another sense, as we navigate a frightening new frontier of cyberthreats, for which there are often no clearly defined geographical or, sometimes, technological boundaries, CISOs and their teams rely on an arsenal of continuously improving current state cyber technologies to secure their organizations.

Indeed, both "current" and "future" technologies are important to the daily work and considerations of today's CISOs, whose role has been largely shaped by the array of technologies they must embrace to deal with the ever-increasingly crowded constellation of threats in cyberspace.

Some of the topics covered here, such as post-quantum cryptography, homomorphic encryption, and unsupervised machine learning are really focused on a future state, simply because practical technologies in these areas are not yet fully developed and are not yet commonplace anywhere. This book also covers many topics within advanced application, cloud, device, and network security, which are continuously being enhanced and are essential to protecting organizations.

I have worked for some of the largest financial, insurance and security service providers in the world. In doing so I have acquired hands-on experience in almost all the security areas that I have covered in the book and I want to share that with my readers. I also want this book to convey the breadth of the multiple facets of evolving CISO leadership: the ability to manage up, working effectively with executive leadership and boards of directors; make a case for appropriate funding for the cyber security program; to manage down, building and maintaining a strong security team, hiring strong talent by leaving no stone of potential unturned; to work cross-functionally with IT and Risk peers; to help the firm win the market place by aiding business development; and, most importantly, to have the technological background for wise decision-making for appropriate cyber risk remediation while dealing with a complex incident, or for mergers and acquisitions. Seasoned CISOs are familiar with security engineering and operations, security architecture, incident response, fraud detection, cyber risk assessment, vulnerability management, and business continuity management, to assess the current deployments and make the necessary upgrades wherever required. They have capability to deal with legacy and existing threats, but also be able to plan for the future, and build protections against the advanced next-generation threats already here or just on the horizon. To be successful, to provide effective, successful leadership, the CISO needs to be adept in most of these fields, and that is only possible through years of hard work, inter-industry exposure, role rotation, and mentorship. The CISO must also pinpoint and fill in knowledge gaps. Hopefully, this book will provide guidance.

Why is such guidance so important? CISOs often come out of niche security backgrounds—perhaps their previous work focused on a single security area, whether engineering, architecture, or operations, or incident management and response, or cyber risk assessment and management, or perhaps they were in the military and focused on physical security and compliance with local, state of federal security, privacy, and compliance regulations. When stepping into a CISO role, there is often a significant learning curve in familiarizing oneself with security subfields. This book is intended to guide a new CISO through that learning curve. This book should also help other cybersecurity professionals specializing in one subfield identify areas for improvement and gain the background knowledge to solicit collaboration with their colleagues in other sub-fields.

This book is also intended for Information Technology leaders (e.g., CIO, CTO, CRO, CDO and CEO), to help them understand the role of security, as they must balance multiple, often competing demands of business efficiency and profitability with security-driven remediations and risk mitigations. It may help the executive leaders of public companies realize the need to have more CISOs join their boards of directors to help them better manage the remediation of the existential threat from sophisticated cyber attackers. It may also help boards of directors for public and private companies better understand the need to have more frequent engagement with CISOs, like they do with the other Business and IT leaders. Most importantly, informing Security and IT professionals and leaders in these broad areas, will place CISOs and their companies in a significantly better position to make risk-based choices to protect both the company and the clients they serve. There are also some chapters in here that talk about basic common sense security paradigms for the Non-IT professional, average consumer, and/or home user.

Will this book make the reader an expert in all the topics discussed? The short answer is – No. Instead, the reader will gain a view of security work from a CISO vantage point, raising general awareness of company-wide security concerns and learn about new aspects of security or cyber risk that may be unfamiliar to some. This book covers a wide variety of carefully selected topics of varying degrees of complexity brought to a uniform level that will be understood by the C-level, senior leaders, and individual contributors alike. Most of the topics are discussed using terms at least somewhat familiar to most cyber security and information technology professionals. However, for topics such as post-quantum cryptography, homomorphic encryption, or unsupervised machine learning, readers may encounter a few new cryptic terms. I have tried to simplify these topics to the best of my ability and also provide secure yet practical solutions to problems wherever possible. What this book will do is raise the reader's awareness and understanding of the range of security issues to be addressed to secure enterprise (and home) environments for today and the near future and advise on practical approaches and techniques.

The 'CISO Take' at the end of each chapter summarizes the CISO's point of view on the subject discussed, generally identifying a security improvement opportunity or elaborating on the steps needed to be secure in the next frontier. Each chapter also has definitions for all the cryptic terms and jargon that may be unfamiliar to many non cyber security folks.

Ashburn, VA, USA   Raj Badhwar

The cyber warfare in the trenches will be won by artificially intelligent security tools aided by advanced encryption and quantum-safe cryptosystems – Raj Badhwar (2021)

Acknowledgement

I would like to thank JP Jesan for helping me with some of the scripts in one of the cloud-security chapters, and Jay Chaudhry for writing the forward.

I would also like to thank Jesus (Laz) Montano, Tejas Jois, Gary Warzala, Jaynie Bunnell, Mahesh Natarajan, Dr. Howie Huang, Harbir Brar, Andy Bonillo and Vishal Salvi for reviewing the initial book proposal, and further taking time out of their busy schedules to respond back to the publisher with their feedback.

I should also thank Gus Ortega for the encouragement he provided and for introducing me to a publisher, and Steven Dick for introducing me to Springer.

Many thanks are also due to Susan Lagerstrom-Fife for bringing me up to speed on the finer points of the book publication process and Arun Siva Shanmugam for reviewing the text.

I must acknowledge my dear wife Michelle Badhwar, without her editing prowess and hard work, this book would not have been possible.

This book was mostly written during the 2020/21 Pandemic and I would like to take this opportunity to acknowledge the good work done by the cyber security professionals worldwide for working tirelessly to enable the secure work-from-home paradigm.

–Raj

Disclaimer

The views expressed and commentary provided in this book is strictly private and does not represent the opinions or work or the state of and/or implementations within the cyber-security or IT programs of my current or former employer(s). Any advice provided here must not be construed as legal advice. If you choose to follow any advice provided in this book, then you must do so at your own risk.

Contents

About the Author

Raj Badhwar has 25+ years of experience within the Cybersecurity and IT indus-try. He is currently the CISO for Voya Financial, and has previously held senior Security and IT leadership roles at AIG, BAE Systems Inc., Bank of America, Time Warner Cable, AOL Time Warner, and Sprint.

Raj is a currently a director and secretary of the board of the National Technology Security Coalition (NTSC). He also serves on the cybersecurity advisory boards of Pace University, Rutgers University, and Ithaca College; the customer advisory board for Venafi; and the CISO advisory council for Infosys.

Raj is a certified information systems security professional (CISSP), a certified ethical hacker (CEH), and a FINRA licensed securities professional (Series 99). He has co-authored 14 security patents, and has written and presented in the areas of advanced encryption, post-quantum cryptography, zero trust networks, cloud secu-rity patterns, and secure remote work paradigms. He has also been interviewed as a cybersecurity subject matter expert by WSJ. Raj is proficient in three languages, and conversant in another three languages.

Raj graduated from George Washington University (GWU) with an MS in Information Systems Technology and also holds a BS in Electrical and Electronics engineering from Karnatak University. Raj is an alumnus of St Francis College, Lucknow.

Raj can be contacted via his email rajb.ciso.mailbox@gmail.com or on his twit-ter handle @Cyber_Sec_Raj

Abbreviations

0-RTT	Zero Round-Trip Time
2PC	Two-phase commit protocol
3DES	Triple Data Encryption Algorithm
AAD	Azure Active Directory
AC	Access Control
ACK	Acknowledgement
ACL	Access Control List
AD	Active Directory
AES	Advanced Encryption Standard
AES 256	Advanced Encryption Standard 256
AET	Advanced Evasion Techniques
AI	Artificial Intelligence
ANQP	Access Network Query Protocol
AP	Access Point
AP	Application Protocol
API	Application programming Interface
API Gateway	Application programming interface gateway
API Key	application programming interface key
API Security	application programming interface security
APT	Advanced Persistent Threat
ARP	Address Resolution Protocol
ASD	Autism Spectrum Disorder
AV	Antivirus
AWS	Amazon Web Services
BCM	Business Continuity Management
BGP	Border Gateway Protocol
BN	Bayesian Network
BYOD	Bring Your Own Device
CA	Certificate Authority
CARTA	Continuous Adaptive Risk and Trust Assessment
CASB	Cloud Access Security Broker

CCA	Chosen Ciphertext Attack
CCPA	California Consumer Privacy Act
CDA	Crash Dump Analyzer
CDS	Cyber Deception System
CEP	Cyber Event Probability
CI/CD	continuous integration/continuous delivery
CISO	Chief Information Security Officer
CKKS	Cheon, Kim, Kim, and Song
CMDB	Configuration Management Database
CMMI	Capability Maturity Model Integration
CNC	Command and Control
CNN	Convolutional Neural Networks
COTS	Commercial off the Shelf
CPA	Chosen Plaintext Attack
CPEP	Cloud Policy Enforcement Point
CPRA	California Privacy Rights Act
CPU	Central Processing Unit
CRL	Certificate Revocation List
CSRF	Cross-site Request Forgery
CT	Certificate Transparency
CVE	Common Vulnerabilities and Exposures
CVP	Closest Vector Problem
CVSS	Common Vulnerability Scoring System
CWSS	Common Weakness Scoring System
CyVaR	Cyber Value-at-Risk
DANE	DNS-Based Authentication of Named Entities
DAST	Dynamic Application Security Testing
DBN	Deep Belief Networks
DC	Domain Controller
DCShadow	Domain Controller Shadow
DCSync	Domain Controller Sync
DDoS	Distributed Denial-of-Service
DGA	Domain Generation Algorithm
DH	Diffie-Hellman
DHS	Department of Homeland Security
DKIM	Domain Keys Identified Mail
DL	Deep Learning
DLL	Dynamic-link library
DLP	Data Loss Prevention
DMARC	Domain Message Authentication Reporting
DMZ	Demilitarized Zone
DN	Domain Name
DNS	Domain Name System
DNSSec	Domain Name System Security
DoH	DNS over HTTPS

DOQ	DNS over QUIC
DoS	Denial-of-Service
DOT	DNS over TLS
DPI	Deep Packet Inspection
DRM	Digital Rights Management
DTLS	Datagram Transport Layer Security
DX	Direct Connect
EC2	Elastic Compute Cloud
ECC	Elliptic Curve Cryptography
ECC	Error Correcting Code
ECDH	Elliptic-Curve Diffie-Hellman
ECDHE	Elliptic-Curve Diffie-Hellman Ephemeral
EDR	Endpoint Detection and Response
ELF	Executable and Linkable Format
EM	Expectation Maximization
EPR	Einstein Podolsky Rosen
ESAE	Enhanced Security Admin Environment
ESNI	Encrypted Server Name Indication
EVT	Extreme Value Theory
EXIF	Exchangeable Image File Format
FAIR	Factor Analysis of Information Risk
FFC	Finite Field Cryptography
FHE	Fully Homomorphic Encryption
FIPS	Federal Information Processing Standard
FQDN	Fully qualified domain name
FS	Forward Secrecy
FS-ISAC	Financial Services Information Sharing and Analysis Center
GAN	Generative Adversarial Networks
GCD	Greatest Common Divisor
GCF	Greatest Common Factor
GDPR	General Data Protection Regulation
GNFS	General Number Field Sieve
GPS	Global Positioning System
GPU	Graphical Processing Unit
GSW	Gentry, Sahai, and Waters
GT	Golden Ticket
HFE	Hidden Field Equations
HMAC	Hash-based method authentication code
HMM	Hidden Markov Model
HOIC	High Orbit Ion Cannon
HPKP	HTTP Public Key Pinning
HSM	Hardware Security Module
HTTP	Hypertext Transfer Protocol
HTTPS	Hypertext Transfer Protocol secure
HVMI	Hypervisor Memory Introspection

IaaS	Infrastructure as a Service
IAM	Identity and Access Management
ICANN	Internet Corporation for Assigned Names and Numbers
ICMP	Internet Control Message Protocol
IDS	Intrusion Detection System
IEEE 802.11	Institute of Electrical and Electronics Engineers 802.11
IETF	Internet Engineering Task Force
IKE	Internet Key Encryption
IOC	Indicators of Compromise
IOT	Internet of Things
IPS	Intrusion Prevention System
IPSec	Internet Protocol Security
IPv4	Internet Protocol version 4
IPv6	Internet Protocol version 6
IRC	Internet Relay Chat
ISO 27001	International Organization for Standardization 27001
ISO/IEC 19794	International Organization for Standardization/International Electrotechnical Commission
ISP	Internet Service Provider
IT	Information Technology
IV	Initialization Vector
JCL	Job Control Language
JSON	JavaScript Object Notation
JVM	Java Virtual Machine
JWT	JSON Web Token
KBA	Knowledge-Based Article
K-NN	K-Nearest Neighbors
KRBTGT	Kerberos Ticket Granting Ticket
L2TP	Layer 2 Tunneling Protocol
LAN	Local Area Network
LDA	Linear Discriminant Analysis
LDAP	Lightweight Directory Access Protocol
LM	LAN man
LOIC	Low Orbit Ion Cannon
LR	Logic Regression
LWE	Learning with Errors
MAC	Media Access Control
MAM	Media Asset Management
MCAS	Microsoft Cloud App Security
MD5	Message-Digest Algorithm
MDM	Mobile Device Management
MFA	Multi-Factor Authentication
MITM	Man-in-the-Middle
ML	Machine Learning
MPC	Multi-Party Computation

MPLS	Multiprotocol Label Switching
MVP	Minimum Viable Product
MVS	Multiple Virtual Storage
NAC	Network Access Control
NAS	Network-Attached Storage
NAT	Network Address Translation
NGAV	Next-Generation Antivirus
NGFW	Next-Generation Firewall
NIST	National Institute of Standards and Technology
NLP	Natural Language Processing
NN	Neural Network
NP	Non-deterministic Polynomial
NPI	Non-public information
NTLM	New Technology LAN Manager
NTP	Network Time Protocol
NTPSec	Network Time Protocol Security
NTRU	Nth Degree Truncated Polynomial Ring Units
NYDFS	New York State Department of Financial Services
OAUTH 2.0	Open Authorization 2.0
OCR	Optical Character Recognition
OCSP	Online Certificate Status Protocol
OEM	Original Equipment Manufacturer
OMS	Operations Management Suite
OOB	Out of Band
OPTH	Overpass the Hash
OSI	Open Systems Interconnection
OSS	Open-Source Software
OU	Organizational Unit
OWE	Opportunistic Wireless Encryption
PaaS	Platform as a Service
PAM	Privileged Access Management
PCI DSS	Payment Card Industry Data Security Standard
PFS	Perfect Forward Secrecy
PGP	Pretty Good Privacy
PHI	Protected Health Information
PII	Personally Identifiable Information
PKI	Public Key Infrastructure
PNS	Photon-Number-Splitting
PPTP	Point-to-Point Tunneling Protocol
PQC	Post-Quantum Cryptography
PRD	Pseudo-Randomness Detection
PSK	Pre-shared key
PTH	Pass the Hash
PTT	Pass the Ticket
QEC	Quantum Error Correction

QFT	Quantum Fourier Transform
QKD	Quantum Key Distribution
QKF	Quantum Key Flipping
QUIC	Quick UDP Internet Connection
RASP	Runtime Application Security Protection
RBM	Restricted Boltzmann Machine
RCA	Root Cause Analysis
RCE	Remote Code Execution
RDP	Remote desktop protocol
RDS	Relational Database Service
RF	Random Forest
RFC	Request for Comment
RIA	Raw Image Analyzer
RNG	Random Number Generator
RNN	Recurrent Neural Networks
RPA 2.0	Robotic Process Automation 2.0
RPC	Remote Procedure Call
RRSIG	Resource record signature
RSA	Rivest, Shamir, Adelman (public-key cryptosystem)
S3	Simple Storage Service
SaaS	Software as a Service
SAM	Security Account Manager
SAML	Security Assertion Markup Language
SAN	Storage area network
SASE	Secure Access Service Edge
SAST	Static application security testing
SBP	Shortest Basis Problem
SCCM	System Center Configuration Manager
SCP	Service Control Policy
SDK	Software Development Kit
SDN	Software-defined networking
SEAL	Simple Encrypted Arithmetic Library
SEC	Securities and Exchange Commission
Secoqc	Secure Communication based on Quantum Cryptography
SHA	Secure Hash Algorithm
SHA-1	Secure Hash Algorithms
SHA-3	Secure Hash Algorithms
SIDH	Super Singular Isogeny Diffie-Hellman
SIEM	Security Incident and Event Management
SIKE	Super singular Isogeny Key Encapsulation
SIVP	Shortest Independent Vector Problem
SKU	Stock Keeping Unit
SMB	Server Message Block
SMLI	Stateful Multi-Level Inspection
SNI	Server Name Indication

SNMP	Simple Network Management Protocol
SOC	Security Operations Center
SSDP	Simple Service Discovery Protocol
SSH	Secure Shell
SSL	Secure Sockets Layer
SSRF	Server Site Request Forgery
SSTP	Safeguard Socket Tunneling Protocol
ST	Silver Ticket
STEM	Science, Technology, Engineering, and Math
SVP	Shortest Vector Problem
TCP	Transmission Control Protocol
TDE	Transparent Data Encryption
TIA	TLS Intercept Application
TLS	Transport Layer Security
TLS 1.3	Transport Layer Security version 1.3
TTP	Tactics, Techniques, and Procedures
UBA	User Behavior Analytics
UDP	User Datagram Protocol
UEBA	User Entity Behavior Analytics
UEFI	Unified Extensible Firmware Interface
UPN	User Principal Name
USG	United States Government
VaR	Value at Risk
VDI	Virtual Desktop Infrastructure
VLAN	Virtual Local Area Network
VM	Virtual Machine
VMM	Virtual Machine Monitor
VOIP	Voice Over Internet Protocol
VPN	Virtual Private Network
WAF	Web Access Firewall
WAN	Wide Area Network
WEP	Wired Equivalent Privacy
WFH	Work from Home
WFP	Web Forward Proxy
WPA	WIFI Protected Access
WPA2	WIFI Protected Access 2
WPA3	WIFI Protected Access 3
WSL	Windows Subsystem for Linux
WSL2	Windows Subsystem for Linux 2
XACML	Extensible Access Control Markup Language
XSS	Cross-site Scripting
ZTA	Zero Trust Architecture
ZTX	Zero Trust Extended

Part I
Post Quantum Cryptography

Are You Ready for Quantum Computing?

1 Introduction

Quantum computing is on the horizon and it may change the computing scene as we know it. I am super excited by this advancement in technology, but as a security technologist I have also reviewed it from a threat lens. On the one hand, quantum computing will exponentially increase the computing power at our disposal, help solve many complex mathematical and IT problems, and also be a boon to medical, weather and space research. On the other hand, security technologists are worried about its supposed capability to break many of the encryption and hashing algorithms that are currently based on computational difficulty, raising concerns about the confidentiality and integrity of our sensitive (PII, PHI, NPI) data at rest and in transit. This has put renewed focus on advanced encryption. Post-quantum data encryption techniques have been discussed within a different chapter (2) in this book, but in the current chapter, I want to further explain what quantum computing is, how it differs from classical computing, and what real short- and long-term security threats it poses.

This chapter does not argue against the viability of quantum computing, but rather attempts to provide an introductory level understanding of the key differences between quantum and classical computing, in order to highlight the looming information security threat. With this in mind, cyber security professionals can start looking for tactical and strategic solutions to mitigate and remediate this risk if the perceived data security threats were to become real in the near (or distant) future.

R. Badhwar, *The CISO's Next Frontier*,
https://doi.org/10.1007/978-3-030-75354-2_1

2   Computational Difficulty

The term computational difficulty or complexity is generally used to portray the large amount of effort or time required by a computer to solve a difficult problem.

Problems are generally classified as "Class P" for which a polynomial function (algorithm) can provide a solution in (deterministic) polynomial time, or as "Class NP" where a solution cannot be found but if one exists then it can be verified quickly in polynomial time (where NP stands for Non-deterministic polynomial time).

The "Class NP" has further sub classifications:

1. NP-hard: problems that are *at least* as hard as the hardest problems in Class NP
2. NP-easy: problems that are *at most* as hard as Class NP
3. NP-complete: problems that are *the hardest* in Class NP

Problems that are classified as computationally difficult (i.e., NP-hard and NP-complete) are the ones that would be the most resistant to brute-force, factoring and search-based attacks by a quantum computer.

3   Classical Computing

In classical computing, the state of a (conventional) computer can be described by the sequence of (two-state) bits (0 or 1) or binary configurations of the individual transistors within the CPU or a storage device, e.g., a two-bit register at any given time can store any one of the (2^2) four binary states (00, 01, 10 or 11), thus with N transistors, there can be 2^N possible (binary) states at any given time.

Thus each 32-bit register can have 2^{32} (i.e., 4,294,967,296) and each 64-bit register can have 2^{64} (i.e., 18,446,744,073,709,551,616) binary states at any given time (e.g., the Intel Core i7 processors have eight registers in 32-bit mode and 16 registers in 64-bit mode, theoretically giving it the capability to store a very large number of binary states).

Currently the industry relies upon encryption to protect sensitive data. Data encrypted with industry standard encryption algorithms (e.g., AES 256) is very safe from malicious and unauthorized decryption because of the sheer length of time it would take a malicious actor to perform a brute force attack.

Let's do some math below. To convey the enormity of the numbers involved here, I am not going to show the numbers as base 10 or base e.

The table below (Fig. 1) shows the number of combinations for AES for each key size in bits.

As of January 20, 2019 [1], the fastest super computer (Summit, unveiled by the US Department of Energy and IBM in mid-2018) had a performance of 200 petaflops, or 200,000 trillion calculations per second = 200 × 1,000,000,000,000,000

Number of flops required (floating point operations per second) per calculation = 750; Number of seconds in one year = 365 × 24 × 60 × 60 = 31,536,000

Key Size	Possible Combinations
1	2
2	4
4	16
8	256
16	65,536
32	4,294,967,296
64	18,446,744,073,709,551,616
128	340,282,366,920,938,463,463,374,607,431,768,211,456
256	115,792,089,237,316,195,423,570,985,008,687,907,853,269,984,665,640,564,039,457,584,007,913,129,639,936
512	13,407,807,929,942,597,099,574,024,998,205,846,127,479,365,820,592,393,377,723,561,443,721,764,030,073,546,976,801,874,298,166,903,427,690,031,858,186,486,050,853,753,882,811,946,569,946,433,649,006,084,096

Fig.1 AES Combinations

Given the number of possible combinations of the AES 256-bit key, it will still take a very long time:

*Number of Years to **crack AES** with 256-bit key* = 115,792,089,237,316,195,423,570,985,008,687,907,853,269,984,665,640,564,039,457,584,007,913,129,639,936/(31536000 × 200 × 1000000000000000 / 750) = 13,769,036,486,553,010,304,000,072,217,229,946,337,090,912,349,593,893,076 **years** *(using the world's fastest computer as of 2019).*

This is a very large number, showing the enormity of the (Class NP) problem and the infinitely large amount of time it would take for a traditional computer to breach AES 256.

4   Quantum Computing

In quantum computing, the two-state (0 or 1) bit within each transistor is replaced by an entity called the qubit (quantum bit), which also has two states and is the physical carrier of quantum information. Although other subatomic particles could also be used, the most basic particle - the electron - can serve as a qubit where its intrinsic angular momentum, or spin (+1/2 aka spin-up, or − 1/2 aka spin-down), can be used to measure its state (0 or 1) generally represented as |0⟩or |1⟩. In addition, in compliance with the quantum law of superposition, an electron can simultaneously exhibit both (spin-up and spin-down) states: a quantum computing system comprising two qubits can have (2^2) four states (spin-up, spin-up; spin-up, spin-down; spin-down, spin-up; spin-down, spin-down); thus, with N qubits it can have 2^N states *simultaneously.*

The difference in these computing models is that while an N-bit register in a conventional computer can store only one of N binary configurations at any given time, an N-qubit register can store all the N states simultaneously.

Thus, a quantum computer with even 500 qubits can have 2^500 (3,273,390,60 7,896,141,870,013,189,696,827,599,152,216,642,046,043,064,789,483,291,36 8,096,133,796,404,674,554,883,270,092,325,904,157,150,886,684,127,560,07 1,009,217,256,545,885,393,053,328,527,589,376) simultaneous states. This is very large number and it gets infinitely larger as the number of qubits increases, making it an extremely powerful computer.

Concerns have been raised about the possibility that error resolution with this many numbers of states could become a problem and render the quantum computer unusable. However, the quantum error-correction (QEC) techniques elaborated by Peter Shor, by which a quantum error correcting code can be created to store the information of one qubit onto a highly entangled state of four and nine qubits, demonstrates that this is not an issue [2, 3].

Theoretically speaking, an exponential increase in computing power (the kind being theorized with the advent of the quantum computer) could drastically reduce the time it would take to compromise an encryption scheme based on mathematical difficulty, such as RSA.

Practically speaking, even if a quantum computer with 2500 qubits were possible, it may take at least 5 years (or more) to achieve. Currently Google has created a quantum computer with 72 qubits and IBM has announced one with 50 qubits. We still have some time to figure out our post-quantum data security paradigms!

The Quantum Advantage
So far, we have generally talked about the superior computing ability of a quantum computer. We will quantify those advantages further.

A quantum computer has two primary advantages over a classical computer:

(a) Its superior speed of performing unstructured search
(b) Its capability to perform faster factoring of semi-primes

4.1 Unstructured Search

The capability for a quantum computer to perform faster unstructured searches has been demonstrated by Grover's algorithm.

This algorithm has been shown to speed up an unstructured search problem quadratically, but it can also be used to provide quadratic run time improvements to other search algorithms.

To search an element × in an unstructured data list of N items or search domain, a classical search algorithm would need to search from N/2 to N elements.

The same search by a quantum computer could be conducted by conducting $\sqrt{N}$ steps using Grover's algorithm built on amplitude amplification.

This algorithm can find an item for a search domain with N items with a max number of evaluations of

$$O\left(\sqrt{N}\right),$$

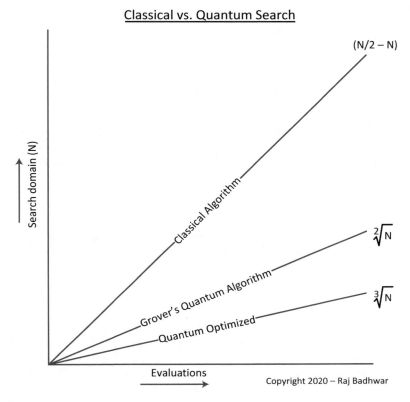

Classical vs. Quantum Search

Fig. 2

where O is the Big O notation and can be considered as a constant for the sake of simplicity for our purposes.

Further improvements have shown that a quantum computer can perform the same search for a domain with N items using a max number evaluation of

$$\left(O\sqrt[3]{N} \right),$$

This would allow the quantum computer to solve problems that are considered NP-hard in polynomial time, much faster than it would take a classical computer. (See Fig. 2).

4.2   *Runtime and Complexity of Factoring*

We begin by asserting that at the current time there is no known algorithm that can factor all known large integers, especially the semi-primes, in polynomial time, making this a class NP problem.

If an integer N with m digits needs to be factored:

(a) A potential basic algorithm could go through all primes number p up to $\sqrt{N}$ to check if p divides N, taking a max runtime of –

$$e^{(O(m))}$$

.

(b) A more efficient algorithm (known as the quadratic sieve) attempts to use integers a, b such that $a^2- b^2$ is a multiple of N. Once each of the numbers a, b is found, they are then checked to find common factors with N by doing $a \pm b$ with a runtime of –

$$e^{(O(m^{1/2}))}$$

(c) A more current and state-of-the-art algorithm is the general number field sieve (GNFS). This has been used with good success on large numbers and has a runtime of –

$$e^{(O(m^{1/3}))}$$

where O is the Big O notation and can be considered as a constant for the sake of simplicity for our purposes, and $e^{(x)}$ the basic *exponential* function (also expressed as exp.(x)), sometimes referred to as the exponential function $f(x)= e^{(x)}$ is the power to which e must be raised to obtain x. The number e sometimes called the Euler's number, is an important mathematical constant approximately equal to 2.718281828459045.

It is obvious from these three basic representations of rather complex equations that however sophisticated a classical algorithm may be, the *time* it requires to factor large semi-primes grows exponentially outside the bounds of polynomial time as the numbers (x) get larger. See Fig. 3 for more details [5].

4.3   *Factoring Methods*

The previous section primarily talks about the exponential relationship between the runtime and the size of a semi-prime being factored, using classical algorithms.

The actual factoring of large semi-prime polynomials is a complex subject and while the full mathematical treatment of it is outside the scope of this book, a simplified approach applying the concepts of greatest common factor (GCF) from Euclid's Theorem and period-finding using Euler's Theorem can be used to find the two non-distinct prime factors for a given number N.

Factorization

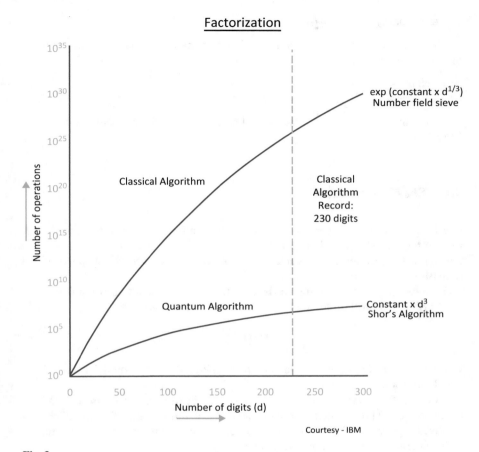

exp (constant x d$^{1/3}$)
Number field sieve

Classical Algorithm

Classical
Algorithm
Record:
230 digits

Number of operations

Quantum Algorithm

Constant x d^3
Shor's Algorithm

Number of digits (d)

Courtesy - IBM

Fig. 3

Given co-prime numbers N and a, the smallest positive integer r such that $a^r - 1$, is a multiple of N, then r is called the *period* of a *modulo* N, and the remainder of a/N is called the *value* of a modulo of N and denoted as a *(mod N)*.

If N = p1.p2 {where p1 and p2 are 2 distinct prime (factors) for N that we are trying to find}

The *GCF* can be calculated using Euclid's, Lehmer's, or the binary GCD algorithm.

Using Euclid's theorem:

GCF of N = (p1, p2);

But since we don't know either *p1* or *p2*, we can find GCF of N and an integer *a* where $2 \leq a \leq N\text{-}1$ and find the period of modulo N (i.e., r), where r is found using Euler's totient theorem (φ) which states if n and a are coprime positive integers then a raised to power of the totient of n is equal to 1 modulo n.

$a^{\varphi(n)} \equiv 1 \bmod(n)$, thus $r = \varphi(n)$.

Given $a^r - 1 = (a^{r/2} - 1)(a^{r/2} + 1)$, if r is odd then start again with another value of a; if r is even, then

$p1 = (N, a^{r/2} - 1)$
$p2 = (N, a^{r/2} + 1)$

Some of the other equations like Fermat's method can also be used for factorization.

4.4 Shor's Algorithm

It is a quantum computing polynomial-time algorithm [4] that states that the 'factoring' problem can be solved exponentially faster on a quantum computer, than by the best known (equivalent) classical algorithm running on a classical computer with a transistor-based central processing unit (CPU).

If an integer N with m digits needs to be factored by a quantum computer:
Per Shor's algorithm, the runtime required to factor N will be

$$\left(O\left(m^3 \right) \right);$$

where O is the Big O notation and can be considered as a constant for the sake of simplicity for our purposes.

Note that the time required to 'factor' large semi-prime increases linearly and not exponentially. Thus, with a sufficient number of qubits, this 'factoring' can be achieved in polynomial-time, making this a class N problem for a quantum computer.

The number of qubits required will be

$$10m;$$

The factorization of a large number by a quantum computer also uses the concept of periodicity (i.e., period-finding), similar to the approach taken by the classical computer. Shor's algorithm uses Quantum Fourier Transform (QFT) to exploit the quantum parallelism and constructive interference to detect and measure the periodicity of a modular exponentiation function [5].

Similar as before, given co-prime numbers N and a, the intent is to calculate r, the *period* of a modulo N. This is done by constructing a unitary operation that implements the modular multiplication function $f(x) \rightarrow a^x \bmod N$ solved by QFT in a quantum computer by making use of quantum gates.

4.5   Quantum Gates

A quantum gate is a basic unit of quantum programing. Unlike a classical logic gate, the operators in a quantum gate must be reversible, i.e., the input and output must have the same number of qubits.

Hadamard (H) gate   This gate acts on a single qubit and can transform a given qubit to either $|0\rangle$ or $|1\rangle$.

Pauli Gates   These gates also act on a single qubit.

(a) The X gate switches the amplitude of the $|0\rangle$ and $|1\rangle$ basis by rotating the vector along the X axis.
(b) The Y gate rotates the vector along the Y axis.
(c) The Z gate rotes the vector by π along the Z axis (i.e., Φ by π).

Phase Shift Gates   These gates rotate the vector around the Z axis.

(a) The Z gate changes its phase by a rotation of π.
(b) The S gate changes the phase by $\pi/2$ rotation around the Z axis.
(c) The T gate changes the phase by $\pi/4$ rotation around the Z axis.

5   The CISO Take

Data protection is one of the key tenets of cyber security. Most of the data security paradigm is built upon mathematical algorithms and computational difficulty involving hard problems.

The mathematical algorithms discussed in this chapter demonstrate how current cryptosystems protect data by relying on mathematical algorithms which are computationally difficult by classical computing standards but will be threatened by the superior computing power of future quantum computing, which will put all current and future data at rest and in transit at risk of exposure.

CISOs are cyber security practitioners and preachers, and they must take appropriate steps to recognize this threat and build in the needed mitigations with a sense of urgency. They must ensure that tactical solutions are in place to provide the protections if they are needed in the near future, while they continue to work with cryptographers and other security engineers to implement the strategic post-quantum cryptosystems described in this book. They must ensure that these new cryptosystems are hardened and free of backdoors, and other known vulnerabilities and weaknesses. They must also work towards creating solutions that would make these new cryptosystems practical to use and backwards compatible, so that all existing data encrypted with the legacy schemes can be ported to and protected using the new cryptosystems without creating any service disruptions.

CISOs must use their bully pulpit to ensure that other senior business and IT leaders are aware of this impending security threat and obtain their concurrence and support, as well as the funding to work towards the implementation of tactical mitigations and strategic remediations.

6 Definitions

AES stands for Advanced Encryption Standard. It is a specification for a symmetric block cipher accepted globally as the standard to protect classified and sensitive information.

Co-prime is a set of numbers with no other common factor other than 1.

Euclid's (first) Theorem states that an even number is a perfect number (one which is a sum of its divisors (e.g., $6 = 3 + 2 + 1$) *if and only if* (2^{p-1}) $(2^p - 1)$ where p is a prime; [e.g., (2^{2-1}) $(2^2-1) = 2.3 = 6$].

Euclid's (second) Theorem is called the theorem of infinitude of primes and states that the number of primes is infinite.

Euclid's Algorithm is a mathematical technique to enable a quick way of finding the greatest common denominator (GCD) of two integers. This is also known as the greatest common factor (GCF).

Euler's Theorem states that if n and a are coprime numbers (i.e., a set of numbers with no other common factor other than 1) then a raised to the power of the totient n is identical to 1 modulo n, i.e., $a^{\varphi(n)} \equiv 1 \bmod(n)$.

Exponential Time this is the run-time that increases by a factor similar to the size of the input as the same is increased, i.e., c^n (where n is the input and c is a constant).

Fermat's Method is based on the representation of an odd integer as the difference of two squares. For an integer n, b can be represented as: $n = a^2 - b^2 = (a + b)(a - b)$, where $(a + b)$ and $(a-b)$ are the factors of the number n.

General Number Field Sieve is the currently the most efficient (and the fastest) classical algorithm to factor very large numbers (i.e., $n > 10^{100}$).

Lehmer's GCD is a more efficient and faster algorithm to calculate the greatest common divider (for larger integers), as compared to Euclid's GCD algorithm.

Modulo it is simply the remainder after a division operation.

NPI stands for Nonpublic Personal Information. It is very similar but distinguished from PII as the information that is not available to members of the public (e.g., some data assets contain data only available for internal use by federal government [3], or data provided by a consumer to a financial institution, including but not limited to banks, insurance companies, credit card processors etc.).

PHI stands for Protected Health Information. It is the personal health information of patients that is held by medical institutions, doctor and pharma houses, and insurance providers, that is federally protected against unauthorized use and disclosure.

Polynomial Time this is the run-time that increases by a constant factor (mathematically as a polynomial function) when the input to an algorithm is increased, i.e., n^c (where n is the input and c is a constant, e.g., n^2).

PII (Personally Identifiable Information) Any representation of information that permits the identity of an individual to whom the information applies to be reasonably inferred by either direct or indirect means. Further, PII is defined as information: (i) that directly identifies an individual (e.g., name, address, social security number or other identifying number or code, telephone number, or email address) or (ii) by which an agency intends to identify specific individuals in conjunction with other data elements, i.e., indirect identification [6].

Quadratic Sieve is currently the most efficient (and the second fastest) classical algorithm to factor small(er) numbers (i.e., $n < 10^{100}$).

Quantum Circuit is a computational model used in quantum computing where the computation is done using quantum gates.

Quantum Gate is a basic quantum circuit that operates on qubits (quantum bits).

Qubit is the physical carrier of quantum information.

Semi-prime is a number that is the product of two prime numbers.

Totient (function) φ **(n)** for a number n, the totient function returns the number of positive integers that are co-prime to n and less than n. $[\varphi (n) = n (1-1/p1)(1-1/p2)\dots]$, e.g., $\varphi (20) = 20 (1-1/2)(1-1/5) = 8$ integers, which would be 1, 3, 7, 9, 11, 13, 17, 19.

References

1. Singleton M (2018) The world's fastest supercomputer is back in America. Available via The Verge, Voxmedia. https://www.theverge.com/circuitbreaker/2018/6/12/17453918/ibm-summit-worlds-fastest-supercomputer-america-department-of-energy. Accessed 2 Dec 2020

2. Shor PW (1995) Scheme for reducing decoherence in quantum computer memory. https://www.cs.miami.edu/home/burt/learning/Csc670.052/pR2493_1.pdf. Accessed 2 Dec 2020.
3. Devitt SJ et al (2013) Quantum error correction for beginners. Rep. Prog. Phys. 76 076001. doi: https://doi.org/10.1088/0034-4885/76/7/076001
4. Shor PW (1994) Polynomial-time algorithms for prime factorization and discrete logarithms on a quantum computer. SIAM J Comput, 26(5), 1484–1509. doi: https://doi.org/10.1137/S0097539795293172
5. Cross A (ed) A field guide to quantum computing. In: Learn quantum computing with Circuit Composer. Available via IBM Quantum Experience. https://quantum-computing.ibm.com/docs/iqx/guide/shors-algorithm Accessed 2 Dec 2020
6. US Department of Labor. Guidance on the Protection of Personal Identifiable Information. https://www.dol.gov/general/ppii. Accessed 22 Nov 2020

Further Reading

Ambainis A (2004) Quantum search algorithms. SIGACT News, 35 (2):22–35.
Bennett et al. (1997) Strengths and weaknesses of quantum computing. SIAM J Comput 26(5):1510–1523. doi: https://doi.org/10.1137/S0097539796300933.
Castelvecchi D (2020) Quantum-computing pioneer warns of complacency over Internet security. Nature 587:189. https://www.nature.com/articles/d41586-020-03068-9. Accessed 22 Nov 2020.
Cross A (ed) A field guide to quantum computing. In: Learn quantum computing with Circuit Composer. Available via IBM Quantum Experience. https://quantum-computing.ibm.com/docs/iqx/guide/. Accessed 2 Dec 2020
Cross A (ed) Figure 3 enhanced from A field guide to quantum computing. In: Learn quantum computing with Circuit Composer. Available via: IBM Quantum Experience. https://quantum-computing.ibm.com/docs/iqx/guide/. Accessed 22 Nov 2020
Grover LK (1996) A fast quantum mechanical algorithm for database search. STOC '96: Proceedings of the twenty-eighth annual ACM symposium on Theory of Computing July 1996, pp 212–219 https://doi.org/10.1145/237814.237866
Grover LK (1999) Quantum computing. The NY Acad Sci 39(4):24–30. https://doi.org/10.1002/j.2326-1951.1999.tb03700.x
Hardy GH and Wright EM (1979) An introduction to the theory of numbers, 5, Oxford University Press, London.
Trevisan L (2012) Stanford University – CS259Q: Quantum Computing Handout 8. https://people.eecs.berkeley.edu/~luca/quantum/lecture08.pdf. Accessed 2 Dec 2020
US Department of Health and Human Services (2013) What is PHI? https://www.hhs.gov/answers/hipaa/what-is-phi/index.html. Accessed 22 Nov 2020

The Need for Post-Quantum Cryptography

1 Introduction

When I talk about post-quantum cryptography, people ask, "Why do we even need it now?" Here is my response:

We need post-quantum cryptography now because there will be a day in the future when cybersecurity professionals will face the fallout predicted by Shor's algorithm (additional details in Sect. 4.4 in Chap. 1), in which quantum computers will have the theoretical capability to break or brute force all encryption and hashing algorithms dependent on the degree of computational difficulty of factoring or of discrete logarithms in our pre-quantum world.

Although post-quantum computers may seem like a future problem, there are compelling reasons to work toward solutions today. First, due to mathematical complexity, it takes time to research, design and develop post quantum cryptographic algorithms, and then subsequently implement associated (post-quantum) cryptosystems designed to prevent quantum attacks. As changes are incremental, our enhancements to existing algorithms should be sufficient to handle attacks from less powerful quantum computers. Secondly, we can start encrypting data sets with effective quantum-resistant encryption technologies available today. Thirdly, if we start encrypting newer data sets with enhanced algorithms shown to be quantum-resistant, then we will have less data to protect or encrypt in the future, when attacks are imminent.

The real question is, "How do we find the algorithms appropriate for the post-quantum world?" This is what we will address below. Cryptographers and other security technologists around the world are working proactively to improve existing crypto mechanisms and also to find alternative mechanisms of encryption resistant to attacks from quantum computers.

R. Badhwar, *The CISO's Next Frontier*,
https://doi.org/10.1007/978-3-030-75354-2_2

For existing crypto schemes, one enhancement is the creation of DH (Diffie-Hellman) replacement with forward secrecy (FS) using the properties of super-singular elliptic curves.

Another option may be to increase the key size of existing algorithms (e.g., AES).

Some of the NEW schemes being looked at are lattice, code, and hash-based cryptographies, as well as multivariate cryptography.

Another option suggested is to employ an encryption cascading or cascade ciphering scheme using existing ciphers.

There are some other interesting possibilities discussed in this chapter.

2   Basic Encryption Concepts

Before we discuss encryption schemes to address post-quantum environments, let's review the basic concepts and existing techniques of encryption developed within our existing pre-quantum environment.

2.1   Symmetric-Key Encryption

For symmetric-key encryption, cryptographic algorithms are based on a shared secret, or a key. The same crypto key which first encrypts the plaintext data subsequently decrypts the ciphertext data.

While this scheme works very well in protecting the data, the major issue with this scheme is that both the sender and receiver of a message must have access to the shared secret (key). Practically speaking, because the sender must provide the shared secret to the receiver using asynchronous secure channels, this presents inherent challenges in maintaining key confidentiality.

2.2   Asymmetric-Key Encryption

Asymmetric-key encryption schemes were developed to overcome the limitations of symmetric encryption.

This encryption scheme uses a key-pair, made up of a public key available to anyone who needs it, and a private key available only to the sender/owner. A given plaintext message encrypted with the public key requires the private key to decrypt it back to its original form from the cyphertext. This provides the capability to maintain the confidentiality and assert the integrity of the message.

The same scheme can also be used to validate the authenticity of the message sender/owner by encrypting the message with the owner's private key and relying on the fact that only the public key for that public/private key pair can decrypt that message. This is also called a providing a non-repudiation service for the owner, generally implemented through the concept of digital certificates.

2.3 Computational Difficulty

The term computational difficulty or complexity is generally used to portray the large amount of effort or time required by a computer to solve a difficult problem (e.g., factoring a (large) prime number).

Problems are generally classified as "Class P" for which a polynomial function (algorithm) can provide a solution in (deterministic) polynomial time, or as "Class NP" where a solution cannot be found but if one exists then it can be verified quickly in polynomial time (where NP stands for Non-deterministic polynomial time).

The "Class NP" has further sub classifications:

NP-hard: problems that are at least as hard as the hardest problems in Class NP.
NP-easy: problems that are at most as hard as Class NP.
NP-complete: problems that are the hardest in Class NP.

2.4 Public Key Infrastructure (PKI)

Asymmetric-key encryption techniques have been used to develop the PKI cryptosystems which rely on the fact that it is not possible to decrypt an encrypted message by just knowing the ciphertext and the public key.

One of the most commonly used PKI cryptosystems is RSA. An explanation of the mathematical basis of RSA will give the reader a better understanding of the inner workings of PKI.

Like most PKI systems, RSA relies on the fact that factoring of a prime number that is a product of two large primes is very difficult. For example, it is easy to check that 397 and 661 can multiply to 262,417 but it is not very easy to try to find factors for 262,417. The problem gets exponentially harder with bigger prime numbers.

In RSA, the public key is generated by multiplying two large prime numbers p & q and the private key is generated making use of modular arithmetic, Euler's (Fermat's) theorem and Euler's totient function that take p and q as inputs. This is a class NP problem where one could easily verify (using basic multiplication) the large prime if one knew the values of p & q but cannot easily determine the factors of the prime number pq. The message is encrypted using the public key (pq) and then decrypted by the receiver using the private key.

The intent of the explanation here is to provide some insight into the inner workings of these cryptosystems, but also, to highlight the fact that while the factoring of a large prime number to help determine the private key for a given PKI cryptosystem may be computationally difficult for our current modern computers,

Shor's algorithm shows this is no longer the case with the exponentially higher parallel computing capability of quantum computers. (Additional details on Shor's algorithm have been provided in Sect. 4.4 in Chap. 1).

We thus need to discover and use other encryption algorithms and cryptosystems resistant to brute force attacks from quantum computers.

3   Enhancing Existing Cryptographic Schemes

The section discusses the various existing cryptographic schemes that can be enhanced and made quantum resistant.

3.1   Diffie-Hellman (DH)

Although RSA is the dominant PKI algorithm, the Diffie-Hellman cryptographic protocol originally discovered in 1976 is another secure public-key protocol available for secure data transfer. This protocol involves the establishment and exchange of a shared secret (key) using the multiplicative group of integers modulo p (where p is a prime number) over an insecure (public) channel. The shared secret (key) is then used to securely encrypt and transmit data between a sender and receiver.

Diffie-Hellman supports perfect forward secrecy (PFS) by providing the capability to establish a new and different secret key for every session. PFS protects past sessions against future compromises of session or secret keys.

Attacks
The Diffie-Hellman (DH) key exchange is known to be vulnerable to man-in-the-middle attacks which allow an attacker to gain unauthorized access to a message or alter the message. This defeats the confidentiality and integrity of the message and the system trying to protect the message. DH is also vulnerable to precomputation attacks, which allow a one-time computation against a multiplicative group of integers to be used to attack all subsequent key negotiations for the same group.

3.2   Elliptic-Curve Diffie-Hellman (ECDH)

The multiplicative group of integers modulo is not safe from brute force cryptanalytic attacks from a quantum computer. The DH algorithm can be made quantum resistant by using an elliptic-curve public and private key pair to establish the shared secret, which is then used to encrypt data within a session using a symmetric key cipher (e.g., AES). The elliptic-curve cryptography (ECC) used in this scheme is based on a set of non-singular elliptic curves over finite fields.

ECDH also supports PFS (by using ECDHE), thereby providing the capability to provide protection against future compromises of session or secret keys.

Attacks
Since ECDH uses ECC and not the multiplicative group of integers modulo which precomputation exploits, its susceptibility to precomputation attacks is greatly reduced.

3.2.1   Elliptic-Curve Diffie-Hellman Ephemeral (ECDHE)

This is an optimization over ECDH where an (ephemeral) key exchange enables the use of a distinct DH key for every handshake and is the key factor in the enablement in perfect forward secrecy (PFS).

One thing to point out is that ECDHE is computationally more intense and may lead to performance impacts. Also, the ephemeral keys are temporary and generally not authenticated, necessitating the need for alternate means (e.g., by using RSA) to perform authentication.

3.3   Super Singular Isogeny Diffie-Hellman (SIDH)

The multiplicative group of integers modulo is not safe from brute force and cryptanalytic attacks from a quantum computer, making both DH and ECDH susceptible to quantum attacks. The DH group of algorithms can be made quantum safe by implementing a SIDH algorithm, which relies on a secret key exchange derived from the isogeny between super singular (elliptic) curves.

Isogenies are used to study the theory and properties of elliptic curves. They are used in algorithms for point counting on elliptic curves and in computing class polynomials for the complex multiplication (CM) method [10].

Attacks
SIDH has been found to be vulnerable to zero-value side channel attacks and other attacks that use the claw finding problem.

3.4   Cascade Ciphering

This is the process to encrypt an already encrypted message, another one or two times, using either the same or a different encryption algorithm. This scheme was initially used with symmetric encryption but has also been used successfully with asymmetric encryption.

Best practices dictate that irrespective of whether the algorithms are the same or different, the keys used for each cipher must be different. Also, the ciphers must use different Initialization Vectors (IV).

Although multiple encryption levels of cascades are theoretically possible, for the sake of performance and practicality, generally a rule of two is followed to perform an outer and an inner layer of encryption using different ciphers.

Although this technique remains vulnerable to meet-in-the-middle attacks and doubles the size of the ciphertext, the availability of faster processors and use of computing concepts like parallel processing makes cascade ciphering a lot more feasible and practical to use.

Although a lot more performance benchmarking and penetration testing needs to be performed to recommend this for mainstream use, this technique can reduce the capability of a quantum computer to brute force the decryption of sensitive data.

Attacks

This scheme is known to be vulnerable to meet-in-the-middle attacks, where an attacker can gain access to intermediate ciphertext and key values from (block cipher) encryption/decryption operations and use them to conduct brute forces attacks to break the encryption and obtain the plaintext.

3.5   Increase Key Size of Existing Algorithms

It has been suggested by some security technologists that increasing the key size of existing cryptographic algorithms would make them quantum-resistant or quantum-safe, and prevent the brute forcing of the given algorithm.

Since AES is one of the most secure encryption algorithms available at the current time, it would make a good candidate to be strengthened further.

Rijndael, the actual cryptographic algorithm on which AES is based, would need to be modified and tested to allow for bigger key sizes of 376 or 512 bits. Currently it only allows for the processing of a data block of 128 bits with a maximum value of 256 bits, and a cipher key (k) with a length of 128, 192, and 256 bits $\{k \in 128, 192, 256\}$.

So, there are 2 options available:

(a) The first and easy option is to increase the data block size to 256 bits and continue to use a key size of 256 bits. This makes the encryption/decryption process computationally more intense and expensive.
(b) The second and more difficult option is to increase the key size (length) to 376 or 512. Some work on this scheme has already been done, e.g., the Rijndael-based Kayla, a 512-bit key cipher, has been implemented and is being used as a standard in Ukraine.

Attacks

Currently there are no known effective cyber-attacks on AES 256. Also, the cyber risks from the proposed increases of the data block or key size increases are currently unknown. There aren't any known attacks on Kayla, but it has not yet been subjected to extensive testing by NIST and has not been FIPS (140–2) validated.

3.6 Increase Number of Rounds of Existing Algorithms

Apart from increasing the size of the cipher keys or blocks, another scheme that has been suggested is to increase the number of transformation rounds that convert the input (plaintext) into encrypted (ciphertext) text for data encryption, and convert the ciphertext back into plaintext for decryption using the same cipher key.

AES has been tested and validated with the following standard:

1. AES-128/10 rounds
2. AES-192/12 rounds
3. AES-256/14 rounds

Suggestions have been made by some cryptographers to increase the number of rounds for AES-256 from 14 to 28 rounds in an attempt to improve its inherent security. This would be a fundamental change to AES and although theoretically it may become stronger, it would have to be tested for feature-set, functionality, and performance, as part of a comprehensive validation by NIST. This would also have to be penetration tested by cyber security professionals. Another side effect would be the performance issues and other unknown issues if new subkeys are not introduced for the additional rounds.

Another proposal is to combine both the schemes mentioned above, i.e., increase the key size and also double the number of rounds.

Attacks

Currently the cyber risks from the proposed transformation round increases are unknown. There are no known attacks or weaknesses that have been presented for these proposed enhancements.

3.7 Other Existing Options – Sponge Functions

A class of existing algorithms called sponge functions is being investigated by cryptographers and mathematicians for their use as quantum-safe algorithms. These functions acting like a sponge can take in (absorb) a large amount of finite data and then output (squeeze) a desired amount of finite data.

The National Institute of Science and Technology (NIST) had released in 2015 the adoption of SHA-3 into the Secure Hash Algorithm (SHA) family, the structure of which is based on Keccak – a sponge function. Another sponge function called Ethash is also of interest, especially for its capability to be implemented as a hardened algorithm for application-specific hardened circuits.

Attacks

The sponge functions (especially belonging to the Keccak family) are susceptible to single-trace side-channel attacks, allowing for the output of secret inputs in certain scenarios. Also, a 'target difference algorithm' has been shown to cause near and actual collisions on reduced-round variants of Keccak.

4   New Cryptographic Schemes

The section discusses the various new quantum-safe cryptographic schemes that have been developed.

4.1   Lattice-Based Cryptography

A lattice can be represented using a group of coordinates in n-dimensional Euclidean space with a periodic structure (with a symmetric array of points).

If R is the field of real numbers and R^n is the (Euclidean) n-dimensional space, then the **lattice L** generated by set of linearly independent vectors $v_1, . ., v_n$ within R^n can be represented by.

$$\mathbf{L}(v_1, \ldots v_n) = \{ \sum_{i=1}^{n} k_i v_i \}$$ where $k_1, \ldots, k_n$ are integers, and the set of linearly independent vectors $v_1, \ldots, v_n$ is called the *basis of the lattice.*

Lattice-based cryptosystems use asymmetric-key cryptography with low-level cryptographic algorithms that make use of lattice-based structures and problems.

The use of Lattices in cryptography may not have been very apparent in the beginning but was theorized in multiple revolutionary papers by Miklos Ajtai [2–4] where a lattice-based cryptographic system could be created with its strength based on the difficulty of lattice problems. Some of the common lattice problems studied were categorized as average-case and worst-case problems; these included but were not limited to the Shortest Vector Problem (SVP), the Closest Vector Problem (CVP), the Shortest Independent Vector Problem (SIVP), or the Shortest Basis Problem (SBP).

It was later shown by Cynthia Dwork and Miklos Ajtai that an average-case lattice problem is at least as hard to solve as a worst-case lattice problem and they used these results to create the first lattice-based public key cryptosystem using the worst-case difficulty of the Shortest Vector Problem (SVP). This was followed by the creation of the well-known public-key cryptosystem, namely, NTRU (Nth degree truncated polynomial ring unit) by Hoffstein, Pipher and Silverman.

Further work in the space was done by Regev, followed by the creation of the first fully homomorphic encryption (FHE) by Gentry using lattice-based cryptography.

NTRUEncrypt (aka NTRU) [1], a PKI-based cryptosystem more resistant to quantum brute force attacks, is the best (lattice-based) alternative to other conventional PKI systems like RSA, ECC, and ECDH and ECDSA variants and is based on the SVP (Shortest Vector Problem) in a lattice-based system.

As the name suggests, this cryptosystem uses a Nth degree truncated ring unit R and each operation that it performs is basically a multiplication of polynomial modulo $x^n - 1$ of integer coefficients of degree $\leq n$-1 (where n is a prime) and can be represented as $R = Z[x] / (x^n - 1)$.

The public and private key creation in this cryptosystem involves two polynomials (f, g) that are $\in R$ and utilize the mathematical processes of convolution multiplication, inversion, and reduction of a polynomial modulo.

The public and private keys are used to perform encryption and decryption activities like any other PKI cryptosystem.

NTRU has been selected as a finalist in the NIST Post quantum cryptography (PQC) standardization effort [7].

Attacks
Lattice-based cryptosystems are being analyzed for attacks enabled by decryption errors based on the Learning with Errors (LWE) problem. NTRU has been found to be vulnerable to side channel and timing attacks.

4.2 Multivariate Cryptography

Multivariate cryptosystems use asymmetric-key cryptography based on multivariate polynomials. Modern multivariate cryptography is based on Hidden Field Equations (HFE) created by Jacques Patarin as an improvement and enhancement of the original C* scheme by Matsumoto and Imai in 1996 [5].

HFE uses polynomials of different sizes over finite and extension fields. Such polynomials contain a finite number of integers on which basic mathematical operations like addition, subtraction, multiplication, and division can be performed.

The private key in this system is a polynomial over an extension field, and the public key is a vector of polynomials over the underlying finite field. It also uses affine transformations to protect the collinearity of the polynomials in an attempt to hide the relationship between the public and private key.

The HFE-based cryptographic systems are based on the difficulty of finding solutions to a system of multivariate polynomial quadratic equations which have been deemed to be of class "NP-Complete" difficulty and thus are considered to be resistant against brute-force attacks from quantum computers.

Attacks
HFE has been found to be vulnerable to private key recovery attacks [9], and also to the algebraic cryptanalysis using Gröbner Bases.

4.3   Hash-Based Cryptography

Hash-based cryptosystems rely on the inherent security capabilities within hash cryptographic functions.

Although hash-based cryptography has been used for digital signatures, its use in constructs like the Merkle signature scheme is of particular interest in post-quantum cryptography due to its inherent capability to resist brute-force attacks from quantum computers.

The Merkle signature scheme uses a combination of a one-time signature creation scheme and a Merkle (hash) tree structure.

The Merkle hash tree is a structure in which each leaf node is labelled with the crypto hash of a data block (e.g., a file), and every non-leaf node is labelled with a crypto hash (SHA-2) which is either the crypto hash of its child node or the concatenation of the crypto hashes of its child nodes such as $Hash(p) = Hash(n1, n2)$, where p is the parent node, and n is a child node such as $1 \leq n \leq 2$. Most Merkle tree implementations are binary (i.e., two child nodes per non-leaf parent node), although more than two child nodes are also (theoretically) supported.

The one-time signature scheme is a technique used to build a digital signature and can be constructed by using a secure one-way cryptographic hash function (e.g., SHA-2) and a secure Random Number Generator (RNG). When used in conjunction with a Merkle hash tree, each one-time digital signature can be used to sign multiple messages to make a cryptosystem resistant to attacks from quantum computers.

Attacks
Merkle signature scheme has been found to be vulnerable to first and second pre-image attacks where an attacker can create a fake document or message with the same cryptographic hash (parent) root using common techniques like brute force or cryptanalysis.

4.4   Code-Based Cryptography

Code-based cryptosystems use an Error Correcting Code (Ecc) in conjunction with a Digital Signature Scheme. Ecc is a data encoding algorithm used to transmit information e.g., a sequence of numbers, such that any transmission errors can be detected and corrected.

One of the best-known code-based cryptosystems is the McElience cryptosystem created by Robert McElience, professor at Caltech. The McElience algorithm is based on the difficulty of decoding an Error Correcting Code (Ecc) which is known to be a NP-hard mathematical problem.

The public and private keys in this scheme are represented as matrices and are fairly large in size. The private key within this scheme is a (Ecc) binary Goppa code described within a matrix that is created using a generator and encoder matrix, for which a decoding algorithm (e.g., the Patterson algorithm) is known. The public key is derived from the private key by using the decoder algorithm and the encoder and generator matrices.

The public and private keys are used to perform encryption and decryption activities like any other PKI cryptosystem.

A variation of this cryptosystem called Classic McElience has been selected as a finalist in the NIST Post quantum cryptography (PQC) standardization effort [7]. This is primarily based on the Niederreiter's dual version of McEliece's cryptosystem using binary Goppa codes.

Attacks
McElience has been found to be vulnerable to brute force attacks where an attacker is able to deduce the plaintext just from the public key and some intercepted ciphertext [8].

4.5 Post-Quantum TLS

Transport Layer Security (TLS) is one of the most widely used and important asymmetric encryption schemes to enable data security. While the enhancement made within the TLS 1.3 implementation has made significant progress in improving the inherent security in the protocol, there are two areas within the protocol that would need to be shored up to prevent attacks from quantum computers.

During the initial handshake, the client and server use asymmetric-key protocols (e.g., RSA and ECDH) to negotiate a symmetric key (e.g., AES-256) that would encrypt the session. So, while AES-256 itself is not so much at risk, protocols like RSA and ECDH need to be replaced by quantum-safe (e.g., lattice-based) algorithms within the TLS protocol.

Also, during the handshake, the server proves its identity to the client by using its certificate's public key involving asymmetric-key algorithms like RSA and ECDH. Since these protocols are at risk, they would also need to be replaced with post-quantum (e.g., lattice-based) algorithms.

At the time of the writing of this chapter, a fork of OpenSSL (1.1.1 h) has already been created to add in prototypes for quantum-resistant key exchange and signature algorithms. Post-quantum key exchange algorithms FrodoKEM and SIKE, and signature algorithms Picnic and qTESLA, co-developed by Microsoft, have already been integrated.

FrodoKEM, Picnic and SIKE have been selected as (alternate candidate) finalists in the NIST Post quantum cryptography (PQC) standardization effort [7].

Attacks
FrodoKEM may be vulnerable to key-recovery timing and generic-hash quantum chosen-ciphertext attacks. Similar to SIDH, SIKE has been found to be vulnerable to attacks that use the claw-finding problem. Picnic has been found vulnerable to multi-target attacks.

4.6 Homomorphic Encryption

Homomorphic encryption has been discussed in greater detail in Sect. 3.1.1 in Chap. 11 in this book, it can be potentially used as an additional security control in conjunction with quantum cryptography and lattice-based encryption, as well as with other conventional symmetrical and asymmetrical encryption techniques.

Attacks
The current homomorphic encryption techniques have been found to be susceptible to chosen cypher text attacks (CCA). They are also vulnerable to private key leakage, and issues with data encoding.

4.7 Quantum Cryptography

This has been discussed in greater detail in chapter (3), is also being considered as an option due to its theoretical ability to provide enhanced capability to detect MITM (man-in-the-middle) attacks. It also limits exposure to certain weaknesses that may exist in conventional cryptosystems due to its ability to restrict the capability to copy data encoded in a quantum state.

Attacks
It has been known to be susceptible to a few types of attacks, such as man-in-the-middle attacks. Additional attack details have been shared in the dedicated chapter (3) on Quantum encryption in this book.

5 The CISO Take

It is the responsibility of CISOs to recognize and find solutions to all cyber threats - both current and those on the horizon. While the threat from quantum computers may not be imminent tomorrow, it is most definitely a threat for which we need to be prepared. It is my recommendation that CISOs start taking tactical steps such as encrypting new data sets with quantum-resistant algorithms or use existing algorithms that have been optimized to add resistance to quantum attacks, while the quantum safe-algorithms of the future are being created and tested for mainstream use in production.

CISOs must impress upon CTOs the urgency to start working on proactive strategies to either create or integrate post-quantum cryptographic SDKs (e.g., NTRU or Microsoft SEAL) into mainstream IT applications.

The CISOs must also impress upon the OEMs like Microsoft to harden the implementations of SEAL, and also work with the open-source community to penetration test and harden implementations like NTRU.

Lasty, the CISO community must take an active role in the testing and validation of the post quantum algorithms by NIST and FIPS.

6 Definitions

Affine Transformations is the technique that can correct for geometric distortions or deformations using transforms like translation, scale, shear, and rotation. When used in multivariate cryptography it is used to protect the collinearity of the polynomials.

Cryptanalysis is the technique used by ethical hackers and threat actors to perform an analysis of cryptographic systems and encrypted data, either in transit or at rest, in an attempt to gain access to encrypted data and convert it to plaintext, sometimes with access to intermediate keys, older session keys or other known information, but most of time, without access to private encryption keys.

ECC Stands for error-correcting code. It is a data encoding algorithm used to transmit information e.g., a sequence of numbers, such that any transmission errors can be detected and corrected.

Ethash is a hash function belonging to the Keccak family. It is the planned proof of work (PoW) algorithm for Ethereum 1.0.

Euler's Theorem states that if n and a are coprime numbers, or a set of numbers with no other common factor other than 1, then a raised to the power of the totient n is identical to 1 modulo n, i.e., $a^{\varphi(n)} \equiv 1 \mod(n)$.

FIPS 140-2 The Federal Information Processing Standard (FIPS) Publication 140-2 is a US and Canadian government standard that specifies the security requirements for cryptographic modules that protect sensitive information.

Goppa code is an error-correcting code used in some cryptosystems.

Gröbner basis is a set of multivariate polynomials where all the leading power products of linear combinations of polynomials in the basis are multiples of at least one of the leading power products in the set [6].

HFE stands for hidden field equations. It is a PKI cryptosystem that is based on the hardness or difficulty to find a solution to solve the MQ (multivariate quadratic equations) problem with the capability to hide the relationship between a public and private key.

Keccak is the family of cryptographic algorithms (Sponge functions and SHA-3 both belong to the Keccak family of cryptographic algorithms).

Merkle Tree is a hash tree structure in which each leaf node is labelled with the crypto hash of a data block (e.g., a file), and every non-leaf node is labelled with a crypto hash (SHA-2) which is either the crypto hash of its child node or the concatenation of the crypto hashes of its child nodes.

NIST stands for National Institute of Standards and Technology. It is a non-regulatory US entity with the mission to promote innovation and industrial competitiveness.

OpenSSL is a general-purpose, open-source cryptographic library that provides an implementation of SSL and TLS used to secure sensitive data in transit, generally used in conjunction with HTTPS.

PFS stands for perfect forward secrecy. It provides the fundamental capability to protect existing or previous session data from compromise, even after the compromise of a long-term secret (e.g., private key).

RSA stands for Rivest-Shamir-Adelman. It is a PKI cryptosystem that is used to protect and secure sensitive data in transit.

SDK stands for software development kit. It is a tool suite that can be used to create and develop applications and integrate with internal or external APIs.

Totient (function) φ **(n)** for a number n, the totient function returns the number of positive integers that are co-prime to n and less than n. $[\varphi$ (n) = n $(1-1/p1)(1-1/p2)...]$ where p1...pn are the distinct primes that can divide n, e.g., φ (20) = 20 $(1-1/2)(1-1/5)$ = 8 integers, which would be 1, 3, 7, 9, 11, 13, 17, 19.

References

1. ntru-crypto and ntru.org (2020) https://github.com/NTRUOpenSourceProject. Accessed 1 June 2020
2. Micciancio D, Regev O (2008) Lattice-based cryptography. https://cims.nyu.edu/~regev/papers/pqc.pdf. Accessed 2 Jan 2021
3. Ajtai M (1996) Generating hard instances of lattice problems. In: STOC '96: proceedings of the twenty-eighth annual ACM symposium on theory of computing, Philadelphia, July 1996. Association for Computing Machinery, New York, p. 99–108. https://doi.org/10.1145/237814.237838
4. Ajtai M (1998) The shortest vector problems in l_2 is NP-hard for randomized reductions, STOC '98: Proceedings of the thirtieth annual ACM symposium on theory of computing, Dallas, May 1998. Association for Computing Machinery, New York, pp 10–19. https://doi.org/10.1145/276698.276705
5. Patarin J (1996) Hidden Fields Equations (HFE) and Isomorphisms of Polynomials (IP): two new families of asymmetric algorithms. In: Maurer U. (eds) Advances in cryptology—EUROCRYPT '96. EUROCRYPT 1996. Lecture Notes in Computer Science, vol 1070. Springer, Berlin/Heidelberg. https://doi.org/10.1007/3-540-68339-9_4
6. Bruno Buchberger and Manuel Kauers (2010) Groebner basis. Scholarpedia, 5(10):7763.
7. NIST (2020). PQC Standardization process: Third round candidate announcement. https://csrc.nist.gov/News/2020/pqc-third-round-candidate-announcement
8. Bernstein D, Lange T, Peters C (2008), Attacking and defending the McEliece cryptosystem. https://eprint.iacr.org/2008/318.pdf. Accessed 2 Dec 2020.
9. Kipnis A, Shamir A (1999) Cryptanalysis of the HFE public key cryptosystem by relineariza-tion. https://link.springer.com/epdf/10.1007/3-540-48405-1_2. Accessed 2 Dec 2020.
10. Galbraith S (2018) Mathematics of public key cryptography, version 2.0. https://www.math.auckland.ac.nz/~sgal018/crypto-book/main.pdf

Further Reading

Adrian D, Bhargavan K, Durumeric Z, et al (2015) Imperfect Forward Secrecy: How Diffie-Hellman Fails in Practice. CCS '15: Proceedings of the 22nd ACM SIGSAC Conference on Computer and Communications Security, Denver, October 2015. Association for Computing Machinery, New York, p. 5–17. https://doi.org/10.1145/2810103.2813707

Becker G (2018) Merkle Signature Schemes, Merkle Trees and Their Cryptanalysis. https://www.emsec.ruhr-uni-bochum.de/media/crypto/attachments/files/2011/04/becker_1.pdf

Bernstein D, Lange T, Peters C (2008), Attacking and defending the McEliece cryptosystem. https://eprint.iacr.org/2008/318.pdf. Accessed 2 Dec 202

Bruno Buchberger and Manuel Kauers (2010) Groebner basis. Scholarpedia, 5(10):7763.

Courtois N (2001) On multivariate signature-only public key cryptosystems. In: IACRCryptology ePrint Archive: Report 2001/029. https://eprint.iacr.org/2001/029.pdf.

Dinur I, Dunkelman O, Shamir A (2012) New Attacks on Keccak-224 and Keccak-256. In: Canteaut A. (eds) Fast software encryption. FSE 2012. Lecture Notes in Computer Science, vol 7549. Springer, Berlin/Heidelberg. https://doi.org/10.1007/978-3-642-34047-5_25

Faugère JC, Joux A (2003) Algebraic cryptanalysis of Hidden Field Equation (HFE) cryptosystems using gröbner bases. In: Boneh D. (eds) Advances in cryptology – CRYPTO 2003. CRYPTO 2003. Lecture Notes in Computer Science, vol 2729. Springer, Berlin/Heidelberg. https://doi.org/10.1007/978-3-540-45146-4_3

Green M (2012) Multiple encryptions. https://blog.cryptographyengineering.com/2012/02/02/multiple-encryption/

Guo Q, Johansson T, Nilsson A (2019) A generic attack on lattice-based schemes using decryption errors with application to ss-ntru-pke. In: IACR Cryptology ePrint Archive: report 2019/043.

Howgrave-Graham N, Silverman J, Whyte W (2003), A meet in the middle attack on NTRU Private key. Accessed 2 Dec 2020.

Kannwischer M, Pessl P, Primas R (2020) Single trace attacks on Keccak. In: IACRCryptology ePrint Archive: Report 2020/371

Kipnis A, Shamir A (1999) Cryptanalysis of the HFE public key cryptosystem by relinearization. https://link.springer.com/epdf/10.1007/3-540-48405-1_2. Accessed 2 Dec 2020.

Koziel B., Azarderakhsh R., Jao D. (2018) Side-Channel Attacks on Quantum-Resistant Supersingular Isogeny Diffie-Hellman. In: Adams C., Camenisch J. (eds) Selected areas in cryptography – SAC 2017. SAC 2017. Lecture Notes in Computer Science, vol 10719. Springer, Cham. https://doi.org/10.1007/978-3-319-72565-9_4

Ladner R (1975) On the structure of polynomial time reducibility. J ACM. January 1975.

Microsoft Seal. https://www.microsoft.com/en-us/research/project/microsoft-seal/

Post-Quantum TLS: the transport layer security (TLS) protocol. https://www.microsoft.com/en-us/research/project/post-quantum-tls/

Silverman J.H., Whyte W. (2006) Timing attacks on NTRUEncrypt via variation in the number of hash calls. In: Abe M. (eds) Topics in cryptology – CT-RSA 2007. CT-RSA 2007. Lecture Notes in Computer Science, vol 4377. Springer, Berlin/Heidelberg. https://doi.org/10.1007/11967668_14

Vates J., Smith-Tone D. (2017) Key recovery attack for all parameters of HFE. In: Lange T., Takagi T. (eds) Post-quantum cryptography. PQCrypto 2017. Lecture Notes in Computer Science, vol 10346. Springer, Cham. https://doi.org/10.1007/978-3-319-59879-6_16

Wikipedia (2020) https://en.wikipedia.org/wiki/Post-quantum_cryptography. Accessed 2 July 2020

Wolf C, Preneel B (2005) Asymmetric cryptography: hidden field equations. In: IACRCryptology ePrint Archive: Report 2004/072. https://eprint.iacr.org/2004/072.pdf

Quantum Encryption Is Not a Paradox

1 Introduction

It is a well-established fact that Quantum Mechanics has many proven and observed paradoxes, e.g., the Schrodinger's cat Paradox [1], Turing Paradox [2], the Einstein-Podolsky-Rosen (EPR) Paradox [3], and Heisenberg's Uncertainty principle [4], among many others. Based on this, when it comes to the topic of Quantum Encryption, one could wonder that it is yet another one of those paradoxes, but such is not the case.

Quantum encryption offers a (theoretically) secure solution to the issue of secure key exchange that may plague (mostly) symmetrical and (to some extent) asymmetrical cryptosystems. It provides some enhanced capability to detect man-in-the-middle (MITM) cyber-attacks. It also limits exposure to certain weaknesses that may exist in conventional cryptosystems due to its ability to restrict the capability to copy data encoded in a quantum state.

2 Genesis

Quantum mechanics is the study of particle physics – it explains the nature and the behavior of atoms and sub-atomic particles at different energy levels.

Within (cyber) security, encryption of data at rest and/or in transit is one of the core tenants of data protection. Traditionally, the data has been "encrypted" using a mathematical algorithm and an (encryption) key, but now a (new) technique of encryption which utilizes quantum mechanics – quantum cryptography, has been implemented.

© The Author(s), under exclusive license to Springer Nature Switzerland AG 2021
R. Badhwar, *The CISO's Next Frontier*,
https://doi.org/10.1007/978-3-030-75354-2_3

3 Prelude

Before we go any further, let's get some basic computing fundamentals out of the way -

(a) In classical computing, the state of a (conventional) computer can be described
    by the sequence of (2 state) bits (0 or 1) or binary configurations of the individual
    transistors within the CPU or a storage device, e.g., a 2 bit register at any given
    time can store any one of the (2^2) four binary states (00, 01, 10, or 11), thus
    with N transistors, there can be 2^N possible (binary) states.
(b) In quantum computing, the 2 state (0 or 1) bit within each transistor is replaced
    by an entity called the qubit (quantum bit), which also has 2 states. Although
    other sub-atomic particles could also be used, the most basic particle, the
    electron, can serve as a qubit where its intrinsic angular momentum or spin
    ($+1/2$ aka spin-up, or $-1/2$ aka spin-down) can be used to measure its state (0
    or 1). In addition, in compliance with the quantum law of superposition, an
    electron can simultaneously exhibit both (spin-up and spin-down) states: So, a
    quantum computing system comprising of 2 qubits can have (2^2) 4 states
    (spin-up, spin-up; spin-up, spin-down; spin-down, spin-up; spin-down, spin-
    down); thus, with N qubits it can have 2^N states *simultaneously*.

The difference in these computing models is that while a N bit register in a
conventional computer can store only one of N binary configurations at any given
time, a N qubit register can store all the N states simultaneously, providing at its
disposal an immense theoretical computing power.

4 Quantum Cryptography

Quantum cryptography provides the capability to perform high speed and to run
parallelized cryptographic tasks using quantum mechanics. Although other
subatomic particles could theoretically also be used, generally photons (light waves)
are the ones that are used to implement this capability. Photons are already used to
carry (large bandwidth) information at high speeds within optical fiber cables and
now they can also encrypt this data if needed.

It theoretically allows for the combination of the concepts of key exchange in
PKI (public key infrastructure) with the security of a one-time pad while providing
the capability to quickly detect any attempt to perform a MITM attack on the
transmitted keys.

4.1 Quantum Key Distribution

The success of any cryptographic system depends upon its ability to protect and
securely distribute its (shared) keys.

In (conventional) cryptography a key is that entity that is randomly generated and determines the functional output of a crypto algorithm for both data encryption and decryption use cases. This key can be a shared secret and must be protected to maintain the confidentiality of data.

Quantum Key Distribution (QKD), the most popular and well-developed application of quantum cryptography, uses components of quantum mechanics to implement a cryptographic ecosystem, enabling capabilities to create and securely share (quantum communication) a random shared secret key and then using the same to perform encryption and decryption of data.

Quantum communication, which utilizes qubits to encode information in quantum states (spin), has been implemented using photons where the quantum communication channel is over the wire (optical fiber) or over the air (radio waves).

The transmission of the shared secret key is done using quantum communication in a linear manner. In addition, the security of the data comes from encoding the information using the state of oscillation (or polarization) of the photon. The sender and the receiver (securely) agree upon a shared secret key using different polarities (e.g., 45°, 135°, 225°, and 315°) or state of oscillation of the photons.

4.2   Quantum Key Flipping

This is a protocol that is used when there is no trust established between the sender and the receiver where they perform quantum communication and exchange information through the transmission of qubits to securely share the key. The key is determined through guessing, responses, and re-transmission of the qubits until success is achieved.

4.3   Quantum Commitment

This protocol is generally implemented using the commitment (cryptographic) Scheme [5] for the purpose of secure transmission of data between distrustful parties by enabling the capability to keep the data hidden to the other party and revealing it later. The scheme has the inherent ability to prevent either of the distrustful parties from changing the data after they have committed to the transfer.

In the quantum paradigm, this scheme is used on a quantum channel to create a secure data transfer protocol to enable the capability to perform an oblivious transfer [6], thereby allowing for the implementation of a secure distributed (quantum) computation in a secure way.

4.4   Other Protocols

Other protocols like the Three-stage [7] quantum cryptography protocol, developed by Prof. Subhash Kak at Oklahoma State University – Stillwater, has also been proposed for secure quantum communications.

5   Post-Quantum Encryption

Apart from providing another secure means of data encryption, quantum encryption is also a candidate for post-quantum cryptography due to its ability to provide resistance to quantum computer brute force attacks to break existing means of classical encryption schemes based on computational difficulty.

6   Threats

Just like conventional encryption, quantum encryption, and quantum key distribution, and quantum commitment-based schemes are susceptible to cyber threats and attacks. We need to better understand these attacks so that we can implement protective schemes against the same. Some of these attacks are described below.

6.1   MITM (Man in the Middle) Attack

The shared key distribution mechanism (quantum key distribution) is susceptible to a MITM attack just like the conventional cryptosystems when used without authentication. This threat can be mitigated by using an initial shared secret to establish a secure communication channel.

6.2   Eavesdropping, Cloning, and Intercept-Resend Attacks

The eavesdropper or the attacker either intercepts or clones the quantum states from the sender and then (re)sends them on to the receiver. Obviously, there are fail-safe capabilities inherently built into QKD as any eavesdropping can introduce errors that can be measured by the sender and the receiver.

6.3   PNS (Photon-Number-Splitting) Attack

This attack is generally used when the sender uses more than one photon to transmit the quantum state, in which case the MITM can split the photons, storing them locally, and still go undetected by the receiver. Later the attacker can use the split data to obtain information on the key. These attacks can be mitigated by using single photons. Other techniques using decoys have also be successfully used.

6.4   DOS (Denial-of-Service) Attack

Given that the systems using quantum encryption rely on a dedicated communication channel (e.g., a fiber optic cable), the attackers can cause a denial-of-service attack by either cutting the fiber optic cable or overwhelming the channel with hijacked or fake (high volume) traffic. Mitigation efforts generally focus on strengthening classical cryptographic algorithms by the use of small amounts of one-time pads, so that these algorithms can be used for an emergency operation during a DOS (Denial of Service) attack.

6.5   Trojan Horse Attack

An eavesdropper may launch a Trojan horse attack on a quantum encryption cryptosystem by sending a bright pulse from the quantum channel into the system and analyzing the back-reflected pulses. Mitigation efforts include but are not limited to installing an auxiliary detector that monitors any incoming light or pulse.

6.6   Dense-Coding Attack

Attackers can potentially steal the session key by sending entangled qubits as the fake signal to the sender. This attack does not introduce any errors to the transmitted information and consequently may not be discovered by the receiver. Mitigation efforts generally focus on adding another shuffle operation to improve the quantum key distribution protocol.

7   Practical Application and Implementations

Most of the implementations of quantum cryptography currently seem to work over the wire (fiber optic), or in air with line of sight, over relatively short distances (up to 40 miles), beyond which bit error rates have made the system unusable. Quantum key distribution networks have been implemented by IBM, DARPA, the Tokyo QKD network, the Los Alamos National Laboratory, and some other European and Chinese networks. There have also been some commercial implementations and many companies also are pursuing some research programs for the implementation and further optimizations, as detailed below.

7.1 Secure Communications Using Quantum Encryption

Quantum encryption was used to provide for confidentiality and integrity of data in Europe by the SECOQC project in 2008. The mission of this project was to develop a global network for secure data transfer and communications based on quantum cryptography, by enabling capabilities to prevent data packets from being sniffed, decrypted, or subject to unauthorized cryptanalysis.

The technology used was enabled by QKD, which was used to provide a secure key over secure point to point or link communication networks.

Similarly, in 2016, China has used entanglement-based QKD to establish secure point-to-point communications between two ground stations about 1210 kilometers apart and a satellite in orbit. The satellite was only used to transmit a pair of secret keys, which was used in turn to establish the secure communication between the two stations [8].

In 2018, NASA initiated the development of a National Space Quantum Lab that used lasers on the International Space Station to achieve secure communications between ground stations [9].

In their latest experiment, researchers from Caltech, NASA, and Fermilab (Fermi National Accelerator Laboratory) built a unique system between two labs separated by 27 miles (44 km). The system comprises three nodes which interact with one another to trigger a sequence of qubits, which pass a signal from one place to the other instantly [10].

8   The CISO Take

It is the belief of some that in a post-quantum computing era, all the encryption algorithms that are based on computational difficulty will fall, and other encryption schemes (like quantum encryption) may be the lone ones left standing. I personally think that both (enhanced) computational difficulty-based, quantum-based encryption algorithms, and other post-quantum encryption like lattice-based encryption will find their rightful place in the post-quantum computing target state.

CISOs need to ensure that they are aware of developments in the quantum encryption arena and partner with technological institutions like MIT and Caltech, and government entities such as NASA and NIST. These technologies must also made available to commercial entities, especially those that build and preserve wealth, such as banks, companies offering other Financial services, trading firms, and Wall Street entities.

9 Definitions

DDoS stands for Distributed Denial of Service. It is a cyber-attack where a threat actor tries to overwhelm a system by flooding it with traffic packets in an attempt to bring it down and make it unavailable to legitimate uses of the system.

MITM stands for man-in-the-middle. It is a type of cyber-attack where an attacker hijacks a secure encrypted connection between a client and server.

PKI stands for public key infrastructure. It is a methodology used to assign or issue digital identities (certificates) to various entities such as users, applications, devices, and systems, and subsequently enables secure (encrypted) communication between these entities.

SECOQC stands for Secure Communications using Quantum Encryption. It was an EU project that was instantiated to develop and promote quantum cryptography in 2008.

References

1. Schrödinger, E. Die gegenwärtige Situation in der Quantenmechanik. Naturwissenschaften 23, 823–828 (1935). https://doi.org/10.1007/BF01491914. English edition: Trimmer JD (1980) The present situation in quantum mechanics: a translation of Schrödinger's "cat paradox paper." In: Proceedings of the American Philosophical Society, 124: 323-38. https://archive.is/20121204184041/http://www.tuhh.de/rzt/rzt/it/QM/cat.html
2. Chaudhry AZ (2016) A general framework for the Quantum Zeno and anti-Zeno effects, Sci Rep 13(6):29497. https://doi.org/10.1038/srep29497. https://www.ncbi.nlm.nih.gov/pmc/articles/PMC4942788/
3. Einstein A, Pqdolsky B, Rosen N (1935) Can quantum-mechanical description of physical reality be considered complete? Phys Rev. 47.777-780. DOI: https://doi.org/10.1103/PhysRev.47.777
4. Heisenberg's Uncertainty Principle, P. Busch, Perimeter Institute for Theoretical Physics, Waterloo, Canada, and Department of Mathematics, University of York, York, UK T. Heinonen and P.J. Lahti Department of Physics, University of Turku, Turku, Finland (Dated: 5 December 2006)
5. Brassard G, Chaum D, Crépeau C (1988) Minimum disclosure proofs of knowledge. J Comput Syst Sci 37(2):156-189. https://doi.org/10.1016/0022-0000(88)90005-0
6. Rabin MO (1981) How to exchange secrets with oblivious transfer. Technical report TR-81, Aiken Computation Lab, Harvard University. https://eprint.iacr.org/2005/187.pdf
7. Perkins W (2006) Trusted certificates in quantum cryptography. arXiv:cs/0603046

8. Yin, J., Li, YH., Liao, SK. et al. (2020) Entanglement-based secure quantum cryptography over 1,120 kilometers. Nature 582, 501–505 https://doi.org/10.1038/s41586-020-2401-y
9. Kwon K (2020) China reaches new milestone in space-based quantum communications. Sci Am Space Phys 3(3). https://www.scientificamerican.com/article/china-reaches-new-milestone-in-space-based-quantum-communications/. Accessed 20 Jan 2021
10. Valivarthi R, Davis SI, Peña C, et al (2020) Teleportation systems toward a quantum internet. In: PRX Quantum 1, 020317. https://doi.org/10.1103/PRXQuantum.1.020317

Further Reading

Pinkstone J (2020) NASA scientists achieve long-distance 'quantum teleportation' over 27 miles for the first time – paving the way for un hackable networks that transfer data faster than the speed of light. https://www.dailymail.co.uk/sciencetech/article-9078855/NASA-scientists-achieve-long-distance-quantum-teleportation-time.html. Accessed 20 Jan 2021

Part II
Artificial Intelligence and Machine Learning for Cyber

AI Code of Ethics for Cybersecurity

1 Preamble

Artificial Intelligence (AI) is one of the most powerful weapons in the CISO's arsenal. AI is built upon algorithms, or a series of instruction sets. In an AI system, machine learning occurs as groups of algorithms modify and create other algorithms without human programmed inputs. This non-human intelligence responds to learned inputs and data, without relying solely on inputs humans designed it to recognize as triggers. The super-human speed of automated AI systems to scan and process massive amounts of data and develop a rapid response is critical to fend off malicious attacks, especially those not seen with the security specialist's naked eye.

Yet, we are all too well aware of science fiction narratives about machines turning against well-intentioned humans and their institutions. While CISOs have yet to encounter any "Transformers" or deal with the "South Park" scenario in which machines decide to destroy humans as the bad actors in anthropogenic climate change, a CISO's AI systems weaponry could be viewed as an armory filled with double-edged swords. Without the proper due diligence of human oversight, which can provide a dose of common sense in a system of relentlessly blinder-driven logic, unchecked AI algorithms may root out and destroy essential company systems. In particular, companies often have to maintain legacy systems for essential company functions, but due to cost or other factors, cannot not constantly update and upgrade them for enhanced cyber resilience. As a result, AI Algorithms may improperly target legacy systems for destruction because of their vulnerability to rapidly evolving malicious threats.

CISOs and their cybersecurity teams have the ethical responsibility to engage in close supervision over the behavior of their AI algorithms, tailoring the specific type of algorithm to the nature of its tasks. To ensure that AI systems uphold the interests and well-being of the business and technology enterprise they serve, cybersecurity teams must make informed choices, using unassisted (or unsupervised) AI

© The Author(s), under exclusive license to Springer Nature Switzerland AG 2021
R. Badhwar, *The CISO's Next Frontier*,
https://doi.org/10.1007/978-3-030-75354-2_4

algorithms for state-of-the-art cybersecurity defense, and using human-assisted (or human-supervised) algorithmic systems to ensure a company's AI does not cannibalize other corporate systems and destroy other non-malicious actors.

2   The Code

To stand on ethical principle, cybersecurity teams must create AI algorithms that can provision for certain principles and processes and against their potential for destructive actions. Here is a basic code of ethics for such AI systems:

Provide for System Preservation   The primary directive behind AI algorithms (or system) is to do no material harm to an Information System or network.

Provide for Algorithmic Transparency   The processing logic and rationale used, the intelligent behavior exhibited, and the input (from training data or other sources) into real-time supervised and unsupervised AI algorithms (or system) to make decisions, should be transparent to cybersecurity administrators. Administrators should ensure that the tools/systems that provide monitoring and (predictive, prescriptive, cognitive and auto-reactive) response for cyber security (synchronous and asynchronous) use cases adhere to these transparent algorithms.

Provide for Algorithmic Accountability   The entities that employ artificially intelligent (supervised and unsupervised) AI algorithms (or systems) for cyber security monitoring and (reactive) response use cases must build in provisions to provide accountability and auditing capability for the decisions made and subsequent actions (detective, protective or otherwise) taken by these algorithms.

Provide for Algorithmic Identification   The AI algorithms (or system) must build in provisions and capability to identify itself (in its current state) to the ecosystem it operates in and protects, and vice-versa.

Provide for Evolutionary Computation   The capability must exist for the AI system to provide for self-correction, optimization and/or healing by the deterministic removal of less desirable algorithmic logic or implementations, but must also have built-in fail-safe provisions to never deviate from this code of ethics.

Provide for Bias Removal   The capability must exist to detect, correct and remove any biases that may develop due to inherent skews within the data sets used to train the algorithms. New and varied training datasets must be used to prevent the biases from developing.

Provide for Verification   The capability must exist to provide for ways to verify the accuracy of the output or outcome. For any instance in which an AI system makes a decision, the system must have the capability to verify the soundness of the decision, which means ensuring compliance with established ethical, moral, and legal guidelines.

Provide for Privacy   When making algorithmic determinations and computations, AI algorithms (or system) are (is) capable of utilizing system data (including PII and NPI) in all forms, whether encrypted, structured, unstructured, or otherwise. When it handles such sensitive data, an AI system must have fail-safe provisions to protect identity and privacy.

Provide for Regulatory Compliance   The AI algorithms (or system) must build in provisions, awareness, and capability to operate within the confines of the corporate, local, state or national regulatory requirements of the ecosystem(s) in which it operates.

3   The CISO Take

CISOs are the custodians of all the security tools and capabilities that are used to protect the integrity and confidentiality of all systems, infrastructure, and data for a given business organization.

As company ramps up its use of AI with cyber security, reaping the benefits of automation and speed, it is the CISO's responsibility to ensure adherence to the AI code of ethics described here, to prevent any intended or unintended misuse or bias, and to prevent any harm to security or IT systems and users.

CISOs also need to work with security product vendor CTOs to ensure that as these vendors incorporate artificial intelligence into their products and security suites, that they follow the code of ethics highlighted in this chapter.

This code of ethics is intended to lay a foundation for the safe and ethical use of AI as it is incorporated into information security programs. This is required to protect the infrastructure, the society, and the commonwealth from the dangers of rogue artificial intelligence.

To get the risk context, please also look at Sect. 7 in Chap. 5.

4   Definitions

PII   stands for Personally Identifiable Information. Any representation of information that permits the identity of an individual to whom the information applies to be reasonably inferred by either direct or indirect means. Further, PII is defined as information: (i) that directly identifies an individual (e.g., name, address, social security number, or any other identifying number or code, such as telephone number or email address) or (ii) by which an agency intends to identify specific individuals in conjunction with other data elements, i.e., indirect identification [1].

NPI stands for Nonpublic Personal Information. It is very similar to but distinguished from PII, as information that is not available to members of the public. (e.g., some data assets contain data only available for internal use by federal government [2], or data provided by a consumer to a financial institution, including but not limited to banks, insurance companies, and credit card processors).

CISO stands for Chief information Security Officer. It is the custodian and executive officer of the first line of defense for the cyber security and information technology security and risk program for a given organization.

References

1. Department of Labor (2020) What is PII, https://www.dol.gov/general/ppii
2. Department of Labor (2020). Data publication process overview. https://www.dol.gov/digital-strategy/publicationprocess.htm

Further Reading

Blackman R (2020) A practical guide to building ethical AI. https://hbr.org/2020/10/a-practical-guide-to-building-ethical-ai. Accessed on 21 Jan 2021.

EC-Council (2020) The role of artificial intelligence in ethical hacking, https://blog.eccouncil.org/the-role-of-artificial-intelligence-in-ethical-hacking/. Accessed on 21 Jan 2021

Ismail K (2018) AI vs. algorithms: What's the difference? https://www.cmswire.com/information-management/ai-vs-algorithms-whats-the-difference/. Accessed on 21 Jan 2021.

Walch K (2020) Ethical concerns of AI. https://www.forbes.com/sites/cognitiveworld/2020/12/29/ethical-concerns-of-ai/

The Case for AI/ML in Cybersecurity

1 Genesis

Before there was any talk of using artificial intelligence (AI), machine learning (ML), and deep learning (DL) for cyber security paradigms in the information technology (IT) world, the implementation of basic security patterns was predicated on diagnostic and reactive manual responses to information from known previous interactions, or from hash-based signatures created from previous infections, attacks, or anomalies. This was the basis of host, network, application, server, device, and perimeter security requirements.

The current environment of more frequent, distributed, sophisticated, and complex cyber-attacks require an artificially intelligent real-time response which is predictive, prescriptive, cognitive and auto-reactive. Only AI-based security can detect previously unknown attack patterns, zero-day attacks, and other challenges posed by ransomware, polymorphic malware and advanced persistent threat (APT).

Also, before we dive in, I'd like to clarify that AI is a bigger and wider concept than ML. AI is a simulation of human-like intelligence, logical thinking, reasoning and learning capability in (hardware and software) machines and systems. In the context of cybersecurity (and IT in general), most of this artificial intelligence is being enabled by the use of machine learning (ML) algorithms.

ML inherits its core principles from AI but technically is a subset of AI and as the name implies, is only relevant to how machines and/or systems may be made artificially intelligent. The terms AI and ML have been used rather interchangeably in the cybersecurity (and IT) world; however, the reader should keep the difference between the two in mind. The usage of the term (AI/ML) in the title and throughout this chapter is to recognize this inheritance, as well as the subtle difference between the two.

R. Badhwar, *The CISO's Next Frontier*,
https://doi.org/10.1007/978-3-030-75354-2_5

2   In the Not-So-Distant Past

The cybersecurity protection schemes (patterns) had humble beginnings and were mostly limited to the following:

Perimeter security was provided by first-generation stateless firewalls implementing the packet filter pattern. The firewalls performed intermediate-level open systems interconnection (OSI) layer 3 and 4 packet filtering based on the Source/Destination IP addresses and (TCP/UDP) source/destination ports.

Similar constructs were used for efficient matching of domains and internet protocol (IP) addresses to implement black and/or white lists, either in the firewall or in a rudimentary implementation of the forward proxy pattern.

The intrusion detection system (IDS) detected network or host-based malicious activity used signature-based techniques (e.g., specific patterns, such as byte sequences in network traffic) or known malicious instruction sequences used by malware. The IDSs suffered from performance issues and thus were not placed in-line, and could generally only detect known attacks.

Anti-Virus (AV) solutions for detection and protection against malware on endpoints and/or servers relied on basic concepts of hash matching or digital signature matching. A hash (mostly MD5) or a digital signature (binary pattern) of an executable was checked to see if it matched the hash or a digital signature of a known piece of malware in a static list.

3   The Current State

The current state of cybersecurity in the IT world has come a long way with advanced security pattern implementations and the beginnings of supervised machine learning. Please note that although robotic process automation (RPA) has helped in the automation of repeatable use cases, most RPA implementations are not artificially intelligent and many don't even have the capabilities to use supervised machine learning paradigms.

A brief description of *some* of the key components that make up the current state has been provided below, since many of these components can be augmented with some artificial intelligence capabilities in the near future.

Perimeter security now has multiple capabilities with the implementation of next generation firewall (NGFW), intrusion prevention systems (IPS), web access firewall (WAF), advanced proxies, and traffic scrubbers (for DDoS mitigation).

The next generation firewall (NGFW) can now perform stateful multi-level inspection (SMLI) and deep packet inspection (DPI) to inspect the entire data packet (including encrypted traffic) across OSI layers 2 through 7, and make rapid comparisons of each packet to known bit patterns (e.g., malware) and other predefined criteria to decide to block or allow data. NGFWs use stream-based detection methodologies, examining the traffic as it is streaming by on the wire.

These deployments have a specific weakness: malware or other threats can get through to the internal network if NGFW doesn't detect the threat in time, or doesn't send out a TCP reset packet in time to disrupt the flow of traffic. In addition, because of the nature of stream-based scanning used by the NGFW, it is possible for malware to be delivered using fragmented packets over a period of time and remain undetected.

Security vendors have also implemented additional capabilities within NGFW (e.g., App-ID by Palo Alto Networks firewalls) to determine what an application is, irrespective of port, protocol, encryption (SSH or SSL) or any other evasive tactic used by the application. It can apply to the network traffic stream multiple classification mechanisms - application signatures, application protocol decoding, and heuristics - to identify applications accurately, making the firewall application-aware.

(Thus, there is a lot of potential for using supervised and unsupervised machine learning in next iteration of NGFWs).

A **web access firewall (WAF)** is an implementation of the reverse proxy pattern, which has the capability to protect HTTP servers hosting web applications from common attacks [e.g., cross site scripting (XSS), cross site request forgery (CSRF), SQL injection] using a combination of rule-based logic, parsing, and signatures. There is potential to use both supervised and unsupervised machine learning algorithms in the WAF. The WAF is one of the first perimeter-based technologies to start leveraging both supervised and (some) unsupervised machine learning paradigms.

Web Forward Proxies (WFP) are designed to protect clients. They provide a "quarantine" service for outbound web traffic wherein they examine all the traffic between (local) client browsers and (remote) HTTP/HTTPS sites (servers), categorizing all URLs so that malicious sites or pages can be identified and blocked while good URLs remain accessible according to custom policies. While NGFW generally only categorizes by domains, the WFP capability to categorize URLs allows for more granular policies that enable IT security teams and administrators to block only malicious content while providing access to the larger site. Web reverse proxies are designed to protect servers and are primarily meant for inbound traffic.

Next generation Intrusion Prevention Systems (IPS) are placed inline and provide the capability to detect and block unknown or new attacks by using anomaly (vulnerability and threat) signature-based detection and prevention techniques. They are 'content aware' and thus have the capability to block detected malicious packets, send a connection (TCP) reset, or block traffic from an offending IP address. They are also 'context aware' and can bring network, application, identity, and behavior-based awareness in decision making required for anomaly detection and blocking. Most IPS implementations still use static white lists to help eliminate false positives, but some have now started using supervised ML constructs. There is potential for the use of both supervised and unsupervised machine learning algorithms in the next generation of IPS systems and there are already some decent implementations of these capabilities.

The **next generation antivirus (NGAV)** solutions can now detect and protect against malware on endpoints and/or servers by using a combination of hash matching or digital signature matching along with heuristic and behavior analysis. Many vendors have also implemented signature-less approaches to prevent malicious code from execution, using supervised ML algorithms to generate signatures, heuristics, hashes, and similar algorithms to scan malicious software. Generally, there is still some human vetting involved to ensure that nothing non-malicious gets blocked. Vendors have also added endpoint discovery and response (EDR) functionality to next gen AV solutions. This functionality is mostly aided by user behavior analysis (UBA) capabilities, which are dependent on some basic forms of supervised machine learning algorithms.

The **next generation traffic scrubbing service** leverages the Border Gateway Protocol (BGP) to route all network traffic for an entity that it is protecting through a globally distributed scrubbing center, giving it the capability to provide dynamic protection against a broad range of DDoS attacks – volume-based attacks (e.g., UDP, ICMP floods), protocol attacks (e.g., SYN flood, ping of death), and application layer attacks (e.g., HTTP GET/POST floods).

Security incident and event management (SIEM) has matured and now has the capability to host and correlate (syslog data) logs and events from all (perimeter, network, mobile, cloud and endpoint) security apparatus and fire alerts for detected anomalies and other pre-configured events. The SIEM would be an ideal platform to implement supervised machine learning algorithms and deep learning paradigms due to the presence of abundant training datasets.

Network access control (NAC) provides the capability to perform policy enforcements using role-based controls to block an endpoint or network device or computing asset from accessing (defined and configured) wired and wireless network resources until a user and/or device-level authentication has been performed. It can also perform encryption of traffic for wired and wireless networks using 802.1X protocols like EAP-TLS and EAP-PEAP, among others.

The **data loss prevention (DLP)** functionality has matured tremendously and now has the capability to provide both logical and physical protection against unauthorized data copying or transfers. Physically, it can block writes to all forms of removable media via known protocols such as USB, SDHC, SDSC, SDXC and UHS. Logically, it can block the transfer of data containing controlled data elements (e.g., PII, NPI, CTI, ITAR) using known protocols such as SMTP/S, FTP/S, HTTP/S. This is a good candidate for supervised machine learning.

SSL/TLS decryption capability, generally enabled by the man-in-the-middle attack pattern, is now being used extensively to provide visibility into encrypted traffic for DLP, forward/reverse proxy, and anomaly detection use cases. Many other network visibility tools also employ this decryption capability to make further deductions by recognizing anomalous patterns within the (decrypted) network traffic.

The **EDR (endpoint detection and response)** capability is now also being extensively used to detect, investigate, and mitigate suspicious activities and issues on hosts and endpoints. This platform has a lot of potential to implement supervised and semi-supervised ML algorithms.

Data protection and malware detection capabilities on mobile devices have come a long way as well and are now available on iOS and Android platforms. Two approaches are common: (a) containerization for data protection (encryption) championed by the likes of Good (now Blackberry) and AirWatch - (although they both use different paradigms of data presentation and protection under the hood); (b) malware scanning and threat detection implemented by companies like Zimperium and Lookout, with potential for the application of semi-supervised ML algorithms.

4   The Not-So-Distant Future

Before we delve any further, I would recommend that you re-read Sect. 1 to understand the subtle difference between AI and ML.

There is a very valid need for the use of artificial intelligence (AI) or machine learning (ML) in cybersecurity. This need will be fulfilled by the use of some supervised and/or unsupervised machine learning algorithms on distributed computing platforms that can provide predictive, cognitive, and automated reactive response and orchestration capabilities, without requiring any data seeding or static signatures, human input, inference, analysis, and/or programming.

5   Artificial Intelligence and Machine Learning

There are four main genres[1] of AI/ML algorithms — supervised learning, unsupervised learning, semi-supervised learning, and reinforcement learning. Supervised learning is useful in cases where a property (or a label) is available for a certain dataset (training set), but is missing and needs to be predicted for other instances. Unsupervised learning is useful in cases where the challenge is to discover implicit relationships in a given unlabeled dataset ("unlabeled" means that items are not preassigned). Reinforcement learning falls between these two extremes – there is some form of feedback available for each predictive step or action, but no precise label or error message.

---

[1] Each genre does have some variants which are outside the scope of this book.

5.1 Supervised Machine Learning

It is defined as an algorithm observing or examining the input and output data pairs (also called labeled data) to deduce a function that can help map the input to the output, thereby giving it the capability to find or predict unseen or missing data. The same capability can be used to determine behaviors or identify anomalies.

"Given a training set of N example input–output pairs - (x1, y1), (x2, y2), . . . (xN, yN), where each y was generated by an unknown function y = f(x), supervised AI can be used to discover a function h that approximates the true function f. Here x and y can be any value; they need not be numbers" [1].

In the world of cyber security today, machine learning most commonly solves the problems of spam and malware detection, OCR (optical character recognition), and facial and speech recognition.

Although still in its infancy, **Active Learning** is a form of Supervised machine learning model that is very promising for its use in cybersecurity where it has the inherent capability to augment existing data-sets that may be missing labels by 'actively' gathering that missing (label) data from various sources. The form of gathering may include active querying.

Classification, regression, and ranking algorithms mentioned below are also useful supervised machine learning models. Most of the supervised machine learning algorithms used for cybersecurity use cases belong to these models.

5.1.1 Classification

The supervised machine learning models that belong to this class use the concept of **data categorization** and **sub-categorization** to classify the data within a given data-set, using pre-defined or known schemes (e.g., credit card or social security numbers). There are two primary types of classifications schemes – binary classifications (i.e., with only two values) and multiclass classifications (i.e., with multiple possible values).

One of the other models in this class are **decision trees** that use their inherent data classification capability of categorizing existing (response) variables to predict future values or discrete *labels* (within this category).

5.1.2 Regression

The supervised machine learning models that belong to this class use the capability to assess and estimate a relationship function (f) between input (x) and output (y) variables–

$$f(x) = y;$$

f can be determined if x and y are known for a known dataset.

Once the function (f) is known then a future output *value* can be predicted given an input value.

5.1.3 Ranking

Ranking is a way of examining a functional relationship between two items within a given set, and assigning them a lower or higher 'rank.'

Some of the kinds of security datasets the supervised ML algorithms are best suited to ingest are real-time network taps, logs, configuration management data, and purpose-built structured data.

5.2 Unsupervised Machine Learning

Unsupervised ML is defined as an algorithm observing or examining unlabeled data (made up of input and output data pairs or otherwise) to deduce a function that can help map the input to the output, thereby giving it the capability to find or predict unseen or missing data. This is easier said than done, as the absence of labeled data makes it difficult to quantitatively evaluate the performance of the (unsupervised) algorithm.

In the world of cyber security today, unsupervised ML most commonly identifies and solves problems through anomaly detection, entity classification leading to attack detection, and data exploration and classification.

Clustering and dimensionality algorithms are also useful in illustrating unsupervised learning. These are outside the scope of this discussion.

5.3 Semi-Supervised Machine Learning

Semi-supervised ML is defined as an algorithm observing or examining both labeled and unlabeled data sets to deduce a function that can help map the input to the output, thereby giving it the capability to find or predict unseen or missing data. This is generally used in situations where unlabeled data is more readily available than labeled data.

In the world of cyber security today, the most common use of semi-supervised ML is for network intrusion detection. These ML algorithms are best suited to ingest security datasets derived from real-time network taps, logs, configuration management data, and purpose-built structured data.

5.4   Reinforcement Machine Learning

With reinforcement ML, a feedback loop is used to channel results from a training phase into the testing phase to deduce a function that can help map the input to the output, thereby giving it the capability to find or predict unseen or missing data. The trick in this technique is to know when to cut over from the training to the actual testing phase, which is generally based on successes and failures encountered during the training. Reinforcement ML algorithms are best suited to ingest security datasets derived from real-time network taps, logs, configuration management data, and purpose-built structured data.

5.5   Bayes' Law

Bayes' Law, widely applied in machine learning algorithms, outlines the probability of the occurrence of an event based on known variables, conditions, or other probabilities related to the event.

This law is a key influence in various machine learning constructs, such as Bayesian models, Bayesian probability, and Bayesian inference.

6   AI for Cybersecurity Use Cases

AI has been used as a buzzword in cyber security for the last decade, and most of the references to it were for schemes that mostly utilized robotic process automation (RPA) or equivalent techniques to automate or augment manual incident response and threat detection processes and use cases.

In the last three to four years, there have been some interesting implementations of supervised machine learning for cyber security uses cases like user and entity behavior analysis (UEBA), threat detection, and network security, but a lot of potential exists to further bring semi-supervised and unsupervised machine learning paradigms into cyber security.

6.1   Generic Requirements

For AI to be used in cybersecurity use cases it must:

(a) Provide the capability to perform the following in REAL TIME (or close to real-time) from live network traffic available on SPAN or TAP ports, or directly over the wire *wherever* possible:

1. Detect security anomalies, abnormal users, system or device behavioral patterns, and/or other deviations from baselines created or learned;
2. Detect (APT) advanced persistent threat or zero-day attacks per pre-established IOCs or through machine learning utilizing supervised or unsupervised learning algorithms;
3. Correlate real-time log data with security logs already resident in the security incident event management (SIEM) to detect threat patterns and anomalies;

(b) Provide the capability to perform after-the-fact (asynchronous) correlation of cross functional application, system and security logs, to identify anomalies or malicious activities.

1. Detect financial fraud, account take overs, illegal or unauthorized money-out, money laundering and other suspicious or fraudulent activity.
2. Algorithms should be tuned to run daily, weekly, monthly and quarterly (batch) jobs.
3. Capability must exist to analyze, train and label large datasets from application and security (log) data.
4. Capability must exist to also examine the actual application data itself in a cross-functional manner.

(c) Map algorithms for threat patterns, anomalies, and user behavior to the optimized cyber kill-chain [reconnaissance, breach (weaponization + delivery), infection (installation, privilege escalation, and code execution), and actions (data exfiltration)], taking appropriate unsupervised reactive alerting or blocking actions defined below:

1. Extend and/or enhance base machine learning algorithms;
2. Detect and mitigate risk proactively, and detect misconfigurations and excessive privileges;
3. Provide for data at rest classification and remediation;
4. Provide for AI-trained steganalysis or other obfuscation detections.

Note: Detailed requirements per phase of the cyber kill-chain, have been provided in Sect. 6.3.

6.2 Existing Models

There are many existing models and algorithms that can be used to enable AI paradigms for cyber security. A list of these AI/ML algorithms that are the best suited for cyber use has been mentioned below:

6.2.1 Decision Tree

This algorithm creates branch-based graphical representations of input data enabling it to *predict* a pictorial outcome or flow, for all possible decisions. A decision tree graphical representation generally comprises a node, edges or branches, and leaf nodes.

There are two types of decision trees:

A **classification tree** is a basic decision tree which primarily provides a yes/no or a binary response as an output.

A **regression tree** is a decision tree which provides continuous values as an output.

In cyber-security, decision trees are used to create ML models to help determine the paths of cyber-attacks. In the past, and in some current implementations, decision trees have been actively used for malware detection. Most of these implementations are now moving to deep learning neural networks.

6.2.2 Naïve Bayes'

This algorithm is based on Bayes' Law and is used to create predictive classifiers to establish the probability of the occurrence of an event based on *strongly independent* known variables, conditions or other probabilities related to the event.

$$\frac{P(A|B)}{P(B)} = \frac{P(B|A)P(A)}{P(B)}$$

Where:

- A and B are strongly independent events;
- P () is the probability, and P (|) signifies conditional probability, so $P(A|B)$ is the probability of A occurring if B is true, and vice-versa.

This algorithm is primarily used for real-time and multi-class (threat) prediction, text-classification and spam filtering, or implementing cyber recommendation systems.

6.2.3 K-Nearest Neighbors

This algorithm uses the concept of multi-class *classification* and *regression* to create one or more class memberships using categorization.

6.2.4   K-NN Classification

Each member of the dataset is assigned membership to a given class. The output of the algorithm is the object being assigned to the class with the k nearest neighbors. k is generally a small odd integer, and if k = 1, then the object is simply assigned to the class that the nearest neighbor belongs to.

For cybersecurity use cases, this algorithm is used to help implement pattern recognition, data mining, and intrusion detection.

6.2.5   K-NN Regression

For regression the input is the k nearest neighbors (same as classification) and the output of the algorithm is an average value of the object from its k-nearest neighbors.

For cybersecurity use cases, this algorithm can be used in statistical estimation and pattern recognition as a non-parametric method.

6.2.6   Deep Learning

Deep Learning is a ML technique which uses output from one or more (lower) level (generally supervised) ML algorithm(s), either as an input into or in combination with another (higher) level (generally unsupervised) ML algorithm to implement cybersecurity functions like pattern analysis (e.g., malware detection) with greater accuracy and a lower rate of false positives.

Deep learning has found widespread use within cyber security in detecting intrusions, malware, and phishing/spam. It is used in image recognition to detect website defacement. It has also been used in speech recognition and natural language processing (NLP).

6.2.7   Restricted Boltzmann Machine (RBM)

RBM is a two-layered randomly determinant generative artificial neural network that has the capability to learn probability distribution (i.e., occurrence of outcomes) over its sets of input. The two layers are comprised of visible and hidden nodes with the restriction that each node within each layer can only have a connection to one or many nodes in the other layer. RBMs are now generally utilized to implement *Deep Belief Networks* (DBN) using an unsupervised learning paradigm.

6.2.8   Neural Networks

Neural networks have been inspired by the human brain to help implement AI unsupervised ML paradigms. Just like the human brain (which has inter-connected neurons), the (artificial) neural network has nodes interconnected to each other and uses a combination of pattern recognition, predictive association, and error correction to produce accurate results.

Neural networks have the capability to learn complex time sequences to enable unsupervised machine learning paradigms, making them good candidates for anomaly detection within data sets derived from close to real-time streaming data.

The algorithms within this class are trained with large volumes of regular (non-malicious) data to help it learn the normal behavior of the system, enabling it to detect a deviation from the normal behavior and thus identify any anomalous activity.

This will be very useful in user entity behavior analysis (UEBA) use cases.

Convolutional Neural Networks (CNN)
These algorithms belong to the feed-forward class of neural networks where the input only moves unidirectionally from one inner layer to another to the output. Generally, there are many hidden layers that form the layers between the input to the subsequent output. This algorithm has found use in detecting certain anomalies in an unsupervised manner.

Recurrent Neural Networks (RNN)
These algorithms belong to the neural network family and are used to perform pattern analysis on long sequences of random numbers or events. They use data from previous rounds of analysis on previous data sets as input to the next round of analysis.

Pseudo-Randomness Detection (PRD)
This algorithm belongs to the neural network family and can be used to implement the capability to correlate random numbers and events and finds extensive use in detecting and correlating random events. These would be beneficial for use within SIEMs.

Extreme Value Theory (EVT)
This algorithm provides the capability to establish a pattern or determine a behavior of a given entity with extreme data availability, i.e., when there is either a very large or very small (sparse) amount of data available. This eliminates the need for data optimization and leads to a faster and more robust pattern recognition capability as it applies for supervised and unsupervised ML scenarios in cyber security use cases.

6.3   Implementation Requirements and Guidance

This section identifies the various cyber security **use cases and subsequent requirements** (mapped to a modified Lockheed Martin cyber kill-chain [3]) that are good candidates to benefit from both supervised and unsupervised machine learning algorithmic implementations using the base algorithms mentioned in Sect. 6.2.

Although this book has chosen to use the Lockheed Martin kill-chain, further enhancements can be done using the popular and more sophisticated MITRE ATT&CK framework, using mapping already established between the two.

The section mentions some existing ML implementations but providing solutions and implementation-level details for all the requirements is outside the scope of this book and may be provided in a further publication.

The guidance and high-level approach used should be as below:

Supervised Machine Learning – Implementation Guidance
To enable supervised ML for some of the cyber kill-chain mapped use cases, train known and new algorithms from existing instances of known malicious activity within each cyber kill-chain phase and use the training data for those activities and events from application, system, and security logs (from the SIEM).

Unsupervised Machine Learning - Implementation Guidance
Unsupervised ML algorithms can be implemented for some of the cyber kill-chain mapped use cases by using already trained supervised ML algorithms as an input for higher-level unsupervised ML algorithms. This creates a Deep Learning paradigm (e.g., using the Expectation Maximization (EM) algorithm to learn the hidden parameters of a hidden Markov model (HMM)).

An implementation approach that may be followed is discussed below:

(a) Classify all supervised ML algorithms into subclasses within the existing kill-chain mapping.
(b) Identify ML constructs and algorithms that can provide mathematical coverage for the various requirements and use classes within each subclass. For example, a pseudo-randomness detection algorithm can be used to detect recon activities like IP and Port scanning.
(c) Exhaustively train each supervised algorithm using labeled data available for the detailed requirements and known use cases mentioned in Sect. 6.3.1–6.3.4.
(d) Create supervised algorithmic variants to cover requirements for the various use cases within each subclass if necessary.
(e) Feed each supervised algorithm trained for each subclass into an unsupervised AI/ML Deep Learning algorithm that can detect an anomaly that falls in a given subclass, even for the events for which its underlying supervised algorithm was not trained. This exhibits real AI.

The below mentioned "Cyber kill-chain" [3] mapped detective algorithms need to be implemented for cyber security domains such as endpoint security, network security, application security, cloud security, data security, perimeter security, monitoring, and incident response.

Note: Many proprietary and some open-source implementations of algorithms are already available and are in active use within the various tools within the current enterprise security stack.

The next few sections identify the AI/ML *requirements* mapped to each phase of the kill-chain.

6.3.1 Reconnaissance

In this phase, the threat actor conducts reconnaissance activities, i.e., scans or scouts the target host or system to identify known vulnerabilities, or exposed ports or services, or other weaknesses that could be remotely exploited. These scanning activities are generally conducted by using tools like nmap or Shodan. In addition to scanning, this phase may include other activities like garnishing information from other platforms like LinkedIn, Twitter, Facebook or other social media platforms, and other publicly available sources. The threat actor may then use this to launch phishing attacks in an attempt to steal employee credentials for the entity targeted for reconnaissance.

The focus of the ML algorithms for this phase is to detect and alert any (mostly) external or internal reconnaissance attempts by threat actors to identify vulnerable systems or services. These would be a good fit for perimeter security appliances and services such as Firewalls, WAFs, and endpoint security behavior analysis engines within EDR tools.

The various **scanning** techniques are covered in detail below and form the basis of the supervised and unsupervised **AI/ML requirements to be implemented** to provide the (primary) detection and (secondary) blocking capabilities.

1. IPSweep

IPSweep is the technique where a given host '*IP Scans*' *one or many* non-local hosts by 'sweeping' across them. Using this technique, the source IP address sends a large number of ICMP echo requests to multiple destinations or target IP addresses (i.e., hosts) within a relatively short time period.

These scans can be done from an IP address external to an entity's private network, referred to as an External IP Scan, or from an IP address internal to the private network, referred to as an internal IP Scan.

There are generally three categories of IPSweeps described below. These should all be detected by AI/ML implementations.

(a) **External IP Scans** are conducted from an external vantage point generally using a transient of an IP address obfuscated through a VPN and tools like nmap or Shodan. Although sophisticated attackers will hide behind a VPN to perform these scans, most of the IPs are immediately recognizable as malicious.
(b) **Internal IP Scans** are conducted from inside the network. The intent of the attacker or insider threat is to hide this traffic into the regular east-west traffic by masquerading as a regular user or application.
(c) **Random (External) IP Scans** are also conducted by an attacker from an external vantage point, but are generally stretched out over a large time scale in an attempt to defeat cyber security (detective) algorithms that look for specific scanning patterns generally over a shorter time period.

2. **PortSweep**

   PortSweep is the technique by which a given host 'scans' ports on *one* non-local host by 'sweeping' across them. Using this technique, the (source) IP address sends a large number of TCP SYN packets to large number of pre-defined ports on a destination or target IP address (i.e., host) within a relatively short time period.

   There are generally two categories of PortSweeps described below. These should all be detected by AI/ML implementations.

   (a) **External Port Scans** are conducted from an external vantage point generally using a (transient) IP address (generally) obfuscated through a VPN and using tools like nmap. Although sophisticated attackers will hide behind a VPN to perform these scans, most of the IPs are immediately recognizable as malicious.

   (b) **Internal Port Scans** - these scans are conducted from inside the network. The intent of the attacker or insider threat is to hide this traffic into the regular east-west traffic by masquerading as a regular user or application.

3. **Other Misc. (incoming/outgoing) Scans**

   In addition to detecting the IP and Port scans, there are various other scanning activities that can be used for malicious recon purposes. Some of these, mentioned below, should be detected by AI/ML implementations.

   (a) Scanning by tools similar to nmap e.g. (Masscan, Solarwinds, Zmap etc.)

   (b) IPv4/v6 wide SSH scans for a given network.

   (c) Malicious use of the H.323 video conferencing (VC) protocol, generally used by various providers like Cisco, Avaya, or Polycom.

   (d) Misuse of google crawler (Googlebot), or of similar or fake crawlers.

   (e) Misuse of the Microsoft IIS tilde character "~" Vulnerability/Feature for Short File/Folder Name Disclosure.

   (f) Malicious UPnP traffic. (UPnP protocol does not require any authentication and thus can be abused to spread malware).

   (g) Simple Service Discovery Protocol (SSDP) amplification scan.

   (h) Firewalls scans (e.g., Firewalk) that use capabilities like traceroute to analyze IP packet responses to help determine gateway ACL filters and map networks.

4. **Insider Recon**

   Some internal users, or guests/partners with intranet access, are also insider threats or users who sometimes perform recon activities to identify either soft targets to spread malware, or sensitive targets with the crown jewels for exfiltration. They must be identified and stopped. Some insider threat behaviors are mentioned below:

   (a) Attempts to visit internal sites, applications, systems, or network segments that they have never visited before, sometimes at odd non-business hours;

   (b) Attempts to gain user privilege;

   (c) Attempts to gain administrator privilege;

   (d) Attempts to profile misconfigurations in o365, AWS, Azure, or other cloud services;

(e) Use of tools like Strobe, NSS, Satan, Portscanner, and Queso.
(f) Use of open-source tools like Ftpcheck and Relaycheck to scan for ftp servers and mail servers that allow relaying;
(g) Use of open-source tools like Bulk Auditing Security Scanner (BASS), which allows for the scanning of a variety of well-known exploits;
(h) Use (local) host scanning tools like cops and tiger, or scripts like check.pl.

5. **Detection of DDoS attacks**

   DDoS bots and other DDoS attempts can be used to perform sophisticated recon to find vulnerable systems. The AI/ML capability must exist to detect attacks that include:

(a) Syn flood and SIP unauthorized flood
(b) Mail bomb and finger bomb
(c) Ping of death
(d) Credential stuffing
(e) Possible inbound SNMP flood
(f) Inbound NTP DoS attempt
(g) Low Orbit Ion Cannon (LOIC) JavaScript inbound DoS
(h) Generic Webserver hashing collision attack
(i) Proxy Authentication required flood

Algorithms –

There is a lot of potential to create detectors using supervised and unsupervised ML algorithms that could detect malicious scans and subsequently attempt to create and orchestra real-time risk mitigation responses in an automatic reactive response manner.

Some existing implementations (of malicious scan detectors and others) are already using the private and open-source implementations of:

1. Restricted Boltzmann Machine (RBM)
2. External Random IP Scanning, and
3. Pseudo Randomness detection (PRD).

6.3.2   Breach (Weaponization + Delivery)

In this phase, the threat actor weaponizes, customizes, or creates a malicious package (malware) designed to exploit one or many known vulnerabilities or known backdoors, and delivers it to the target host or system. Generally, sophisticated attackers will make use of polymorphic or metamorphic malware to evade detection by the perimeter defenses of the target. Other techniques like phishing, spoofing, or drive-by-download can be used to defeat the email and web security defenses and deliver the malicious package right through the front door.

By employing user, endpoint, application, and system behavioral patterns and using training data from system and application logs from known malicious activity,

ML algorithms can detect the various malicious activities that generally occur in this phase of the cyber kill-chain.

Here are *some* of the various malicious known behaviors or patterns within this phase of the cyber kill-chain that should be detected by the AI/ML algorithms:

1. Exploit Kit and Webshell detection

    (a) Webshell in a webroot
    (b) shell bot code download
    (c) Powershell checking for virtual host and internet connectivity
    (d) reverse Webshell
    (e) Webshell accessed on remote server
    (f) backdoors (Win32 and others).

2. VPN-related anomaly detection

    (a) VPN IP failed logins
    (b) VPN user failed logins
    (c) Concurrent VPN logins

3. Detection of Privilege Escalation gain (remote-to-user, and user-to-root attacks)

    (a) Outbound responses from Windows Management Interface Command (WMIC)
    (b) A local (Windows or Linux) firewall disabled
    (c) Outbound traffic after the execution of the windows SysInternals suite (e.g., sc.exe)
    (d) The transfer or download of the executable (e.g., metsrv.dll) for Metasploit/Meterpreter that loads this tool into system memory on a compromised host
    (e) Suspicious opening of the shell (e.g., cmd or /bin/sh) on local host
    (f) kadmind buffer overflow attempt
    (g) non-local burp proxy error

4. Detection of Privilege Escalation attempts (remote-to-user, and user-to-root attacks)

    (a) Heap and buffer overflow
    (b) NNTP overflow attempts
    (c) Use of known backdoors
    (d) Auth bypass attempts
    (e) DNS (TCP and UDP) inverse query overflow
    (f) Procdump dump file exfiltration
    (g) Windows NETAPI stack overflow

5. Detection of unauthorized/non-compliant network nodes

    (a) Unauthorized switches, hubs, repeaters and routers.
    (b) Unauthorized Wi-Fi access points
    (c) Unauthorized devices with spoofed MAC address of an IP phone or video conferencing equipment.

6. Detection of malicious activity using advanced network deception technology and sophisticated honeypots

7. Rogue (application or process) instance detection

   (a) Unauthorized (branded) applications
   (b) Malicious svhost.exe (process)
   (c) Unsigned applications
   (d) Rogue certificate usage

8. Network Trojan detection

   (a) Obfuscated eval string
   (b) Hiloti loader requesting payload URL
   (c) Possible whitelotus exploit
   (d) Metasploit Meterpreter reverse HTTPS certificate request

9. Attempted information leak or exfiltration

   (a) Transfer of password files (e.g.) /etc./passwd via HTTP/S, SMTP
   (b) Transfer of UPnP discovery search output
   (c) Transfer of ipconfig response output
   (d) DNS zone transfer

10. Attempt to login with a default user-id and password

    (a) Using FTP without a password
    (b) Using anonymous FTP

11. Attempt to login with a suspicious user-id

    (a) Logging into FTP with password wh00t (generally an attempt to install a rootkit)
    (b) Attempting other brute force logins using default user-ids.

12. Non-standard protocol detection

    (a) Detection of protocol independent multicast (e.g., Protocol number - 103, keyword – PIM; or number 77, keyword – SUN ND)
    (b) Discovery of unassigned/reserved or non-standard IP protocol
    (c) IRC DCC file transfer on non-standard port

Note Many supervised and semi-supervised ML algorithms for the above use cases is already in use in WAF, EDR, Network Visibility, AV, NGFW, IPS, and NAC tools.

Algorithms –
There is a lot of potential to create detectors using supervised and unsupervised ML algorithms that could detect malicious breaches and subsequently attempt to create and orchestra real-time risk mitigation responses in an automatic reactive response manner.

Some existing implementations (of malicious breach detectors and others) are already using the private and open-source implementations of:

1. DNS Tunneling
2. Hidden Markov Model (HMM)
3. Expectation Maximization (EM)

6.3.3 Infection (Installation, Privilege Escalation, Remote Command and Control, and Code Execution)

In this phase, the threat actor installs and subsequently executes a malicious package (malware) designed to exploit one or many known vulnerabilities, on a target host or system. Other malicious activities including but not limited to privilege escalation or establishing connectivity with a remote command control center (CnC) that give full administrative access and local/remote control on a local/remote host/system are also part of this phase.

Here are some of the various malicious known behaviors or patterns within this phase of the cyber kill-chain that should be detected by the AI/ML algorithms:

1. Command and control (CnC) detection

    (a) Known CnC server/IP/domain or DNS query
    (b) CnC beacon and server messages
    (c) CnC downloading configuration file
    (d) Blacklist (Malicious) SSL cert detected
    (e) Known CnC domain in TLS SNI

2. Executable (malicious) code detection

    (a) Generic ShellExecute in Hex or URLEncode
    (b) Powershell bypass attempt
    (c) Powershell executing base64 decoded VBE from temp directory or saving base64 decoded payload to temp
    (d) Office file with embedded executable

3. User entity behavior analysis (UEBA) for malicious activities (such as failed or simultaneous logins) and insider threat type use cases

    (a) Behavioral anomalies of a user, machine, or process

4. Beaconing (periodic or random)

    (a) Adware and CnC beacons
    (b) PUP install beacon

5. Network protocol anomaly detection

    (a) Anomalous traffic on assigned network ports
    (b) RFC violations

6. Lateral movement detection

    (a) malicious use of psexec, powershell, and remote desktop
    (b) token stealing and pass-the-hash attacks
    (c) Network sniffing, ARP spoofing
    (d) Active Directory attacks like pass the hash (PTH), pass the ticket (PTT), kerberoasting, gold or silver ticket, dcysnc, or dcshadow
    (e) Powershell command with execution bypass or hidden windows argument over SMB
    (f) wmic wmi request over SMB

7. HTTP request-based anomaly detection

    (a) buffer overflow in HTTP URI
    (b) buffer overflow in HTTP header
    (c) buffer overflow in HTTP body
    (d) Directory Traversal in HTTP URI
    (e) information gathering in HTTP URI
    (f) XPath Injection in HTTP URI

8. Worm attack detection (only a few examples are mentioned below)

    (a) Worm:Win32/Rimecud
    (b) Worm:Win32/Dorkbot.AR
    (c) Worm:Win32.Socks.s

9. SQL injection detection

    (a) Boolean-based blind (sql) injection
    (b) Time-based sql injection
    (c) Error-based sql injection

10. Phishing

    (a) Vishing (voice based)
    (b) Smishing (SMS based)
    (c) Malicious URL in content
    (d) DGA-generated (new) domains
    (e) Zero-day attacks (that will not be caught by signature-based detection)
    (f) Patient Zero (needs sandboxing or heuristical analysis)

11. Cloud-based file-shares

    (a) Used to host malware
    (b) Use to host infected documents

12. Fake access logins

    (a) Look alike logins use for phishing

13. Web application attack detection

    (a) Web app scan in progress
    (b) Unicode directory traversal attempt
    (c) Unauthenticated Remote command execution attempt
    (d) Cross-site Scripting (XSS) & Cross-site Request Forgery (CSRF)
    (e) Sql injection
    (f) Request URI too large
    (g) Remote file inclusion attempt
    (h) /bin/bash in URI
    (i) Struts OGNL expression injection
    (j) Java deserialization RCE attempt
    (k) Server-side Request Forgery (SSRF)

14. Successful Administrator Privilege gain detection

    (a) UDP/TCP inverse query overflow
    (b) Server heap overflow attempt
    (c) Authentication bypass attempt
    (d) CGI stack buffer overflow
    (e) Certificate request length overflow
    (f) Procdump dump file exfiltration
    (g) Remote code execution attempt

15. Decoding of a remote procedure call (RPC) query

    (a) Exploit of these RPC calls: portmap, ypserv, yppasswd

16. Suspicious file name

    (a) Certain system or key files being uploaded, copied or transferred – e.g., authorized_keys .forward, .rhosts, /etc./hosts
    (b) Hidden zip files - .pif, .scr, .cpl,

17. Suspicious system calls

    (a) Detection of Shellcode

Algorithms
Some existing implementations (of infection and code execution detectors) are already using the private and open-source implementations of:

1. Lateral Movement Chains
2. Anomaly detection using Markov-chain model
3. Frequency Extraction
4. Domain Generation Algorithm (DGA) detection (Shannon Entropy and N-Grams)
5. Usual day
6. Extreme Value Theorem (EVT)-based anomaly detection

Note: Many supervised and semi-supervised machine learning algorithms for the above use cases are already in use in WAF, EDR, Network visibility, AV, NGFW, IPS and NAC tools.

6.3.4   Mission Goals / Malicious Actions (Data Exfiltration, Data Destruction)

In this final phase of the cyber kill-chain, the threat actor performs various activities such as data exfiltration, data encryption (ransomware), and data destruction (virus/worm). Generally, the data is encrypted to evade detection and transferred to an external location (per instructions from the CnC) on the dark web. The threat actors may use other evasion techniques like protocol tunneling (e.g., DNS tunneling) to hide their tracks so that resident cyber security incident and response teams cannot detect and block unauthorized data transfers or exfiltration attempts.

Here are some of the various malicious known behaviors or patterns within this phase of the cyber kill-chain that should be detected by the AI/ML algorithms:

1. DNS tunneling detection

    (a) HTTP, HTTPS, FTP, SCP, and POP3 tunnels
    (b) script-based backdoors
    (c) DNS zone transfer

2. Unauthorized data encryption detection (ransomware)

    (a) torExplorer certificate or user-agent
    (b) ransomware DNS query
    (c) ransomware CnC beacon
    (d) ransomware payment or onion domain
    (e) ransomware domain in SNI
    (f) ransomware geo ip
    (g) writing encrypted files over SMBv1 and v2
    (h) ransomware transferring encrypted data
    (i) suspicious encryption (start/end) activity

3. Unauthorized data destruction or corruption activities detection
4. Unauthorized Data access and manipulation (alteration) detection
5. Cloud lateral movement

    (a) wmic wmi request over smb (Azure)
    (b) Lateral movement through DCOM Pass the hash functionality
    (c) Download or usage of lateral movement tool that enable capabilities like semi-interactive shells (e.g., WMIExec and SMBExec), and remote command execution capabilities (e.g., PSExec and WMI) (in Azure)
    (d) Rundll command over SMB (in Azure)

6. Cloud data exfiltration
7. Cloud resource consumption (unauthorized)

8. Client using an unusual port

   (a) TLS-encrypted application data, or client key exchange, server certificate exchange on usual port

Note: Many supervised and semi-supervised machine learning algorithms for the above use cases are already in use in WAF, EDR, Network visibility, NGFW, and IPS tools.

Algorithms
Some existing implementations (of data exfiltration detectors) are already using the private/proprietary and open-source implementations of:

1. DNS Tunneling (DT)
2. Naïve Bayes (NB)
3. Support Vector Machine (SVM)
4. Decision Tree (DT)
5. Logic Regression (LR)
6. Bayesian Network (BN)
7. Neural Networks (k-NN)
8. Random Forest (RF)
9. Convolutional Neural Networks (CNN)
10. Linear Discriminant Analysis (LDA)

6.4   Quantum AI/ML

A lot of supervised ML is based on classical algorithms. Generally, the value proposition of ML is in its capability to train the supervised or semi-supervised algorithms with test data, and then subsequently use them to create artificially intelligent systems.

Using Grover's algorithm, these classical ML algorithms (especially search-based functions) can be made to run much faster on a quantum computer (see 'Chap. 1 - Are you ready for quantum computing'), giving rise to a new ML work-stream called Quantum AI.

Some of the classical ML algorithms like k-nearest neighbor, k-means clustering, and support vector machines are a good fit to use the efficient quantum approach of calculating classical distances on a quantum computer. Neural networks and decision trees are being investigated to create equivalent quantum models. Also, Bayesian theory and hidden Markov models are being converted to be represented in the language of open quantum systems. [2]

Quantum AI generally encodes data used by a classical algorithm into qubits for quantum processing and measurement by exploiting the quantum capability of superposition, parallelism, and constructive interference by executing multiple states at the same time.

Both IBM and Google have recently launched capabilities that allow for quantum ML. IBM now provides the IBM Q Experience – a cloud-based platform that allows users to gain access to their prototype quantum processors.

Regetti computing is now providing Forest (1.3) – a tool set for quantum computing.

There is also Xanadu, a startup with the first photonic hardware-based cloud.

From a cyber security perspective, Quantum AI is a watch area to ensure it is not misused to launch attacks.

6.5   Model Risk Scoring

In an effort to reduce the 'noise' and false positives and false negatives, each of the AI/ML models must implement a risk score-based alerting model for cyber security use cases.

A proposed scheme that could be used is elaborated below:

(a) **Risk score range** –

A risk score range of 0–100 can be used.

(b) **Alert category** –

Alert events may be classified as low, medium, high, and critical. The category can also be used to establish priority of event handling by the incident response team.

(c) **Event Risk** –

A security risk determined for an individual event.

(d) **Cumulative Risk** –

Score at an entity level calculated as an average of multiple individual but associated events for a given entity (e.g., detection of a DNS tunneling activity, malware, or privilege escalation).

(e) **Risk Threshold** –

If the cumulative risk for a given entity or configured alert (supervised ML) is exceeded then either an incident alert is raised or a blocking action is taken by an automated workflow pre-created by an orchestrator.

Machine Learning

Supervised AI/ML algorithms may use a configuration scheme to define the risk threshold and risk categorizations for entity events. With appropriate training data sets, these algorithms can learn the risk alerts and categorizations. Most algorithms may need frequent reinforcement learning to ensure that the false positives or the noise from the alerts stays at a minimal level.

Unsupervised AI/ML algorithms generally learn the cumulative risk treatment and associated alerting through deep learning and inherent error resolution capability. They can also make appropriate decisions on new alerts or events independently.

7 AI/ML Risks

While AI/ML have found widespread adoption in cyber security use cases, their use does bring forth some risks that need to be understood and mitigated.

Lack of Domain Awareness - Currently the ML algorithms are not domain aware, i.e., they do not have knowledge or awareness about a given IT or Security domain in which they may be operating. This can cause skewed decision making, leading to both false positives and false negatives.

Inherent Bias – Since all the supervised machine learning algorithms use training data to learn, they can develop many biases including sampled data, knowledge and correlation biases, which can lead to errors in judgement, algorithmic-induced discrimination, and wrong decisions. Thus, any decision made by such an algorithm has the potential to become biased, based on the data used to train the algorithm.

Verification – It is very difficult to verify the accuracy of the output or decisions, especially for unsupervised machine learning algorithms, leading to a creation of untrustworthy (or unjust) systems.

Probability – AI/ML use predictive analysis of previous (training) data to predict future behavior. While previous events can predict a future event with high probability by discovering the functional relationship between interacting entities, there is no guarantee of accuracy all the time, due to anomalies in the data patterns that can lead to erroneous results.

Without providing a complex mathematical proof, simply speaking, if (f) is a function that describes the relationship between two elements (x, y), such that $f(x) = E + y$, where E is the error factor, then generally $E \rightarrow 0$ due to the training of the data from repetitive feedback loops, but even an infinitesimally small value of E while it is tending to 0 can still introduce mathematical anomalies for f that can lead to inaccurate results.

Statistical correlation – AI/ML uses statistical correlation between two or more variables to predict future events, but a statistical correlation alone is not always deemed sufficient to demonstrate causation when it comes to complex systematic or even human actions, often leading to preemption, or erroneous predictions that are hard to validate.

8 Attacks on AI/ML

Just like any other system, AI/ML can be attacked. Given the inherent trust placed in AI/ML systems and the lack of visibility into their inner workings, these attacks can be difficult to detect and can have a devastating effect on the security of an AI-reliant system.

Data Poisoning - is the process by which an attacker can poison the training data set to trick the algorithm into making incorrect decisions. For example, an attacker can poison the geolocation data to classify IP addresses from a rogue nation or a dark web domain as safe, allowing them to circumvent a black-list or other AI/ML-enabled conditional access controls.

Generative adversarial networks (GAN) –generally comprises two AI systems which, while taking adversarial postures against each other, collaborate to create duplicative or representative data or functions to defeat an AI system.

The scheme generally has two primary actors: a generator and a discriminator AI system, with the final goal of replicating or duplicating some content or a function (f) being used by some supervised ML algorithm. The generator starts off with random content, and the discriminator provide feedback to the generator to improve upon the function or data being replicated. This cycle is repeated until the generator has created the content or a function that is indistinguishable from the original.

The GAN has been used by threat actors as an adversarial entity to crack passwords, evade malware and forge facial detection to defeat supervised ML systems used for biometric authentication.

Manipulating RPA Bots – The second-generation RPA agents that have been augmented by supervised machine learning, can be manipulated either to make a wrong decision or to take an erroneous decision (tree) path.

There have been instances of bots or augmented RPA agents being defeated or tricked. This can lead to disastrous consequences when an RPA agent (bot) being used for high frequency (stock) trading, or to provide self-service for password changes, is breached.

9 The CISO Take

The increased use of ML and other AI paradigms in cyber security use cases is undeniable. It provides us the capability to detect and block advanced threats from sophisticated attackers, many of which may be using AI augmented tools to launch those attacks. The reduction in the total time for an attacker to launch an attack and exploit a known or unknown (zero day) vulnerability necessitates that the response be automated and immediate, something that is only possible with artificially intelligent cyber threat detection and mitigation tools.

AI/ML augmented security tools has been found to be effective in detecting advanced malware, including polymorphic and metamorphic malware, ransomware and other malware that use advanced evasion techniques (AET). (see chap. 35).

AI/ML enhanced algorithms used asynchronously are being used very effectively for fraud detection within organizations that provide financial services.

CISOs need to impress upon product vendors regarding the urgent need to implement the various requirements of next generation AI-augmented cyber security and identity and access management tools.

Also, rather than relying on (proprietary) implementations and solutions by product vendors, the CISOs must stand up their own data science programs and implement (some) core AI/ML algorithms for each security domain (e.g., endpoint security, network security etc.) to create SDKs that they should be able to integrate with vendor products (where possible), or run independently.

As the basis of security toolset capability shifts from supervised to unsupervised AI/ML, CISOs should also be aware of the many associated risks and issues– the development of biases, false positives and the lack of capability to verify the decisions made by an artificially intelligent response system, to name a few. They must push for compliance with the code of ethics defined in another chapter in the book, to be built into the next generation tools.

10   Definitions

AV – stands for Anti-Virus. It is computer software that has the capability to detect, prevent, block, and remove malware. Most legacy AV uses static (hash-based) signatures to perform the detection.

Bot – is a short form for robot. It has the capability to perform certain high volume, manual, and repeatable tasks that were previously performed by humans. Bot perform these tasks much faster than humans.

CnC – stands for command and control (server). Generally, a cloud-hosted server/ system often working in tandem with the usage of DGA-generated domains, the CnC is used by threat actors to control and manage infected and breached endpoints and servers (generally resident) on private networks.

CSRF- stands for Cross-Site Request Forgery. It is an attack where a user's session is hijacked using a vulnerability within the application, and is then used to submit forged transactions that the user neither made nor intended to make.

DDoS – Distributed Denial of Service. It is generally used to represent a network-based attack that has the capability to overwhelm the target application or system with a flood of (TCP/UDP) traffic packets or even basic TCP acknowledgements like an ack.

DBN – stands for deep belief networks. They are a sub-class of deep neural networks. They are composed of algorithms that use probabilities and unsupervised learning to produce outputs, similar to a human brain.

DLP – stands for Data Loss Prevention. It is a technology that prevents the unauthorized access to or exfiltration of company and customer sensitive data.

EDR – stands for Endpoint Detection and Response. It is the next generation malware detection system. Rather than relying on the legacy static signature provided by/generated by legacy AV detection products, it has the capability to provide visibility into endpoint user, machine and process behavior, and perform dynamic heuristical analysis, which it then uses to detect and block advanced malware.

IPS – stands for Intrusion Prevention System. It is a network security tool that provides monitoring (detection) and protection against network-based attacks and intrusions, including lateral movement.

Label – It is the annotation of known data or the value of the entity being predicted (y) where y = f(x). An element can have multiple labels.

MD5 – stands for message digest. It is a legacy 128-bit hash function which has been deprecated due to security issues and is no longer recommended for use.

NAC – stands for Network Access Control. A concept inherited from the principle of Zero Trust, NAC manages device (and user) access to private networks, primarily through the enforcement of authentication and authorization controls. Other controls like (geo) location, role, and patching level are also used.

NGAV – Stands for Next Generation Anti-Virus. It is the AV engine with modern ML-enabled AI algorithms to perform behavioral threat detection and remediation and malware sandboxing in conjunction with legacy techniques like malware (static hash based) signatures.

NGFW – Stands for Next Generation Firewall. It uses third-generation firewall technology with capabilities such as deep packet inspection, network device filtering, application awareness, threat detection, and intrusion prevention.

NLP – stands for natural language processing. It is the branch of artificial intelligence that enables a computer to read, understand, and speak human languages.

OSI – stands for Open Systems Interconnection. It is a reference model that establishes a standard for how a given application, system, or device may communicate and interoperate with others over a network. The OSI layer has 7 layers – Application (layer 7), Presentation (layer 6), Session (layer 5), Transport (layer 4), Network (layer 3), data-link (layer 2), and physical (layer 1).

SIEM – stands for Security Incident and Event Management (system). It has the capability to aggregate, correlate, and cross reference security (log) data and events from various systems.

Steganalysis – is the steganography-based technique for detecting and discovering data hidden within unsuspecting data sources such as digital media.

Steganography – is the technique of secretly and securely storing sensitive data within digital media.

WAF – stands for Web Access Firewall. It is primarily an application firewall that protects an HTTP/S-based (web) application against advanced attacks like cross-site scripting, cross-site forgery, and SQL injection.

XSS – stands for Cross-Site Scripting. It is an attack where an attacker can inject and/or execute malicious code (generally JavaScript) within a user's browser.

References

1. Russell S, Norvig P (2010) Artificial Intelligence: A Modern Approach, 3rd. Prentice Hall
2. Schuld M, Sinayskiy I, Petruccione F (2014) An introduction to quantum machine learning. Contemporary Phys 56:2, 172-185. https://doi.org/10.1080/2F00107514.2014.964942
3. Lockheed Martin (2015) Gaining the Advantage: Applying Cyber Kill Chain® Methodology to Network Defense. https://www.lockheedmartin.com/content/dam/lockheed-martin/rms/documents/cyber/Gaining_the_Advantage_Cyber_Kill_Chain.pdf. Accessed 20 Nov 2020

Further Reading

Choubey V (2020) Text classification using CNN. https://medium.com/voice-tech-podcast/text-classification-using-cnn-9ade8155dfb9. Accessed 21 Nov 2020

Cybersecurity and Infrastructure Security Agency (2017) Alert (TA15-314A): Compromised Web Servers and Web Shells – Threat Awareness and Guidance https://us-cert.cisa.gov/ncas/alerts/TA15-314A.Accessed 20 Nov 2020

Deep Learning Tutorials: https://github.com/lisa-lab/DeepLearningTutorials. Accessed 8 Nov 2020

Delplace A, Hermoso S, Anandita K (2019) Cyber Attack Detection thanks to Machine Learning Algorithms COMS7507: Advanced Security. University of Queensland, Brisbane

Deng L, Yu D (2014) Deep Learning: Methods and Applications, Foundations and Trends® in Signal Processing 7(3–4): 197-387. https://doi.org/10.1561/2000000039

Doedhar S (2017) Authentication and Encryption in PAS Web Shell Variant. In: Trustwave Spider Labs Blog. https://www.trustwave.com/en-us/resources/blogs/spiderlabs-blog/authentication-and-encryption-in-pas-web-shell-variant/. Accessed 20 Nov 2020

GitHub (2020) SharpExec. https://github.com/anthemtotheego/SharpExec.Accessed 21 Nov 2020

Internet Assigned Numbers Authority (2020) Assigned Internet Protocol Numbers. https://www.iana.org/assignments/protocol-numbers/protocol-numbers.xhtml. Accessed 18 Nov 2020

Klimek T (2018) Generative adversarial networks: what are they and why we should be afraid. https://www.cs.tufts.edu/comp/116/archive/fall2018/tklimek.pdf. Accessed 18 Nov 2020

Lanier J, Weyl G (2020) AI is an Ideology, Not a Technology. https://www.wired.com/story/opinion-ai-is-an-ideology-not-a-technology Accessed 7 Dec 2020

MahaLakshmi A, Swanpa Goud N, et al (2018) A Survey on Phishing and It's [sic] Detection Techniques Based on Support Vector Method (SVM) and Software Defined Networking (SDN). Int J Eng Adv Technol 8(2S):498-503. https://www.ijeat.org/wp-content/uploads/papers/v8i2s/B11031282S18.pdf

mIRC (2020) mIRC Help: send and receive files. https://www.mirc.com/help/html/index.html?send_receive_files.html. Accessed 18 Nov 2020

Monjor A (2019) An exploration of machine learning cryptanalysis of a quantum random number generator https://umm-csci.github.io/senior-seminar/seminars/fall2019/monjor.pdf Accessed 21 Nov 2020

Nguyen VH (2018) Using Deep learning model for network scanning detection. In: ICFET'18: Proceedings of the 4th International Conference on Frontiers of Educational Technologies, Moscow Russian Federation, June 2018, pp 117–121. https://doi.org/10.1145/3233347.3233379

Rigetti C (2017) Introducing Forest 1.0 https://medium.com/rigetti/introducing-forest-f2c806537c6d. Accessed 7 Dec 2020

Stratos K (2017) Unsupervised Learning 101: the EM for the HMM. http://www.cs.columbia.edu/~stratos/research/em_hmm_formulation.pdf. Accessed 21 Nov 2020

Theodoridis S, Koutroumbas K (2009) Pattern Recognition, 4th. Academic, London

Wikipedia (2020) Machine Learning. https://en.wikipedia.org/wiki/Machine_learning. Accessed on 15 Dec 2020

Xanadu (2020) How Xanadu's chips work. https://www.xanadu.ai/hardware. Accessed 7 Dec 2020

Part III
Secure Remote Work

Security for Work-From-Home Technologies

1 Introduction

The impact from the novel coronavirus (Covid-19) has been devastating to the world's economy. This outbreak has become a global Pandemic forcing the business continuity management (BCM) protocol for each company to go into effect, testing each company's capability for normal, disruption-free business operations.

Apart from the need for redundant, highly available and disaster recoverable IT infrastructure, human capital is key to a successful BCM strategy for any global or local company. If the employees and users cannot go into the traditional office and work facilities due to travel restrictions stemming from a local viral outbreak or global pandemic, then in an effort to maintain normal business operations, they must all be able to continue to work from home or other remote locations without compromising the confidentiality and integrity of business sensitive data and operations.

2 Problem Statements

In the likelihood of a local or global pandemic, there are several problems every modern company must proactively consider and solve…

(a) How to enable a secure mechanism for employees, users and business associates to work remotely for a prolonged period?
(b) How to handle a 100–500% increase in workload on systems (and services) that enable the current secure work from home paradigms? Namely, how to handle: remote access enabled by VPN (virtual private network); Virtual Desktop infrastructure (VDI); and any enhanced volumes in supporting security systems, such as perimeter security appliances like firewalls, authentication and

© The Author(s), under exclusive license to Springer Nature Switzerland AG 2021
R. Badhwar, *The CISO's Next Frontier*,
https://doi.org/10.1007/978-3-030-75354-2_6

authorization systems which are part of IAM, soft phone systems, and Incident Response.

(c) How to securely handle sensitive data that is/was generally only processed or handled in a controlled and protected office environment?

(d) How to ensure that the confidentiality and integrity of sensitive data is maintained while it is being transmitted from employees' workstations (generally laptops and mobile devices) while they are working from remote locations (generally their homes) for prolonged periods?

(e) How to ensure that all authorized vendors, suppliers, partners and contractors for a given company can also work remotely in a secure manner from on-shore and off-shore locations?

(f) How to assess the risk to business operations from the inability to provide the services to maintain normal business operations?

(g) How to comply with local, state, federal government and client security and compliance requirements while majority of the workforce is working remotely (from home)?

(h) How to provide rapid and effective Incident Response for a potential increase in the number of security and privacy incidents due to large number of employees working from remote locations for prolonged periods with no in site supervision?

This chapter may not answer all the questions raised but will try to focus on the current state technological capabilities that can be used to enable secure work from home (WFH) paradigms – i.e., VPN and VDI, in more detail. It will elaborate upon the various protocols and technologies available, cite the risks from their usage and makes some recommendations on secure usage of the same.

RDP (remote desktop services) is another technology that can be used to work from home, but it is not being mentioned in detail here as it does not belong in my future state for *secure* work from home.

Also, there are three additional Chaps. 7, 8 and 9 in this book which will try to answer some of the remaining questions (a) First, on the additional security controls required to maintain the confidentiality and integrity of sensitive data, and also to provide enhanced monitoring and response capabilities for employees that are going to WFH for prolonged periods using VPN and VDI technologies. (b) Second, on the future state improvements that need to be made to VPN, VDI and other WFH enabling technologies to continue to serve the needs of work from home paradigms in an attempt to provide better data security and protections.

3   Secure Remote Access – Current State Options

VPN (Virtual Private Network) The capability must exist to provide remote access to employees and authorized partners, vendors, suppliers and contractors so that they can access the required IT Application and Systems in order to maintain the current level of business and technology operations. This capability is generally provided through a capability called as VPN. Simply speaking a VPN extends a private (corporate) network across a public network (e.g., the internet), assigning a remote user a private IP address and enabling a remote user or employee to send and receive data as if he/she were onsite at a corporate facility. Under the hood, the data is encrypted when entering a secure tunnel created between the remote client and on-premise or cloud hosted corporate VPN system, and decrypted upon exiting the tunnel when it reaches a recipient.

Some of the commonly used VPN protocols that are available now are detailed below.

1. **L2TP (Layer 2 Tunneling Protocol)** – It provides the capability to securely send data across a point-to-point tunnel (using PPP [point-to-point protocol]) over an IP (internet protocol) network. The original RFC for L2TPv2 is detailed in RFC2661. The current version of this standard in the industry is referred to as L2TPv3 and its RFC is detailed in RFC3931.
2. It is extremely important to note the limitations of L2TP. It provides only one layer of security. It "hides" the data as it travels through the tunnel over a public network (e.g. the internet), but it does not encrypt the data. In other words, if the security of the tunnel is compromised, the data can be easily read.
3. **IPSec** – Given the limitations of L2TP, the industry generally uses IPSec (a protocol that is used to secure network traffic between two peers) to "secure" the L2TP traffic. IPSec generally uses AES 256 among other options like 3DES as the encryption algorithm to maintain confidentiality of data and a hashing algorithm like SHA256 for data integrity.
4. **L2TP+IPSec** – This combination of L2TP+IPSec works for both UDP and IP traffic and the usage scheme for these is elaborated in the RFC3193. **This is the bare minimum or baseline scheme that must be used for transmission of sensitive data over a VPN.** (Under the hood, IPSec uses IKE [internet key exchange] for mutual authentications and establishing and maintaining security associations. IKE has 2 versions – IKEv1 and IKEv2, both of which can be used in conjunction with L2TP, although IKEv2 is preferred because of its inherent ability to reestablish a VPN connection).
5. **PPTP** – A basic VPN protocol based on the PPP (point to point tunneling) protocol. It uses the MS CHAPv2 for authentication, MPPE (Microsoft point to point encryption) protocol for encryption, which in turn uses the RSA RC4 data (128 bit) encryption algorithm. While this is the best performing VPN protocol, it is no longer deemed secure enough for transmission of sensitive data, primarily due to the sub-standard, faster-to-compute encryption schemes. I would recommend that this NOT be used for commercial/office use.
6. **OpenVPN** – This is an open source and customizable VPN scheme that utilizes the OpenSSL library and TLSv1/TLSv2 protocols. It is deemed very safe as long as you keep the version of the OpenSSL library used up-to-date, and also use secure cryptographic algorithms (AES, 3DES, Blowfish, Twofish etc.) within the library. While this is very secure, it is harder to detect and block, much to the chagrin of security folk like myself.

7. **SSTP** – Safeguard Socket Tunneling Protocol that is built on top of the SSLv3/ TLSv1 protocol. It is primarily a Microsoft offering and thus only works (well) in the Microsoft ecosystem. In a nutshell, although this is proprietary to Microsoft, it is deemed safe for use from a security perspective for a small-medium (mostly Microsoft) shop, or if no other options are available.

4 Basic Security Requirements

(a) VPN systems must use strong authentication paradigms with 2FA (two-factor authentication) performed for every login.
(b) The 2FA/MFA (Multi-Factor Authentication) scheme must preferably use modern techniques, including but not limited to biometric authenticators; geo-location-aware, hardware-based authenticators; and conditional access.
(c) The VPN systems must have advanced logging, monitoring, and alerting capabilities.
(d) The VPN systems must be hardened and penetration tested on a frequent basis.

5 Security Issues with Current VPN Options

(a) Generally speaking, VPN can provide unfettered access to a company's private corporate network. Providing VPN capability to a large user base that is going to WFH for a prolonged period increases the risk of unauthorized access and exposure of private and sensitive data. This risk can be tactically remediated by implementing micro-segmentation to implement the concepts of Zero Trust with least privilege. The strategic approach generally used these days to remediate this risk is to go towards newer paradigms of providing selective and restrictive application-based access rather than the traditional approach of network-based access. Also, other data security techniques like DRM (digital rights management) can be used to further protect the data that may be accessible through a VPN system.
(b) VPN infrastructures can be susceptible to man in the middle and brute force attacks.
(c) VPN infrastructures are susceptible to configuration errors and mistakes that can be exploited by hackers and threat actors.
(d) VPN infrastructures have been found exposed through zero-day exploits, and also some of them have been known to contain back-doors.

6 Security Recommendations for VPN

(a) To ensure the confidentiality and integrity of sensitive data, the minimum requirement for a VPN system is to use L2TP+IPSec either with IKEv1 or IKEv2 (preferred), or use SSLVPN.
(b) In commercial use, avoid using a VPN system that uses the PPTP protocol.
(c) OpenVPN is okay to use as long it is officially supported and an effort is made to ensure that the OpenSSL library remains current and patched.
(d) SSTP is okay for use as long the caveats with its usage are understood.
(e) Any other proprietary VPN scheme should NOT be used.
(f) Avoid the use of VPN for use cases, where using a VDI would suffice (e.g., basic email and basic internet surfing)
(g) It is recommended that VPN systems use behavioral analysis-based machine learning paradigms to detect misuse and insider threats.

6.1 Other Comments

(a) VPN systems are much easier to scale than VDI systems.
(b) Although the use of internet facing RDP is highly discouraged, it can still be used securely when used in conjunction with (or over) VPN.

7 Secure Virtual Desktop Infrastructure (VDI)

VDI virtualizes the desktop experience, which includes the OS and all the native apps that get installed on a local desktop, by running it in a public or private cloud environment and making it available in a way that is appears to be local to each user. The VDI paradigm generally applies to the Windows OS, but can also be made available for Linux and other operating systems. Also, there are two approaches to VDI. In a "persistent," or "stateful" VDI session, a given user's settings, configuration, state, and data are stored and can be retrieved when the user comes back later. In a "non-persistent" or "stateless" VDI session, a given user's access to data is considered transient, for one-time use only, with the user's data footprint destroyed once the session expires or is terminated.

VDI is a very useful capability that allows workers to work remotely in a secure manner. This has a lot of security benefits as it provides for better endpoint control, governance and monitoring capabilities.

7.1 Secure VDI – Private Interface

There are three primary ways VDI can be made available to (private) remote users:

(A) **Dedicated Private VDI infrastructure Pool with fixed internet circuit**– This is generally done when there is a large number of remote users, generally offshore, who need to work remotely from an office setting for back office IT functions with an expectation of a high-quality connection and user experience. In this scheme, a dedicated VDI pool is created and made available to a group of remote users by providing a MPLS (multi-protocol label switching) connection over an internet circuit with fixed (high) bandwidth and speed (at least 1 Gbps). In this scheme, the VDI pool is only available through the dedicated and private connection and is not available through the internet. This type of scheme can support both stateless or stateful VDI sessions, depending upon need. In theory, this scheme can also support a remote user that may be working from home and is using a VPN connection to get to the office site/hub from where it can then subsequently ride the secure dedicated MPLS connection. Generally speaking, one dedicated (VDI) pool is setup for each set/group of remote users (generally belonging to a given remote site or partner).

(B) **Dedicated Private VDI infrastructure Pool with dedicated site-to-site VPN**– This is generally done when there is a medium number of remote users (generally offshore or in a distant office location) who need to work remotely from office setting for back office IT functions without an expectation of a high-quality connection and user experience. In this scheme, a dedicated VDI pool is created and made available only through a dedicated private connection, not through the Internet, to a group of remote users using a dedicated IPSec tunnel with a bandwidth of at least 5-50 mbps. This type of scheme can support both stateless or stateful VDI sessions depending upon need, although stateless sessions are preferred. Generally speaking, a single dedicated pool is setup for each set of remote users, generally belonging to a given remote site or partner.

(C) **Dedicated Private VDI infrastructure over MPLS**– this is used when a remote office worker already on a corporate network (not through VPN) wants to utilize VDI rather than a desktop or laptop. Generally, these are transient workers who travel to various offices or sites for a given employer but do not have dedicated workstations at each office location. In this situation, they can login through a dumb terminal or a thin client into a (stateful or stateless) VDI session to get their basic computing needs met (e.g., corporate email and basic internet/intranet surfing). Depending upon setup and configuration, these workers can also make use of the VDI infrastructures setup for (A) or (B).

7.2   Secure VDI – Public Interface

Dedicated Public-facing VDI infrastructure (D) – is generally made available over the internet for local or in-country remote users, often working from home, who want a VDI experience rather than a VPN. This VDI connection requires strong encryption algorithms to secure the VDI connection, in conjunction the use of hardware-based authenticators for MFA (multifactor authentication). Because VDI generally requires a lot of bandwidth, this scheme cannot guarantee a good quality VDI experience unless the user has access to a high-speed internet connection with good QOS (quality of service). Reliance on a public network also creates additional risk to the confidentiality and integrity of the transmitted data. Due to the inherent high risk of breaches and unauthorized access, the public VDI infrastructure on the server needs to be physically separated or logically segmented from the rest of the private VDI stack, and additional security apparatus need to be setup to provide monitoring and other perimeter-based security controls. Stateless sessions are more appropriate for this scheme.

7.3   Basic Security Requirements

(a) Publicly facing or available VDI systems must use strong authentication paradigms with 2FA (two factor authentication) performed for every login.
(b) The 2FA/MFA scheme must preferably use modern techniques, including but not limited to biometric authenticators, hardware-based, geo-location aware authenticators, and conditional access.
(c) The VDI systems must have advanced logging, monitoring, and alerting capabilities.
(d) The VDI systems must be hardened and must run all the required endpoint security software, including but not limited to AV and EDR, either at the hypervisor (preferred) or within each VM (virtual machine).

7.4   Security Issues with VDI

(a) VDI environments are prone to common cyber threats like ransomware and other sophisticated malware, traffic sniffers, privilege escalation, vulnerability exploits, and insider threats.
(b) Due to the high cost of compute and memory, performance concerns, resource contentions, and vendors' unreasonable software licensing schemes, IT administrators often discourage the use of endpoint security software within the VDI sessions, leading to higher cyber risk.

(c) Patching cycles require the update of the golden images and thus are slower, leading to higher risk from un-patched critical or high vulnerabilities.

7.5   Security Recommendations for VDI

(a) Dedicated Private VDI infrastructure Pool with a fixed internet circuit is the recommended approach to service the remote desktop needs for large remote users doing business critical work.
(b) Dedicated Private VDI infrastructure Pool with dedicated site-to-site VPN can be used for large to medium group of remote users performing standard back office functions.
(c) Dedicated Private VDI infrastructure over MPLS is recommended for on shore users to service their basic computing needs.
(d) Dedicated Public facing VDI infrastructure is discouraged for use by remote users performing business critical work involving sensitive data.
(e) VDI should be used in place of VPN, if the user only needs access to corporate email, access to corporate time entering software and/or the capability for basic intranet access.
(f) VDI should use dynamic host checking, where a user's machine is dynamically checked for malware and other security hygiene items (like patches and a recent AV scan etc.) before they are allowed to connect (every time they try to make a connection).

7.6   Other Comments

(a) VDI is a resource intensive capability and is thus harder to scale with a multi-fold increase in user count.
(b) Stateless VDI sessions, which are less resource intensive than stateful sessions, should be considered where the use case supports it.

8   The CISO Take

The expanding use of work from home paradigms can be enabled by using VPN and VDI technologies, but the global cyber security community led by their CISO's must ensure that we collectively assess the risk of their expanded use and work collaboratively to remediate and mitigate the additional security and compliance risks that their usage brings forth.

The CISOs have defined and designed multiple ways to mitigate the risk and additional details on those has been shared in subsequent chapters.

9   Definitions

MFA – stands for multi factor authentication. It is an authentication technique used to grant access to a restricted resource (application, system, website, device etc.) only after the user requesting the access has successfully presented two or more factors of information asserting possession (what a user has) and inherence (who a user is) to an authenticator.

MPLS – stands for Multiprotocol Label switching. It is a label-based data routing technology that enables much faster data transfer and control in a network. It is very scalable and protocol independent i.e., works with both IP and ATM traffic.

RDP – stands for remote desktop service. Initially known as terminal services, RDP is the remote work capability made available by Microsoft which allows users to log in from a corporate or personal device using a public (internet) or private (VPN) network.

Thin client – is a virtual end user computing asset hosted on a virtual machine on remote server. The thin client utilizes a shared pool of multitenant computing resources like CPU, RAM and storage.

Zero Day – is an unknown exploit that is used to expose and subsequent take advantage of a software or firmware vulnerability or weakness and then maybe subsequently used to launch a cyber-attack or breach a network or a system.

Zero Trust – is a security architecture and implementation paradigm that reduces enterprise risk by performing secure implementations in compliance with the principal that all assets inside and outside a perimeter firewall are not to be trusted and thus access control for users, devices, systems and services must be provided using least privilege.

Further Reading

Patel B, Aboba B et al (2001). Securing L2TP using IPsec. https://tools.ietf.org/html/rfc3193

Townsley M, Lau J (2005). Layer Two Tunneling Protocol - Version 3 (L2TPv3). https://tools.ietf.org/html/rfc3931

Townsley W, Valencia A (1999). Layer Two Tunneling Protocol "L2TP". https://tools.ietf.org/html/rfc2661

Secure Video Conferencing and Online Collaboration

1 Introduction

In the wake of the coronavirus pandemic, companies must rely upon collaboration and video conferencing software and services to ensure business continuity. Given the exponential rise in the usage of collaboration platforms such as Microsoft's Skype and Teams, Cisco's WebEx, and, Zoom, it is imperative to understand underlying security issues, patch vulnerabilities and implement the appropriate mitigating controls to maintain the confidentiality and integrity of business sensitive audio video and chat data shared on these platforms.

2 Common Platforms

Recently, Zoom has received a lot of media attention due to several Zero-day types of vulnerabilities that have cropped up, as well as renewed privacy concerns from the supposed sharing of user (Meta data) with Facebook that have lingered on for a while (a practice that Zoom claims it has now stopped).

Both Microsoft (Skype) and Cisco (WebEx) have had their own share of documented security issues and problems within their respective collaboration platforms.

This is my second chapter on the topic of enabling **secure** work-from-home paradigms. The previous chapter focused on the technologies used to work from home and there are three additional chapters that continue to discuss other aspects on how-to securely work from home.

R. Badhwar, *The CISO's Next Frontier*, https://doi.org/10.1007/978-3-030-75354-2_7

2.1   Skype for Business and Teams

Skype for business is a hybrid, on-premise or cloud (o365) hosted platform that has served the collaboration and messaging needs of the business enterprises for the last decade. I am not going to get into too much detail on the Skype vulnerabilities, since Skype is susceptible to most of the windows SMB and RCE related vulnerabilities, (e.g., **CVE-2020-0674** and **CVE-2020-0601**). Microsoft has been pretty good about releasing emergency patches or patching these on a monthly basis as part of their Patch Tuesday. Whether you are a corporate or a home user, please ensure that your Windows workstation is patched for these above-mentioned (and other) vulnerabilities.

Although the Skype for business platform is still being used across the world, its end-of-life dates have been released. Microsoft has already released its replacement – Microsoft Teams, which is a modern (o365 hosted) platform with better functionality, but already has some known security issues and vulnerabilities that have been released.

Teams has been found to be vulnerable to authentication (oauth) token stealing, and worm-able remote code execution (RCE) vulnerabilities delivered via malicious links (.LNK files) similar to the vulnerability described in **CVE-2020-0729**. While Microsoft has fixed many of the RCE vulnerabilities earlier in 2020, there is no solution to token stealing but the better enforcement of conditional access policies and using the newer paradigm of continuous evaluation (authentication) currently (Q42020/Q12020) available in preview mode.

2.2   WebEx

WebEx is one of the most popular web conferencing platforms but has lost share to Microsoft and Zoom in the last 1 year or two. Just in 2020, Cisco issued multiple security patches for the vulnerabilities below and one should ensure that all of these are patched in the given instances of WebEx that you may be running.

(a) **CVE-2020-3127** and **CVE-2020-3128** – "Multiple vulnerabilities in Cisco WebEx Network Recording Player for Microsoft Windows and Cisco WebEx Player for Microsoft Windows could allow an attacker to execute arbitrary code on an affected system. The vulnerabilities are due to insufficient validation of certain elements within a WebEx recording that is stored in either the Advanced Recording Format (ARF) or the WebEx Recording Format (WRF). An attacker could exploit these vulnerabilities by sending a malicious ARF or WRF file to a user through a link or email attachment and persuading the user to open the file on the local system. A successful exploit could allow the attacker to execute arbitrary code on the affected system with the privileges of the targeted user".

(b) **CVE-2020-3142** – "The vulnerability is due to unintended meeting information exposure in a specific meeting join flow for mobile applications. An unauthorized attendee could exploit this vulnerability by accessing a known meeting ID or meeting URL from the mobile device's web browser. The browser will then request to launch the device's WebEx mobile application".

(c) **CVE-2020-3116** – "A vulnerability in the way Cisco WebEx applications process Universal Communications Format (UCF) files could allow an attacker to cause a denial of service (DoS) condition. The vulnerability is due to insufficient validation of UCF media files. An attacker could exploit this vulnerability by sending a user a malicious UCF file through a link or email attachment and persuading the user to open the file with the affected software on the local system. A successful exploit would cause the application to quit unexpectedly".

From what I know, Cisco continues to invest in WebEx and is striving to make this a better, stable and secure platform.

2.3 Zoom

Since the onset of the pandemic, Zoom has rapidly become one of the most popular and widely used web conferencing and collaboration platform worldwide. Due to this rapid growth, they've had their own share of weaknesses and vulnerabilities that have been discovered and exploited.

A) It was reported that the chat feature within the Zoom Windows client is vulnerable to UNC (universal naming convention) path injection, enabling attackers to steal the Windows credentials of domain joined users who click on the link (which would make use of the SMB file sharing protocol to open/ execute the remote script/payload). This vulnerability affects all Zoom instances. Although this Windows hack, is well known (e.g., you can do the same attack via a Windows Explorer link) it is especially troubling because it can also be used to launch programs on the local host/machine and infect it with malware (I am not going to provide too much detail here and avoid sharing ideas that can be misused).

All Zoom needs to do to stop this hack is to prevent its chat client from converting the UNC links into hyperlinks. Many other chat clients have already fixed this vulnerability). While Zoom implements a fix, the other things that the firms using Zoom need to do is to –

1. Set a value of 'deny all' either individually (gpedit) or systematically (gpmc) for the value of the said policy – 'Network security: Restrict NTLM: Outgoing NTLM traffic to remote servers'.
2. Set a value of 2 for registry value RestrictSendingNTLMTraffic under HKEY_ LOCAL_MACHINE\SYSTEM\CurrentControlSet\Control\Lsa\MSV1_0 key.

3. Block or Restrict outbound NTLM traffic either in the local firewall or the perimeter firewall(s). [This should be the preferred approach with various other benefits.]

Note Due to the various Windows-based SMB vulnerabilities, outbound NTLM traffic should already be blocked for all domain joined windows machines. If the traffic is not blocked, then the Zoom chat client weaknesses should be the least of your worries.

B) The second issue is something called 'Zoom Bombing' where users can iterate the Zoom numbers and randomly join meetings midsession. While Zoom figures out a way to limit their exposure to this weakness, the easiest way to prevent unauthorized joining of meetings is by ensuring that every **meeting request is using a random meeting id and a meeting password**. This needs to be enforced for the account being used to send the meeting/sharing invite. In addition, the following additional steps may be taken to provide protection against known vulnerabilities and weaknesses (especially if all you want to do is to enable video conferencing) –

(a) Disable Chat and recording.
(b) Disable file sharing for the account being used.
(c) Disable feedback to Zoom.
(d) Only allow application sharing and disable desktop sharing in meetings.

Note These instructions will come in handy for any collaboration platform, including but not limited to Zoom, Skype, WebEx, Gotomeeting, and Chime.

C) It has also been reported that although all the (TCP and UDP) network traffic between a Zoom client (i.e., a meeting participant) and its server infrastructure is encrypted, the video, audio and chat traffic is theoretically visible to the Zoom service and its administrators on their internal network, leading to the potential of unauthorized access or (voluntary or involuntary) sharing or disclosures.

If you require end-to-end encryption or FIPS 140-2 compliance, then you should reconsider your choice of secure collaboration and request a dedicated tenant from one of the other providers discussed above. (**NOTE**: End-to-end encryption is not that easy. Even well-established players like Skype will have a hard time asserting end-to-end encryption and FIPS compliance for all use cases involving audio, video and text data, especially when you mix in data from PSTN/SS7 networks).

If you are worried about the security and privacy issues, please note that if configured correctly, following the threat and risk mitigation steps that I have provided above, then Zoom is as safe to use as any other video conferencing and collaboration service.

[Since this chapter was originally written during the summer of 2020, Zoom has released multiple patches to fix and resolve most of the issues highlighted and reported earlier, but we should remain vigilant and continue to monitor for any future weaknesses or vulnerabilities that may manifest themselves due to the constant evolution of this platform].

3 The CISO Take –

While the software and services for video conferencing and online collaboration are key in enabling the recent work from home paradigm, the users must be aware of the security pitfalls and take steps to ensure that their audio, video or chat data is not subject to unauthorized access, exposure, snooping or disclosures.

Another factor to keep in mind is that most of these platforms have moved from the legacy on-premise hosted environments to SaaS and thus any vulnerability and remote code exploits discovered puts all the customers at risk simultaneously irrespective of any local security controls in the traditional walled garden.

The CISOs must highlight the renewed risk from SaaS exploits and the stealing of authentication and refresh tokens which can be misused by threat actors to authenticate to these cloud hosted platforms as the compromised user. They must ensure that conditional access and continuous evaluation and authentication paradigms are enabled for these platforms using inherent capabilities in Azure and Office 365 (for Microsoft) or through other capabilities enabled by platforms like ZScaler or other CASB platforms.

All the three video conferencing vendors referenced in his chapter have done a good job of remediating vulnerabilities as they were discovered and have collaborated with the CISOs to ensure that the capabilities exist to ensure the secure work from home paradigm, and I applaud them for that.

4 Definitions

CASB – stands for Cloud Access Security Broker. It is an on-premise or cloud hosted security policy enforcement point, generally resident between the flow of network or application traffic and cloud-hosted or based services (e.g., SaaS, IaaS or PaaS). The security policies enforced include but are not limited to DLP, SSO, MFA, logging, and malware detection.

FIPS 140-2 – stands for the Federal Information Processing Standard. (FIPS) Publication 140–2 is a US and Canadian government standard that specifies the security requirements for cryptographic modules that protect sensitive information.

MPLS – stands for Multiprotocol Label switching. It is a label-based data routing technology that enables much faster data transfer and control in a network. It is very scalable and protocol independent i.e., works with both IP and ATM traffic.

NTLM – stands for NT Lan manager. It is the replacement for LM. It is a Microsoft security protocol primarily used to provide authentication services to client and server sessions. NTLM v1 is considered insecure and the current recommend version of NTLM is v2.

Zero Day – is an unknown exploit that is used to expose and subsequent take advantage of a software or firmware vulnerability or weakness and then maybe subsequently used to launch a cyber-attack or breach a network or a system.

Further Reading

BRODKIN J (2020). Zoom lied to users about end-to-end encryption for years, FTC says. https://arstechnica.com/tech-policy/2020/11/zoom-lied-to-users-about-end-to-end-encryption-for-years-ftc-says/ Accessed on 23 December, 2020

CISCO WebEx Meeting. https://www.cisco.com/c/en/us/products/conferencing/webex-meetings/index.html

CVE Search List. https://cve.mitre.org/cve/

Hutchinson A (2020). Zoom Releases New Update to Address Security Concerns. https://www.socialmediatoday.com/news/zoom-releases-new-update-to-address-security-concerns/576585/ Accessed on 23 Jan, 2021

Khalili J (2020). Microsoft Teams may have downplayed a disastrous security issue. https://www.techradar.com/news/microsoft-may-have-downplayed-a-disastrous-teams-security-issue Accessed 23 December, 2020

Krohn M (2020). Zoom Rolling Out End-to-End Encryption Offering. https://blog.zoom.us/zoom-rolling-out-end-to-end-encryption-offering/ Accessed 23 December, 2020

Lee M, Grauer Y (2020). ZOOM MEETINGS AREN'T END-TO-END ENCRYPTED, DESPITE MISLEADING MARKETING. https://theintercept.com/2020/03/31/zoom-meeting-encryption/ Accessed 23 December, 2020

Microsoft (2020). Skype End of life dates. https://support.microsoft.com/en-us/lifecycle/search?alpha=Skype

Microsoft. Skype for Business. https://docs.microsoft.com/en-us/skypeforbusiness/

O'Flaherty K (2020). Are Zoom Chats Private? Here's Why You Should Think Before Opening the App. https://www.forbes.com/sites/kateoflahertyuk/2020/03/31/are-your-zoom-chats-private-heres-why-you-should-think-before-opening-the-app/?sh=325260171979 Accessed 23 December, 2020

Paul K (2020). Zoom releases security updates in response to 'Zoom-bombings'. https://www.theguardian.com/technology/2020/apr/23/zoom-update-security-encryption-bombing Accessed Aug 22, 2020.

Wagenseil P (2021). https://www.tomsguide.com/news/zoom-security-privacy-woes . Zoom security issues: Here's everything that's gone wrong (so far). Accessed 23 Jan, 2021.

Yuan E (2020). Zoom Acquires Keybase and Announces Goal of Developing the Most Broadly Used Enterprise End-to-End Encryption Offering. https://blog.zoom.us/zoom-acquires-keybase-and-announces-goal-of-developing-the-most-broadly-used-enterprise-end-to-end-encryption-offering/ Accessed 23 December, 2020

If You Must Work from Home, Do It Securely!

1 Introduction

Given COVID-19 induced business continuity needs, every security technologist is being asked about the ways to enable the capability to work securely from home, right? This question would remain a very valid question in a post pandemic world.

I am going to provide a perspective here that is shared by me and many of my hands-on technical CISO peers. Another chapter in this book is focused on technological capabilities to enable corporate IT and business users to work from home in a secure manner. Using that chapter as the basis, I am going to provide some very basic yet effective guidance that can be used by any employer, from a small business owner to a large corporation, needing its employees to securely work from home.

Please note that most of these capabilities and services are based on infrastructure. Most individual users may not be able to implement these by themselves in their homes.

2 Secure Network Connectivity

There must be security in the network connectivity between a user's device and the remote application services infrastructure to maintain the confidentiality and integrity of sensitive data as it is being transmitted from user workstations (generally laptops and mobile devices) while employees are working from remote locations (generally their homes) for prolonged periods.

I have covered in a great amount of technical detail the two primary paradigms to securely connect while working from home in my previous chapter, but here's a quick recap of Virtual Private Networks and Virtual Desktop Infrastructure:

Virtual Private Cloud (VPN) – When used in conjunction with MFA, VPN is the primary technology which provides the capability to extend a private (corporate) network across a public network (e.g., the internet) assigning a remote user a private IP address and enabling a remote user or employee to send and receive data as if he/she were onsite at a corporate facility. Under the hood, the data is encrypted/decrypted and traverses a secure tunnel created between the remote client and on-premise or cloud hosted corporate VPN system.

Virtual Desktop Infrastructure (VDI) – The other commonly used technology is the one that virtualizes the desktop experience (the OS and all the native apps that get installed on a local desktop) by running it in a public or private cloud environment and making it available in a way that is appears to be local to each user. The VDI paradigm generally applies to the Windows OS but can also be made available for Linux and other operating systems. Also, some of the other terms that one may hear in the VDI space is that of a persistent vs non-persistent, aka Stateful vs Stateless VDI, where a persistent/Stateful VDI session stores a given user's settings, configuration, state and data and thus allows for retrieval when the user comes back later, as compared to a non-persistent/stateless VDI session where all the user data is considered transient, one-time use only, and is destroyed once the session expires or is terminated.

VDI is a very useful capability that allows workers to work remotely in a secure manner. This has a lot of security benefits as it provides for better endpoint control, governance and monitoring capabilities.

Remote desktop Services (RDP) – This is still being used by mid to smaller size firms and must be discontinued as it is not considered a secure way to work remotely. All internet exposed RDP services and ports must be blocked with immediate effect. In some cases, to support certain use cases, making an RDP connection over VPN may be allowed if other mitigating and monitoring security controls (mentioned in this chapter) are present.

3   Implement Application Segmentation with Zero Trust

While VPN is a time trusted technique and has served the information security community around the world very well in the past in providing secure remote access, it also carries the risk of providing unfettered access to a company's network, especially in case of a flat network with very little or no network (micro) segmentation. The lack of segmentation becomes very problematic if a user's VPN credentials were ever to be compromised or breached by a threat actor.

The modern way to provide secure access is to use software-defined networking (SDN) techniques to enable application segmentation, not network segmentation. A user gets remote access only to needed applications rather than to the entire internal network, all applications, and the intranet, thereby reducing the threat surface and associated risk in case the remote access credentials of a user working from home were to ever get compromised.

4   Close Device Side Doors

Split Tunnel – Disable all split tunneling and dual homing on a device and thereby enable the closure of any side channels that could be compromised to exfiltrate data by insider threats, bad actors or malware.

Please note these are generally done either within the VPN configurations or through Windows GPO (group policy object) and generally are not something that the user can implement themselves.

Block RDP ports – All internet exposed RDP ports must be blocked. All internal use of RDP must be discouraged and restricted to specific users using custom security policies implemented along with other security controls like MFA, network segmentation and access with least privilege.

5   Implement Advanced Monitoring and Blocking

Working from home for prolonged periods does increase the risk of data exfiltration and unauthorized access. While there is no silver bullet to eliminate this risk altogether, here are a couple of things that can be implemented as mitigating controls –

Internet Proxy (On-premise and Off-Premise) – All internet bound traffic from all devices in off-premise (home or other remote) locations must also traverse through an internet proxy all the time, just like it does while a device is on-premise. The proxy monitors all off-premise internet traffic usage from company assets and devices, and can also block all data exfiltration attempts using web-based email and cloud-based file sharing (e.g., Microsoft OneDrive, Google Drive, Box, etc.). Modern internet and cloud proxies also have the network DLP (data loss prevention) capability and can even block the transfer of sensitive data based on pre-configured DLP rules.

Always on VPN connection – Alternatively you could use a VPN client that will auto (force) connect to a VPN server at login time, forcing all (off-premise) internet traffic through your VPN infrastructure and providing the equivalent monitoring and blocking capability discussed above (i.e., Internet Proxy). This technique is even more effective when used in conjunction with disabled split tunneling.

6   Manage BYOD

Bring your own device (BYOD) – It should only be used when risks are low. If you must use BYOD to connect remotely into a VDI or VPN service, then only allow the use of (secure) VDI+MFA from a BYOD device to connect to a said corporate network. The VDI must be configured to disable all copy/paste/download/print functionality, and must run at a minimum with an AV, DLP and EDR agent (preferably at the hyper-visor). To provide further security, all VDIs must use biometric based (preferably Face-ID) authentication token as the second factor of authentication.

7 Implement Dynamic Host Checking

The remote device must be subject with dynamic host checking every time it tries to connect to the VDI (or VPN) service. This would provide a real-time dynamic check to ensure that the remote device is free of malware, has all the recent security patches, has all the updated AV signatures, and has good overall security hygiene.

8 Implement End Point Controls

Visibility – Deploy a capable EDR (Endpoint Detection and Response) agent armed with some sophisticated behavioral analysis machine learning algorithms to gain good visibility on your endpoints.

It is preferred that a corporate owned EDR tool be installed on partner and contractor machines to provide uniform and centralized endpoint telemetry that can be correlated with other machines and devices for threat analysis.

Dynamic White-listing – Make use of application control techniques (like white-listing) to reduce malware and other harmful security attacks by only allowing approved and trusted (i.e., digitally signed) files, applications, and processes to be installed and run on a system (endpoint, server or otherwise). The modern way of doing this is to use **real-time** dynamic white-listing.

9 The CISO Take

CISOs and their cyber-security teams face big challenges in maintaining security as company employees work from home. Using guidance from the techniques elucidated in this article, they can set up infrastructure in a manner that upholds the fundamental cyber-security principles of data confidentiality, integrity, and availability.

The CISOs need to make sure that the security programs they run have the capability to perform enhanced monitoring and should strive towards an implementation state that closely aligns with Zero Trust to reduce the increased cyber risk from this pandemic induced expanded work from home paradigm.

10   Definitions

AV – stands for Anti-Virus. It is computer software that has the capability to detect, prevent, block, and remove malware. Most legacy AV uses static (hash-based) signatures to perform the detection.

DLP – stands for Data Loss Prevention. It is a technology that prevents the unauthorized access to or exfiltration of company and customer sensitive data.

Dual Homing – it is the capability that provides a networked device (computer) with more than one network interface (generally ethernet).

EDR – stands for Endpoint Detection and Response. EDR is the next generation malware detection system. Rather than relying on the legacy static signature provided by/generated by legacy AV detection products, it has the capability to provide visibility into endpoint user, machine and process behavior, and perform dynamic heuristical analysis, which it then uses to detect and block advanced malware.

RDP – stands for remote desktop service. Initially known as terminal services, RDP is the remote work capability made available by Microsoft which allows users to log in from a corporate or personal device using a public (internet) or private (VPN) network.

SDN – stands for software defined networking. It is a modern approach to network architecture and design that uses uniform software defined and managed controls rather than the hardware-based controls of the past, to enable the capability of centralized management, including but not limited to faster delivery and reconfigurations, better monitoring and alerting, and reduced cost of maintenance.

Split Tunneling – it is a networking capability which allows a user to connect to two separate networks at the same time.

Zero Trust – is a security architecture and implementation paradigm that reduces enterprise risk by performing secure implementations in compliance with the principal that all assets inside and outside a perimeter firewall are not to be trusted and thus access control for users, devices, systems and services must be provided using least privilege.

Further Reading

Ahrens M (2018), The Risks of Remote Desktop Access Are Far from Remote. https://www.darkreading.com/endpoint/the-risks-of-remote-desktop-access-are-far-from-remote/a/d-id/1331820. Accessed July 4 2020.

Brook C (2020). The Ultimate Guide to BYOD Security https://digitalguardian.com/blog/ultimate-guide-byod-security-overcoming-challenges-creating-effective-policies-and-mitigating. Accessed 20 Jan 2021.

BYRES E (2010). Dual Homed Machines are the Juiciest Targets. https://www.tofinosecurity.com/blog/dual-homed-machines-are-juiciest-targets , Accessed Dec 25, 2020.

Givati M (2018). Application Segmentation, https://www.guardicore.com/micro-segmentation/application-segmentation/. Accessed Dec 6, 2020.

Hein D (2019). Five BYOD Management Best Practices for Enterprises, https://solutionsreview.com/mobile-device-management/five-byod-management-best-practices-for-enterprises/   . Accessed July 6 2020.

Jeffery E (2020) VPN Split-Tunneling – To Enable or Not To Enable. https://www.infosecurity-magazine.com/opinions/vpn-split-tunneling/ . Accessed Dec 25, 2020.

Katz B (2013). The right way to manage BYOD, https://www.infoworld.com/article/2614836/the-right-way-to-manage-byod.html. Accessed on July 6 2020.

NIST. Securing Network connections – https://www.nist.gov/itl/smallbusinesscyber/guidance-topic/securing-network-connections. Accessed Dec 15, 2020.

Seshadri N (2020). How Micro segmentation Differs from Network Segmentation, https://www.zscaler.com/blogs/product-insights/how-microsegmentation-differs-network-segmentation. Accessed Dec 6, 2020.

Zscaler staff writer (2020). What is network segmentation, https://www.zscaler.com/resources/security-terms-glossary/what-is-network-segmentation. Accessed Dec 24, 2020.

Security Controls for Remote Access Technologies

1 Introduction

This chapter shares some details about the basic yet effective security controls for remote access technologies used either by commercial firms or individuals at home.

2 Virtual Private Network (VPN)

The below mentioned security controls must either be in place or implemented for VPN.

2.1 Local Device Authentication

Ensure a strong authentication scheme for login into the (local) device used to connect to the VPN Service. Ideally, use a hardware or biometric based authenticator for this purpose, especially for regulated entities or the ones that carry inherently higher than normal cyber-risk.

2.2 Endpoint Checking

The VPN client (or browser plugin) must have the native capability to perform dynamic and real-time checks on the actual device being used to connect to the remote VPN service such as checks for updated AV signatures within the last 48 h,

© The Author(s), under exclusive license to Springer Nature Switzerland AG 2021
R. Badhwar, *The CISO's Next Frontier*,
https://doi.org/10.1007/978-3-030-75354-2_9

updated security patches within the last 7 days, and verification of the status of whole disk encryption (e.g., Bitlocker). If the client device fails any of these checks, then the VPN access must not be granted. In some cases, given the cyber-risk posture for a given business or firm, temporary access can be granted by quarantining the machine and only allowing access to certain applications (e.g., email, time reporting system, or any other system required per local, state of federal regulations).

To login into the VPN client, use a unique user id and strong password. Enable two-factor authentication and employ a strong virtual or hard token – biometric authenticators are preferrable. Certificate based authentication to enable dual or mutual authentication can also be used to augment the user/pass authentication, to further bolster the security posture.

An EDR (endpoint detection and response) and NGAV (next generation antivirus) agent must be resident on the endpoint to detect, alert, and prevent against any malware or behavioral anomalies.

Routinely penetration test the endpoint to detect and patch vulnerabilities such as dynamic code injection and man-in-the-middle attacks.

2.3   Data Encryption

You must ensure that the technologies used to create the VPN connection (tunnel) are approved by the resident information security team and secured such as [L2TP (layer 2 tunneling protocol) + IPSec + IKEv2], PPTP (Point to Point tunneling protocol), OpenVPN or equivalent, and SSTP (safeguard socket tunneling protocol). Also ensure that strong data encryption algorithms like AES 256 or 3DES and masking/hashing algorithms like SHA 256 are used by the respective VPN scheme.

2.4   VPN Service Hardening

Harden the remote VPN Service using the concept of least privilege, patching all known critical and high vulnerabilities and disabling all unnecessary ports and protocols.

The VPN Service must be routinely penetration tested to identify and remediate any vulnerabilities, susceptibility to man in the middle attacks, or remote exploits.

2.5   Network Segmentation

Drawing from the concept of Zero Trust and depending upon the level of network micro segmentation implemented, the profile for a user can be used to only allow access to certain network segments once they get on VPN. This is generally done by assigning an IP range that only has access to certain network segments or subnets allowing them access to only certain applications or systems based on their need.

2.6   Split Tunneling and Dual/Multi Homing

To prevent data exfiltration scenario's, split tunneling and dual/multi homing must be disabled for the client machine from which a VPN connection is made to the corporate network. Thus, while the user device is using a (corporate) VPN, its connection to any other network must be disabled.

3   Virtual Desktop Infrastructure (VDI)

The below mentioned security controls must either be in place or implemented for VDI.

3.1   Local Device Authentication

Have a strong authentication scheme to login into the local device used to connect to the remote VDI service. Basic authentication (i.e., user ID and password) for a thin client is generally considered acceptable, but use a hardware or biometric based authenticator for non-thin clients.

3.2   Endpoint Checking

The client (e.g., the VMWare horizon client) used to connect to a remote VDI service from any device other than a thin client must have the capability, either natively or with the aid of supporting software, to perform a dynamic and real-time check on the actual device being used to connect to the remote VDI service, including checks for updated AV signatures within the last 48 h and updated security patches within the last 7 days. If the client device fails either of these checks, then deny access to the VDI service. In some cases, given the cyber-risk posture for a given business or firm, limited access to certain basic applications (e.g., email, time reporting system) can be provided for a non-persistent/stateless instance.

Ensure a strong authentication scheme. To login into the remote VDI service, use a unique user id and strong password. Enable two-factor authentication (2FA) employing a strong virtual or hard token – biometric authenticators are preferrable.

An EDR (Endpoint detection and response) and NGAV (next generation antivirus) agent must reside on the endpoint to detect, alert and prevent against 'screenshot malware'used to steal PII customer data or account information via screenshots.

Routinely penetration test the endpoint to detect and patch vulnerabilities such as dynamic code injection attacks.

3.3   Data Encryption

Ensure the VDI client uses TLS 1.2 or higher to create an encrypted session to the remote service. Use strong data encryption algorithms like AES 256 or 3DES and masking/hashing algorithms like SHA 256 in the initial handshake and session negotiation, and then for subsequent data transmissions.

3.4   VDI Service Hardening

Harden the VDI Service using the concept of least privilege, patch all known critical and high vulnerabilities and disable all unnecessary ports and protocols.

Routinely penetration test the VDI Service to identify and remediate any vulnerabilities or remote exploits.

3.5   DLP Controls

The VDI (client) should have local data loss prevention (DLP) controls implemented preventing users from functionality like copy/paste or printing (if needed per compliance requirements). The VDI server must have DLP enabled for every VDI session.

4   Remote Desktop Services (RDP)

Initially known as terminal services, remote desktop service is the remote work capability made available by Microsoft which allows users to log in from a corporate or personal device using a public (internet) or private (VPN) network. They basically remote into either a centralized server or their physical desktop to gain access to the corporate network and applications.

Exposing RDP directly over the internet is highly discouraged and the RDP ports (typically 3389) are generally blocked in the perimeter firewalls.

I am not a big fan of RDP but *internal* use of this capability may be allowed if proper security controls of network micro segmentation, application segmentation, user access with least privilege and continuous (authentication) evaluation are in place.

4.1 RDP Over VPN

The use of RDP over VPN (i.e., RDP in after establishing a VPN connection), has been allowed in some firms. This is generally done if the remote users do not have corporate issued laptops and want to login into their corporate (physical) desktops remotely by using their personal devices (BYOD). This practice must be discontinued to account for business continuity concerns, as it hampers the remote employees' ability to work independently if his/her work desktop goes offline due to power outages or other network issues. The laptops are a commodity these days and must be procured and distributed to all employees that need to work remotely. This also enables the security teams to get the corporate endpoint security stack on the endpoint to help enable the needed monitoring and response capabilities.

Many enterprises are blocking RDP ports even in the local host (windows) firewalls, which will cause any use of RDP to break.

5 The CISO Take

The 2020 pandemic has set the future state of remote work, at least for the near future. With a large majority of our users working remotely (from home) the use of VPN and VDI as the technologies that enables this remote has sky rocketed – and so have the attacks.

It is thus imperative that the security controls elaborated in this chapter be implemented. They will help to maintain the confidentiality, integrity and availability of data being transmitted from a remote device connecting to a company network using either VPN or VDI.

The CISOs have to continue to find ways to improve the security of VPN and VDI technologies, as new threats evolve.

6 Definitions

3DES – stands for triple data encryption algorithm (DES). It is a symmetric data encryption algorithm that applies 3 rounds of the (56 bit) DES algorithm to each data block.

AES 256 – stands for advanced encryption standard. It is the AES data encryption algorithm with the use of a 256 key bit key.

Dual Homing – it is the capability that provides a networked device (computer) with more than one network interface (generally ethernet).

EDR – stands for Endpoint Detection and Response. EDR is the next generation malware detection system. Rather than relying on the legacy static signature provided by/generated by legacy AV detection products, it has the capability to give visibility into endpoint user, machine and process behavior, and perform dynamic heuristical analysis, which it then uses to detect and block advanced malware.

NGAV (Next Generation Anti-Virus) – Is the AV engine with modern ML-enabled AI algorithms to perform behavioral threat detection and remediation and malware sandboxing in conjunction with legacy techniques like malware (static hash based) signatures.

RDP – stands for remote desktop service. Initially known as terminal services, RDP is the remote work capability made available by Microsoft which allows users to log in from a corporate or personal device using a public (internet) or private (VPN) network.

SHA 256 – It is part of the SHA-2 family and is used to denote the 256-bit cryptographic hash SHA algorithm.

Split Tunneling – it is a networking capability which allows a user to connect to two separate networks at the same time.

TLS – stands for transport layer security. It is used to provide data in transit encryption for various use cases including but not limited to web browsing, email, instant messaging, file transfers etc.

Thin client – is a virtual end user computing asset hosted on a virtual machine on remote server. The thin client utilizes a shared pool of multitenant computing resources like CPU, RAM and storage.

Further Reading

BYRES E (2010). Dual Homed Machines are the Juiciest Targets. https://www.tofinosecurity.com/blog/dual-homed-machines-are-juiciest-targets, Accessed Dec 25, 2020.

Cloudflare (2020). What are the security risks of RDP? https://www.cloudflare.com/learning/access-management/rdp-security-risks/. Accessed Dec 24, 2020.

Craven C (2020), Virtual Private Network (VPN) Best Practices, https://www.sdxcentral.com/security/definitions/what-are-vpn-best-practices, Accessed 24 Dec, 2020.

Hickman M (2018). Security meets flexibility: A checklist for virtual desktop infrastructure, https://www.bai.org/banking-strategies/article-detail/security-meets-flexibility-a-checklist-for-virtual-desktop-infrastructure/, Accessed 7 July, 2020.

Jeffery E (2020) VPN Split-Tunneling – To Enable or Not To Enable. https://www.infosecurity-magazine.com/opinions/vpn-split-tunneling/. Accessed Dec 25, 2020.

Lohr H et al (2020). Security best practices, https://docs.microsoft.com/en-us/azure/virtual-desktop/security-guide. Accessed 24 Dec, 2020.

Ringold J (2020). Security guidance for remote desktop adoption. https://www.microsoft.com/security/blog/2020/04/16/security-guidance-remote-desktop-adoption/.   Accessed   Dec 25, 2020.

VMware staff writer (2020). VMware Security Hardening Guides, https://www.vmware.com/security/hardening-guides.html. Accessed 24 Dec, 2020.

Specialty Malware and Backdoors for VDI

1 Introduction

Virtual desktop infrastructure (VDI) is a technology that provides a secure remote desktop offering, enabling users to work securely from remote locations (e.g., working from home due to COVID-19-induced social distancing). This technology protects against endpoint malware and other endpoint cyber-threats, and prevents data exfiltration, since no data is actually stored locally on an endpoint device. It also prevents data theft because it does not generally allow the use of removable media, outbound internet access and printing.

VDI is susceptible to malware that has been specially crafted to be used on this platform. Also, it does have some exposure to backdoors as well. Both these topics have been discussed in this chapter.

2 Risk Analysis

Security professionals love VDI for its excellent data security. If there is one weakness, it is the capability to take pictures of the data visible on the desktop. Both humans and malware can exploit this screenshot capability. We all know about the human capability to exploit this through cameras, but we also know these could be prevented through policy, and by using controlled and monitored environments for desktops; however, in this chapter, I am going to shed some light on the much higher risk posed by malware that can also exploit this weakness. We will also review risk from backdoors in the VDI environments.

© The Author(s), under exclusive license to Springer Nature Switzerland AG 2021
R. Badhwar, *The CISO's Next Frontier*,
https://doi.org/10.1007/978-3-030-75354-2_10

3   Malware

There are a few types of specialty malware used to target VDI systems.

3.1   SquirtDanger (SD)

There is one type of malware called SquirtDanger, which is a commodity botnet. It is written in C# and has multiple layers of embedded code. Once resident on a host (victim) system, it persists through a scheduled task which is generally set to run every minute. It then uses raw TCP connections to communicate with a remote command and control (CnC) server to receive commands and also transfer/exfiltrate data. This malware has the uncanny ability to take screenshots and upload them to the remote CnC server or other servers upon the commands of the CnC servers. It defeats the data protection provided by VDI by using its capability to take screenshots (primarily to steal customer PII data or other account data to further its financially motivated operations).

It can also perform various other activities to avoid detection: it can list and kill processes, list drives and get directory information, steal passwords stored in a browser, and execute commands and code. It has also been known to have a special affinity for stealing wallets for bitcoin and other cryptocurrencies.

Palo Alto's Unit52 researchers have published pioneering research on SquirtDanger. [1]

3.2   Disk Wipers

This family of disk wiping malware (Shamoon or Disttrack), which targets VDI systems, has been used to launch successful attacks against a Middle Eastern country and subsequently against a large US corporation.

This malware generally spreads to other computers on a local network using stolen or compromised credentials. In the past it has generally used breached credentials for windows domain controllers (DCs) but has also used default credentials for some common virtual desktop platforms.

The next-generation variant of Shamoon is also known to have capabilities to destroy the VDI backup snapshots which may make it impossible for the VDI to recover from the initial attack.

4   Backdoors

There are two types of backdoors that can exist in a VDI environment.

4.1 Golden Image

This is an illicit backdoor that can be embedded by attackers inside the golden image of a VDI image (full or linked clone). Attackers generally embed themselves by using a stolen (but valid) digital certificate to sign a compromised (trojanized) library or system component of the VDI image file used to create full or linked clones. Once the VMs are created from the VDI images, the backdoor activates and reaches out to the CnC server under the control of the attacker to establish a communication with preconfigured or DGA-generated malicious domain(s).

This is especially dangerous, as it has the potential to create a backdoor into each VM created from the VDI image. How these backdoors could further make use of 'host VM escape' vulnerabilities and exploits to run exploit code on the hypervisor or parent host of the VM is discussed below in 4.2.

4.2 Host VM Escape

An attacker will use this technique from an unprivileged account to escape from a VM to the host, resulting in the capability to execute code or achieve residency on the host, thereby overriding all inherent isolation assurances.

The attacker generally achieves this by exploiting the backdoor communication between the host and the VM, many times using the tools (e.g., open-vm-tools) provided by the hypervisor OEM, and by writing malicious fuzzers and exploits.

Although the backdoor is ultimately the means by which the attacker escapes the VM to get to the host, the term 'backdoor' is not a reference to something malicious here; rather, it is what is initially established as the legitimate communication channel between the VM and hypervisor.

I have provided some known VMWare vulnerabilities that have been exploited (in the past) for the above-mentioned purposes –

(a) **CVE-2017-4904** – An unpatched XHCI controller in VMware ESXi has a vulnerability with uninitialized memory usage. This issue may allow a guest to execute code on the host. The issue can also be used to conduct a Denial of Service of the guest on the host [2].
(b) **CVE-2017-4905** – An unpatched VMware ESXi has a vulnerability with uninitialized memory usage. This issue may lead to an information leak [3].
(c) **CVE-2017-4901** – The drag-and-drop (DnD) function in VMware Workstation and Fusion has an out-of-bounds memory access vulnerability. This may allow a guest to execute code on the operating system that runs Workstation or Fusion [4].
(d) **CVE-2020-3981** – VMware ESXi contains an out-of-bounds read vulnerability due to a time-of-check time-of-use issue in the ACPI device. A malicious actor with administrative access to a virtual machine may be able to exploit this issue to leak memory from the vmx process [6].

(e) **CVE-2020-3982** – VMware ESXi contain an out-of-bounds write vulnerability due to a time-of-check time-of-use issue in ACPI device. A malicious actor with administrative access to a virtual machine may be able to exploit this vulnerability to crash the virtual machine's vmx process or corrupt the hypervisor's memory heap [5].

While most of the above-mentioned vulnerabilities have been patched, there are various other ways to perform (malicious) host VM escape and thus every new hypervisor release must be penetration tested to ensure that new vulnerabilities using backdoor communications (that can be exploited using fuzzers) have not been inadvertently introduced.

5 Protections

The indicators of compromise (IOCs) for this malware are known and are loaded into our next-generation (application aware) firewalls, which use threat intel from Wildfire and other endpoint application control and whitelisting security agents. However, we need to keep a close eye on this, as there is always the possibility for new malware variants that can evade detection. Additional capability provided by endpoint detection and response (EDR) security agents is also used in the industry to detect this malware. EDR security agents can rely on IOCs and examine the behavioral traits of malware as it executes on an endpoint or servers, detecting and blocking any new variants.

Another way to protect sensitive data is to watermark the data or add custom tags to every page, so that any image taken would carry the watermark with it, making it easier to identify or recover.

Users logged into VDI sessions should be continuously authenticated; to ensure that any behavioral change or anomaly detected triggers another step-up authentication event.

For all environments (prod/pre-prod/test/dev), one must never use any default credentials for VDI platforms, especially for the admin or root accounts.

Any data exfiltrated by means such as taking screenshots generally finds its way onto the dark web. It is prudent to scan known dark web frequently to identify and act to remediate (or take down) this exfiltrated data to protect any further exposure from misuse of this data.

In addition, the VDI images used to create linked or full clones should be tested and analyzed for malware by using sandboxing or equivalent techniques.

6 The CISO Take

The intent of this chapter is to create an awareness that even safe technologies like VDI have some risks, which means we should always be vigilant. Specifically, we should ensure all our endpoints are continuously and regularly patched for vulnerabilities and exploits and have a modern endpoint security stack that includes next-gen antivirus (NGAV), EDR, application controls, and dynamic whitelisting to protect against advanced malware.

Security technologists should be aware of the threat of backdoors within the popular VDI platforms used in the industry and must apply the principle of Zero Trust by scanning all the software components that make a golden VDI image for vulnerabilities, and subsequently sandbox VMs created from VDI images before they are released in production for general availability. They must also ensure that security patches for all known hypervisor vulnerabilities are implemented to fix the various exploits used to perform host VM escape.

7 Definitions

CnC – stands for command and control (server). Generally, a cloud-hosted server/ system often working in tandem with malware using DGA-generated domains, the CnC is used by threat actors to control and manage infected and breached endpoints and servers (generally resident) on private networks.

EDR – stands for Endpoint Detection and Response. EDR is the next-generation malware detection system. Rather than relying on the legacy static signature generated by legacy AV detection products, it has the capability to provide visibility into endpoint user, machine, and process behavior, and perform dynamic heuristical analysis, which it then uses to detect and block advanced malware.

ESXi – stands for Elastic Sky X (now just known as ESXi), a type 1 hypervisor created by VMware. It runs directly on the hardware of the physical host and has the capability to control and manage the OS and hardware.

Full Clone – is an independent copy of a virtual machine (VM) and does not access or maintain an ongoing connection to the parent virtual machine. These do not share virtual disk with the parent and thus have better performance. They do take much longer to instantiate than a linked clone.

Fuzzing – is a technique used to find security bugs in software. It is generally used for testing untrusted interfaces and inputs. It can also be used to discover vulnerabilities and create exploits.

IOC – stands for indicator of compromise. It is either a unique signature, log entry, or an event that indicates that a network or system breach has occurred. These can be used as forensic evidence, either individually or in combination with other IOCs.

Linked Clone – is generally a copy (snapshot) of a parent virtual machine (VM). These share virtual disks with the parent which can lead to disk contention and performance issues. This cloning technique allows multiple VMs to use the same software installation which helps to conserve disk space. These are also much faster to instantiate (spin up), and provide better security monitoring and cleanup capabilities.

NGAV – stands for Next-Generation Antivirus. It is the AV engine with modern ML-enabled AI algorithms to perform behavioral threat detection, remediation, and malware sandboxing in conjunction with legacy techniques like malware (static hash-based) signatures.

References

1. Grunzweig J, et al (2018) SquirtDanger: the swiss army knife malware from veteran malware author TheBottle. Available via Palo Alto Networks. https://unit42.paloaltonetworks.com/unit42-squirtdanger-swiss-army-knife-malware-veteran-malware-author-thebottle/ Accessed 10 Dec 2020
2. CVE Details: The Ultimate Security Vulnerability Datasource (2021) The MITRE Corporation, McLean. https://www.cvedetails.com/cve/CVE-2017-4904/. Accessed 13 Jan 2021
3. CVE Details: The Ultimate Security Vulnerability Datasource (2021) The MITRE Corporation, McLean. https://www.cvedetails.com/cve/CVE-2017-4905/. Accessed 13 Jan 2021
4. CVE Details: The Ultimate Security Vulnerability Datasource (2021) The MITRE Corporation, McLean. https://www.cvedetails.com/cve/CVE-2017-4901/. Accessed 13 Jan 2021
5. Common Vulnerabilities and Exposures (2021) The MITRE Corporation, McLean. https://cve.mitre.org/cgi-bin/cvename.cgi?name=CVE-2020-3982 . Accessed 13 Jan 2021
6. Common Vulnerabilities and Exposures (2021) The MITRE Corporation, McLean. https://cve.mitre.org/cgi-bin/cvename.cgi?name=CVE-2020-3981. Accessed 13 Jan 2021

Further Reading

VMWare Documentation (2020). VMware Workstation 5.0 Understanding Clones https://www.vmware.com/support/ws5/doc/ws_clone_overview.html , Accessed Jan 4, 2021.
Godefroid P (2020) Fuzzing: Hack, Art, and Science. Comm of the ACM 63(2):70-76. https://doi.org/10.1145/3363824 . Accessed Jan 4, 2021
Kurth O (2020) https://github.com/vmware/open-vm-tools/blob/master/open-vm-tools/lib/backdoor/backdoor.c
Security VDI. Available via SentinelOne. https://assets.sentinelone.com/vdi1/sentinel-one-vdi-2 , Accessed 12 Dec 2020
What is VDI security? Available via VMWare. https://www.vmware.com/topics/glossary/content/virtual-desktop-infrastructure-security Accessed 12 Dec 2020
Wiggenhorn R (2017) Busting the non-persistent VDI security myth! Available via HP Bromium Blog. https://threatresearch.ext.hp.com/busting-non-persistent-vdi-security-myth/. Accessed 12 Dec 2020
Zhang Y K (2017) Analyzing a patch of a virtual machine escape on VMware, https://www.mcafee.com/blogs/other-blogs/mcafee-labs/analyzing-patch-of-a-virtual-machine-escape-on-vmware/.
Zhao HQ, et al (2019) Breaking turtles all the way down: an exploitation chain to break out of VMware ESXi., In: WOOT'19: Proceedings of the 13th USENIX conference on offensive technologies, https://www.usenix.org/system/files/woot19-paper_zhao.pdf

Part IV
Data Security

The Future State of Data Security

1 Introduction

Data security is paramount in cyber security. If a given business entity could some-how protect all their sensitive data, then their cyber risk from a data breach, unau-thorized access, or an exfiltration event would reduce tremendously – much to the liking of security and risk professionals worldwide.

Data breaches occur almost daily, yet with some promising solutions on the hori-zon, we can make this future state a current one. It is the responsibility of security technologists to start enabling the work and adoption required to improve data security.

This chapter will speak about the current state of data protection, review some common techniques and offer a vision into the future state with some promising implementations.

2 Current State

First let's talk about the current state which has served the cyber security and infor-mation technology communities very well so far.

Currently, there are three primary paradigms of logical and physical data protec-tion for both structured and unstructured data: data obfuscation (masking), digital rights management of data, and data encryption.

2.1   Data Obfuscation

This data protection method is generally used to mask or obfuscate sensitive data either at rest and/or in motion. Data obfuscation can be computationally intense, although a lot depends on strength of the masking algorithm. E.g., computing times required for SHA-256 and SHA-512 are higher than (the now broken) SHA-1 and MD-5. Data obfuscation is only useful for certain use cases where the original sensitive data is not required in plaintext (e.g., passwords) once it has been obfuscated, because generally speaking obfuscation is done using a one-way hash.

Data masking and de-personalization techniques also find widespread use in quality assurance and testing use cases, where production data has to be masked before it is allowed to be used in lower-level environments (e.g., unit, integration, pre-prod etc.), to comply with information security and privacy requirements.

2.2   Digital Right Management (DRM)

This data protection method provides the capability to categorize and digitally manage access and rights at a granular level on the said data to be protected. It is the newest and the most practical way to provide protection to sensitive data. DRM uses data encryption to protect the said data along with creative key management and authentication techniques.

2.3   Data Encryption

This data protection method is the primary method to provide physical and logical level protection to sensitive (structured and unstructured) data while at rest and/or while in motion. The encryption methods comprise of both symmetric and asymmetric encryption techniques depending upon the data protection use case. While data encryption has many benefits, it comes with its own problems and limitations, including but not limited to:

(a) Computation cycles: The computing cycles needed to encrypt the data, are very high and require extensive processing power leading to higher costs.
(b) Computation time: Due to the heavy computing cycle need, data encryption can also take a good deal of time, asymmetric encryption taking more time than symmetric encryption.
(c) Usage: Using current encryption paradigms, the encrypted data has to be decrypted before it can used. This creates a problem as eventually the data is available in the clear (even though for a short period in memory or on disk etc.) and can lead to unauthorized access.

(d) Key Protection: The cryptographic key used to encrypt the data has to be pro-
     tected, and also needs to be provided for decryption, leading to additional costs
     and the risk of key exfiltration.

3   Future State

The future state is on the horizon. We expect many improvements in the next
2–4 years as production ready implementations become more available.

A key issue in the current data encryption paradigm is that data has to be
decrypted prior to performing mathematical computation or using it for data processing purposes. The next generation of encryption technologies is trying to fix this
problem by developing encryption techniques that enables data computation on
encrypted data. This paradigm will also help with the post quantum computing data
security scenarios.

Currently there are two primary next-generation encryption techniques, Fully
Homomorphic Encryption (FHE) and Multi part compute (MPC). These techniques
have delivered promising results in performing data computation while the data is
still encrypted. This chapter takes a deeper look at both – FHE and MPC techniques.

3.1   Encryption Basics

In the world of computation, data encryption is the technique which provides the
capability to encode (encrypt) and decode (decrypt) plaintext data using a key.
Generally speaking, mathematical algorithms (Fn) are used to perform the encryption (encoding) and decryption (decoding) of data. When plaintext data is encrypted
the resulting data is called Ciphertext.

To put this into simple equations (let's leave asymmetric encryption out for the
sake of simplicity) –

ciphertext = Fn$_{encrypt}$(key, data);
data = Fn$_{decrypt}$(key, ciphertext);

3.1.1   Fully Homomorphic Encryption (FHE)

FHE allows computations to be carried out directly on input encrypted data yielding
a ciphertext containing the encrypted output. These computations generate a result
which is the same as if the computations were done on unencrypted data or plaintext. FHE has its roots in lattice-based cryptosystems (details of which have been
discussed in another chapter (2) in this book). The previous generations of FHE
technologies suffered from extremely slow performance and only supported a

limited number of mathematical operations, but significant improvements have been made in the capabilities of the current (3rd and 4th) generation FHE algorithms.

Let's look at this on an introductory level, beginning with a very basic explanation of how FHE works using the example below.

(i) Financial institution (X) wants to share some personally identifiable information (PII) with an external third-party service data processing provider (Y) which requires some mathematical computation.
(ii) X sends (FHE) encrypted data to Y (but does not provide a decryption key for the said data)
(iii) Y performs data processing on the encrypted data
(iv) Y returns the encrypted data results back to X
(v) X decrypts the encrypted data result to read the processed data.

Company X was able to maintain the confidentiality and integrity of its data, while still successfully obtaining the data processing results required in a highly secure manner, as the data decryption key never left its premises.

Theoretically speaking the computation works as follows:

$$C1 = FHE_{encrypt}(D1);$$
$$C2 = FHE_{encrypt}(D2);$$
$$D1+D2 = FHE_{decrypt}(C1+C2);$$
$$D1*D2 = FHE_{decrypt}(C1*C2);$$

The second generation of FHE offers some promising implementations, namely NTRU (Nth degree truncated polynomial ring unit) a scheme based on lattice-based cryptography, CKKS (Cheon, Kim, Kim and Song) and BFV (Brakerski, Gentry and Vaikuntanathan) cryptosystems.

The NTRU [1] cryptosystem is open-source with multiple implementations and consists of two algorithms, NTRUEncrypt and NTRUSign. Given the scope of our discussion, the primary cryptography interest lies in NTRUEncrypt due to its capabilities to support homomorphic data encryption.

Both BFV and CKKS (4th gen) has been used in Microsoft's Simple Encrypted Arithmetic Library (SEAL) implementation [2].

(a) The BFV [3] encryption scheme provides the capability to perform modular arithmetic on encrypted integers and is used for applications where exact values are necessary.

Microsoft has reported major improvements in performance of homomorphic encryption with the use of artificial intelligence (AI) CryptoNets [5] based optical recognition systems. This deep-learning neural network uses the homomorphic encryption capabilities powered by SEAL.

The third generation of FHE offers two promising implementations of particular interest, namely FHEW (fully homomorphic encryption with Bootstrapping), and TFHE (Fast fully homomorphic encryption). These are based on the GSW [8] (Gentry, Sahai and Waters) method of building FHE techniques with the enhanced capability to perform homomorphic multiplications with constructs that would (previously) only support homomorphic additions, and also reduce the ciphertext size after a homomorphic multiplication.

The fourth generation of FHE offers some promising implementations but the one of particular interest is the CKKS (Cheon, Kim, Kim and Song) cryptosystem. The CKKS [4] encryption scheme provides the capability to perform mathematical operations like addition and multiplication on encrypted real or complex numbers. It's capability to support efficient rounding operations on encrypted data (built upon its characteristic to operate on approximate values) provides the capability to perform noise reduction while doing multiplication (on encrypted data). It can also enable the capability to train supervised machine learning models using encrypted data, and also to compute distances between two vectors.

SEAL – It is an open-source homomorphic encryption library written in C++ that has been developed by Microsoft, licensed by Massachusetts Institute of Technology (MIT). The library is easy to use, run and compile, and has the capability to execute in multiple environments and operating systems. The most recent version of Microsoft SEAL as of the writing of this chapter is version 3.6 and has been cloud enabled using Azure, providing the said homomorphic encryption capability with the agility and computing power of the cloud. Additional details are available for reference at [9].

3.1.2 Multi-party Computation (MPC)

Although the mathematics behind FHE is extremely complex with huge computational overheads, the concept of performing computation on encrypted data is easy to understand.

MPC on the other hand is not so easy to understand, even conceptually. This chapter provides a simplistic treatment of the same.

Theoretically MPC can enable the capability to be additively homomorphic i.e., having the capability to compute the secret from other parts by computing on a minimum number of secret parts without having to use cryptographic keys to perform decryption operations, but not as FHE would do it. (Then there is also the case of using both FHE and MPC together, which is an optimization that is mentioned later in this chapter but not discussed in detail within this book).

Using a simple example to help provide an explanation, let's say we have three high-school students – u1, u2 and u3, who each have their own private SAT scores – s1, s2 and s3. They want to compute a function (fn) which tells them which of them got the highest SAT score without disclosing their own score. This can be depicted using the below equation –

fn(s1, s2, s3) = max(s1,s2,s3);

Using this scenario, the goal of MPC is to enable the students to find max (s1, s2, s3) by only interacting with each other but without disclosing their private data score to each other. Each student will know their own score and the max score. The data (i.e., s1, s2 and s3) could be plaintext or encrypted (in which case it would be decrypted fetching a key if required to calculate the function, or we could use FHE to perform computation on the encrypted data itself).

Thus, MPC enables the capability to ensure

(a) Confidentiality of the input – The private input data of each party cannot be inferred from the data exchanged during the execution of the MPC protocol. Their private data and the output are the only things visible to each party using this computation protocol.

(b) Integrity of the output – Any deliberate or malicious sharing of their private data by parties does not force the honest parties to output an inaccurate result, either leading to an accurate result or an abortion of the computation process.

There are two main ways to implement MPC – garbled circuits and shared secrets, both of which are not very intuitive and require serious understanding of graduate level math. For that reason, a simpler treatment to these two topics has been provided.

Garbled Circuit: A garbled circuit follows a two-party compute (2PC) protocol. It is simply a crypto-protocol implemented as a Boolean circuit that enables secure computation between two parties where they can provide their private inputs to a function (fn) and obtain an output without exposing their input data to the other party. The most common Garbled circuit was implemented by Andrew Yao [6].

Shared Secrets: The garbled circuit concept only works for two party compute (2PC). Most multi-party compute (MPC) protocols use shared-secrets based techniques. The most popular is *Shamir Secret Sharing* [7] method, a crypto-algorithm where a secret is divided into many parts and stored separately. The reconstruction of the original secret requires either all or least a minimum of secret parts. The proof of this method has successfully been provided using finite field mathematics and it outside the scope of this book.

One of the most common practical use cases of Shared Secret in the world of cyber security is the splitting of a private key in two or more key-parts and storing it in two or more hardware security modules (HSM). The key-parts are not never combined at any point and never exist in the clear. The actual key will be computed by a function that would take the two or more inputs of the key-parts to calculate the actual key. In the case of a compromise, the attackers would have to take control of all the HSMs at the same time to get their hands on the real key, which is very difficult to do.

4   Attacks and Issues

Just like any new technology or capability, we need to make sure that the implementations of homomorphic encryption (e.g., SEAL) are hardened and secure from attacks from threat actors. Some known attacks and weaknesses have been discussed below:

4.1   Susceptibility to CCA Attacks

The current homomorphic encryption implementations have security features built to prevent (active) chosen plaintext attacks (generally referred to as CPA or IND-CPA) giving them the plain text distinguishability. It has been theorized by security researchers that to be fully secure they need to also have the capability to protect against chosen cypher text attacks (generally referred to as CCA or IND-CCA), something that they do not have in most of the current implementations, and thus making them susceptible to CCA attacks.

4.1.1   Private Key Leakage

Due to their susceptibility to CCA attacks as explained above, it has been theoretically shown that either the full or part of the secret or private key can be recovered during decryption operations for a given homomorphic encryption implementation. This is a very serious problem and needs to be resolved before these implementations are made mainstream.

4.1.2   Approximation Schemes

Homomorphic encryption schemes like CKKV that are built upon the characteristic to operate on approximate (encrypted) values rather than exact values, have been found susceptible to passive attacks also leading to the recovery of the private key. This problem has been classified as a class P problem, making it very easy and practical for an attacker to use this (passive) attack to perform full key recovery.

As discussed above (in 4.1), the inherent capability within the current gen homomorphic cryptosystems to provide protection against (active) chosen plaintext attacks (IND-CPA) giving them the plain text distinguishability does not provide the same protection against *passive* IND-CPA attacks when performed on homomorphic schemes (like CKKV) that use approximations.

4.2   Data Encoding Issues

Some security researchers have pointed out issues with the (homomorphic) data encoding functions (e.g., IntegerEncoder in SEAL) used to encode integer or floating-point numbers, which could cause it to leak operand information.

4.3 Data Integrity

The current homomorphic encryption schemes do not have good provisions built in for asserting that the integrity of the data has been maintained. Currently there isn't a good way to detect if any changes were made to the ciphertext by a malicious entity. Apart from the information security risk, this will become a compliance issue if this is not resolved before these schemes are used in production.

5 The CISO Take

The data encryption based data security paradigms are only as good as the safety of the keys used to encrypt the data. Even if the keys are stored securely, the data is available in plaintext in memory or on disk and is susceptible to exfiltration or unauthorized access through various sophisticated memory-based exploits, both in the application or server stack, or in the firmware itself.

In the future, data processing will be done either directly on encrypted data (FHE) or by not sharing all the private data itself (MPC). This new paradigm will greatly reduce the cyber risk from data exfiltration, breaches and unauthorized access. Security technologists are at the forefront of emerging technologies in this arena, and considering the current state of the threat scene and emerging cyber risk, are our best line of data security defense.

It is the responsibility of the CISOs to ensure that they aid the development and then subsequently enable the adoption of newer data protection technologies like homomorphic encryption and multi-party compute that are on the horizon. They also need to ensure that homomorphic encryption schemes are hardened against all known attacks, and any data integrity issues have been resolved by product companies like Microsoft before these schemes are made generally available.

6 Definitions

2PC – stands for two-party-compute. It is a protocol that enables two mutually distrustful parties A and B to evaluate an arbitrary function using their own private inputs (x, y) and only revealing the result $z = f(x,y)$.

Bootstrapping – it is the process to self-start a system or a process that may include self or auto configuration but generally without any external input.

Class P – Problems are generally classified as "Class P" for which a polynomial function (algorithm) can provide a solution in (deterministic) polynomial time.

HSM – stands for hardware security module. It is a physical or virtual computing device whose primary function is to provide secure storage and management of cryptographic keys and other critical security parameters (CSP).

MD5 – stands for message digest. It is a legacy 128-bit hash function which has been deprecated due to security issues and is no longer recommended for use.

One-way Hash – A one-way hash is an algorithm that generates a unique message digest of the input. The algorithm always creates the same output (hash) for the same input. Once a digest (hash) has been created, then there is no way to get back to the original input (hence one-way).

NIST – stands for National Institute of Standards and Technology. It is a non-regulatory US entity with the mission to promote innovation and industrial competitiveness.

SHA – stands for secure hashing algorithm. It is a family of cryptographic (one way) data hashing or obfuscation algorithms that have been approved for use by the National Institute of Standards and Technology (NIST). SHA1 has been deemed as breached and has been deprecated. SHA2 and SHA3 family of functions are approved for use.

References

1. NTRU-CRYPTO (2020) NTRU. https://github.com/NTRUOpenSourceProject. Accessed 28 June, 2020
2. Microsoft (2020) SEAL. https://github.com/microsoft/SEAL, Accessed 30 Dec, 2020
3. Halevi S, Polyakov Y, Shoup V (2018) An Improved RNS Variant of the BFV Homomorphic Encryption Scheme. Accessed June, 2020
4. Cheon J, Kim A, Kim M, Song Y (2017) Homomorphic Encryption for Arithmetic of Approximate Numbers. Accessed 30 June, 2020
5. Dowlin N, Gilad-Bachrach R, Laine K et al (2016) CryptoNets: Applying Neural Networks to Encrypted Data with High Throughput and Accuracy. Accessed 30 June, 2020
6. Prof and Dean at the Institute of Interdisciplinary information sciences at Tsinghua University, China.
7. Posner (2020), Shared Secret, https://github.com/posener/sharedsecret. Accessed 30 Dec 2020
8. Gentry C, Sahai A, Water B (2013) Homomorphic Encryption from Learning with Errors: Conceptually-Simpler, Asymptotically-Faster. Accessed 27 June 2020
9. Microsoft (2018) Seal. https://www.microsoft.com/en-us/research/project/microsoft-seal/. Accessed 30 Dec 2020

Further Reading

Li B, Micciancio D (2021) On the Security of Homomorphic Encryption on Approximate Numbers. https://eprint.iacr.org/2020/1533.pdf. Accessed 16 Jan 2021
Peng Z (2019) Danger of using fully homomorphic encryption: A look at Microsoft SEAL. https://arxiv.org/pdf/1906.07127.pdf. Accessed 30 Dec 2020
Wikipedia (2020) Homomorphic Encryption. https://en.wikipedia.org/wiki/Homomorphic_encryption. Accessed 30 Dec 2020

Cybersecurity Enabled by Zero Trust

1 Introduction

Cybersecurity professionals have all heard of the buzzword "Zero Trust," but few know what it means. The Zero Trust concept has come a long way in a decade, from the original 2010 Zero Trust model by John Kindervag of Forrester, the first implementation by Google (BeyondCorp) in 2013, followed by the Continuous Adaptive Risk and Trust Assessment (CARTA) model by Gartner in 2017, the Zero Trust extended (ZTX) Model by Forrester in 2018, to the Zero Trust Architecture (ZTA) by NIST. In spite of the various proposed models and architectures, and a proliferation of costly complex proprietary products from vendors who often fail to deliver, there is no single tool to achieve Zero Trust. Instead, "Zero Trust" calls for a fundamental shift in a firm's security paradigm across many levels. CISO's must make it their mission to provide clear and concise requirements for Zero Trust, along with practical guidance on implementations to secure their enterprise.

2 Tenets

I have highlighted the fundamental tenets of Zero trust below, along with commentary on how they may be implemented to provide better security.

2.1 All Assets inside and outside a Perimeter firewall Are Not to Be Trusted

Whether users, systems, or services are inside or outside the firewall, all must be treated as untrustworthy assets, which means they must be authenticated and authorized before use. This is enforced for external entities by a perimeter firewall, and for internal entities by higher-level network segmentation of (internal and external) DMZ, the Extranet, and the Intranet, as well as by also performing application segmentation.

In network micro-segmentation, the intranet is further segmented into smaller segments based on risk profiles or to meet network/application/work-load isolation needs. This concept can be applied to any part of the internal network using a combination of host-based and network-based firewalls. Although physical network micro-segmentation is possible, it is difficult to implement manually and very difficult and complex to maintain, manage and audit. Instead, it is generally implemented through concepts of VLAN on physically networked compute platforms and components, and through implementations like NSX at the hypervisor level on virtual compute platforms like VMware.

Here are guidelines for network based micro-segmentation:

(a) Enable distributed stateful firewalling at a per server or work-load (VM) level, regardless of the underlying physical or logical network overlay.
(b) Enable and programmatically define logical level micro-segmented networks, regardless of the underlying compute and network overlay.
(c) Programmatically create, provision and subsequently manage fine grained security and access control policies across multiple micro segments using a single pane of glass.
(d) Perform full SSL/TLS decryption and network packet inspection and also integrate with advanced intrusion prevention system (IPS) capabilities.

Application segmentation limits the attack surface for a given application by using layer 4 controls. Here are guidelines to secure applications:

(a) Perform intra-application segmentation by enforcing a distinct separation between the n tiers of an individual application and using the principle of least privilege to allow only the least amount of access to each tier (e.g., web tier, application tier, database tier)
(b) Isolate a given application from other applications and systems, to restrict vulnerability exploitation and lateral movement from other apps within or outside the network segment in which the app resides.

Network segmentation can further enable application segmentation.

2.2 Accurate Asset Inventory Must Exist for All Systems and Services

The capability should exist to create and maintain an accurate asset inventory of all hardware, software, systems, and services within an application (preferably a CMDB) with API and programmatic access. To be effective, dynamically detect and inventory (i.e., adding or updating) all physical and virtual systems and services as they may come on or go off the network.

2.3 All Traffic for All Systems and Services Must Be Authenticated and Authorized

The traditional way of hauling all authentication and authorization requests to a traditional data center to comply with a Zero Trust model is achievable, but is becoming increasingly difficult to manage and maintain with the advent of distributed computing. An alternative means of proper authentication and authorization is to ensure that secure access decisions are made at the entity (user, system, device, service, or location) initiating the connection itself, generally at the edge computing location. This can be achieved using the concepts defined in Secure Access Service Edge (SASE), which extends the existing concept of identity built upon users, groups and roles to include edge computing and wide area networks (WAN). The SASE paradigm uses a combination of security capabilities defined in software defined wide area network (SD-WAN), cloud access security broker (CASB), secure web gateway (SWG), next generation anti-virus (NGAV), virtual private network (VPN), next generation firewall (NGFW) and data loss prevention (DLP) – all delivered as a single service at the network edge.

2.4 Access Control for Users, Devices, Systems and Services Must Be Provided Using Least Privilege

Access for all users, devices, systems and serviced must be continuously assessed and always be provided using the principle of least privilege with continuous re-assessments.

2.5   All Data in Transit and at Rest Must Be Encrypted End to End

Encrypt data in transit end-to-end using technologies such as TLS, IPSec using FIPS compliant initial handshake and key management. Data at rest must be encrypted using techniques such as TDE for structured data (e.g., databases), and symmetric encryption algorithms such as AES (128 or 256 bit) for unstructured data (e.g., file shares).

2.6   Full Traffic Packet Inspection Capability for North-South and East-West Traffic

Although all traffic is expected to be encrypted end-to-end, the capability must still exist to be able to inspect all (north-south and east-west) traffic to look for anomalous patterns and indicators of compromise for use cases like insider threat. This is generally done using an approved man-in-the-middle SSL/TLS decryption and re-encrypt + forward scheme.

2.7   Step-Up Authentication Aided by Strong Authenticators Using Dynamic Transaction Level Risk Calculation

The capability must exist to enhance security controls for (primarily) a web or mobile application, by dynamically performing a step-up authentication in response to a detection of a risky user action or behavior, on the web application. The strength level of the step-up authentication must be adaptive to a user risk profile generated in real time for each user session and an action risk profile generated for the user action on the web application. This scheme can also be implemented for internal (high risk) applications or transactions.

3   Challenges

While there are many advantages as explained in the previous section, there are some challenges and pitfalls from the adoption of a zero-trust approach of which one needs to be aware so that it does not become a blind spot.

3.1   Partial Implementations

Partial implementations done just to protect specific datacenters, sites, applications, or even certain network segments can create a false sense of security, allowing blind spots to develop, and may lead to the creation of security gaps that can be exploited by insider threats.

3.2   Complexity

Zero trust implementations like network micro segmentation, least privilege access, and continuous access reviews can lead to significant complexity. Such complexity requires skilled engineering and operational skills, increases administrative and operational costs, delays implementations and lengthens recovery times from outages.

4   The CISO Take

From my experience, imposing a Zero Trust paradigm onto a legacy network and security framework can prove to be very difficult, complex, and costly. The best practice is to do the implementation right the first time, when the opportunity for new implementations or redesign of existing networks and implementations presents itself.

Also, do not chase shiny new tools, focus on requirements, and see if you can use a firm's existing toolset to create hybrid solutions, whether they be a next gen firewall, a CASB system, a hypervisor platform that could be retrofitted with new segmentation capability, an existing reverse proxy, an existing privileged access management (PAM) solution, or a next generation VPN system with app segmentation capability and otherwise.

Zero Trust (with least privilege) significantly mitigates the risk from insider threats and advanced (polymorphic and metamorphic) malware. It is very effective in providing adequate protections against third party breaches and attacks like SolarWinds.

Lastly be aware that zero trust is a journey and the work cannot stop after the initial implementation. Because the threats keep changing, evolving, and getting more sophisticated, zero-trust implementations need continuous assessments and improvements.

5 Definitions

AES – stands for Advanced Encryption Standard. It is a specification for a symmetric block cipher accepted globally as the standard to protect classified and sensitive information.

API – stands for Application Programming Interface. It is an intermediate layer that enables software applications to talk to other applications, systems, and users.

CASB – stands for Cloud Access Security Broker. It is an on-premise or cloud-hosted security policy enforcement point, generally resident between the flow of network or application traffic and cloud-hosted or based services (e.g., SaaS, IaaS or PaaS). The security policies enforced include DLP, SSO, MFA, logging, and malware detection.

CMDB – stands for configuration management database. It is used to store configuration records for entities within an org that include but are not limited to hardware, software (including SaaS), systems (physical and virtual) and facilities, throughout their lifecycle and maintain relationships between them.

DLP – stands for Data Loss Prevention. It is a technology that prevents the unauthorized access to or exfiltration of company and customer sensitive data.

DMZ – is a "demilitarized zone," a restricted subnet between the intranet and the internet, and is generally used to host the external facing sites and services.

Extranet – is generally partly hosted inside the DMZ and is used to provide secure access to certain intranet applications to external partners, suppliers, or even customers.

NIST – stands for National Institute of Standards and Technology. It is a non-regulatory US entity with the mission to promote innovation and industrial competitiveness.

PAM – stands for Privileged Access Management. It generally used to refer to a solution that is used to protect, manage, and monitor privileged access and credentials to critical computer systems and applications.

TDE – stands for Transparent Data Encryption. It provides for logical level encryption of data both at the column, table, or tablespace level.

VPN – stands for virtual private network. It provides the capability to extend a private (corporate) network across a public network (e.g., the internet) assigning a remote user a private IP address and enabling a remote user or employee to send and receive data as if he/she were onsite at a corporate facility.

Zero Trust – is a security architecture and implementation paradigm that reduces enterprise risk by performing secure implementations in compliance with the principal that all assets inside and outside a perimeter firewall are not to be trusted and thus access control for users, devices, systems and services must be provided using least privilege.

Further Reading

Arntz P (2020) Explained: the strengths and weaknesses of the Zero Trust model. https://blog. malwarebytes.com/explained/2020/01/explained-the-strengths-and-weaknesses-of-the-zero-trust-model/. Accessed 29 Dec 2020

Cloudflare (2020) What's a Zero Trust Network? https://www.cloudflare.com/learning/security/glossary/what-is-zero-trust/. Accessed 29 Dec 2020

Crowdstrike (2020) What is Zero Trust? https://www.crowdstrike.com/epp-101/zero-trust-security/. Accessed 29 Dec 2020

Keary E (2020) Security Think Tank: Facing the challenge of zero trust. In: ComputerWeekly. com. https://www.computerweekly.com/opinion/Security-Think-Tank-Facing-the-challenge-of-zero-trust. Accessed 29 Dec 2020

Kindervag J (2018) Four myths of Zero Trust Architecture. https://edge.siriuscom.com/security/4-major-myths-of-zero-trust-architecture. Accessed 29 Dec 2020

National Cybersecurity Center of Excellence, National Institute of Standards and Technology (2020) Zero Trust Architecture https://www.nccoe.nist.gov/projects/building-blocks/zero-trust-architecture. Accessed 29 Dec 2020

Advanced Active Directory Attacks and Prevention

1 Introduction

Active Directory (AD) is the windows domain directory services implementation that is used to provide user and identity management, authentication, and policy administration services. It is the most common directory services implementation and is used across the windows ecosystem.

Within Active Directory, user and identity management services for the windows domain, such as user authentication and authorization, are provided by a server running the Active Directory domain service called Domain Controller (DC or AD DC).

A Domain Controller (DC) natively speaks the two primary protocols, Kerberos and LDAP. Clients use these protocols to communicate with the DC and with various services it exposes for user and account management. Other capabilities exposed by a DC include but are not limited to a global catalog that contains information about every object in the directory, a query service that can be used by users or applications to search for (directory) objects and their properties, and a replication service that replicates directory data across a network.

2 Security Threats

Due to its primary role in management of user credentials and other authentication and authorization services within the windows ecosystem, the AD DC is the crown jewel every malicious actor wants to compromise. To orchestrate an attack on a windows ecosystem, a threat actor generally needs to gain privileged access to the DC, often accomplished by either stealing (domain) administrative credentials, or stealing user or system credentials, and then subsequently escalating the privilege of these credentials.

For obvious reasons, access to these administrative credentials is restricted to domain admins, who use various access management-based protective schemes, including credential vaulting and multi-factor authentication, to gain access to these credentials.

Apart from the basic credential stealing or sniffing credentials over a wire in a compromised ethernet network, there are many other complex and sophisticated exploits and attacks that are used by attackers and malicious entities. Understanding these attacks is important to design and implement appropriate protective schemes. Some of these attacks and protection options are detailed below.

The creation of certain penetration testing and hacking tools (like MimiKatz) and their easy accessibility have made most of these attacks very possible and easily achievable without developing deep expertise into the inner workings of Active Directory.

Most of the attacks can be broadly classified as Kerberos, password, or DC-based attacks as explained below.

2.1 Pass the Ticket (PTT)

In this attack, an attacker impersonates a valid user by stealing their Kerberos token from a compromised system, and re-uses that stolen token to authenticate as that user.

Many tools (e.g., MimiKatz) are used to steal or harvest these tokens, which may be resident in memory caches of compromised systems.

These stolen tokens generally have a max validity of 600 min and can be used to gain access to multiple systems as long the token remains valid.

This attack requires the attacker to be resident on a host or machine for it to be able to steal the token. Under the hood within AD, the Key Distribution Center (KDC) issues a Ticket Granting Ticket (TGT) – a user authentication token which is then used for initial authentication and subsequent requests for access tokens for other services. The stealing of this token provides the attacker access to the network resources without stealing the user's password.

2.1.1 Protection Options for PTT

The best way to detect these attacks is to detect the re-use of user authentication tokens by different IP addresses or systems. This is generally done by auditing Kerberos traffic on DCs and on user endpoints such as laptops by using newer techniques such as endpoint detection and response (EDR).

The use of supervised machine learning (ML) algorithms within the EDR and other network monitoring tools has also provided better detection and blocking capabilities.

2.2 Pass the Hash (PTH)

This is a standard exploit where an attacker impersonates a user by stealing the cryptographic hash of their password and uses it to authenticate as the user. In the AD context, generally this hash is the NTLM or the (legacy) LanMan hash of the user's password.

Apart from sniffing the hash over the wire, an attacker can use the Security Account Manager (SAM) to harvest cached hashes of users currently or previously logged into a compromised machine. The users' cached passwords can also be dumped from the SAM account database on the compromised machine.

The users' credentials can also be dumped from within the memory of the lsass. exe process. This technique is more effective since it allows access to domain admin or other system admin credentials rather than just the local user credentials within the SAM.

2.2.1 Protection Options for PTH

Since this attack technique relies upon domain admin or system administrative privileges, the accounts with these privileges must be protected by vaulting them in a privileged access management (PAM) system, in addition to drastically reducing the total number of admins with these credentials.

All LanMan/NTLM authentications must be disabled and only NTLMv2 should be allowed.

Another technique is to prevent windows from storing cached credentials so that they cannot be dumped from memory. This can be achieved by modifying the below mentioned (windows) registry entry to 1 (please note a value of 0 may cause some clustered nodes to fail):

HKEY_LOCAL_MACHINE\Software\Microsoft\WindowsNT\Current   Version\
    Winlogon\ CachedLogonsCount

Microsoft has also introduced the Restricted Admin Mode feature (originally in Windows 8.1 and Windows Server 2012 R2) in their attempt to limit these attacks by preventing the storage of the RDP users' credentials in the memory of the machine on which the connection was made.

2.3 Overpass the Hash (OPTH)

The attack technique takes the previously discussed PTH exploit to the next level by using the harvested or stolen password hash to acquire a Kerberos user authentication token (from the KDC) which is subsequently used to gain access to the user's account (as described in the PTT attack).

2.3.1 Protection Options for OPTH

A combination of protection techniques for PTH and PTT can be used to protect from this exploit.

2.4 Golden Ticket (GT)

For this attack to work, the attacker generally needs to gain access to the AD DC for a given domain.

Using this attack technique, the attacker gains total and complete access and control over an AD domain. These attacks are generally carried out against AD domains that use Kerberos tickets for user and admin authentications (similar to the PTT attack). These tickets are issued by the Kerberos Distribution Service (KDS) and if the attacker can gain control over the KDC by taking over the KRBTGT account (generally by stealing its LM/NTLM hash), then it allows the attacker to generate TGTs for any account in the AD domain.

With valid TGTs, the game is over, as now the attacker can request access to any system service or resource within the AD domain.

2.4.1 Protection Options for GT

These attacks are very hard to detect, since the attackers use a valid TGT token encrypted and signed by a domain Kerb account (KRBTGT). These are some of the techniques that can be used to protect against this attack:

Drastic reduction of the total number of accounts with domain admin privilege or other accounts with elevated privileges.

Full traffic packet capture and analysis to detect any later movement and other suspicious activity.

Implementation of the capability to detect the re-use of user authentication tokens by different IP addresses or systems. This is generally done by auditing Kerberos traffic on DCs and on laptops and other user endpoints by using newer techniques such as EDR.

Use of dynamic whitelisting capability on DCs to prevent the execution of unauthorized software or tools.

It is recommended that the KRBTGT account be changed every 40 days.

2.5 Silver Ticket (ST)

This attack is similar to PTT and GT. Unlike GT, in this case, the attacker gets access to a Ticket Granting Service (TGS) token (rather than the KRBTGT), giving it access to a single service (rather to all the DC services) within a given AD domain.

For this attack to work, the attacker generally needs to be able either to harvest or to dump SAM credentials, using those credentials to forge a TGS token. If possible, the attacker then uses the TGS to elevate access to privileged access (e.g., domain admin).

This attack is like a mini-GT attack but is generally used to run malicious code on a target host of interest. This attack is even more difficult to detect when compared to GT, since technically it does not need to establish any communication with the DCs. – All token forging activity is done on a local system.

2.5.1   Protection Options for ST

One option to protect against STs is to use a Privilege Attribute Certificate (PAC), which enables the capability of the KRBTGT to sign the TGS token. This configuration, already made available by Microsoft, disables the capability to perform this exploit by just getting access and dumping credentials on a local system.

Another option is to implement the capability to detect the re-use of user authentication tokens by different IP addresses or systems. This is generally done by auditing Kerberos traffic on DCs and on user endpoints like laptops by using newer techniques like EDR.

The use of dynamic whitelisting capability on domain controllers can prevent the execution of unauthorized software or tools.

It is recommended that the KRBTGT account be changed every 40 days.

2.6   DCShadow (DCS)

For this attack to work, the attacker generally needs to gain access to one DC for a given AD domain. As the name suggests, it provides the attackers the capability to register a (shadow) rogue or compromised AD DC to an AD domain and then subsequently use it to push changes (e.g., fake credentials, ACLs) to other domain controllers within that AD domain using standard domain replication.

This capability was introduced via the MimiKatz tool located within the lsadump module.

2.6.1   Protection Options for DCS

This attack is difficult to detect as it uses the legitimate domain replication capabilities and the standard Directory Replication Service, but steps can be taken to reduce the likelihood of a DCS attack.

One method of protection is to monitor any API call (especially for replication functions) from a non-domain controller, as it may be a rogue host pretending to be a DC.

Requests from domain controllers in other lower-level environments must also be logged and monitored, as they could be compromised and try to join a production AD domain.

Another method of protection is to rely on pre-established DCS-related IOCs to monitor all intra-domain controller replication requests for AD objects.

An additional protective measure would be to monitor the use of use of Kerberos SPNs by computers or hosts that are not part of the DC organizational unit (OU). Any such use must be alerted upon for further investigation.

Drastically reducing the total number of accounts with domain admin privilege or other accounts with elevated privileges would also decrease the risk of a DCS attack.

2.7   DCSync (DCSy)

This attack requires the attacker to get access to a domain admin credential or another credential with elevated rights.

It allows the attackers to 'mimic' a domain controller by using the stolen domain admin credentials and prompting the primary domain controller (within an AD domain or forest) to replicate user credentials back to the attacker using the standard AD directory replication service.

2.7.1   Protection Options for DCSy

Just like DCS, this attack is difficult to detect as it uses the legitimate domain replication capabilities using the standard Directory Replication Service.

The best way to detect these attacks is to detect the re-use of user authentication tokens by different IP addresses or systems. This is generally done by auditing Kerberos traffic on DCs and on laptops and other user endpoints by using newer techniques like EDR.

Also, the enforcement of standard and common-sense security controls such as risk-based vulnerability management and network monitoring can be effective in detecting and stopping these attacks.

Lastly, the reduction of the total number of accounts with domain admin privileges or other accounts with elevated privileges is highly recommended.

2.8   Kerberoasting

This is another Kerberos-based attack and is used by the attackers to harvest Active Directory service account credentials (or even user credentials) and then crack them offline.

Once the attackers gain residence on the internal network and perform reconnaissance, they then compromise the account of a domain user, either by sniffing the password or using social engineering techniques like phishing. They then use the domain user account to request a (Kerberos) service ticket for a given service. These tickets are encrypted with the service accounts LM/NTLM(v2) hash. Once they have the ticket (generally from memory), they crack the hash of the password using one of the many available tools (e.g., Hashcat). Once they have the password of the Service ID for the service, then it's game over.

2.8.1 Protection Options for Kerberoasting

Kerberoasting can be detected by noticing a spike in service ticket requests from a baseline. This can only be done effectively by using ML-enabled detection algorithms.

The best protection against Kerberoasting is to enforce a hardened password policy for service accounts. Microsoft recommends that all service account passwords be at least 25 characters long. These should be changed frequently, every 30 days. Additionally, the service accounts must be placed in a dedicated OU within AD to enable separation from user accounts, separate management, and separate password policy.

The security teams must deploy decoy accounts, also referred to as honey accounts. These accounts are primarily used for threat detection purposes and to build threat intel. The honey (decoy) accounts do not provide access to any real services. Once these accounts are compromised, they fulfill their sole function of sending alerts to the incident response team about an account security breach.

2.9   Skeleton Key

This is a post-exploitation attack. Once an attacker achieves domain admin credentials, it can then install malicious code to bypass the local security authority subsystem service, which runs as lsass.exe in the windows operating system, allowing the security authority subsystem to accept a new (weak) password for any user. This new (fake and weak) password is called the skeleton key, which basically allows the attacker to login into a DC with any known user or service account.

2.9.1 Protection Options for Skeleton Key

Skeleton key attacks can be detected by scanning for weak passwords or passwords that do not comply with the password policy for a given OU or domain.

The detection of an encryption downgrade during the logon process can also help detect the use of skeleton keys.

3   Future Protection Challenges and Techniques

Legacy techniques of doing AD and endpoint log parsing to look for anomalies, manually auditing AD user and service accounts, and relying on Microsoft patching capabilities have all served us fairly well, but are not sufficient to protect against sophisticated threat actors and malware.

3.1   New Challenges

Some of the new(er) challenges that have come to the forefront are mentioned below.

3.1.1   Sophisticated Tools

Easy access to sophisticated hacking tools such as MimiKatz, John the Ripper, Hashcat, MetaSploit, Windows Credentials Editor (WCE), and FGDump that were originally designed to aid with penetration testing and red teaming exercises are now at the disposal of threat actors, providing them with advanced hacking capability.

3.1.2   Hybrid Environments

Before the office 365 (o365) era, building the capability to deploy and enforce security controls for complex on-premises AD environments with multiple domains within a single forest or multiple forests was not an easy task, but now that has become even more difficult and complex with the introduction of hybrid environments with uni- or bi-directional replication of data from the on-premises AD in a cloud-based Azure Active Directory (AAD) environment.

3.1.3   Hybrid Join

The need to perform hybrid domain join of on-premises AD and AAD creates many security and monitoring challenges for cyber security teams from (hybrid) domain joined on-network/off-network devices.

3.2   Better Solutions

Due to its pivotal role as a key component that is responsible for authentication and authorization of users and service in a windows ecosystem, any compromise or breach of AD can be catastrophic.

Given the high risk from their compromise any attacks to AD have to be detected in as close to real-time as possible, although in some cases slower analytical solutions may be the only option available.

As threats have become more sophisticated, security teams should avail themselves of newer defensive and detective schemes improved by the introduction of supervised and unsupervised ML algorithms.

3.2.1 Real-Time Synchronous Detection

Rule-based engines have often been employed to perform log analysis on readily available AD authentication and authorization log data. This would create alerts to flag suspicious events based on known IOCs. The problem with these rule-based engines is that they are slow and also generate a large number of false positives. Even if these rule-based engines performed log analysis close to real-time (within 15 min), the high rate of false positives is such that these alerts are just recorded and sampled for further analysis and action, causing further delays. Rule-based engines are best used simply for monitoring, as they lack real-time enforcement capability.

Fortunately, with the improvement in supervised ML algorithms, the large amount of existing log data and alert events can now be raised as training data sets to refine and reduce the false positives. If this is done on live data on the wire through a network span or tap, then ML algorithms for specific detection use cases can provide near real-time threat detection with a very small number of false positives, which can be further reduced by tweaking the training data sets. This provides the capability to move beyond basic monitoring mode to enforcement mode, which makes blocking suspicious service account logins or other activities in a timely fashion possible.

This method of threat identification in the detection and enforcement mode can be used to detect and block many of the Kerberos-based attacks.

3.2.2 Asynchronous Detection

Even though there has been improvement in the reduction of false positives with the use of supervised ML for real-time traffic and event analysis, there are still many use cases that need asynchronous analysis and event correlation to detect malicious activities (e.g., kerberoasting) after the fact. This is generally done by taking log data from various sources such as domain controllers, user end points, suspicious lateral movement alerts, threat intel sources, and honey accounts and honey pots, and subjecting them to analysis by a special group of ML algorithms that are used to detect anomalous events from large data sets. This data can come from the source systems but are generally sourced from the SIEM.

This method of threat identification in the detection and enforcement mode can be used to detect and block many of the AD replication-based attacks.

3.2.3 Endpoint Discovery and Response (EDR)

The new generation of EDR tools can perform behavior analysis from established baselines to detect suspicious user and system behavior. These EDR alerts can be further correlated with events and network monitoring tool alerts to detect suspicious and anomalous events, many of which could be further classified as lateral (east-west) movement. These events are generally bubbled into the SIEM as alerts, but can also be used by SOC threat hunters and blue teamers to look for suspicious activities stemming from many of the AD-based attacks discussed earlier this chapter.

3.2.4 Implement a Red Forest Design, aka ESAE

The risk from the various credential theft attacks can be drastically reduced by limiting the exposure of the domain admin and other credentials with privileged access. This can be achieved by implementing the Enhanced Security Administration Environment (ESAE) for privileged accounts by setting up buffer zones within AD using an administrative tier model comprised of three levels – Tier 0 through Tier 2. ESAE is generally referred to as a Red Forest.

Tier 0 contains the highest risk accounts that are the prime target of threat actors. This tier holds privileged accounts (e.g., domain admins and system admins), as well as groups and assets (workstations) that provide direct and indirect administrative access to a given AD forest, domain or domain controllers, and any assets within it.

Tier 1 contains the medium risk accounts, through which there is access to enterprise and applications servers for on-premises and cloud environments and associated operating systems and applications. This includes the application and server administrative accounts, the compromise of which can do serious damage to business applications.

Tier 2 contains the lower risk accounts, or the type of accounts which provide access to domain-joined user laptops, workstations, and mobile devices, and control over software—such as the software for the operating system or security patching—that may run on these endpoint (user) assets.

Update: During the writing of this book, Microsoft has deprecated the Red Forest design. Driven by the rapid adoption and migration of services to Azure. It has been replaced by the modern privileged access strategy [2] and rapid modernization plan (RAMP) [1] guidance for providing secure workstations for privileged users. It is my opinion that the Red Forest is still a very relevant and valid design for on-premises AD implementations, but the newer guidance should be actively considered for all solely Azure-based or hybrid scenarios.

3.2.5   Sophisticated Backup and Recovery System

An AD outage either from hardware failure, network (replication) issues, or a debilitating malware attack (e.g., ransomware) can have a catastrophic impact on business operations.

Given the risk, the Active Directory instances must be protected using modern and fault-tolerant backup and recovery schemes. Some details of these schemes have been provided below:

AD object-level restores are the standard in most implementations.

AD database-level restores provide the capability to recover from failed schema updates or an AD database corrupted at a forest level. Most implementations have some basic capability provided inherently by Microsoft system state backups and/or restores, but there are some sophisticated tools that can do this better and faster.

AD server-level restores provide complete disaster recovery, restoring capability from completely compromised AD servers with bare metal backups.

4   The CISO Take

An Active Directory breach is one of the most severe forms of cyber risk that an enterprise can face. It is the responsibility of CISOs to ensure that the security monitoring and response systems they oversee can detect and block all of the various attacks discussed in this chapter. They must use all the tools at their disposal – rule-based log analyzers or supervised ML-augmented synchronous and asynchronous techniques, and blue and red team exercises using the same tools that the hackers use, among the other tools discussed here, to detect, mitigate, and remediate these threats.

I am frequently asked by other security and IT technologists about how to protect ourselves from these attacks. There are so many hacking tools; there are hundreds of windows processes that would need to be monitored across thousands of users and tens of thousands of servers and applications, and millions of log lines and thousands of events. My answer is this: apart from our standard security controls and cyber risk management practices, cybersecurity is also the science of pattern recognition and detection. We cannot block every hacking tool (some of which are used by our own penetration testers) or chase down every unique signature or variation of every infected file, system or process, or review every log line. However, we do need to identify as many of the malicious patterns and indicators of compromise as possible. Only once security teams are fully informed with a uniform knowledge of these malicious patterns will they be capable of identifying malicious threats and preventing those attacks.

Lastly, if you had the capability or funding to implement just one or two protective measures, then I would recommend that you implement Red Forest or the equivalent modern privileged access strategy [2] and rapid modernization plan (RAMP) [1] guidance for providing secure workstations for privileged users, followed by the capability to recover AD at the database and server levels.

5   Definitions

DC– it stands for Domain Controller. It is a server that authenticates a user's request to join a (Microsoft) active directory domain and enforces other configured security controls and policies. These are generally deployed in a cluster mode to enable (local) high availability and (remote) disaster recovery.

ESAE – stands for Enhanced Security Administrative Environment. Also known as the Active Directory Red Forest Design, it tries to implement a risk-based segregation of privileged accounts within AD.

Kerberos – is an open client/server network authentication protocol that uses encryption to maintain the confidentiality of the transmitted data tickets which are issued by an authentication service (KDC) and used to perform secure authentication over an untrusted network. It is the default authentication mechanism used by Microsoft to authenticate users to an Active Directory Domain Controller.

KRBTGT – stands for Kerberos ticket generating ticket account. It is a (critical) service account within each Active Directory domain. The hash of this account's password is used to encrypt and sign all Kerberos tickets (TGTs) exchanged with domain-joined clients. The domain controllers use this account's password (i.e., hash) to decrypt Kerb tickets for validation. This account and its password are shared between the KDC services of DCs within a domain. The compromise of KRBTGT allows an attacker to gain control over all the resources of the given domain.

LDAP – stands for Lightweight Directory Access Protocol. It is an open and cross-platform client/server protocol for interacting with X.500-based directory services (e.g., Active Directory) over a TCP/IP network.

LM – stands for Lan Manager, aka Lan Man. It is an obsolete authentication protocol primarily used by Microsoft windows. It is known for the LM Hash, which is a breached (and obsolete) password hashing function also used by Microsoft. LM was replaced by NLTM.

NTLM – stands for NT Lan Manager. It is the replacement for LM. It is a Microsoft security protocol primarily used to provide authentication services to client and server sessions. NTLM v1 is considered insecure and the current recommend version of NTLM is v2.

OU – stands for organizational unit. It is generally used to denote a subdivision within a Directory, and to place specific logical group of users, computes and devices (among other entities) into their own specific unit (OU) in an effort to serve their unique needs (whether related to geography, a business unit or something else) together.

SAM – stands for Security Account Manager. It is basically an encrypted database file within the Microsoft operating system that stores user passwords and authenticates users.

SIEM – stands for Security Incident and Event Management (System). This started out as log repositories but now have the capability to provide real-time cross-platform correlated analysis of security events and alerts from all the security systems and applications within an enterprise environment.

SOC – stands for Security Operations Center. The SOC represents the combined capabilities provided by security professionals (generally resident in a secured physical space), processes and technologies with a mission to provide 24x7 security, network and application monitoring services for a given enterprise.

References

1. Flores J (2020) Security rapid modernization plan. In: Microsoft documentation, Microsoft security best practices. https://docs.microsoft.com/en-us/security/compass/security-rapid-modernization-plan Accessed on 26 Dec 2020.
2. Flores J (2020) Privileged access: strategy. In: Microsoft documentation, Microsoft security best practices. https://docs.microsoft.com/en-us/security/compass/privileged-access-strategy. Accessed 26 Dec 2020

Further Reading

Berg L (2019) What is DCSYNC? An introduction. In: StealthBits Active Directory Attacks Blog. https://stealthbits.com/blog/what-is-dcsync-an-introduction/, Accessed 20 Dec 2020

Chen K (2019) Do You Need to Update KRBTGT Account Password? https://www.kjctech.net/do-you-need-to-update-krbtgt-account-password/. Accessed 20 Dec 2020

DCShadow. https://www.dcshadow.com/. Accessed 20 Dec 2020

Delpy B (2020) mimikatz. https://github.com/gentilkiwi/mimikatz. Accessed 20 Dec 2020

DelSalle L (2018) DCShadow explained: A technical deep dive into the latest AD attack technique. In Alsid Blog 2. https://blog.alsid.eu/dcshadow-explained-4510f52fc19d. Accessed 20 Dec 2020

Flores J (2020) Enterprise access model. In: Microsoft documentation, Microsoft security best practices. https://docs.microsoft.com/en-us/security/compass/privileged-access-access-model. Accessed 21 Dec 2020

Flores J (2021) ESAE Retirement – https://docs.microsoft.com/en-us/security/compass/esae-retirement. Accessed 25 Jan 2021

Metcalf S (2014) Kerberos & KRBTGT: Active Directory's Domain Kerberos Service Account. In: Trimarc's Active Directory Security. https://adsecurity.org/?p=483, Accessed 20 Dec 2020

Petters J (2020) Kerberos Attack: Silver Ticket Edition. In: Varonis Inside Out Security Blog. https://www.varonis.com/blog/kerberos-attack-silver-ticket/. Accessed 20 Dec 2020

QOMPLX Staff (2020) QOMPLX Knowledge: Golden Ticket Attacks Explained. https://qomplx.com/qomplx-knowledge-golden-ticket-attacks-explained/. Accessed on 26 Dec 2020

The MITRE Corporation (2020) Steal or Forge Kerberos Tickets: Kerberoasting, https://attack.mitre.org/techniques/T1558/003/ , Accessed 20 Dec 2020

The MITRE Corporation (2020) Steal or Forge Kerberos Tickets: Silver Ticket. https://attack.
    mitre.org/techniques/T1558/002/ , Accessed 20 Dec 2020
The MITRE Corporation. Golden Ticket. In: Stealthbits Attack Catalog. https://attack.stealthbits.
    com/how-golden-ticket-attack-works. Accessed 20 Dec 2020
Varghese B (2020) Kerberos Silver Ticket Attack. In: Attivo Networks Active Directory Blog.
    https://attivonetworks.com/kerberos-silver-ticket-attack/, Accessed 20 Dec 2020

Cyber Deception Systems

1 Genesis

To thwart the ever-evolving and increasingly sophisticated internal and external cyber threats, cyber security technologists have improved their threat detection capabilities by developing the modern cyber deception stack, which is primarily based on network deception and honeypots. Compared to honeypots and network deception capabilities that came into existence almost two decades ago, the modern (cyber deception) stack is far more powerful and sophisticated, with the capability to detect sophisticated threats and also provide real-time alerts.

Let's take a **step back** and understand some of the basics here first –

A **honeypot** is generic term used for a set of (generally hardened) systems or services, sitting on physical or virtualized hardware within a company's network, used as a trap to bait (both internal and external) cyber criminals into conducting malicious hacks, breaches, data exfiltration's, or other activities classified as part of the cyber kill-chain, i.e., reconnaissance, breach (weaponization + delivery), infection(installation, privilege escalation, remote CNC, and code execution), or mission goals (data exfiltration, data destruction).

Honeypots are generally hardened systems, which means that most critical services and ports are actually disabled, residing in a segmented network segment while exposing a façade that exhibits those critical services to be running with multiple exploitable (application, operating systems or network) vulnerabilities or weaknesses. Other techniques include using monitored open IP addresses/ranges, internet/intranet web pages, and fake network share or SharePoint sites with decoy sensitive documents. These all help create simplistic yet effective honeypots.

Network deception is basically a segmented network or a protected and monitored subnet used to lure hackers into traversing it and launching attacks on it, allowing security specialists and incident responders to study hacker tools and techniques passively. Generally speaking, a honeypot and network deception work together,

© The Author(s), under exclusive license to Springer Nature Switzerland AG 2021
R. Badhwar, *The CISO's Next Frontier*,
https://doi.org/10.1007/978-3-030-75354-2_14

where a honeypot is installed on a network segment that is using network deception.

Honeynet is basically a collection of honeypots working together in a cluster type of configuration used in large deployments.

2 Cyber Deception

In use for the last 4 or 5 years, cyber deception is the evolved state of the honeypot and network deception put together. Cyber deception provides protections from internal and external human threats and hackers, malicious or compromised systems, sophisticated malware, compromised robotic processes, or other adversaries (e.g., hacktivists).

Generally speaking, the current generation of cyber deception techniques use either a portion of a network subnet segmented from the rest of the corporate network by a dedicated (physical network or host-based) firewall, or a dirty line within a deception lab enabled by a completely separate network circuit.

Alternatively, security specialists could set up a standalone and segmented virtual private cloud (VPC) in a (public or private) cloud environment connected via a dirty line with no connectivity back to the corporate network.

Modern cyber deception techniques today have the capability to spin up applications using virtualization or container technologies and orchestrate network-based services on demand using software defined networks (SDN), giving the impression of a full-blown network with real applications, network appliances, databases, and file stores, with known exploitable OS, network, and application vulnerabilities.

Cyber deception is also frequently used to analyze how **malware** may behave against company systems that house sensitive data on various operating systems with varying controls and permission levels, or how would it try to circumvent or defeat security controls and implementations.

In many cases, cyber deception is primarily used for gathering **intelligence** about adversaries and imposters and their tools, tricks, and techniques to launch attacks or conduct other malicious activities. This can lead to the generation of many **IOCs** (indicators of compromise) that can then further be leveraged in the security teams' UEBA, IDS/IPS or WAF systems. Cyber deception also gathers intelligence to identify and collect evidence against insider threat.

There are generally two types of cyber deception paradigms: high risk and low risk. Whether a security researcher relies upon the high risk or low risk model depends upon risk tolerance and research goals.

(a) In the **high risk** (high reward) paradigm, the goal is to gather the maximum amount of information on the attacker's techniques and toolsets. Why is it high risk? The cyber deception deployment environment, generally in either a production or non-production segmented network, has almost all the capability of an equivalent application environment with a full theoretical command line or portal capabilities available to the hacker if they were to breach the system through compromise and/or privilege escalation. This could potentially disclose too much information about the internal systems, or incur the risk that protections are defeated to allow the threat actor on the actual corporate network.

(b) Conversely in a **low risk** (low reward) paradigm, the goal is to just detect the source of potential compromises or breaches (e.g., insider threat vs. an external connection). This type of cyber deception environment only exposes a limited amount of application of infrastructure capability, thus reducing its exposure to a compromise by an attacker.

2.1 Next Generation

There are three primary requirements that are being factored into creating the next generation Cyber Deception Systems (CDS).

2.1.1 Dynamic Plug and Play

Next generation CDS should have the capability for dynamic plug and play, in order to stand them up in different network segments to increase visibility into different application and infrastructure ecosystems. These CDS can maintain their elusiveness without compromising their security posture.

2.1.2 AI and ML

The combination of an entity risk scoring and configuration-based packet analyzer rules (e.g., snort) can lead to a brittle implementation plagued by false positives needing constant correction or filtering of alerts and event.

With the advent of Machine learning (ML) and artificial intelligence (AI) paradigms, the next gen cyber deception stack will have the ability to conduct behavior analysis on malicious activities (human, malware or otherwise) in real time, without human (analyst) intervention. It will apply the information gathered into real-time intrusion detection and prevention scenarios in production through reactive response.

Naïve Bayes and Hidden Markov Models
Some work has been done using supervised machine learning algorithms such as Decision Trees, Support Vector Machine (SVM), Naïve Bayes, and Hidden Markov Models (HMM).

Algorithms like Decision Trees and SVM are generally used to train the algorithms using data from existing CDS results and help them detect threats with previously known behavioral patterns.

This data can subsequently be fed into deep learning algorithms like Naïve Bayes and HMM algorithms to enable unsupervised ML by using inherent error correction functionality within these algorithms.

AI Risks

Although the use of AI and ML algorithms can enable the detection of sophisticated threats, these algorithms can also be used by the threat actors to identify CDS and take evasive actions, making it difficult for the incident response teams to detect internal or external threats.

2.1.3 Cybernet

A Cybernet is basically a network of CDS working together in a cluster type of configuration, which can be used if dynamic plug and play capability is not available.

This has also been used as an upgrade path from honeynets to more modern CDS, while keeping the network connectivity and associated infrastructure intact.

3 Deployment Use Cases

Cyber deception has become a workstream within some cyber programs with formal deployment and management strategies.

3.1 *Deployment Use Cases*

The cyber deception systems (CDS) are generally deployed for four primary cases discussed below:

3.1.1 Research and Development (R&D)

Several security research firms use some cyber deception R&D to get a better understanding of the modus operandi and techniques of hackers and malware, such as exploiting application, infrastructure, and system vulnerabilities; performing privilege escalation and data exfiltration; and beaconing. This information may be used to create IOCs (indicators of compromise), understand behavioral patterns and signatures, as well as to develop better detection and mitigation techniques for their various product and incident response offerings that provide malware detection, mitigation, and remediation capabilities.

3.1.2 Threat Detection

CDS are used for Threat Detection from internal and external threats and malicious entities. Once a threat is detected, the CDS may either alert, block, defuse, or slow it down.

3.1.3 Monitoring and Response

CDS generally have (API Level) integrations with the Security Incident and Event Management (SIEM) systems to provide active monitoring and response capabilities for the systems or applications being attacked.

3.1.4 Threat Blocking

Modern CDS have the capability to block the threats that they detect. This capability is similar to that of an intrusion prevention system (IPS). This capability is only exercised if the threat level is determined to be high, since blocking that threat may disclose the identity of the system as a deception system, alerting the threat actor.

3.2 Production Deployment

Cyber deception in production is primarily deployed in production environments or networks in a hardened or air-gapped network segment. The cyber deception system is generally part of the production Intrusion Prevention System (IPS) and Cyber Threat Intelligence (CTI) ecosystems and gives the impression of a full-blown network with real applications, network appliances, databases, and file stores. The sole aim is to gather intelligence in an attempt to learn more about the tools, tricks, and techniques used to launch attacks, breach or compromise a system, or conduct other anomalous activities.

3.3 Taxonomy

In an effort to bring uniformity to the various proprietary and open-source cyber deception systems, a standardized taxonomy similar to the one described below is generally used for the development and implementations of the same.

Class	Value	Description
Interaction level	High	All designed functionality is exposed (high-risk/high reward)
Interaction level	Low	Only limited functionality is exposed (low-risk/low reward)
Data Capture	Event	An action that creates a change of state
Data Capture	attack	Attempting to breach security policy or control
Data Capture	Intrusion	Violation of security policy
Data Capture	None	No activity recorded
Containment	Block	Attackers Actions are blocked
Containment	Defuse	Actions permitted, but rendered harmless
Containment	Slow Down	Actions are slowed down
Containment	None	No action taken
Distribution Appearance	Distributed	Operates as a cluster of servers.
Distribution Appearance	Standalone	Is stand-alone as one system.
Communication Interface	Network	Listens on a network interface (e.g., ethernet)
Communication Interface	Non-network hardware	Uses a hardware interface (e.g., USB)
Communication Interface	Software API	Listens using an API interface
Role in n tier	Server	CDS acting as a Server listening for connections.
Role in n tier	Client	CDS acting as a client launching connections to servers.

Fig. 1 CDS Taxonomy

For a given Cyber Deception system (CDS), the taxonomy proposed by Seifert, Welch and Komisarczuk [1] provides the capability to classify the object being analyzed as a member of one of the six classes below (See Fig. 1).

3.3.1 Basic Design and Implementation

The key components of a cyber deception system are:

Packet analyzer component – This is the key component of the system and analyzes regular and encrypted input traffic (tcp/udp) packets to detect (known and unknown) attacks or abnormal/malicious behavior per the configured ruleset.

In use in the industry are both commercial and open source (e.g., snort, zeek) implementations of the main analyzer engine within CDS.

Protection component –prevents the exposure of the cyber deception entity by hiding its system and services, removes any malicious rootkits installed in the kernel, and replaces them with a non-malicious kit that can return fake results to the hacker trying to breach the cyber deception system.

Configuration component – provides the needed configurations to all the components that make up the cyber deception system mentioned above. It also performs dynamic class loading to inject new and/or updated configuration items during run-time.

Logging component – provides the capability to store the events that are generated from the real-time packet analysis conducted by the packet analyzer. Events are stored for cross-reference, cumulative risk analysis, event batch processing by ML algorithms, or for reporting purposes.

Cyber deception has many benefits but also has some drawbacks.

3.3.2 Benefits

(a) Because cyber deception systems analyze real traffic, the IOCs they generate are more accurate, reducing the number of false positives that have plagued the IDS/IPS systems of the past.
(b) System-generated training datasets can be fed into supervised and semi-supervised machine learning algorithms, leading to the reduction of human labor required for analysis and interpretation.
(c) Because cyber deception systems do not need to be pre-populated with IOCs and attack (hash) signatures, they can be more effective than IPS/IDS systems.

3.3.3 Drawbacks

(a) Identifiability – Cyber deception systems can be identified using system fingerprinting and pattern analysis techniques especially utilized by sophisticated malware, hackers, or artificially intelligent (anomalous) systems.
(b) Segregation – Due to their segmented existence on the company network, these have no way to detect anomalous activities on other production systems or networks.
(c) Limited Data – They can only see traffic that comes their way which may sometimes be too limited to establish patterns.
(d) Justification – sometimes it is hard to justify the budget required to implement and maintain these systems.
(e) Misuse – if not properly protected, the cyber deception could be misused to launch attacks on other systems.

3.4   Implementations

There are now a variety of commercial and open-source implementations of cyber deception systems, *some* of which are mentioned below:

3.4.1   Open Source

There are plenty of open-source implementations that have been done. These are ideal for lab environments and should primarily be used for research and development purposes. Although this space is dynamic and changes very frequently, I have provided a list of names of some products with which I am familiar:

1. Honeysens
2. Google Hack Honeypot
3. HoneyC
4. Honeyd
5. Honeymole
6. Nepenthes
7. Dockpot

3.4.2   Commercial

Most of these are production ready with good vendor support and professional services available. Security practitioners should quantify the (cyber) risk they carry and use that number in the business case to justify their implementation. Generally, if a firm adheres to Zero Trust and has both macro and micro segmentation across the board, then the value proposition of commercial cyber deception implementation decreases.

This space has seen a lot of investment from commercial security product developers in the last 3 years, leading to the delivery of some good products. Some of the current leaders in this space include:

1. Cybertrap
2. Cymmetria
3. Trapx
4. Attivonetworks
5. Acalvio
6. Alluresecurity
7. kFSensor

Note It is recommended that the reader write security requirements specific to their needs and a conduct proof-of-concept (POC) with some of the above-mentioned providers. The author has provided the above-mentioned products list in no specific order and is not making any assertions on their performance, capability or maturity.

Also, since this is a fast-evolving space, there are other interesting products in the market that have emerged recently. I also recommend that the readers look at the Gartner Magic quadrant for this space before they make a selection.

4   The CISO Take

Cyber threats have become increasingly persistent, complex, and sophisticated. CDS can be used to better understand internal and external threats and the tools and techniques employed by malicious actors. Cyber deception can also help create IOCs (indicators of compromise) which then subsequently can be used within the IPS (intrusion prevention systems) to help provide better detection and mitigation of advanced threats and other anomalous activity.

Also, the possibility of unsupervised machine learning paradigms has the potential to make CDS more effective, while reducing operational and maintenance costs and improving the return of investment into the technology. I recommend that every cyber program dealing with the protection of very sensitive data deploy a cyber deception system in strategic network segments to become aware of the cyber risk or malicious behavior.

5   Definitions

IOC – stands for indicator of compromise. It is either a unique signature, log entry, or an event that indicates that a network or system breach has occurred. These can be used as forensic evidence, either individually or in combination with other IOCs.

IPS – stands for intrusion prevention system. It is a network security tool that provides monitoring (detection) and protection against network-based attacks and intrusions, including lateral movement.

SDN – stands for software-defined networking. It is a modern approach to network architecture and design that uses uniform software-defined and managed controls rather than the hardware-based controls of the past, to enable the capability of centralized management, with faster delivery and reconfigurations, better monitoring and alerting, and reduced maintenance costs.

Snort – is an open-source (legacy) network intrusion detection system (IDS) and intrusion prevention system (IPS) tool.

UEBA – stands for user and event behavior analysis – previously also known as user behavior analysis (UBA). It has the capability to examine and analyze user, application, process, and machine behavior and any system events within a network to identify threats and other anomalous behavior.

WAF – stands for web access firewall. It is primarily an application firewall that protects an HTTP/S-based (web) application against advanced attacks like cross-site scripting, cross-site forgery, and sql injection.

Reference

1. Seifert C, Welch I, et al (2006) Taxonomy of Honeypots, http://www.mcs.vuw.ac.nz/comp/Publications/archive/CS-TR-06/CS-TR-06-12.pdf . Accessed 22 Nov 2020

Further Reading

Rowe N (2019) Honeypot Deception Tactics, http://faculty.nps.edu/ncrowe/honeypot_deception_tactics.htm , Accessed 22 Nov 20

Spitzner L (2001) The Value of Honeypots, Part One: Definitions and Values of Honeypots https://community.broadcom.com/symantecenterprise/communities/community-home/librarydocuments/viewdocument?DocumentKey=a8da0d16-65ae-405a-abeb-325af33a393d. Accessed 22 Nov 2020

Unknown Threat Detection with Honeypot Ensemble Analysis Using Big Data Security Architecture, Michael Eugene Sanders Illinois State University, https://ir.library.illinoisstate.edu/cgi/viewcontent.cgi?article=1359&context=etd Accessed 22 Nov 2020

The Cybersecurity-Driven Need for Hypervisor Introspection

1   Introduction

The advent of software virtualization – i.e., the creation of virtual servers, desktops, applications, storage and networks has indeed introduced the functionality to better utilize the underlying hardware, thereby improving agility and scalability and generating significant cost savings. Software virtualization also has provided these additional capabilities:

(a) **Partitioning** is the running of multiple operating systems (OS) on one physical machine and dividing/sharing system resources between/across Virtual Machines (VMs);
(b) **Isolation** provides for fault and security isolation at the hardware level;
(c) **Encapsulation** provides the capability to save the entire state of a VM, and move/copy VMs to other VMs;
(d) **High Availability** refers to better local high availability and disaster recovery capabilities; and
(e) **Automated Provisioning** leads to faster provisioning of applications and system resources.

All leading to the ultimate goal of establishing a software-defined network, perimeter, and data center. The technology component that enables all the above is called a hypervisor, also known as a virtual machine monitor (VMM) which creates and runs the virtual machine on the host machine.

2 Genesis

Despite its many advantages, software virtualization can be problematic under a variety of different circumstances, such as with applications that have high compute needs (I/O, CPU, or GPU) or require specialist hardware or firmware, where time synchronization is critical (across VMs), where CPU, memory, or disk capacity is limited, or where encryption or other cryptographic keys need to be managed.

Due to the need to optimize the underlying hardware and system sources like RAM and CPU, the virtualization of applications does also create a bit of a problem from an information security perspective - especially for cyber security applications/agents (e.g., AV, EDR, DLP, eDiscovery agents) that now have to run within each VM and contend for system resources with other business applications. In addition, running a security agent inside a VM leaves it vulnerable to attacks. It would be advantageous if, instead of running within each VM, security applications could be agentless, running instead at the hypervisor level. From the centralized location of the hypervisor, security applications will have full visibility into each VM, and can provide all security monitoring or blocking previously handled by agents running within individual VMs.

3 Hypervisor Memory Introspection (HVMI)

The capability to introspect or perform high-fidelity monitoring inside each VM running on a hypervisor is called Hypervisor Memory Introspection (HVMI). This enables the capability to create agent-less technology, especially for security purposes, by allowing for the security monitoring of a VM or multiple VMs simultaneously from outside each VM, directly from the hypervisor itself. HVMI has direct access to physical memory thus enabling it with better visibility from outside than a security agent running inside the VM. Also, unlike VM-based security monitoring agents, HVMI can also impose memory or register access restrictions.

Having said that, implementing and operating/running HVMI can prove to be very complicated and complex. Due to the lack of standardization in the virtualization space, separate implementations would need to be written for separate commonly used hypervisor implementations (Citrix Xen, VMWare vSphere, Microsoft HyperV, etc.). In addition, the need for HVMI to operate at the kernel level and utilize many documented and undocumented OS features can lead to bugs and instability.

3.1 Advantages of HVMI

(a) Running a security agent or daemon at the hypervisor and not inside the VM, **reduces the attack surface**.

(b) Using the API level integration with the various internal components such as raw memory and cache, virtual disk, and the system and application processes, HVMI provides better monitoring capability from outside the virtual machine.
(c) A singular HVMI instance/agent can provide the monitoring and enforcement capability over multiple virtual machines, thereby eliminating the requirement to install security agents within each individual VM.

3.2 Disadvantages of HVMI

(a) The HVMI instance/agent only gets visibility into those components that are available to it through the API integration, leaving it to infer other systems information and necessitating frequent upgrades to the API integration as more visibility is made available.
(b) Suboptimal integrations of the HVMI instance/agent with a given hypervisor can cause significant performance impacts for VMs.
(c) The HVMI implementations have high complexity owing to the system-level integration at the hardware and firmware level for different hardware configuration and operating systems.
(d) The undocumented features within closed operating systems (e.g., windows) pose significant issues to the integrity of some HVMI integrations.

3.3 HVMI Security Risk

Hyper Introspection does have some security risks that need to be mitigated with proper implementation of security controls.

(a) Hypervisor introspection without fine-grained access and security controls can lead to undocumented functionality and backdoor access into the data processing by a VM.
(b) A hypervisor that has either been breached or compromised can lead to unauthorized access to sensitive data or processing in the VM.
(c) Malware at the hypervisor could use the introspection capability to spread further into the VMs.
(d) Introspection without full API-level integration or testing can lead to VM corruption, potentially causing crashes, restarts, performance issues, and general system instability.

3.4 Using AI/ML with HVMI

HVMI is an evolving technology and while the API-level integrations are getting better with each new functionality release, there are some known system visibility issues. Currently it overcomes the lack of full visibility into the system resources by inferring the missing information. This an area where ML paradigms like deep learning can be used to infer data based on training data from the other (memory) data and patterns that are indeed visible to the HVMI instance/agent.

4 The CISO Take

The hypervisor OEMs need to standardize the APIs required to support HVMI. This will improve security monitoring, reduce performance impacts caused by multiple security agents running inside VMs, and enable the capability to repulse sophisticated malware and threats. CISOs need to assert the inclusion of this requirement in the writing of new security software which can be either virtualized or containerized. They also need to ensure that all HVMI implementations are secure, are not prone to attacks from threat actors, and disallow any unauthorized monitoring of systems or visibility of sensitive data within a given VM.

CISOs also need to ensure that the lessons learned from the implementation and hardening of hypervisor introspection are now also applied to container introspection.

5 Definitions

AV –stands for Anti-Virus. It is computer software that has the capability to detect, prevent, block, and remove malware. Most legacy AV uses static (hash-based) signatures to perform the detection.

Agentless – generally refers to the capability where a process, daemon, agent or service is not required to deliver the needed functionality. In cyber security many services like AV or Monitoring can be delivered using this paradigm by running at the hypervisor rather than running a process within a VM.

DLP – stands for Data Loss Prevention. It is a technology that prevents the unauthorized access to or exfiltration of company and customer sensitive data.

EDR – stands endpoint detection and response. It is the next generation malware detection system. Rather than using the legacy static signature of legacy AV detection products, it has the capability to provide visibility into endpoint user, machine, and process behavior and rely on dynamic heuristical analysis to detect and block advanced malware.

Virtual machine (VM) – is a software representation or emulation of a physical computer system. Just like a physical computer, a VM runs an operating system and applications. The implementation of a VM is generally done using specialty hardware and software. Generally, multiple VMs run on a hypervisor and an underlying physical host system/computer.

Hypervisor – is an entity generally composed of software, hardware, and firmware components assembled as a unit, and creates and manages new VMs.

Further Reading

Bitdefender (2020) Bitdefender releases groundbreaking open source HVI technology through Xen project. https://www.prnewswire.com/news-releases/bitdefender-releases-groundbreaking-open-source-hvi-technology-through-xen-project-301102819.html. Accessed 23 Nov 2020

Bitdefender (2020) Bitdefender hypervisor introspection: a transformative approach to advanced attack detection, https://www.bitdefender.com/business/enterprise-products/hypervisor-introspection.html, Accessed 23 Nov 2020

Bitdefender, Intel et al (2019) Virtual machine introspection. https://wiki.xenproject.org/wiki/Virtual_Machine_Introspection. Accessed 23 Nov 2020

Kurth L (2016) Virtual machine introspection: a security innovation with new commercial applications. https://www.linux.com/news/virtual-machine-introspection-security-innovation-new-commercial-applications/. Accessed 23 Nov 2020

Tuzel T, Bridgman M, et al (2018) Who watches the watcher? Detecting hypervisor introspection from unprivileged guests. Digital Investigation 26(Supp): S98–S106. https://doi.org/10.1016/j.diin.2018.04.015

Bitcoin Is a Decade Old, and So Are the Threats to the Various Blockchain Ecosystems

1 Introduction

In October of 2018 we celebrated the tenth anniversary of Bitcoin: a public blockchain – a digitized, decentralized, public ledger crypto-currency implementation. There is enough material on how blockchain has created a new ecosystem for micro-payments and crypto-currency transactions and has found widespread use in supply chain management, accounting, smart contracts, voting, the stock exchanges, insurance, shipping and peer-to-peer global transactions, but today I want to take a moment to document SOME of the various security issues that have also plagued this ecosystem, and defeated the basic premise of blockchain immutability.

2 BlockChain Attacks

1. The "51% Attack" on public and private blockchains is where either a singular malicious entity or a group of miners gain control of 51% of the blockchain network's mining hash-rate or computing power. This allows the attackers to prevent new transactions from gaining confirmations, halting payments between some and/or all users and potentially also gaining the capability to reverse transactions that may have completed previously.
2. "Sybil Attack" works on the same construct as the 51% attack, where the attackers (or, generally, a singular attacker) gains control of the majority of the blockchain network by creating multiple fake identities.
3. "Penny-Flooding Attack" is where an attacker floods a blockchain network with (generally free) transactions that achieve nothing (basically making crypto transactions between controlled account or nodes that they own).

4. "Penny-spend attack" is similar to a penny-flood attack where an attacker sends very small value transactions to a large number of accounts in order to overwhelm the storage and computing resources of the nodes.
5. "Transaction flooding" is another DDoS (*Distributed Denial-of-Service*) type attack where an attacker sends a large number of valid transactions to other accounts (generally controlled by the attacker) leading to the saturation of the blockchain network.
6. "Time-jacking attack" is one where an attacker can plant fake nodes in a blockchain network and report inaccurate timestamps from those. Using this technique, they can either slow down or speed up the time counter for the entire blockchain network, giving them the ability to cheat the network into accepting an alternate block-chain.
7. "Eclipse attack" is one where an attacker takes control over a victim's egress and ingress network connections, thereby causing network isolation and computing resource wastage and or exhaustion, and leading to situations like engineering block races, splitting mining power, selfish mining or double spend – all of which benefit the attacker.
8. "Steganographic attack" is the one where the attackers may embed malicious or illegal data in crypto blockchain transactions.
9. "Silkroad attack" is the one where the attackers have control of a victim while the victim is trading with a merchant. Upon the completion of a given transaction, the attacker uses the client address to request a fraudulent refund from the merchant.

3   Some Threat Mitigation Techniques for Block-Chain Systems

I am going to very briefly mention some of the techniques available to mitigate some of the attacks mentioned in the previous section:

1. Penny-flooding attacks can be prevented by continuous rate-limiting of free transactions.
2. A way to prevent Sybil attacks is to require some sort of trust before allowing a new identity to join the network.
3. Time jacking attacks can be prevented by changing how nodes calculate the current time.
4. One of the ways to prevent the 51% attacks would be to implement merged mining, which would allow for the miner's pool to mine several crypto-currencies (e.g., Bitcoin, Ethereum etc.) simultaneously, as long as they are implemented on the same algorithm.
5. There are various techniques to prevent DDOS (distributed denial of service) attacks –

    (a) Not to forward the same block, transaction or alert twice to the same peer.

(b) Not to forward orphan or double-spend transactions or blocks.

(c) A signature cache can be used to prevent attacks caused by continuous re-verification of stored orphaned transactions.

6. Sybil attacks can be prevented by only allowing an outbound connection to one IP address per /16 (x.y.0.0).

7. A rather drastic solution to prevent long-term attack by malicious entities on a given block-chain is a hard-fork to change the proof-of-work function which would result in a removal of the current miners.

8. The attacks on block-chains from quantum computers can be prevented by changing the crypto schemes within proof-of-work algorithms from ECC to Momentum (based on finding collisions in a hash function).

9. Double spend attacks can be prevented by utilizing a third-party transaction validation service before the transactions are committed to the ledger.

4 The CISO Take

Blockchain was made possible by cryptography. The immutability of a blockchain and its whole trust model will be called into question if the platform gets breached or if the immutability is proven to be false or defeated.

Apart from its apparent use in various use cases to aid the financial and business driven use cases, blockchain can also be used in cyber security using its inherent capability to track and record every change to an information system. Also, it can prove very helpful in other areas like data security, peer to peer sharing of indicators of comprise (IOC) or other threat intel data, secure messaging, or even a new way of securing DNS.

It is the responsibility of the CISOs to take a leadership role in these conversations, firstly to ensure that all blockchain systems are secured properly so that the confidentiality integrity and availability of blockchain data is maintained, and secondly to ensure that they take the first steps in using this technology for cybersecurity use cases.

5 Definitions

Blockchain – is an immutable and distributed digital ledger. The records (blocks) are linked to each other using a Merkle tree – where each block contains a cryptographic hash (e.g., SHA2) of the previous block, a timestamp and ledger (transaction) data.

Cryptocurrency – is digital (or virtual) currency built using blockchain technology that can be used to pay for goods and services (just like the paper currency).

DDoS – stands for Distributed denial of Service (attack). It is a cyber-attack where a threat actor tries to overwhelm a system by flooding it with traffic packets in an attempt to bring it down and make it unavailable to legitimate uses of the system.

DNS – stands for Domain Name System. It is a global naming system which enables the mapping and the subsequent syncing of a website or other internet/intranet-hosted resource name, to an IP address.

ECC – stands for elliptic curve cryptography. It is used to build an PKI cryptosystem that uses the mathematical structure of discontinuous elliptic curves over finite fields.

IOC – stands for indicator of compromise. It is either a unique signature, log entry, or an event that indicates that a network or system breach has occurred. These can be used as forensic evidence, either individually or in combination with other IOCs.

Further Reading

Aggarwal D, Brennen G et al (2017) Quantum attacks on Bitcoin, and how to protect against them. https://www.researchgate.net/publication/320727053_Quantum_Attacks_on_Bitcoin_and_How_to_Protect_Against_Them, Accessed 13 July 2020

Aruba. 10 Blockchain and New Age Security Attacks You Should Know. https://blogs.arubanetworks.com/solutions/10-blockchain-and-new-age-security-attacks-you-should-know/. Accessed July 13, 2020

Deloitte. Quantum computers and the Bitcoin blockchain, https://www2.deloitte.com/nl/nl/pages/innovatie/artikelen/quantum-computers-and-the-bitcoin-blockchain.html, Accessed July 13, 2020

Kanal E (2019) Could blockchain improve the cybersecurity of supply chains? https://insights.sei.cmu.edu/sei_blog/2019/11/could-blockchain-improve-the-cybersecurity-of-supply-chains.html, Accessed July 13, 2020

Orcutt M (2019) Once hailed as unhackable, blockchains are now getting hacked, https://www.technologyreview.com/2019/02/19/239592/once-hailed-as-unhackable-blockchains-are-now-getting-hacked/, Accessed July 13, 2020

Wikipedia (2020). Blockchain. https://en.wikipedia.org/wiki/Blockchain

Yeomans M (2019) Security Think Tank: risk mitigation is key to blockchain becoming mainstream, https://www.computerweekly.com/opinion/Security-Think-Tank-Risk-mitigation-is-key-to-blockchain-becoming-mainstream, Accessed July 13, 2020

The Advanced Malware Prevention Playbook

1 Introduction

This chapter talks about Ransomware and other forms of Advanced Malware – the one existential threat to information systems worldwide that has become front and center for all cyber security professionals.

Malware is generally categorized as software that has the capability to enable unauthorized access to a system, make unauthorized system calls, or execute malicious code or inject it into an existing process or into memory. It is generally hidden from normal monitoring and can cause irreversible harm to an information system.

Like worms and viruses, malware has been in existence since the birth of systems with open assembler architecture (i.e., 8086 and 80,386 families) adopted by operating systems like windows, UNIX and Linux. Just a decade ago most malware could be detected by using a signature list of hashes used to identify the offending software, but the advent of advanced Malware is a most recent occurrence and uses polymorphic techniques to evade detection.

2 What Is Ransomware?

Ransomware is generally categorized as malware that has the capability to perform unauthorized encryption of data with the intent of extorting a ransom from the victim before providing a decryption key for the said (encrypted) data, among other things.

Ransomware infestations have become cyber attackers' and criminals' weapon of choice for money extortion schemes. They are also used to cause reputational damage and to destroy and delete data in an attempt to cause irreversible infrastructural damage to the victim, generally a business entity.

© The Author(s), under exclusive license to Springer Nature Switzerland AG 2021
R. Badhwar, *The CISO's Next Frontier*,
https://doi.org/10.1007/978-3-030-75354-2_17

Ransomware kits are now also available on the dark web to other (unsophisticated) threat entities.

3   Threat Prevention and Mitigation

Prevention against Ransomware can be achieved by using a combination of the following techniques:

3.1   Perform Continuous Patching

Since ransomware is generally spread through the exploitation of known vulnerabilities (primarily on Windows systems), the proactive and continuous patching of all critical and high-risk vulnerabilities for all systems is the best way to prevent the spread of ransomware and reduce the attack surface.

I would also recommend not to ignore the medium and low severity vulnerabilities. Cumulatively these present higher risk to an organization and sometimes these can also be exploited by insiders or other threat actors and used as a jumping off point to perform privilege escalation.

3.2   Perform Proactive Hardening

Since ransomware is also spread through the exploitation of open ports e.g., Remote Desktop Protocol, or RDP, it is imperative that all internet-facing systems be hardened using the principle of least privilege, and all unnecessary or risky services like RDP be blocked.

All unnecessary ports and services must be turned off in the base operating system and application server images, with monitoring turned on in case they are enabled using privilege escalation attacks.

The same posture must also be used for any endpoint and mobile device (e.g., laptops, iPads, and mobile phones) in addition to the proper configuration of local firewalls for public, private, and domain- joined networks.

3.3   Enable Secure Backups

Ensuring that daily and weekly backups are done of all critical data repositories is a key recovery mechanism in case of a ransomware attack.

All backups must be stored on an air-gapped or segregated network (either on spinning disk or on tape) that is different from the network housing the database or data repository. All access to the data backup network and storage devices must be restricted to authorized personnel. All access credentials must be vaulted, and must require multifactor authentication.

All the backed-up data must be **encrypted** with the encryption keys stored in a dedicated (tenant) hardware security module (HSM).

Other schemes such as taking backup storage offline or making the network interfaces of the backup systems/appliances unavailable when not being used are additional (simpler) ways of (quasi) air-gapping the backup infrastructure.

The capability to recover breached or compromised Active Directory Domain Controllers with clean backups is crucial to help recover an environment from a ransomware attack. (Please see Chap. 13 for additional information on Active Directory attacks and prevention).

3.4 Enable Detect and Block

The capability to proactively detect and block ransomware is another important means of preventing the spread of ransomware. This is generally done by ensuring that appropriate indicators of compromise (IOC's) are available and used to detect patterns in all incoming north-south and east-west traffic flows.

This end goal is generally achieved by using a combination of endpoint discovery and response (EDR) and user and entity behavior analysis (UEBA) tools. The EDR uses dynamic and static IOCs and other sources of threat intel to provide visibility into the various endpoints and server machines on the network and has the capability to discover, detect and block anomalous activity by a user, system or process.

The UEBA creates baselines of user, machine, and process behavior across the network and endpoints, and can alert for any deviations from baselines behaviors using a risk-based thresholding approach.

3.5 Enable Application Control

In making use of application control techniques to reduce malware (including ransomware) and other harmful security attacks, the best practice is to allow only approved and trusted (i.e., digitally signed) files, applications, and processes to be installed and run on a system. The modern way of doing this is to use real-time dynamic application and executable white-listing (also see Chap. 32).

3.6 Implement DNS Sinkholing

One of the other ways to detect the presence of ransomware on your network is to detect any CnC bound traffic by implementing a **DNS Sinkhole**. It is a technique that helps with the identification of infected hosts on a private (or public) network. It enables the redirection of malicious internet-bound traffic by entering a fake entry into a DNS server to change the flow of a malicious URL. The sinkhole allows to control any CnC bound traffic and other malicious traffic routed to a DGA generated (malicious) domain across a private network.

This can be used to build a list of impacted local/global workstations and servers. These can also be used to deploy kill switches against the said ransomware.

3.7 Reduce Reliance on Third-Party Patching

The best practice is to reduce reliance on third party patching (directly in production) as much as possible and still try to use the time-tested approach of 'trust but verify' wherever possible.

Some ideas of reducing this reliance are below -

(a) **Old School**: The tried and tested security paradigm of the past - '**Trust but Verify**', where any software update (OS, application, Browser, AV updates, etc.) is thoroughly tested in a lower-level environment, then turned into a **gold image** and subsequently pushed through or deployed into production systems through a well-established software update mechanism (e.g., using SCCM). If done right, there is a pretty high chance of catching any application compatibility issues or malware infestation during the testing before any product deployment.

(b) **New School**: In this model, the responsibility of ensuring the creation of secure patches free of any malware or exploitable vulnerabilities lies with third parties. In today's world, reliance on third-party patching is unavoidable. Our current environment often makes it difficult for IT and security teams to go through full-blown testing cycles to create golden images of software. Applications and software update on their own, automatically. Next generation malware and threats are morphing and spreading at record pace. OS and application exploits and vulnerabilities requiring rapid patching have proliferated. With these challenges to the old school testing paradigm, software now may get updated and patched directly in some production environments. Unfortunately, live production environment updates make products prime targets for supply chain attacks.

With this school of thought, behavior-based endpoint discovery and response (EDR) tooling and network traffic analysis aided by Machine Learning (ML) are used to detect anomalous behavior potentially introduced by third-party patching.

There also opportunities to use sandboxing and other forms of heuristics analysis for malware scanning and dynamic behavior analysis for high-risk applications or for third party applications or systems that have fallen victim to breaches in the past (e.g., Solarwinds).

3.8 Deploy Kill Switch

The kill switch in this context is a technique used to kill or terminate a ransomware process. Sometimes these can work in tandem with a sinkhole to kill ransomware processes. There are few techniques available –

(a) It is generally a file which when enumerated by the ransomware process crashes the shell or process. This technique can work against a generic class of ransomware, and can be proactively deployed. These files are generally pushed to high-risk endpoints or servers by security teams as defensive measures.
(b) It can also be another file that can also crash the process when the process tries to encrypt it.
(c) It could be a backdoor into the malware that the attacker may have left open to kill the process if/when needed.
(d) It could be command that the malware can use to kill (itself) or any in progress encryption process(es) in case it is detected. This can also be used by the cyber defense teams through threat intelligence information they may have gathered.

4   Protections from Other Advanced Malware

Advanced malware has caused serious damage in the recent past (e.g., Petya, NotPetya, WannaCry) amounting to billions of dollars of damage to corporations worldwide.

I have also written a separate chapter (35) on Polymorphic and Metamorphic malware in this book.

In addition to the ransomware prevention techniques already mentioned above, most of which are also very relevant for prevention against other advanced forms of malware, some other generic techniques for the *prevention* of other forms of advanced malware are described below.

4.1 Implement a Cyber Threat Intel Platform

The best practice is to implement a threat intel platform with intel feeds and IOCs from various open source (e.g., VirusTotal etc.), government (e.g., DHS, FS-ISAC), and private sources (e.g., Palo Alto Wildfire, Symantec, Crowdstrike, Lookout, Proofpoint) and then run the hashes of (all) the updates and patches through the threat intel platform which has a consolidated and up-to-date list of IOCs and hashes of all malicious software and malware.

4.2 Implement Endpoint Detection and Response

Another best practice is to make use of EDR capability to detect, investigate, and mitigate suspicious activities and issues on hosts and endpoints. The next-generation EDR platforms now use supervised and semi-supervised ML algorithms aided by training data from SIEMs and IOCs from threat intel platforms to detect and flag malicious and anomalous (software) behavior to be blocked from execution.

4.3 Deploy Advanced Quarantine Capability

Have advanced quarantine capability (where the user device is automatically segregated into a restricted subnet) for all end-user devices (including but not limited to laptops, tablets and smart phones) to stop malware infestation from spreading or moving laterally, once detected.

4.4 Employ Forensics Examination

An eDiscovery agent on the endpoint or server can come in very handy to aid with forensic examination of infected or breached systems. Modern eDiscovery agents can perform real-time 'memory forensics' (generally done by creating a raw image and/or a crash dump image of system memory) from live processes to analyze suspicious endpoint, application or process behavior alerted by an EDR agent, host or network based UEBA agent. Some additional details on this topic have also been provided in Sect. 5.6 in Chap. 35.

5 The CISO Take

Although there is already a lot of good material available on this subject, I have provided some additional baseline insight from a CISO perspective that others in the industry may want to incorporate into their cyber risk assessment, mitigation, and remediation practices.

I recommend that every business, corporate or government entity that has sensitive data targeted by threat actors must implement the above-mentioned security controls to protect themselves from ransomware attacks and advanced malware infestations.

Apart from implementing good security controls, the other recommended approach to prevent against sophisticated cyber-attacks is to gain awareness about the adversaries and the techniques they may use to attack us by establishing a cyber threat intelligence program and using it to gain actionable threat intel. Once we have this threat awareness and visibility, then the cyber security people can design, develop, and implement preventative and defensive measures especially against advance malware.

The CISOs must also ensure that they have a good insider threat program since insiders are being used to seed internal networks with ransomware in an attempt to spread it without having to defeat perimeter security apparatus.

6 Definitions

CISA – stands for cybersecurity and infrastructure security agency. It is the Nation's risk advisor, working with partners to defend against today's threats and collaborating to build more secure and resilient infrastructure for the future.

CnC – stands for command and control (server). Generally, a cloud-hosted server/system often working in tandem with the usage of DGA-generated domains, the CnC is used by threat actors to control and manage infected and breached endpoints and servers (generally resident) on private networks.

EDR – stands for Endpoint Detection and Response. EDR is the next-generation malware detection system. Rather than relying on the legacy static signature generated by legacy AV detection products, it has the capability to provide visibility into endpoint user, machine, and process behavior, and perform dynamic heuristical analysis, which it then uses to detect and block advanced malware.

FS-ISAC – stands for Financial Services Information Sharing and Analysis Center. It is a cyber intelligence sharing community solely focused on financial services.

SCCM – stands for System Center Configuration Manager. It is a Microsoft utility that provides the capability to administer and manage a large number of domain attached windows-based computers. The services within the SCCM suite include patch management, OS deployment, remote control, among some others.

Further Reading

Alex Hern (2017) WannaCry, Petya, NotPetya: how ransomware hit the big time in 2017, https://www.theguardian.com/technology/2017/dec/30/wannacry-petya-notpetya-ransomware. Accessed Dec 24, 2020

CISA (2020) Ransomware guidance and resources, https://www.cisa.gov/ransomware

FireEye Staff (2020) Ransomware – attacker's top choice for cyber extortion, https://www.fireeye.com/current-threats/what-is-cyber-security/ransomware.html, Accessed Dec 24, 2020

Sood K, Hurley S (2017) NotPetya technical analysis – a triple threat: file encryption, MFT Encryption, Credential Theft, https://www.crowdstrike.com/blog/petrwrap-ransomware-technical-analysis-triple-threat-file-encryption-mft-encryption-credential-theft/

Krebs B (2020) Malicious domain in solarwinds hack turned into 'Killswitch.' Available via Krebsonsecurity. https://krebsonsecurity.com/2020/12/malicious-domain-in-solarwinds-hack-turned-into-killswitch/

Lord N (2018) What is advanced malware? https://digitalguardian.com/blog/what-advanced-malware. Accessed Dec 24, 2020

Joven M (2017) A technical analysis of the petya ransomworm, https://www.fortinet.com/blog/threat-research/a-technical-analysis-of-the-petya-ransomworm

Rashid FY (2020) Stopping Solarwinds backdoor with a killswitch. Available via Decipher. https://duo.com/decipher/stopping-solarwinds-backdoor-with-a-killswitch. Accessed Dec 24, 2020

Staff Writer (2020) The biggest ransomware threats, https://www.kaspersky.com/resource-center/threats/ransomware-threats-an-in-depth-guide. Accessed Dec 24, 2020

Staff Writer (2020) What is ransomware. https://www.mcafee.com/enterprise/en-us/security-awareness/ransomware.html. Accessed Dec 24, 2020

What is advanced malware protection (AMP)? https://www.cisco.com/c/en/us/products/security/advanced-malware-protection/index.html. Accessed Dec 24, 2020

Part V
Network Security

The 768K Precipice

1 Introduction

Remember the 512 K day (outage) on Aug 12, 2014? No? Well let me now refresh the memory of those who forgot or missed this major outage.

This chapter will provide some tactical steps ISP's can take to either mitigate or resolve this issue, and will also share the current state as of Feb 7, 2021.

2 Genesis

On August 12, 2014, there was a widespread internet outage experienced by many ISPs (e.g., Verizon, ATT, Sprint) and their customers, potentially causing millions of dollars' worth of lost business and productivity. This outage was attributed to network packet loss, primarily caused by the memory exhaustion (512 K) of the border gateway protocol (BGP) global routing tables, which could not store any additional (IPv4) routes.

3 Tactical Resolution

This issue was resolved by making firmware updates to the impacted routers and increasing the BGP routing table size to 768K and by manually configuring the routers with a BGP routing table memory big enough to store 768,000 (IPv4) routes.

Almost six years later, the BGP routing table size for most ISPs is close to that 768K limit, with the clock ticking for some smaller ISPs running older network gear susceptible to this problem (e.g., the Cisco 6500/7600 product line).

© The Author(s), under exclusive license to Springer Nature Switzerland AG 2021
R. Badhwar, *The CISO's Next Frontier*,
https://doi.org/10.1007/978-3-030-75354-2_18

So technically speaking now the new boundary is 786,432 routes and I am sure that there are some ISPs out there that are susceptible to this new limit.

Thankfully, all the larger ISPs in the US have addressed this issue, either with better networking gear with built-in resiliency or with configuration and/or firmware patch implementations. But this is a global problem and I am not sure of the state of affairs for smaller ISPs or the ones in other parts of the world that is less economically or technologically developed and may still be using older hardware.

Another solution is to prevent the addition of large /24 routes to your BGP routing table, tactically discard or disallow /24 network routes, or point all outbound traffic to /24 routes onto upstream network providers who have advanced networking gear to handle this situation (which is what probably is already the case for many of us).

BGP Route filtering is yet another option, but in that case one should use prefix lists instead of access lists in the filtering commands.

The best practices for configuring prefix lists are listed at [2].

The clock is ticking and only time will tell, sooner rather than later, if this BGP routing table size precipice will cause another widespread internet outage or not.

4   Current State

Ripe Labs (part of Ripe Network Coordination Center (aka Ripe NCC)) has done some good work to track the current state (and size) of the IPv6 and IPv6 route tables [1].

They have published a whois type interface called riswhois which provides the capability to perform some monitoring of the IPv4/v6 tables. This is a peer query and can show the number of IPv4 and v6 routes of their peers over the last 8 hours. Their interface can be used with the whois command and can be run from any Linux or Apple (MacOS) machine – whois -h riswhois.ripe.net peers

Or you can view the equivalent output data at their web site where this data has been made available in JSON format by making a data call to their database via this URL – https://stat.ripe.net/data/ris-peers/data.json

When I looked at this data, I saw that there are some peers that were still below the 786,432 limit, some that are almost at the number, and some that were higher, which tells me that many ISPs and equivalent entities have successfully mitigated the risk but some may have not.

Because this command and associated data is publicly available, this also runs the risk of being used by the threat actors or insider threat actors to launch a denial-of-service attack for the entities that may be below the limit and are running older hardware. It is thus imperative that the ISPs and other entities that are exposed take proactive steps to mitigate this risk before they face an outage of their network inconveniencing their users and business that use them for network and internet connectivity.

5 The CISO Take

Although this is primarily a network issue which is going be further compounded by the wider adoption of IPv6, it is also very much a security issue since this weakness can be exploited to launch a denial-of-service (type) attack. It is thus upon the CISOs to ensure that this issue is treated as a security issue by promoting the adoption of some of the tactical fixes mentioned in this chapter and prioritizing the upgrade of the network stack to the next generation where this issue has been handled.

This is another simple item that highlights the breadth of the CISO role. CISOs have to make sure they are aware of the various ways the eco system they protect could be attacked, and have also found ways to remediate, mitigate or transfer that risk. This is yet another reason why the CISOs should be responsible for all the network infrastructure and not just the security of that (network) infrastructure.

6 Definitions

BGP – stands for border gateway protocol. It is the routing protocol of the internet and is used to provide routing information between an ISP and an autonomous system (AS).

IPv4 – stands for internet protocol version 4. It is the fourth version of the internet protocol and the far the most used today. It is one of core network protocols that powers the internet. Its successor, IPv6, has been implemented, but has not yet been widely adopted.

ISP – stands for internet service provider. It is an entity that provides internet access to a private customer or a business enterprise.

JSON – stands for JavaScript Object Notation. It is a lightweight and compact data interchange format that can be easily parsed or generated by systems but equally easy for humans to read and write.

Whois – it isn't an acronym. It is a record listing implemented as a request/response query that identifies and tracks internet domain (and IP address) ownership.

/24 (subnet) – can have 254 hosts in this (sub) network.

References

1. Aben E (2019) 768k day. Will it happen? Did it happen? Available via RIPE NCC.https://labs.ripe.net/Members/emileaben/768k-day-will-it-happen-did-it-happen. Accessed on Dec 24, 2020
2. Parkhurst W R, Ph.D. "Cisco BGP-4 Command and Configuration Handbook." April 27, 2001. BGP Time To Live Security Check, https://tools.cisco.com/security/center/resources/protecting_border_gateway_protocol#8

Further Reading

Introducing JSON (2020) https://www.json.org/json-en.html. Accessed 20 Jan 2021

Ripe NCC (2021) RipeEstat. https://stat.ripe.net/data/ris-peers/data.json. Accessed 21 Jan, 2021

Singh S (2014) Catalyst 6500 switches ternary content addressable memory customization.https:// www.cisco.com/c/en/us/support/docs/switches/catalyst-6500-series-switches/116132- problem-catalyst6500-00.html. Accessed 21 Jan, 2021

Turner F (2020) 768k day: the importance of adaptable software. Available via Cumulus Networks Engineering Blog. https://cumulusnetworks.com/blog/768k-day-importance- adaptable-software-growing-internet/

MAC Address Randomization to Limit User/Device Tracking

1 Introduction

The debate and the need to find a healthy compromise and balance between privacy and security has continued. This chapter provides an interesting discussion on the matter.

2 Genesis

The topic of MAC Address randomization originally came into the lime light with Edward Snowden, when he reported that the NSA may have been using Mac Addresses to track the movement of devices in a given area. This should not have been earth shattering or new information. MAC addresses have long been used and are still being used for various (similar) purposes – ISP and cable providers used MAC addresses to authorize devices behind a cable modem to connect to services long before the use of identity federations and protocols like SAML became mainstream. Many corporate networks and other network providers like hotels and airports have used MAC filtering techniques to authorize and track users on their networks for various use cases, such as guest user authorization and management, time-bound restriction enforcement, and checks for compromised devices.

This chapter addresses the steps taken by device OEMs to prevent MAC address filtering and discusses the pros and cons of this enhancement with some recommendations about a future state.

© The Author(s), under exclusive license to Springer Nature Switzerland AG 2021
R. Badhwar, *The CISO's Next Frontier*,
https://doi.org/10.1007/978-3-030-75354-2_19

3 MAC Address Randomization

MAC randomization prevents listeners (snoopers or traffic sniffers) from using MAC addresses to build a history of device activity and thus limits the capability to "track" them, thereby increasing user privacy. Both iOS and Android have taken active measures to promote user privacy through randomization. Also, both Windows (10) and recent Linux kernels have built in support for MAC Address randomization as well in the last couple of years but its use has been fairly limited and under the covers so far.

"Starting in Android 8.0, Android devices use randomized MAC addresses when probing for new networks while not currently associated with a network. In Android 9, you can enable a developer option (it's disabled by default) to cause the device to use a randomized MAC address when connecting to a Wi-Fi network. In Android 10, MAC randomization is enabled by default for client mode, SoftAp, and Wi-Fi Direct." [1].

With the release of iOS 14, iPadOS 14, and watchOS 7—currently all in Beta— Apple will release the capability called "Private Address." This uses the capability of MAC address randomization by enabling the usage of a different MAC address every 24 hours for a given Wi-Fi network.

4 Issues

Changing an historically static value of the MAC Address can cause some serious issues with existing security and access management processes.

4.1 MAC Address Filtering

This is a legacy security access control process that uses the MAC address of a wireless or Ethernet LAN adapter or card of a given device to authenticate to a given network, and also to enforce other security constructs like port security and wireless client isolation. Although these techniques can by defeated by hacks like MAC Address spoofing, this "poor person's NAC (Network Access Control)" capability is still widely used. Changing the MAC address will most definitely break these legacy access control processes impacting user experience and business processes for enterprises around the globe.

This will also break access controls parents implement in home networks to enforce some rudimentary parental controls, network security, and VLAN separation for their kids.

4.2 *Detecting Stolen or Breached Devices*

The MAC address is still used to detect devices reported as stolen or breached. Changing the MAC address of such devices can cause these detection processes to break and make it even harder to detect and block these devices from joining a controlled network.

4.3 *False Sense of Privacy*

Security researchers have already proven that sophisticated users (you know who they are) can use "other" information elements in probe requests to create device fingerprints while looking to track devices or associate users to devices.

For example, commodity WiFi devices use predictable MAC address scrambling seeds to create predictive de-randomization algorithms.

Also, the sophisticated trackers or threat actors can induce WiFi devices to connect to compromised hot spots and figure out their real MAC addresses. They can also make use of the 802.11u standard where the ANQP (Access Network Query Protocol) requests are sent using the device's real MAC address.

5 Potential Compromise Solution (Device Anonymization)

If privacy is the sole concern of individual users, and security is the concern of organizations, then a standard can be developed to accommodate the needs of both parties. Such a standard would create a secure one-way hash (e.g., using SHA 256) of a device's MAC address, allowing corporations to register and track a device to enforce their standard device authentication and authorization processes, including but not limited to filtering, port security and client isolation, without storing or disclosing the actual individual MAC address, the device name and the user identity.

6 The CISO Take

The usage of MAC addresses to uniquely identify and track devices is a legacy construct that is longer considered safe and is known to have many flaws. This chapter highlights the problems that MAC address randomization may cause to existing Information Security and Identity & Access management processes, while also giving a false sense of privacy to users.

Device certificates, not MAC addresses, are the best authoritative device identifiers to enforce corporate information security and compliance policies.

Enterprises that can't afford to deploy certificates on devices, because of complexity or cost, must consider using better constructs like MAC address anonymization, rather than MAC address randomization, to enable user privacy. Having said that, MAC address-based filtering is considered to be an acceptable security measure for noncommercial private use home networks.

It is the responsibility of the CISOs to ensure that all MAC address-based filtering is deprecated and the new paradigms of device and machine identities provided by certificates are used for device authentication and authorization purposes.

7 Definitions

ANQP – stands for access network query protocol. It is a query and response protocol for Wi-Fi hotspot services, and is generally used to discover network information that is not identified in beacons.

MAC address – stands for media access control (address). It is a unique identifier assigned to every network interface.

NAC – stands for network access control. It performs policy enforcements using role-based controls to block an endpoint or network device or computing asset from accessing (defined and configured) wired and wireless network resources until a user and/or device level authentication has been performed.

Reference

1. Android (2020) Privacy: MAC Randomization. https://source.android.com/devices/tech/connect/wifi-mac-randomization, accessed on 13 September 2020

Further Reading

Burton M (2020) Wi-Fi MAC randomization – privacy and collateral damage, https://www.extremenetworks.com/extreme-networks-blog/wi-fi-mac-randomization-privacy-and-collateral-damage/, accessed Sep 17, 2020
Cisco. Hotspot 2.0, https://www.cisco.com/c/en/us/td/docs/wireless/controller/9800/17-1/config-guide/b_wl_17_11_cg/hotspot2.pdf, accessed 13 Sept 2020
Peterson M (2020) iOS 14 MAC randomization privacy feature may cause Cisco enterprise network issues, https://appleinsider.com/articles/20/09/17/ios-14-mac-randomization-privacy-feature-may-cause-cisco-enterprise-network-issues, accessed Sep 17, 2020

Transport Layer Security 1.3

1 Introduction

Approved as an Internet Engineering Task Force (IETF) standard (RFC 8446) in Aug 2018, Transport Layer Security (TLS) 1.3 is a key component of the security paradigm for enterprise data in transit. The link to RFC 8446 has been provided in reference item [1].

TLS 1.3 brings forth significant enhancements and improvements, and quite a number of deviations from TLS 1.2. The RFC provides a detailed list of all major differences from 1.2, details which have been provided in reference item [2].

This chapter provides a technology, business and cyber security perspective.

2 Impact Analysis

Although there are many changes in the protocol, one key takeaway and additional security and business impact analysis have been provided below:

2.1 Key Takeaway

Perfect Forward Secrecy (PFS) Ciphers (DHE-RSA, ECDHE-RSA, ECDHE-ECDSA) will be the only ciphers used in TLS 1.3:

> Static RSA and Diffie-Hellman cipher suites have been removed; all public-key based key exchange mechanisms now provide forward secrecy. [1] – (Section 1.2 (Page 8), RFC 8446)

© The Author(s), under exclusive license to Springer Nature Switzerland AG 2021 183
R. Badhwar, *The CISO's Next Frontier*,
https://doi.org/10.1007/978-3-030-75354-2_20

Before we go any further, let's get some fundamentals out of the way regarding PFS:

Forward Secrecy is that functionality in a given cryptosystem to generate a key without the use of a deterministic algorithm, thereby protecting the past (n − m) or future (n + m) session keys from compromise if a given current session key (n) is compromised. Generally, this mechanism is used to generate a new (session) key thereby (theoretically) making the data transmission very secure from unauthorized access, even if some sessions keys get compromised.

So, in a nutshell, PFS provides the fundamental capability to protect existing or previous session data from compromise even after the compromise of a long-term secret (e.g., a private key).

PFS implemented with elliptic curve Diffie-Hellman ephemeral key exchange (EC DHE) finds widespread use in TLS and (instant) message security.

Now back to TLS 1.3.

3 Cybersecurity Operational Impact Analysis

The introduction of TLS 1.3 creates significant impacts to cyber security operations:

(a) PFS has both benefits and drawbacks from a security perspective. On the one hand, the capability to better protect existing or previous session data from being misused is clearly a boon to data security. On the other hand, the cyber security teams will find it difficult to decrypt historical or saved session data even with access to the private key, unless they somehow save or get access to the ephemeral keys, which would defeat the purpose of PFS.

(b) The capability to decrypt live (session) data for sanctioned TLS intercept can only be performed with control over the endpoint and the forwarding proxy. This will prove beneficial to corporate cyber security programs as it would prevent any unauthorized or malicious TLS eavesdropping or man in the middle attacks.

(c) This may impact some security tools unable to handle PFS ciphers, either forcing costly upgrades or loss of functionality until an upgrade can be performed or is even available.

(d) This may lead to the downgrading of many session connections to TLS 1.2.

(e) This may also lead to modifications or minor tweaks of the existing TLS 1.2 implementation(s). For additional details, please review [1] – Section 1.3 (Page 9), RFC 8446.

(f) The X.509 certificate is no longer sent in plaintext, impacting other (security) applications that may not be doing a TLS intercept, but still need (to read) the certificate to make policy decisions, thereby forcing them to perform the intercept.

4   Security Issues

Both TLS 1.3 and PFS have some security issues to be resolved either in future implementations or through the creation of suitable mitigations in the near future.

4.1   TLS 1.3

(a) **0-RTT (Zero round trip time) data is not adequately protected**.

This data is not forward secret, as it is encrypted solely under keys derived using the offered PSK. [1] – (Section 2.3.1, Page 18, RFC 8446)

Although 0-RTT is only meant to be used at the beginning of the connection for initial data exchange, there is a still the possibility that this exchange may contain some very sensitive data such as passwords, cookies, or authorization tokens, and can be better protected using PFS.

(b)**Susceptibility to replay attacks**

There are no guarantees of non-replay between connections. Protection against replay for ordinary TLS 1.3 1-RTT data is provided via the server's Random value, but 0-RTT data does not depend on the ServerHello and therefore has weaker guarantees. This is especially relevant if the data is authenticated either with TLS client authentication or inside the application protocol.

The same warnings apply to any use of the early exporter_master_secret. [1] – (Section 2.3.2, Page 18, RFC 8446)

The replay of data within 0-RTT can be prevented by deleting the session cache after use but the same is not mandated in the RFC.

4.2   Security Issues with PFS

(a) PFS may protect past data from the future compromise of a long-term secret, but it can't really protect against the successful breach or cryptanalysis of the actual cryptographic cipher itself—either due to a vulnerability or inherent weakness of the cipher, or an attack, say, from a powerful (quantum) computer.

(b) While PFS works very well to protect data encrypted by past or future session keys from compromise of a current session key, it is susceptible if the private key itself gets breached, especially if the attacker also had access to intermediate ciphertext or other sensitive cryptographic material due to man-in-the-middle attacks for previous sessions.

5 The CISO Take

TLS 1.3 presents an interesting challenge to CISOs. On the one hand, it improves the data-in-transit security posture by mitigating the risk from man-in-the-middle attacks for multiple use cases like web browsing, email, instant messaging, or VoIP, On the other hand, it does create operational impacts limiting the capability of cyber security teams to enforce corporate security policies and restricting their ability to detect and block data exfiltration attempts by malicious entities and insiders.

There have been some reports in the media about the need for back doors with TLS 1.3; for the record, I am against back doors. Once you build a back door for restricted use, attackers generally find ways to walk through it. What I do recommend is that the capability for secure ways to perform SSL/TLS inspection be built into the protocol itself.

I have covered some other advanced aspects of TLS 1.3 security, extensions and features in one other chapter "The Use of ESNI with TLS 1.3: Is It a Boon to Privacy, or Does It Raise Security Concerns?" in this book.

6 Definitions

EC DHE – stands for elliptic curve Diffie Hellman ephemeral key exchange. It enables PFS. The (ephemeral) key exchange enables the use of a distinct DH key for every handshake (making it a more secure but operationally expensive process).

IETF – stands for Internet Engineering Task Force. It is an open standards organization, which develops and promotes voluntary Internet standards; in particular, the standards that comprise the Internet protocol suite [4].

PSK – stands for pre-shared key. It is a client authentication method that uses a small passphrase to generate unique encryption keys to authenticate wireless clients that use WPA2 encryption. It is not recommended for commercial use.

RFC – Request for comments. It is a document from the IETF and covers many technical aspects of computer networking, including protocols, procedures, programs, and concepts [3].

TLS – stands for transport layer security. It is used to provide data in transit encryption for various use cases including but not limited to web browsing, email, instant messaging, and file transfers.

X.509 – is a cryptographic standard that defines the format of PKI certificates.

References

1. Rescorla E, (2018) The Transport Layer Security (TLS) Protocol Version 1.3 (RFC 8446) Internet Engineering Task Force, https://tools.ietf.org/html/rfc8446. Accessed 27 Jan 2019.
2. Rescorla E, (2018) The transport layer security (TLS) protocol version 1.3: section 1.2, major differences from TLS 1.2 (RFC 8446). Internet Engineering Task Force. https://tools.ietf.org/html/rfc8446#section-1.2. Accessed 27 Jan 2019.
3. RFCs, Memos in the RFC document series contain technical and organizational notes about the Internet. Internet Engineering Task Force. https://www.ietf.org/standards/rfcs/. Accessed 27 Jan 2019.
4. The internet engineering task force (IETF) is the premier internet standards body, developing open standards through open processes. Internet Engineering Task Force. https://www.ietf.org/about/.

Further Reading

Juniper Networks (2019) Understanding PSK authentication. https://www.juniper.net/documentation/en_US/junos-space-apps/network-director3.1/topics/concept/wireless-wpa-psk-authentication.html
Salowey J, et al (2019) TLS 1.3: one year later. Available via Internet Engineering Task Force. https://www.ietf.org/blog/tls13-adoption/

The Use of ESNI with TLS 1.3: Is It a Boon to Privacy, or Does It Raise Security Concerns?

1 Preface

It is a pretty well-known fact amongst the security technologists within the industry that some nation states, governmental entities, ISPs, or information security teams in financial services, defense, or other critical sectors enforce some corporate or other acceptable use security or compliance policies by using the server name indication (SNI) available within the TLS protocol to conduct *selective* blocking on internet bound web traffic right before an HTTPS connection is established. They are able to do this because the SNI is still in the clear (i.e., not encrypted) during the TLS handshake process. This allows them to enforce the policies without having to eavesdrop inside the SSL/TLS traffic, allowing for a good compromise between privacy, data security and acceptable use of the internet connection.

TLS 1.3 has further enabled the capability to encrypt the SNI used to perform the blocking, thereby preventing its use in the enforcement of the above-mentioned policies.

In an effort to continue the enforcement (I assume), there have been media reports that some nation states have started the outright blocking of web traffic secured by TLS 1.3 traffic when it also uses the encrypted server name indication (ESNI) extension.

(Note: this section assumes the reader has some pre-existing knowledge about SSL/TLS, certificate management and associated terminology).

R. Badhwar, *The CISO's Next Frontier*,
https://doi.org/10.1007/978-3-030-75354-2_21

2   Introduction

In a previous chapter "Transport Layer Security 1.3", I wrote about the security advancements made with the release of TLS 1.3. Using that chapter as the context, I am going to address some of the lingering security issues and residual concerns that still existed (with TLS 1.3). These security issues included but were not limited to the fact that (a) 0-RTT (Zero round trip time) data was still not properly protected (b) and there was still a susceptibility to replay attacks.

There is one other specific item (SNI) that I did not explicitly cover in that chapter that still presents a security concern that I am elaborating further here. I am also going to provide some additional commentary on Subject Alternate Name (SAN), SNI, ESNI and KeyShareEntry, as these are relevant to the conversation.

3   Background

I am going to provide a brief overview about the need that led to the invention of SNI and ESNI [1]. This will help explain how ESNI can be used to achieve a total privacy posture for web browsing.

3.1   Server Name Indication (SNI)

For HTTPS to work, the client has to create a Transport Layer Security (TLS) connection with the server. Per the TLS protocol, the client requests a digital certificate from the server. Once the server sends a digital certificate to the client, that client must only make a connection to the server if the name of the URL it is trying to connect matches the one in the digital certificate (although not everyone follows it completely due to non-standardized implementations or the lack of enforcement of the RFC that governs this behavior). However, if the server hosts multiple URLs then it can be very difficult to create a certificate with all the names of the URLs that may be hosted by the server, or provide just the certificate for a given URL among many other certificates. This led to the invention of SubjectAltName (SAN), a X.509 extension that allows for various values to be associated with one certificate which could be presented by the server when requested by a client. The values supported are IP addresses, URIs, DNS names, DNs and UPNs. The SAN is more of a hack than an elegant solution since these certificates have to be reissued when the list of domains mentioned in the SAN changes.

The advent of 'name-based virtual hosting,' in which multiple host names use the same IP address, created further complications, necessitating the presentation of individual certificates for each domain to the client before it could make a successful HTTPS connection. This problem was solved by using SNI, where the client presents the name of the domain to which it is trying to connect amongst many domains virtually hosted on a given virtual host. SNI has now been built as part of the TLS protocol as an extension, enabling the server to present the appropriate digital certificate to the client.

The problem with this approach is that prior to TLS 1.3, the SNI was sent in the clear and thus could be sniffed by a man in the middle, which could either be 'big brother' in some countries, a company/corporate proxy server, the web hosting provider, your cable company, or your VPN provider. It could also be used to perform selective blocking, which can often aid information security efforts, but at the expense of the privacy of the client making the connection. As previously stated, there had been reports of some other nation states selectively blocking sites as they snooped and eavesdropped on SNI within HTTPS traffic.

3.2   Encrypted Server Name Indication (ESNI)

With TLS 1.3 the capability now exists to encrypt the SNI with a symmetric encryption key derived from the server's public key (that the browser needs to know in advance) as part of the initial TLS handshake between a client and server. Obviously, the server has the private key and thus can decrypt the SNI. TLS 1.3 is a prerequisite for ESNI, as it relies on the KeyShareEntry (to share the encryption key) which is only available with 1.3.

As of May 2020, approx. only 30% of sites worldwide were found to be support TLS 1.3, but I predict that the TLS adoption will steadily increase within the next 1–2 years. Also, the adoption of the ESNI TLS 1.3 (extension) is also in its infancy, but its use is also going to steadily increase due to advocacy for privacy.

Consensus is still emerging on the proper use of ESNI within the cyber security teams. Meanwhile rather than taking an extreme posture of the outright blocking of TLS 1.3 when used in conjunction with ESNI, the cyber security teams do have the option of either downgrading the TLS 1.3 connection to 1.2 (although the protocol has provisions to prevent that) if their SSL/TLS intercept tools have the cooperation of the possible endpoints under their legal control, or configuring their TLS intercept tool to act as a man in the middle although there are various complications with that approach due to the inherent security built into the 1.3 protocol to prevent that.

4   The CISO Take

TLS has always provided good security for data in transit. However, certain gaps have always existed where a man in the middle or an eavesdropper could (at least) figure out the destination to which you were going to connect, with the data encrypted only once the connection was made. Although eavesdroppers could not see inside the data being transmitted, they could at least see your intended destination (URL) and block it if it violated a policy.

Using TLS 1.3 in conjunction with the ESNI extension enables the capability to have a totally secure and private connection, eliminating any eavesdropping whatsoever. This is a boon to privacy advocates but may lead to ESNI being blocked by nation states or corporations, as it may prohibit them from getting the visibility, they need to enforce their acceptable use of technology and internet access policies. It will also break any valid use of SSL/TLS inspection to enforce DLP and prevent the exfiltration of sensitive or proprietary company data.

CISOs must work with their peers to engage in a dialog on how best to use this technology going forward to maintain the privacy of users while still being able to enforce corporate security policies, but in the meanwhile I propose a compromise with this dual approach – (a) allow TLS 1.3 with ESNI if the TLS interception (TIA) capability within an enterprise allows for the legitimate and legal inspection of TLS 1.3 with ESNI, else downgrade TLS 1.3 to 1.2 for all outbound connections from internal users (b) Fully support TLS 1.3 with ESNI for inbound connections (wherever possible and supported by the perimeter security stack) i.e., for external clients and consumers that are trying to connect into our internet exposed high risk (digital) applications, portals and services.

5 Definitions

DN – stands for domain name. It identifies the owner or requester (subject DN) in a certificate, or the CA that issues the certificate (issuer DN).

DNS – stands for Domain Name System. It is a global naming system which enables the mapping and the subsequent syncing of a website or other internet/intranet-hosted resource name to an IP address.

KeyShareEntry – It is a TLS extension as specified in the RFC 8446. It is included in the ServerHello message, generally suggesting which group and key exchange values may be used in the handshake.

SAN – stands for subject alternative name. It is an extension to the X.509 certificate standard and provides the capability to specify additional host names (IP addresses, common names, sites) to be protected by a single SSL certificate.

TIA – stands for TLS Intercept Application. It is the term generally used when MITM or equivalent techniques are used for SSL/TLS inspection in a legitimate and ethical manner.

UPN – stands for user principal name. It is a user name attribute generally used to identify user objects such as logon names and IDs.

VPN – stands for virtual private network. It provides the capability to extend a private (corporate) network across a public network (e.g., the internet), assigning a remote user a private IP address and enabling a remote user or employee to send and receive data as if he/she were onsite at a corporate facility.

X.509 – is a cryptographic standard that defines the format of PKI certificates.

Reference

1. Rescorla E, Oku K, et al (2020) TLS encrypted client hello. https://tools.ietf.org/html/draft-ietf-tls-esni-07

Further Reading

Rescorla E, (2018) The Transport Layer Security (TLS) Protocol Version 1.3 (RFC 8446) Internet Engineering Task Force, https://tools.ietf.org/html/rfc8446. Accessed 27 Jan 2019.

Prince M (2018) Encrypting SNI: fixing one of the core internet bugs. Available via The Cloudflare Blog. https://blog.cloudflare.com/esni/.

Cimpanu C (2020) China is now blocking all encrypted https traffic that uses TLS 1.3 and ESNI. Available via ZDNet. https://www.zdnet.com/article/china-is-now-blocking-all-encrypted-https-traffic-using-tls-1-3-and-esni/.

Rescorla E, (2018) Encrypted SNI comes to Firefox. Available via Mozilla Security Blog. https://blog.mozilla.org/security/2018/10/18/encrypted-sni-comes-to-firefox-nightly/.

Chai Z, Ghafari A, et al. (2019) On the importance of encrypted-sni (ESNI) to censorship circumvention. https://www.usenix.org/system/files/foci19-paper_chai_0.pdf.

TLS 1.3: One Year Later, https://www.ietf.org/blog/tls13-adoption/. Accessed 10 Jan, 2021.

Roelof Du Toit, https://docs.broadcom.com/doc/responsibly-intercepting-tls-and-the-impact-of-tls-1.3.en, accessed Jan 10, 2021.

Using FQDN vs IP Addresses in FW Rules and App Configs

In this chapter I want to discuss a very basic topic essential to effective cybersecurity operations.

1 Introduction

Traditionally speaking, firewalls and other servers have used IP addresses in firewalls rules, to address external/internal servers, and within other application-specific configuration files. There has been a movement to start using fully qualified domain names (FQDN) in some of these application configuration files and FQDN-based network objects in firewall rules. When I put my CISO and cybersecurity professional hat on, I am still on the fence when it comes to using FQDNs in firewall rules; but when I wear my CTO hat, I may be swayed to use FQDNs in configuration files (and even firewalls), as that may provide the capability to reduce outages from changing (dynamic) host IP addresses in load-balancers and firewalls. The nature of this debate is defined by risk. If we can mitigate the known risk from using domain name service (DNS) based capabilities, then using FQDNs may be fully authorized for some use cases.

2 Analysis

A quick analysis reveals some advantages and disadvantages for using FQDNs vs IP addresses.

© The Author(s), under exclusive license to Springer Nature Switzerland AG 2021
R. Badhwar, *The CISO's Next Frontier*,
https://doi.org/10.1007/978-3-030-75354-2_22

2.1 Disadvantages of FQDN in Server/App Configs and Firewalls

(a) Using a FQDN forces reliance on a DNS server, creating an additional point of failure, and potential performance and security issues (discussed later in the DNS Security chapter "Domain Name System (DNS) Security" in this book).
(b) When FQDN gets in the middle of critical services such as firewalls or application or server configurations, then issues with DNS can be especially hard to debug.
(c) Using a FQDN adds potential exposure to various forms of common DNS attacks, such as DNS spoofing, poisoning, and hijacking. (Additional attacks have been discussed in the DNS Security chapter "Domain Name System (DNS) Security" in this book).
(d) Compared to using FQDN/DNS, an IP address is better suited for some situations, such as for linking two machines which are both on private IP address ranges (192.168.1.x). Setting up a DNS zone just for linking these would not be ideal.
(e) Using FQDNs in routing tables is not feasible or practical.
(f) If the frequent changing of IP addresses or usage of dynamic IP addresses by cloud computing providers is the sole reason for using FQDNs in firewalls, then a good workaround is to use static IP addresses instead.
(g) Support for IPv6 is limited.
(h) Older generation firewalls do not support FQDN-based network objects.

2.2 Advantages of FQDN in Server/Application Configurations and Firewalls

(a) Using a FQDN instead of an IP address provides the capability to reduce or eliminate outages stemming from IP address changes, caused either by the migration of services from one host/server to another, or by a change of the virtual host or service. With FQDN, making simple changes to a DNS record is all that is required to prevent outages. This approach is pretty effective in reducing the amount of work that needs to be performed in editing application configuration files or firewall rules. This also reduces complexity and improves agility and speed.
(b) FQDNs are very helpful for name-based virtual hosting.
(c) Static IP addresses are expensive and also may not be able to support all auto-scaling scenarios. They may not be able to replace the need for all FQDN-based network objects in firewalls and in some other application configuration use cases.

3 The CISO Take

The usage of FQDN-based network objects in firewalls, FQDNs to address external (or internal) servers, and FQDNs in application (and some server) configurations can all be authorized if proper monitoring and mitigating security controls (e.g., DNSSEC and NTPSEC) have been implemented.

The use of FQDN-based network objects in firewalls is faster to implement, convenient, and easy to use, but can introduce additional cyber risk due to the increase in DNS-based (hijacking) attacks.

CISOs have to take a leadership role in this decision to ensure that appropriate mitigating security controls and better firewall management solutions (e.g., Firemon or Tufin) have been implemented before we start making active use of FQDNs instead of IP address in firewalls and application configurations.

4 Definitions

DNSSEC – stands for Domain Name System Security Extensions. It provides the hardening guidelines and specifications to secure DNS by adding cryptographic signatures to existing records.

DNS – stands for Domain Name System. It is a global naming system which enables the mapping and the subsequent syncing of a website or other internet/intranet-hosted resource name, to an IP address.

NTPSEC – stands for Network Time Protocol system secure. It provides a secure and hardened version of NTP.

IPv6 – stands for Internet Protocol version 6. It is the most current version of Internet Protocol and is considered an upgrade from the more popular and used version (IP) v4. It solves the problem of IP address exhaustion (in v4), and also has many security improvements and benefits.

Further Reading

Donato R (2015) Cisco ASA – How to Permit/Deny Traffic based on DomainName (FQDN). https://www.fir3net.com/Firewalls/Cisco/cisco-asa-domain-fqdn-based-acls.html. Accessed 1 Dec 2020

Horne V, Kurianski J et al (2020) Use FQDN filtering in network rules. In: Microsoft Azure Product Documentation. https://docs.microsoft.com/en-us/azure/firewall/fqdn-filtering-network-rules Accessed 1 Dec 2020

Ionos (2019) Fully Qualified Domain Name (FQDN) explained In: Ionos Digital Guide. https://www.ionos.com/digitalguide/domains/domain-administration/fqdn-fully-qualified-domain-name/. Accessed 1 Dec 2020

Pepelnjak I (2016) Using DNS Names in Firewall Rulesets- https://blog.ipspace.net/2016/10/using-dns-names-in-firewall-rulesets.html. Accessed 1 Dec 2020

Network Time Protocol (NTP) Security

1 Introduction

Although many of you may have either not heard about NTP or realized its importance or the need to protect it, trust me when I tell you it plays an extremely critical role in synchronizing the system time for all the various systems and servers in an enterprise.

The legacy implementation of network time protocol (NTP), still the most widely used version in the industry today, has many vulnerabilities and weaknesses. Not only is it exposed to many cyber-attacks, to make matters worse, this vulnerable version of NTP has also been used to launch attacks on DNS/DNSSEC (another critical network component that has also been discussed in a separate chapter in this book).

This chapter provides a brief introduction to NTP, asserts the importance of network time synchronization, and details the various attacks and the protections against those attacks.

2 NTP

NTP is a network-based protocol used to synchronize computer clocks connected to data networks within a few milliseconds of UTC (coordinated universal time). The protocol is UDP-based on port 123 and works in two modes: (a) client-server mode, where clients connect to a NTP server; and (b) peer-to-peer mode, where each computer treats its peer computer as a time source.

NTP has built-in fault tolerance, with a high rate of accuracy within one to five milliseconds on local area networks, and a good rate of accuracy rate between 10 and 50 milliseconds over the public internet, but has the susceptibility for that accuracy to fall to more than 100 milliseconds or higher due to network congestion.

Although NTP works very well and is widely used, it has been known to have multiple vulnerabilities and security weaknesses that can be and has been exploited to launch various types of attacks on unsuspecting victims.

3 Importance of Network Time Synchronization

Network time synchronization is a critical requirement for various IT and Security operational areas:

3.1 Security Forensic Analysis and Troubleshooting

The SIEM is the repository of all (syslog) log data received from disparate security and identity management systems. To conduct a root cause analysis (RCA) of an issue or forensic analysis on a security event or incident, a security analyst may need to review the logs from various systems including the firewall, VPN system, authentication and authorization systems (e.g., active directory), and DNS logs, among other systems. It is imperative that the time stamps from all these systems be synchronized, otherwise, it would be next to impossible to troubleshoot.

The synchronization of log time stamps is also a must for many other security auditing or monitoring activities, and for the debugging of any network issues.

3.2 Hybrid Computing

The distributed nature of security and IT systems with hybrid hosting in on-premise and cloud environments makes it extremely important that the clocks on these hosts be synchronized. A difference in the clocks on two hosts resident on different environments can lead to the failure of time-sensitive processes such as authentication or identity federation.

3.3 System Operations

Many daily operational activities such as scheduled jobs (e.g., cron or JCL) on hosts need to be executed at specified times, with downstream dependencies and impacts. If the clocks of the hosts are not synchronized, then it may cause jobs to run out of schedule or step over each other causing operational failures and issues.

4 Network Time Protocol Secure (NTPsec)

NTPsec is a forked version of NTP and claims to be "a secure, hardened, and improved implementation of Network Time Protocol derived from NTP Classic."

The problem is that the 'sec'in NTPSec [7] does not provide integrity and confidentiality of NTP data as it traverses the internet/intranet. It is basically a hardened implementation of NTP. It also does not provide authenticity of the NTP Server.

5 NTP Attacks

Here are some of the documented attacks:

5.1 NTP DDoS Amplification Attack

This attack comprises an attacker using the monlist command and sending data packets to a NTP server with a spoofed IP address of the intended victim. The NTP server provides an amplified response to the victim (the monlist command give details of the last 600 clients that have connected to the NTP time service) basically leading to a DDoS attack if this command is repeatedly sent to the server.

CVE-2013-5211: The monlist feature in ntp_request.c in ntpd in NTP before version 4.2.7p26 allows remote attackers to cause a denial of service (traffic amplification) via forged (1) REQ_MON_GETLIST or (2) REQ_MON_ GETLIST_1 request, as exploited in the wild in December 2013.

5.2 Buffer Overflow Attack

This attack allows an attacker to execute malicious code at the same privilege level of the ntpd process using buffer overflow in the ntpd daemon, which can be triggered by a single crafted data packet.

CVE-2014-9295: Multiple stack-based buffer overflows in ntpd in NTP before 4.2.8 allow remote attackers to execute arbitrary code via a crafted packet, related to (1) the crypto_recv function, when the Autokey Authentication feature is used; (2) the ctl_putdata function; and (3) the configure function.

CVE-2014-9293: The config_auth function in ntpd in NTP before 4.2.7p11, when an auth key is not configured, improperly generates a key, which makes it easier for remote attackers to defeat cryptographic protection mechanisms via a brute-force attack.

CVE-2014-9294: util/ntp-keygen.c in ntp-keygen in NTP before 4.2.7p230 uses a weak RNG seed, which makes it easier for remote attackers to defeat cryptographic protection mechanisms via a brute-force attack.

5.3   Delay Attack

This attack allows an attacker to introduce an artificial time delay before a data packet from a client reaches the NTP server or vice-versa.

5.4   Man-in-the-Middle Attack

This is the classic MITM attack where an intruder intercepts and potentially tampers with the data packets between a client and a NTP server.

5.5   Attack on DNSSEC

DNSSEC is highly susceptible to NTP attacks, where an attacker can 'shift' the time of a resolver. This causes the expiration of all the timestamps in the crypto keys and signatures, resulting in the resolver (and its clients) losing connectivity to any domains secured with DNSSEC.

6   Complete List of Vulnerabilities

The complete list of NTP vulnerabilities is available at the link below [8]. (Also see [4]). Many of these vulnerabilities remain unpatched in most production deployments worldwide, either due to the lack of realization on the cumulative high risk these bring to a given enterprise or the lack of appetite for firms to upgrade to NTPsec. However, some measures security teams can and should take to address these vulnerabilities/prevent attacks are discussed below.

7 How to Prevent Various (NTP) Attacks

(a) Update all ntpd server versions to the latest version, especially those that are older than version 4.2.7.
(b) Disable the monlist command, which is not very useful, by adding the noquery directive to the restrict default command in the ntp.conf file.
(c) Enable capabilities to detect and block traffic with spoofed IP addresses.
(d) Implement NTPSEC, a hardened version of NTP (especially for internet-facing NTP Servers).
(e) Conduct POC's for the other secure implementations available.

8 Other Secure NTP Implementations

(a) **Network Time Security** (draft-ietf-ntp-network-time-security-15) – a secure variant of NTP that provides for integrity and authenticity, but not confidentiality. It has an RFC draft which seems to have stalled [1].
(b) **Tlsdate** – this solution [2] uses the date within TLS. Originally championed by Google, this seems to have fallen out of favor and does not work with TLS 1.3.
(c) **OpenNTPD** – Part of OpenBSD, it uses NTP for the time synchronization and HTTPS to validate the NTP time with a certain fault tolerance and range. This can work for specific use cases but cannot be used as an industry standard [3].
(d) **Roughtime** – This is from our good friends at Google. Quoting from their site "Roughtime is a protocol that aims to achieve rough time synchronization in a secure way that doesn't depend on any particular time server, and in such a way that, if a time server does misbehave, clients end up with cryptographic proof of it." [5]

This is the best new solution available to meet the integrity, confidentiality and authenticity requirements. I am not sure of its future, as Google does tend to abandon projects. However, Google currently operates a public Roughtime server, although without any uptime assurances.

A roughtime client implementation by Cloudflare based on Google's implementation is available at [6].

9 The CISO Take

Similar to solving DNS security issues with DNSSEC, the industry needs to take the threats to NTP very seriously and find ways to harden the legacy NTP implementation by implementing NTPsec. The industry also needs innovative solutions and implementations like Google's roughtime to establish much-needed integrity, confidentiality and authentication of NTP data.

Both DNS and NTP are network security services and must be part of the security stack. IT teams have traditionally not invested in the security aspects of DNS and NTP, leading to deployments that continue to remain vulnerable to attacks. It is a CISO's responsibility to make the case for these to be owned, run, and managed by network security teams, and ensure that these are prioritized for security upgrades and improvements.

10 Definitions

DNS – stands for Domain Name System. It is a global naming system which enables the mapping and the subsequent syncing of a website or other internet/intranet-hosted resource name to an IP address.

MITM – stands for Man-in-the-middle (attack). It is a form of cyber-attack where an attacker hijacks a secure encrypted connection between a client and server.

Monlist – is a command generally used for debugging purposes. It allows the retrieval of a list of hosts with which the NTP daemon (ntpd) communicated recently.

RFC – stands for request for comments. It is a document from the IETF and covers many technical aspects of computer networking, including protocols, procedures, programs, and concepts [9].

SIEM – stands for Security Incident and Event Management (system). It has the capability to aggregate, correlate, and cross-reference security (log) data and events from various systems.

References

1. Sibold D, Roettger S, Teichel K (2016) Network Time Security: draft ietf-ntp-network-time-security-15. Available via Internet Engineering Task Force Trust. https://tools.ietf.org/html/draft-ietf-ntp-network-time-security-15. Accessed 06 Dec 2020
2. ioerror/tlsdate. https://github.com/ioerror/tlsdate. Accessed 06 Dec 2020
3. Open NTPD. http://www.openntpd.org/ Accessed 06 Dec 2020
4. National Vulnerability Database. https://nvd.nist.gov/ National Institute of Standards and Technology, Gaithersburg. Accessed 06 Dec 2020
5. Roughtime (2019). Google Git. https://roughtime.googlesource.com/roughtime. Accessed 06 Dec 2020
6. cloudflare/roughtime. https://github.com/cloudflare/roughtime. Accessed 06 Dec 2020
7. NTPsec. https://www.ntpsec.org/. Accessed 06 Dec 2020
8. Recent Vulnerabilities (2020) Network Time Foundation NTP Support Wiki. http://support.ntp.org/bin/view/Main/SecurityNotice#Recent_Vulnerabilities. Accessed 06 Dec 2020
9. RFCs (2020). https://www.ietf.org/standards/rfcs/

Further Reading

CISA Alert (TA14-013A) (2016). NTP Amplification Attacks Using CVE-2013-5211. https://us-cert.cisa.gov/ncas/alerts/TA14-013A. Accessed on Dec 24, 2020

Malhotra A, Cohen I et al (2017). Attacking the Network Time Protocol. https://www.ndss-symposium.org/wp-content/uploads/2017/09/attacking-network-time-protocol.pdf. Accessed on Dec 24, 2020

Domain Name System (DNS) Security

1 Genesis

The risk from DNS poisoning, tunneling and hijacking has gone up exponentially due to some high-profile breaches and incidents. For example, Mandiant recently, identified a wave of DNS hijacking attacks affecting dozens of domains belonging to government, telecommunications, and internet infrastructure entities [2, 3].

This has led to a lot of chatter about protection schemes like Domain Name System Security Extensions (DNSSEC) and associated or alternative technologies like DNS over TLS, also known as DOT, and DNS over HTTP/s, also known as DOH (DNS over HTTP/s) in the recent past.

It is well known that DNSSEC has been around for a decade or more with very little adoption, but for the Feds and other USG agencies. I believe the new security threat from DNS Hijacking episodes has also led The Internet Corporation for Assigned Names and Numbers (ICANN) to call for a full deployment of DNSSEC [1].

I believe there is also a school of thought that is not on-board with DNSSEC – they talk about better protecting and hardening how DNS is administered, prevent privilege escalation and also focus on better architectural paradigms.

This is a call to arms for CISOs to review available technologies and options, and come to a consensus on how best to solve this problem with global implications.

In this chapter, I will talk about the problem statement, then introduce the technologies that can provide the needed security hardening and protection, the implementation challenges, some security issues with these technologies themselves, and a final recommendation.

R. Badhwar, *The CISO's Next Frontier*,
https://doi.org/10.1007/978-3-030-75354-2_24

207

2 Problem Statement

DNS Hijacking and poisoning incidents that were on a steady rise for the last decade have now spiked with some high-profile cases coming into the lime light. For the typical corporation that lets folks work from home using a VPN connection, (apart from DNS Hijacking and Poisoning) there have been instances when their security teams have observed external IPs being returned for internal servers. This generally happens due to the mixing of DNS servers used while a user is off-network and then it becomes resident in their local DNS cache and persists after a VPN connection is made. Then there is our (not so) good friend – DNS tunneling, which is used by anomalous entities for data exfiltration and beaconing purposes.

3 Recap of DNS and Available Protection Technologies

DNS (RFC 1034) – is used to perform domain name translation to an IP address (e.g., translating www.google.com to 172.217.18.206). Under the hood this information is fetched from an A record published by google.com (in this example).

DNSSEC (RFC 4033, 4035, 4036, 5155 and 6840) – DNSSEC provides a set of security extensions to DNS which authenticate DNS records using PKI (cryptography and digital signatures) and thus ensure that the lookup data is accurate. (To facilitate signature validation, DNSSEC added a few new DNS record types: RRSIG, which contains a cryptographic signature; DNSKEY, which contains a public signing key; DS, which contains the hash of a DNSKEY record; NSEC and NSEC3 for explicit denial-of-existence of a DNS record; and CDNSKEY and CDS for a child zone requesting updates to DS record(s) in the parent zone).

Apart from proving the authenticity of records (IP addresses and other DNS records like AAAA, CNAME, MX, or NS) it returns, it also provides the capability to assert the non-existence of records. Thus, DNSSEC not only provides data integrity by ensuring the client that nothing has edited or tampered with the data received from the DNS server, but also asserts that the data is current.

Please note that DNSSEC does not provide confidentiality of data (e.g., by encryption or otherwise) and thus, although the data being returned is accurate, it can still be sniffed, leading to unauthorized data access or disclosure.

DNS over TLS (DOT) – **(RFC 7898)**: DOT provides for the capability for the DNS transactions to occur within a (secure) encrypted (TLS) tunnel or channel using port 853. This enables the integrity and confidentiality of the data to be maintained while it is in transit. The encrypted (TLS) tunnel also provides some inherent PKI based authentication of the remote party (although there are complications due to the complex path or hops a DNS request may take from the client to the recursive resolver(s) to the authoritative name server for the zone in question, leading to the trusting of multiple CAs in the process).Please note that while DOT does provide data integrity and confidentiality while in transit, it still does not provide protection again DNS poisoning or hijacking. For the client to be absolutely sure that nothing has modified or tampered with the responses received, it needs to DNSSEC-validate the requests itself.

DNS over HTTPS (DOH) – (RFC 8484): DOH provides for the capability for DNS transactions to occur over HTTPS. DOH is similar to DOT, but uses HTTPS as the secure channel. This solution also needs a web server and operates over port 443.

DNS over Quic UDP Internet Connections (DOQ): (QUIC) (Draft) – DOQ provides for the capability for the DNS transactions to occur over the QUIC protocol over port 784. (QUIC is an optimized transport layer protocol developed by Google that provides the reliability of TCP with multiplexed connections and performance optimizations).

DNS over datagram transport lawyer security (DTLS) – (RFC 8094): DTLS provides for the capability for the DNS transactions to occur over datagram transport layer security. This has been found susceptible to OpenSSL induced vulnerabilities.

DNSCrypt – It provides for the authentication of communications between a DNS client and a DNS resolver, but is a non-standard, in-the-wild implementation with little or splintered adoption, making it an unsuitable implementation for a commercial entity because of its incompatibility and in-supportability.

Note: DOH, DOT, DOQ etc. are currently all in the Request of Comments (RFC) comments stage and have not been finalized.

4   Security (and Misc.) Issues with DNSSEC –

(a) There are known performance issues with DNSSEC. There is a 250–300 ms delay when a recursive resolver makes an initial validation (the subsequent validations are cached). Also, since DNSSEC introduces additional records, there is a multi-fold increase in the traffic from queries, eventually leading to congestion and increased mitigation cost.

(b) The adoption of DNSSEC has been sector driven. There has been widespread adoption in the federal government and other (semi-) public sector entities, but minimal in the banking, insurance, and finance sectors.

(c) DNSSEC was designed to work with RSA with PKCS1v15 padding using 1024-bit keys. In 2019, these are considered to be cryptographically weak.

(d) DNSSEC is expensive to deploy (and manage) due to the high-end skillset needed to deal with the inherent complexities.

(e) DNSSEC adds many complexities to the fundamentally simple DNS protocol, leading to additional failure use cases that are very hard to debug. This would be an added burden for a typical corporate IT and Security ecosystem already dealing with networking problems.

(f) As previously stated, apart from the additional records that DNSSEC adds, it can also assert the non-existence of records (through an NSEC record) which provides the anomalous capability to expose any obscured zone content, thereby exposing subdomains previously kept secret for a security or business reason. (This exposure occurs by walking a zone by following one NSEC record to the next, until all subdomains are revealed).

(g) DNSSEC is also susceptible to reflection and amplification attacks due to its usage of rather large DNSKEY and RRSIG records, which can amplify the effects of a UDP based DDOS attack by querying the name servers and sending the reflected traffic to the victim.

(h) DNSSEC is highly susceptible to NTP attacks, where an attacker can 'shift' the time of a resolver, causing the expiration of all the timestamps in the crypto keys and signatures, leading the resolver (and its clients) to lose connectivity to any domains secured with DNSSEC. (Hence, the need for NTPSec, which has been discussed in great detail in chapter "Network Time Protocol (NTP) Security" within this book)

4.1   Other Impediments

(a) It has been observed that in most of the industry sectors, DNS is generally run by the network teams in IT (and not by the security team) and thus, in many cases, they may not be able to prioritize security improvement initiatives (like DNSSEC, NTPSEC) over network centric ones either due to funding constraints or capacity.

(b) The slow rollout of IPv6 has not helped matters much. With an IPv6 deployment, all the DNSSEC induced resolver validation issues would be non-existent and thus, hopefully, IPv6 deployments will spur the adoption of DNSSEC in the not-so-distant future. (Note: DNSSEC interoperability with IPv4 and IPv6 (and NAT64 and DNS64) is a complex topic and is outside the scope of discussion within this book.)

5   Potential Solutions to the Security Issues

(a) One way to mitigate the susceptibility to reflection and amplification attacks is to make use of the elliptic curve digital signature algorithm (ECDSA) which reduces the size of the keys, thereby producing smaller signatures, and thus reducing the size of the DNSKEY and RRSIG records returned.

(b) Using ECDSA also reduces the risk from cryptographic weakness resulting from the previous usage of RSA (1024-bit) keys.

(c) **Note**: Using ECDSA does have a side effect – it increases the CPU consumption on the DNS resolvers (by approximately 3%, which is well within tolerance range due to the increase in computing power of modern-day CPUs). Additionally, there is very little support for ECDSA in the current recursive DNS resolvers.

6 The CISO Take

I sincerely think that no action is not really an option. DNSSEC is the industry standard and is recommended and supported by the USG and ICANN. I recommend that DNSSEC be implemented along with DOT, to provide for both the integrity and confidentiality of DNS data. In an effort to reduce the complexity, I would recommend a phased approach of first doing a DOT implementation, followed by DNSSEC.

Having said this I have to assert that these patchwork-based solutions have to stop. Getting a hodgepodge of IPv4, IPv6, NAT, NAT64, DNS, DNS64 and DNSSEC is not really working. The industry has to step back and look at this problem holistically to design solutions that are easier to implement and maintain.

There is also a call to the industry to simplify and standardize DNSSEC and other alternative yet compatible technologies to simplify the implementations and their subsequent maintenance.

Last but not the least I have to assert that both DNS and NTP are network security services and must be part of the security stack. The IT teams have traditionally not invested into the security aspects of DNS and NTP leading to deployments that continue to remain vulnerable to attacks. It is the responsibility of the CISOs to make the case for these to be owned, run and managed by the network security teams and ensure that these are prioritized for the needed security upgrades and improvements.

7 Definitions

ECDSA – stands for Elliptic Curve Digital Signature Algorithm. It is a variation of digital signature algorithm that uses elliptic curve cryptography.

ICANN – stands for the internet corporation for assigned names and numbers. It is responsible for the allocation of IP address space allocation and protocol identifier assignment among a few items.

NAT – stands for network address translation. It is a technique used to map multiple local private IP addresses to a public IP address. This technique is now common practice with organizations due to the shortage of public IPv4 addresses.

NTP – stands for network time protocol. It is a network-based protocol used to synchronize computer clocks connected to data networks within a few milliseconds of UTC (coordinated universal time).

RRSIG – stands for resource record signature. These are required for DNSSEC and store digital signatures of resource record sets (RRSets).

RSA – stands for Rivest-Shamir-Adelman. It is a PKI cryptosystem that is used to protect and secure sensitive data in transit.

VPN – stands for virtual private network. It provides the capability to extend a private (corporate) network across a public network (e.g., the internet) assigning a remote user a private IP address and enabling a remote user or employee to send and receive data as if he/she were onsite at a corporate facility.

References

1. ICANN (2019). ICANN Calls for Full DNSSEC Deployment, Promotes Community Collaboration to Protect the Internet – https://www.icann.org/news/announcement-2019-02-22-en. Accessed Dec 6 2020.
2. O'Donnell L (2019). Unprecedented' DNS Hijacking Attacks. https://threatpost.com/unprecedented-dns-hijacking-attacks-linked-to-iran/140737/. Accessed Dec 24, 2020.
3. Hirani M, Jones S et al (2019), Global DNS Hijacking Campaign: DNS Record Manipulation at Scale. https://www.fireeye.com/blog/threat-research/2019/01/global-dns-hijacking-campaign-dns-record-manipulation-at-scale.html, Accessed Dec 24, 2020.

Further Reading

Ariyapperuma S, Mitchell C (2007), Security vulnerabilities in DNS and DNSSEC, doi: https://doi.org/10.1109/ARES.2007.139. Accessed 6 December, 2020.

Chung T (2017). Why DNSSEC deployment remains so low. https://blog.apnic.net/2017/12/06/dnssec-deployment-remains-low/, Accessed 6 December, 2020.

Cloudflare (2020). How DNSSEC Works. https://www.cloudflare.com/dns/dnssec/how-dnssec-works/, last Accessed 6 December, 2020.

Constantin L (2020), DNSSEC explained: Why you might want to implement it on your domain, https://www.csoonline.com/article/3569277/dnssec-explained-why-you-might-want-to-implement-it-on-your-domain.html, Accessed 6 December, 2020.

Fieldhouse M (2020). Time to Stop Overlooking DNS Security. https://www.infosecurity-magazine.com/opinions/stop-dns-security/, Accessed 6 December, 2020.

ICANN (2019). DNSSEC – What Is It and Why Is It Important? https://www.icann.org/resources/pages/dnssec-what-is-it-why-important-2019-03-05-en, Accessed 6 December, 2020.

Next Gen Wi-Fi and Security

1 Introduction

The IEEE 802.11 specifications enable network connectivity for wireless local area networks (WLAN). The exponential increase in intranet and internet-dependent devices has driven research and development to achieve higher speeds in data streaming, from the rather basic implementations of 802.11b and 802.11a with humble streaming data rates ranging from 1–54 Mbps, to the next generation of 802.11g and 802.11n, with faster streaming data rates up to 600 Mbps operating in various frequencies in 2.4, 5, and 60 GHz frequency bands.

2 Genesis

The most current specification in use (802.11 ac) operates in the 5 GHz frequency range with bandwidth in the range of 20-160 MHz and average streaming rates of 1733 Mbps with the capability to burst up to 3466 Mbps, making it infinitely faster than those achieved with 802.11a or b. Even 11 ac has not been able to keep up with the demand (stemming from IOT), with especially sub-optimal performance in crowded environments such as airports, trains, and sports stadiums. These limitations led to the development of 802.11ax and 80211ay.

© The Author(s), under exclusive license to Springer Nature Switzerland AG 2021   213
R. Badhwar, *The CISO's Next Frontier*,
https://doi.org/10.1007/978-3-030-75354-2_25

3   The Future Is Here

802.11ax can operate in both 2.4 and 5GHz frequency ranges, with the capability to almost quadruple the data streaming speeds from what was made available with 802.11ac. Theoretically, it can provide streaming rates in the range of about 10,530 Mbps, with an average rate of about 4803 Mbps – not bad, eh? 802.11ax is specifically designed to perform better in high density environments, especially with the proliferation of IOT devices, with the added capability for cellular data offloading (obviously causing security concerns).

Then there is 802.11ay which will operate in the greater-than-45 GHz WLAN. It will be an enhancement to 802.11ad (primarily used for the relatively unknown WiGig networks) with the theoretical capability to provide data streaming rates in the range of 20,000 Mbps.

3.1   Let's Not Forgot About Security

We can't really talk about Wi-Fi speed without discussing how to secure the data that is transmitted over these wireless networks. While WPA2 has been satisfactory for securing 802.11 a, b, g, n, and ac networks, with the advent of 802.11ax and 802.11ay, I recommend that the usage of WPA2 be deprecated (in a phased manner) and WPA3 (and WPA3 enterprise) be made standard and mandatory due to its enhanced authentication ability and much improved encryption. This is especially important given the large number of IOT devices that solely rely on Wi-Fi for their network connectivity and data transmissions. Another security advancement that should be made standard with ax and ay is that of Opportunistic Wireless Encryption (OWE) for improved security in public networks in use at airports, schools, universities, and hotels. OWE can provide automatic encryption with no user intervention, basic transport level data security in an open public network, and some basic protection from data sniffers.

4   Opportunistic Wireless Encryption (OWE)

This section discusses the general state of Wi-Fi security and the capabilities of OWE.

4.1 Genesis

Today it would not be far-fetched to argue that internet access has become a basic human right like air, water, shelter, clothing, electricity, and food. Apart from new paradigms such as Internet of Things (IOT) forming the backbone of an information aware and internet-connected eco-system, internet is an essential information and educational resource for people. It is the great equalizer putting a wealth of knowledge at the hands of everyone –whether rich or poor, young or old, novice or expert. While free internet access is still not commonplace in all parts of the world, its availability has been greatly improved through public Wi-Fi sources offered either by philanthropic efforts e.g., Google Loon [1] or at many public and educational institutions and free Wi-Fi hotspots.

While information security professionals can't solve the problem of free internet for all, when access is indeed universal, we can ensure that it is used in a secure manner so that a user's data is secure from various forms of attacks and snooping.

4.2 Background

Let's talk a little more about Wi-Fi data security today, which involves/concerns encryption of data while it is in transit. The cryptographic algorithm in use to provide data security (encryption) for the first Wi-Fi implementations (802.11b and 802.11a) was WEP, which was subsequently breached in 2004. Since the breach of WEP, the cryptographic algorithms that have been in use are the IEEE 802.11i-2004 standard (implemented and known as WPA2) and then subsequently the new and improved 802.11i-2016 standard (implemented and known as WPA3). Today's modern Wi-Fi implementations (802.11g, 802.11n, and 802.11ac) use AES 128-bit keys for data encryption and EAP for authentication.

Although the data encryption and authentication capabilities of current and previous Wi-Fi implementations meet data security needs fairly well by WPA2 and now WPA3, there is still a significant portion of the Wi-Fi traffic that is open with no encryption whatsoever. From recent analysis (in 2018) at least 20% of the world's Wi-Fi traffic is open, another 10% still uses cracked or legacy cryptographic algorithms like WEP or WPA, and the remaining 65% uses WPA2, with a small minority using WPA3. The percentages vary by country, but one thing is certain: as large numbers of people connect to open Wi-Fi networks in public places such as hotels, airports, coffee shops, and sports stadiums, they are transmitting their personal and business sensitive data through an exposed medium. There are various reasons why people use open Wi-Fi, the primary one being that they don't want to make use of their cellular signals with monthly data caps and expensive overage charges; or sometimes, unaware of the data security risk, they connect to any access point (AP) that offers them connectivity. There are cases when a Pre-Shared Key (PSK), aka "password," is made available by restaurants, coffee shops, hospitals, or doctors' offices. Generally, the password is available on a wall, a menu, or from the front desk receptionist. This provides a mere semblance of security. The PSK, which is used in a basic 4-way handshake, is known to everyone, enabling an attacker to calculate the encryption keys used by the client and AP. There are secure remedies available, the primary one being the use of a VPN service, but most folks don't use them, either due to the complexity of setup, or monthly recurring cost, or the lack of their understanding of the risk they incur when they transmit their data on an open Wi-Fi channel or on one where the PSK is publicly known.

4.3   Opportunistic Wireless Encryption

Just as browsers have made HTTPS transparent to its users, with many of them not even realizing that a secure (TLS) tunnel is used to transmit their sensitive data, security technologists have been hard at work on an advancement called opportunistic wireless encryption (OWE). OWE can provide automatic encryption with no user intervention required whatsoever, providing decent transport level data security in an open public network, giving users basic protection from data packet sniffers.

OWE works on the premise of *some best effort protection all the time*. Like the name itself suggests, the protocol is designed on the principal of opportunistic encryption and can work with and without authentication, thereby providing the capability for it to be used in a widespread manner on the internet and intranets.

OWE can be discovered using two techniques. AP can advertise their presence using "beacons," wherein they share information about the security policy in use, the symmetric ciphers supported, or QoS information. Alternatively, the client can discover APs with support for OWE by issuing the usual probe requests and listening for responses which carry the same response as a beacon. OWE is achieved by performing a Diffie-Hellman (DH) key exchange during the authentication phase of 802.11 association and then utilizing the resulting secret for a four-way handshake. OWE supports both Elliptic Curve Cryptography (ECC) and Finite Field Cryptography (FFC). It uses a hash algorithm (SHA-256 and others in the SHA family) for the generation of a secret key and identifier. Additional technical details are outside the scope of this chapter but can be read within the RFC for OWE [2].

OWE does not provide authentication by default (although it can be turned on if required), but it does provide the capability to maintain the confidentiality and integrity of the data being transmitted between the client and the AP. However, application-level security paradigms need to be used for total end-to-end security as OWE only solves one part of the overall end-to-end security puzzle.

Also, please note that OWE is susceptible to impersonation attacks. An attacker can impersonate an AP and induce a client to connect to it. At that point, the client provides the attacker with the capability to read and update operations on the data being transmitted.

5 The CISO Take

The improvement in the capability to encrypt data in transit is essential to continue to maintain the confidentiality and integrity of sensitive data. This has become critical with the increased usage of IOT devices leading to a high-density population of devices requiring secure wireless internet connectivity and faster data transfer speeds.

Also, whenever and wherever possible, security professionals should make seamless information security their mission. Data security should be woven into the fabric of the internet, enabled by default, always available, and adaptive, with self-configuring data encryption capabilities. OWE is a step in that direction.

6 Definitions

AP – stands for access point. It is a device that creates a wireless local area network (WLAN). It connects to a cable modem or a router, via an ethernet cable, and projects a WIFI signal.

ECC – stands for elliptic curve cryptography. It is used to build an PKI cryptosystem that uses the mathematical structure of discontinuous elliptic curves over finite fields.

FFC – stands for Finite Field Cryptography. It is a more classic approach of using a Galois field for data encryption.

IEEE – stands for institute of electrical and electronics engineers. IEEE and its members inspire a global community to innovate for a better tomorrow through highly cited publications, conferences, technology standards, and professional and educational activities.

IOT – stands for internet of things. It is used to describe a system where ubiquitous sensors and smart devices are continuously connected to the internet.

PSK – stands for pre-shared key. It is a client authentication method that uses a small passphrase to generate unique encryption keys to authenticate wireless clients that use WPA2 encryption. It is not recommended for commercial use.

VPN - stands for virtual private network. It provides the capability to extend a private (corporate) network across a public network (e.g., the internet) assigning a remote user a private IP address and enabling a remote user or employee to send and receive data as if he/she were onsite at a corporate facility.

WPA – stands for Wi-Fi protected access. The WPA protocol implements the IEEE 802.11i standard and is used to encrypt Wi-Fi traffic. It has now been superseded by WPA2 and WPA3.

References

1. Google loon https://loon.com/ Accessed 15 Nov, 2020.
2. D. Harkins, Kumari W (2017). Opportunistic Wireless Encryption. https://tools.ietf.org/html/rfc8110. Accessed 15 Jan 2021

Further Reading

Benvenuto CJ (2012) Galois Field in Cryptography. https://sites.math.washington.edu/~morrow/336_12/papers/juan.pdf. Accessed 14 Nov 2020

Calhoun P, Montemurro M, Stanley D (2009) Control and Provisioning of Wireless Access Points (CAPWAP) Protocol Binding for IEEE 802.11. Available via Internet Engineering Task Force https://tools.ietf.org/html/rfc5416. Accessed 15 Nov 2020

IEEE (2020). https://www.ieee.org/about/index.html

Shao C, Deng H, et al (2015) IEEE 802.11 Medium Access Control (MAC) Profile for Control and Provisioning of Wireless Access Points (CAPWAP). Available via Internet Engineering Task Force. https://tools.ietf.org/html/rfc7494 . Accessed 15 Nov 2020

Wi-Fi Alliance® introduces Wi-Fi 6 (2018) https://www.wi-fi.org/news-events/newsroom/wi-fi-alliance-introduces-wi-fi-6 . Accessed 15 Nov, 2020

The Next Frontier for CA/Certificate Security - DANE and Certificate Transparency

1 Introduction

If a certificate authority (CA) is compromised or breached, then any certificates that it may have issued in the past and any more it will issue in the future, cannot be trusted.

2 Known Issues

There are various problems with this scenario that one needs to contend with –

(a) If an impostor John uses data mined from social media or other publicly available data sources to convince a publicly trusted CA to issue it a (X.509) certificate claiming to be Jane, then he can assume the digital identity of Jane and use the certificate to encrypt data, send signed emails pretending to be Jane or launch man-in-the-middle attacks. Even if by some miracle, Jane discovers and reports the impersonation, the certificate revocation list (CRL) process to revoke the malicious certificate and make that information known to all has many issues of its own: first, the revocation process relies upon an authoritative source (generally the compromised CA itself) to maintain an updated CRL list; also, if a CRL has to be consulted before a given certificate is accepted, then the CRL has to be highly available and fault tolerant, or else it may lead to a denial of service simulation. CRLs are fundamentally problematic because the X.509 certificates are theoretically self-authenticating - introducing a CRL defeats that purpose. For these reasons, most browsers are moving away from CRLs to another validation protocol called Online Certificate Status Protocol (OSCP), which is more efficient and provides real-time status checks.

R. Badhwar, *The CISO's Next Frontier*,
https://doi.org/10.1007/978-3-030-75354-2_26

(b) If the same impostor John breaches the CA and gets hold of the private key used by the CA to issue and sign certificates, then it can issue malicious certificates signed by it that would be trusted by users, systems, and browsers. The same impostor (John) can now also issue certificates for ANY domain, which creates very big data integrity, privacy and confidentiality problems. If the CA breach is discovered, then an authority revocation list (ARL) process (similar to CRL) to revoke certificates issues to CAs is used and has issues similar to those faced by CRLs.

3   Solutions

I'd like to highlight two solutions and one best practice to deal with the issues cited above.

3.1   DNS-Based Authentication of Named Entities (DANE)

The issue of a compromised CA being able to issue certificates for any domain can be solved by using DANE, which allows the X.509 certificates to be bound to domain names using Domain Name System Security Extensions (DNSSEC). This works best and is commonly used for TLS, and provides the domain admin for a given domain the capability to certify the keys used by its TLS clients or servers connecting to that domain, by storing them within its Domain Name Service (DNS) server(s). The DNS records have to be signed with DNSSEC (creating a dependency on it, which is a bit of a problem due to its poor adoption rate outside of the US government apparatus). DANE also enables the capability for a domain owner to specify which CA is authorized to issue certificates for a given domain resource, thus reducing the threat surface of a compromised CA issuing certificates for any domain.

While DANE is very sound theoretically, it has not found widespread adoption and its days seem numbered, primarily because of its dependency on DNSSEC. Google Chrome does not support it and is going the route of supporting certificate transparency.

3.2   Certificate Transparency (CT)

This works on the fundamental belief that while it is difficult to prevent the threat actors from issuing malicious certificates, it is certainly possible to get good monitoring, auditing and alerting established for all certificates, eventually leading to the discovery of malicious or mis-issued certificates. This standard is based on the concept of a 'public log' which is a repository of all certificates issued by all publicly trusted CAs. Under the hood, the 'public log' uses a 'Merkle Tree' which provides a cryptographic construct for the logs to be added to an infinite, ever-growing (hash) tree structure, and verifies that each submitted certificate has been appropriately signed by the trusted root CA before adding it to the tree. Certificate Transparency also uses the concept of 'observers' who have the capability to check the 'public logs' and ensure that all data is valid and current, and also verify that all certificates being used by browsers from trusted CAs are indeed present in the public logs.

While CT provides the capability for a browser to check a certificate with the 'public log' before establishing a trusted connection with it, it is still a non-preventative detective control. Because it is not fool-proof, it can also create issues like missing certificates or simulating conditions similar to a denial of service. It does introduce a lot of organizational and CA hygiene by detecting and highlighting bad processes and practices being used to issue certificates and pre-certificates by organizations and certificate authorities.

Another noteworthy fact is that even CT does not have full support and adoption in the industry. Google is pushing it, but other browser providers like Microsoft (Edge), Mozilla (Firefox) and Apple (Safari) are not entirely on board yet.

3.3   Hardware Security Module (HSM)

An HSM must be used to maintain the confidentiality, integrity and availability of all cryptographic keys and variables. In a nutshell, all private keys must be stored in an HSM to protect them from being misused, stolen, or compromised.

4   The CISO Take

Both DANE and CT are much needed improvements required to provide security to certificates and CAs from various security threats. I personally like and support DANE as a better solution, as it not only provides certificate security, but also much needed security to otherwise attack-vulnerable DNS implementations by adding DNSSEC as a dependency.

It is the responsibility of CISOs to ensure that any new implementations, adoptions or optimizations of public or private CAs used to issue public facing or private self-signed certificates support these new enhancements, and any sensitive crypto key or variable is secured within an HSM.

5 Definitions

DNS – stands for Domain Name System. It is a global naming system which enables the mapping and the subsequent syncing of a website or other internet/intranet-hosted resource name, to an IP address

Merkle Tree - is a hash tree structure in which each leaf node is labelled with the crypto hash of a data block (e.g., a file), and every non-leaf node is labelled with a crypto hash (SHA-2) which is either the crypto hash of its child node or the concatenation of the crypto hashes of its child nodes.

DNSSEC – stands for Domain Name System Security Extensions. It provides the hardening guidelines and specifications to secure DNS by adding cryptographic signatures to existing records.

CA – stands for certificate authority. Is an entity that issues digital certificates.

HSM – stands for hardware security module. It is a physical or virtual computing device whose primary function is to provide secure storage and management of cryptographic keys and other critical security parameters (CSP).

X.509 – is a cryptographic standard that defines the format of PKI certificates.

Further Reading

Dukhovni V, Hardaker W (2015) The DNS-Based Authentication of Named Entities (DANE) Protocol: Updates and Operational Guidance. Internet Engineering Task Force, https://tools.ietf.org/html/rfc7671. Accessed August 7, 2020.

Laurie B, Langley A, Kasper E (2013) Certificate Transparency. Internet Engineering Task Force, https://tools.ietf.org/html/rfc6962. Accessed August 7, 2020.

Staff Writer (2020). What is Dane, https://www.infoblox.com/dns-security-resource-center/dns-security-faq/what-is-dane/ Accessed August 7, 2020.

Staff Writer (2015) "WHAT'S IN A NAME?" USING DANE FOR AUTHENTICATION OF INTERNET SERVICES, https://blog.verisign.com/security/whats-in-a-name-using-dane-for-authentication-of-internet-services/, Accessed August 7, 2020.

Man-in-the-Middle Attack Prevention

1   Introduction

Man-in-the-middle attack is the one thing that breaks the security paradigm for encrypted data in transit. Protective schemes must be designed to maintain the confidentiality and integrity of data in transit using transport-level encryption.

This chapter provides further details on the man-in-the-middle attacks, along with some attack prevention and protection mechanisms. It also discusses some valid (ethical) use scenarios.

2   Man-in-the-Middle-Attack (MITM)

A MITM attack occurs when an attacker hijacks a secure encrypted connection between a client and server. The attacker could:

(a) Be a proxy that intercepts the active traffic, examines it by decrypting the traffic, and then re-encrypts the traffic and forwards it;

(b) Be a proxy that reroutes the traffic to another system/server, which pretends to be a legitimate system but is actually controlled by the attacker;

(c) Use a phishing site to gain access to user credentials and then use privilege escalation to gain administrative access to a site and reroute incoming connections to a malicious site or decrypt incoming traffic, and subsequently perform packet analysis using readily available tools (e.g., tcpdump) to read (or exfiltrate) sensitive data;

(d) Compromise the domain name service (DNS) system (generally, the local DNS cache) to make a domain name resolve to a malicious IP address (DNS spoofing and poisoning);

(e) Use malware to hijack not just the local cache, but the entire DNS system;

(f) Register a fake or malicious domain meant to look similar to a site that is regularly used by unsuspecting developers;
(g) Use malicious techniques like IP spoofing on a company's local network (intranet);
(h) Perform passive MITM attack if an active attack is not possible.

3   Background Information

Protections against DNS hijacking and spoofing have been discussed in the chapter (24) on DNSSEC in this book.

This chapter focuses on certificate-based techniques that are key to implementing protections for MITM attacks.

3.1   SSH Handshake Basics

To better understand how certificate-based techniques can be used to protect again MITM attacks, one first needs to understand some fundamental concepts on SSL connectivity, SSL handshakes, and the security issues therein that can be exploited for MITM attacks.

Before a client and server establish an SSL/TLS connection between themselves, they must first perform an "SSL Handshake," a technique by which the client and the server agree on the data security aspects of their connection. Specifically, they agree on the cryptographic ciphers they would use to secure (encrypt) the communication, verify the identity of the server, and establish a secure connection.

The *simplified* chain of events is as follows:

(a) The client requests an encrypted connection with the server and shares its list of cryptographic ciphers that it can use to secure the traffic.
(b) The server responds with its lists of cryptographic ciphers it supports.
(c) The client and server agree upon the ciphers to be used for the encrypted connection.
(d) The server sends its digital certificate and public key to the client.
(e) The client verifies the server certificate and exchanges keys with the server to negotiate a shared secret, which would be used to encrypt and decrypt the traffic. A different shared secret is negotiated for each session.

3.1.1 SSL Handshake Issues

During the SSL handshake, the client checks that the certificate presented to it by the server is valid by performing a certificate chain of trust verification. This ensures that it originates from a trusted source by comparing its issuer to a list of trusted Certificate Authorities (CA) and that it has been signed by the trusted root CA or an intermediate root CA in the trust chain.

Although not always enforced, the client also tries to verify the hostname of the certificate.

This verification scheme is not foolproof since the server-provided trusted root CA or trust store can be breached and the hostname spoofed.

Using the MITM capability, the attacker introduces a proxy within the client and the server, the client does a handshake with the proxy and receives the proxy's (fake) certificate instead of the server's real certificate. Generally, the attackers use a root CA that is either already present in the client's local trust store or is installed there by the attacker using various malicious techniques.

Additional commentary on this subject has been provided in a different chapter (26) on certificate transparency.

4 Protective Schemes

There are two primary techniques that are available to provide protection from man-in-the-middle attacks.

4.1 *Certificate Pinning*

This technique enables the client to detect MITM attacks. There are two types of certificate pinning: Client Certificate Pinning and Server Certificate Pinning. I have also mentioned some other alternative approaches as well.

With **Server Certificate Pinning**, the client knows exactly which server certificate is exclusively required for a secure connection. Even if the server certificate presented to it by the server has a verifiable trust chain and hostname, it rejects the connection if it isn't the specific server certificate it is configured to expect (generally, in the format of a hash of the public key of the cert). All clients for a given domain name can use the same server certificate. Generally, the pinning can be done (a) at the certificate level, thereby enforcing a stricter control where a mismatch will cause the connection to fail; or (b) at the certificate authority (CA) level, for which any server certificate issued and/or signed by a specific CA will be trusted and the connection will be made.

The certificate level pinning is the preferred Zero Trust-compliant approach, although it can cause initial setup challenges and outages from expired certs, rotations, or revocations. By contrast, the CA pinning approach, although easier to setup, is much riskier due to the potential for a CA to become compromised and then used to sign rogue SSL certificates.

Client Certificate Pinning involves the issuance of unique certificates which must be pinned to each client with a matching unique private key. During certificate verification by the server, the client needs to present the pinned certificate, or else the server will refuse the connection. Although this approach is similar to that of server certificate pinning, the multiple steps required of both client and server make it harder to implement. The need to revoke or reissue a certificate (to the client) adds to the complexity.

Other Schemes – Pinning the public key, rather than the certificate, can help improve usability challenges posed by periodic rotations of pinned certificates. The public key remains the same through certificate rotations. This does pose the new challenge of programmatically extracting the public key from the digital cert for some programming languages.

4.2 Mutual Authentication

This technique enables the server to detect MITM attacks. Theoretically speaking, this technique allows for both the client and server to validate and trust each other's certificates before a successful SSL/TLS connection can be made.

Mutual authentication builds upon the simplified chain of events for SSL/TLS previously discussed in Sect. 3.1, and is described below:

(a) The client requests an encrypted connection with the server and shares its list of cryptographic ciphers that it can use to secure the traffic.
(b) The server responds with its lists of cryptographic ciphers it supports.
(c) The client and server agree upon the ciphers to be used for the encrypted connection.
(d) The server sends its digital certificate and public key to the client, *and also requests the client certificate – the client obliges.*
(e) The *server and client* verify each other's certificates and exchange keys to negotiate a shared secret to be used to encrypt and decrypt the traffic. A different shared secret is negotiated for each session.

While this approach works very well, it does require the server to distribute unique certificates to each client, which sometimes is not very feasible. The need to revoke and reissue certificates adds to the complexity.

4.3 HTTP Public Key Pinning (HPKP)

Although HPKP has been deprecated, it is good to talk about this to understand the rationale why it was pursued and implemented in the first place.

This primary purpose of this technique was to implement a pseudo-public key pinning approach in browsers to provide protection against the use of fraudulent certificates or the compromise of the CA that issues the server certificates for a given web-based application. In simple terms, the server would send a client a public key hash which must appear in the certificate chain of future connections for the same domain name, through an HTTP header. The client would store the key in its cache. Subsequently, if the client visits the same site/URL later and the server provides a different public key than the one previously obtained by HPKP, then the browser raises an alert to the user about the possibility of a man-in-the-middle attack.

The technique was found to be at risk of compromise if the first key hash itself was fraudulent, or if an attacker were to perform a MITM attack on the first hash of the public key sent by the server, thereby using it to send the client to a fraudulent domain.

HPKP has been replaced by Certificate Transparency, which has been discussed in another chapter (26) in this book.

4.4 TLS Downgrade Detection

MITM attacks become a lot more difficult to conduct with TLS 1.3, and thus the threat actors try to get around this problem by downgrading the TLS 1.3 connection to TLS 1.2. The protocol designers foresaw this issue and have provided a downgrade marker within the protocol itself. When a TLS 1.3 client (or server) sees this marker, it should immediately abort the (handshake) connection.

5 Valid Use of MITM

So far, we have used the man-in-the-middle scenario to highlight various malicious use cases. But this concept can also be used ethically to enforce corporate security policies, to prevent employees from visiting malicious sites, or to enforce data loss prevention (DLP) policies against the exfiltration of company sensitive data primarily by insiders. Internet proxies, cloud proxies, and cloud access security brokers (CASB) solutions basically use a man-in-the-middle approach to examine encrypted internet-bound traffic by decrypting it, reviewing it, and forwarding it on after re-encrypting it (aka SSL Inspection).

To avoid any confusion, security technologists generally use the term TLS Intercept Application (TIA) when they use MITM in a legitimate and ethical manner.

If you read the fine print of most employment contracts, generally there is verbiage in it that authorizes employers to inspect internet- bound traffic when it originates from a company issued computing asset (e.g., laptop) or while on a private company network. There are still ethical boundaries and privacy concerns of which both the employers and employees should be aware so that those are understood and not violated, especially as most of the SSL inspection may be performed by artificially intelligent processes in the near future [1].

6   The CISO Take

By now it should be obvious that MITM attacks are a serious security threat and can raise significant doubts in the minds of our customers and users about our capability to secure their data in transit.

The mitigations laid out in this chapter are all proven techniques and very possible to implement. However, implementation complexity and cost often result in pushback from CIOs and other IT leaders, who also cite these to be the cause of delays to their project or product releases and other application implementations. Higher maintenance costs are also attributed to reduced adoption and implementation of these capabilities.

Thus, it is the responsibility of CISOs to ensure that they make these implementations easier by using automation wherever possible, and also impress upon their IT leadership peers and other business leaders the importance of mitigating this cyber risk, even though it may be more complex to implement and cost slightly more to maintain.

7   Definitions

CA – stands for Certificate Authority. Is an entity that issues digital certificates.
CASB – stands for Cloud Access Security Broker. It is an on-premises or cloud-hosted security policy enforcement point, generally resident between the flow of network or application traffic and cloud-hosted or based services (e.g., SaaS, IaaS or PaaS). The security policies enforced include but are not limited to DLP, SSO, MFA, logging, and malware detection.
DLP – stands for Data Loss Prevention. It is a technology that prevents the unauthorized access to or exfiltration of company and customer sensitive data.
DNS – stands for Domain Name System. It is a global naming system which enables the mapping and the subsequent syncing of a website or other internet/intranet-hosted resource name, to an IP address

---

[1] Please also read the 'The AI Code of Ethics for Cyber security'.

DNSSEC – stands for Domain Name System Security Extensions. It provides the hardening guidelines and specifications to secure DNS by adding cryptographic signatures to existing records.

TIA - stands for TLS Intercept Application. It is the term generally used when MITM or equivalent techniques are used for SSL/TLS inspection in a legitimate and ethical manner.

Further Reading

Akamai (2021) Mutual Authentication. Available via Akamai Documentation. https://learn.akamai.com/en-us/webhelp/iot/internet-of-things-over-the-air-user-guide/GUID-21EC6B74-28C8-4CE1-980E-D5EE57AD9653.html . Accessed 10 Jan 2021

Contini S (2020). Understanding certificate pinning. https://littlemaninmyhead.wordpress.com/2020/06/08/understanding-certificate-pinning/ . Accessed 10 Jan 2021

Du Toit R (2017) Responsibly intercepting TLS and the impact of TLS 1.3. Symantec Technical Brief. https://docs.broadcom.com/doc/responsibly-intercepting-tls-and-the-impact-of-tls-1.3.en . Accessed 10 Jan 2021

Evans C, Palmer C, Sleevi R (2015) Public Key Pinning Extension for HTTP. Available via Internet Engineering Task Force. https://tools.ietf.org/html/rfc7469. Accessed 10 Jan 2021

Imperva. Man in the middle (MITM) attack. https://www.imperva.com/learn/application-security/man-in-the-middle-attack-mitm/. Accessed 10 Jan 2021

Microsoft (2019) 2.5.4.1.3 Mutual authentication. In: documentation, open specifications. https://docs.microsoft.com/en-us/openspecs/windows_protocols/ms-authsod/1691cf8a-2049-49f5-8940-3cf5640496fe . Accessed 10 Jan 2021

Mozilla (2020) HTTP public key pinning. In: MDN Web Docs. https://developer.mozilla.org/en-US/docs/Web/HTTP/Public_Key_Pinning. Accessed 10 Jan 2021

Oiwa Y, Watanabe H, et al (2017) Mutual Authentication Protocol for HTTP. Available via Internet Engineering Task Force. https://tools.ietf.org/html/rfc8120. Accessed 10 Jan 2021

Piątek K (2020) Certificate pinning in iOS. Available via netguru. https://www.netguru.com/codestories/certificate-pinning-in-ios . Accessed 10 Jan 2021

Rashid FY (2017) Warning: your network tools are weakening your web security. Available via InfoWorld. https://www.infoworld.com/article/3182192/warning-your-networking-tools-are-weakening-your-web-security.html. Accessed 10 Jan 2021

Rowley J (2020) What is certificate pinning? Available via DigiCert. https://www.digicert.com/dc/blog/certificate-pinning-what-is-certificate-pinning/. Accessed 10 Jan 2021

Samuel J (2018) Can we stop intercepting user traffic (aka man-in-the-middle) please? https://medium.com/@joelgsamuel/can-we-stop-intercepting-user-traffic-aka-man-in-the-middle-please-2a00de208d4b . Accessed 10 Jan 2021

Square, Inc. (2019) CertifcatePinner. https://square.github.io/okhttp/4.x/okhttp/okhttp3/-certificate-pinner/. Accessed 10 Jan 2021

Wikipedia (2020) Mutual authentication. https://en.wikipedia.org/wiki/Mutual_authentication . Accessed 10 Jan 2021

Wikipedia (2020). Man in the middle attack. https://en.wikipedia.org/wiki/Man-in-the-middle_attack . Accessed 10 Jan 2021

Distributed Denial of Service (DDoS) Protection

1 Introduction

A Distributed Denial of Service attack has become a very common technique used by attackers and malicious entities to attack internet-facing web applications, web services, exchange (email) infrastructure, DNS and NTP servers, and VOIP infrastructure.

2 DDoS

DDoS attacks are generally used to bring down critical perimeter security apparatus and other internet-facing high-risk applications in an effort to gain unauthorized access, cause reputational damage and perform other malicious activities including the exfiltration of sensitive data and the spread of malware.

DDoS attacks are generally launched simultaneously from multiple global locations such as rogue nation states in Eastern Europe, the Far East, and Africa; by extortionists, advanced persistent threat (APT), or by individual criminals or organized crime syndicates. Attackers rely on virtualized servers with short life-spans, which make them hard to detect and block. They have also been known to hijack and use a wide swath of IOT devices to launch these attacks.

Cyber criminals are now making DDoS attack capability available (DDoSaaS) to anyone who wants it by selling subscriptions on the dark web.

R. Badhwar, *The CISO's Next Frontier*,
https://doi.org/10.1007/978-3-030-75354-2_28

2.1   Layer 7 Attacks

DDoS attacks at Layer 7 of the OSI model use common protocols like HTTP to conduct the attack. The technique generally utilizes an HTTP packet flood to exhaust the target with HTTP GET and POST requests.

These attacks are hard to detect for a commercial site, as the attack blends in with the valid HTTP requests.

Although there are many open-source tools available, generally these attacks are conducted by a Low Orbit Ion Cannon (LOIC) tool, which primarily uses the UDP and TCP protocols. This technique allows the attacks to be launched using a command line or a browser.

Sometime other Layer 7 attacks, such as a rapid password-spray attack, can also simulate a DDoS attack.

2.2   Layer 3 Attacks

The DDoS attacks at Layer 3 down the OSI model generally use protocols like UDP to conduct the attack, sending a UDP flood to a targeted server in an attempt to overwhelm the server.

These attacks are also hard to detect due to the valid usage of UDP for streaming media by ISPs, cable companies, and content providers like Netflix, Amazon and Hulu.

Although there are many open-source tools available, generally these attacks are conducted by the High Orbit Ion Cannon (HOIC) tool, which primarily uses the HTTP protocol. Traditionally this required a coordinated effort by multiple individuals to launch this type of attack, but now unattended bots have been used to replace the humans.

There are some other Layer 3 attacks that are also used:

(a) NTP Amplification (which uses amplified UDP traffic)
(b) Syn and ACK flood attacks
(c) DNS Flood attacks
(d) ICMP Flood attacks

3   Prevention Techniques

Several techniques to detect and prevent DDoS attacks are described below.

3.1 Traffic Scrubbing

This provides the capability to detect and scrub malicious IP (generally UDP or TCP) data packets. An external provider will generally perform this service, which can operate in two modes:

(a) A monitoring mode, with the capability to detect and manually enable traffic scrubbing. Once an attack is detected, manually starting the scrubbing of traffic can take at least 15–45 min.

This technique is still the most widely available and implemented option and requires a lot of manual intervention and coordination between the on-premise network security teams and the scrubbing service provider. This capability is generally offered by commercial internet service or circuit providers as an add-on service (generally with a third-party scrubber) but is not very effective any more, given the large amount of damage that can done by sophisticated attacks in a very short time, requiring proactive and sustained real-time response. Additional delays can be caused if the network security team does not have the rights to make network routing changes.

(b) 'Always on' in an inline mode with the capability to dynamically detect and scrub traffic with minimal lag and performance issues.

This is the best possible implementation option at the current time for medium-large enterprises with critical internet facing high risk applications. It provides near real-time detection and protection from large and small DDoS or equivalent attacks. This technique has been known to provide protection against some very large (>1 Tbps) attacks.

Most cloud providers at least have some rudimentary protection enabled by default, although sophisticated detection and scrubbing, and the capability to provide protection against large (Tbps) attacks requires additional services to be purchased.

3.2 Firewall

A next generation (application aware) firewall is a key perimeter appliance that has the capability to block malicious data packets and forms the first line of defense against DDoS attacks. Firewalls are capable of blocking small DDoS attacks but should not be used for big attacks that persist for prolonged periods. One of the main objectives of the attackers is to bring down a firewall with a sustained high-volume DDoS attack, often ranging from 50 Mbps to 1 Tbps, to gain unauthorized access to a private network (and thus the firewalls should always be configured in a HA configuration).

Using a firewall in conjunction with a real-time traffic scrubbing service, provides the best defense against DDoS attacks.

3.3 Throttling

This technique limits the number of requests that a server can handle by throttling them as the volume increases beyond a configured threshold.

This technique can slow down an attack to provide some tactical mitigation but cannot be used as a strategic solution, as this would also impact the incoming connection from genuine users.

3.4 Web Application Firewalls (WAF)

The WAFs have an inherent capability to provide rudimentary protection against UDP/TCP or HTTP floods, but cannot provide protections against large DDoS attacks.

A WAF would have to be configured in enforcement mode rather than the more common monitoring mode for it to be able to block an attack.

3.5 High Availability (HA) and Disaster Recovery (DR)

The best practice is to ensure that all the internet-facing high-risk systems have local HA and remote DR to provide mitigation against DDoS attacks on a given site or geographic location.

This would enable the capability to provide local or site level redundancy required to ensure business continuity after the loss of a primary data center or site due to a catastrophic network (DDoS) event.

4   The CISO Take

The DDoS attacks instances have gone up exponentially over the last 5 years. CISOs have to ensure that all internet-facing high-risk (digital) applications, their cloud environments, their VOIP infrastructure, and other digital properties are adequately protected against these attacks using dynamic traffic scrubbing and filtering techniques.

DDoS attacks are also often used as decoys and façades to launch malware attacks or data exfiltration events by malicious insiders or other threat vectors.

CISOs must have good threat intelligence for both external and internal threats to ensure that protection capabilities are available across various domains.

CISOs also have to ensure that they do frequent (at least quarterly) table-top exercises and other attack simulation exercises to verify their threat detection and mitigation capabilities can (still) provide the needed protections.

Also, the migration to the cloud has accelerated the convergence of network and network security and thus it is my recommendation that the network teams be merged with the network security teams under the leadership of the CISO to help provide more pro-active mitigation to DDoS attacks among other security posture improvements.

5 Definitions

Disaster Recovery – It is the capability to provide site level redundancy by enabling the recovery of all critical systems and applications at a secondary or alternate data center or site, after the loss of a primary data center or site due to a catastrophic network event or natural disaster.

DNS – stands for Domain Name System. It is a global naming system which enables the mapping and the subsequent syncing of a website or other internet/intranet-hosted resource name, to an IP address.

High Availability – It is the capability to provide local redundancy by enabling standby secondary or tertiary instances of a given application, system or server, in case of failure of the primary instance.

ICMP – stands for Internet Control Message Protocol. It is a protocol within the internet protocol suite and is generally used by network devices like routers to diagnose network communication issues.

ISP – stands for internet service provider. It is an entity that provides internet access to a private consumer, or to a business enterprise.

OSI – stands for Open Systems Interconnection. It is a reference model that establishes a standard for how a given application, system, or device may communicate and interoperate with others over a network. The OSI layer has seven layers – Application (Layer 7), Presentation (Layer 6), Session (Layer 5), Transport (Layer 4), Network (Layer 3), Data-link (Layer 2), and Physical (Layer 1).

VOIP – stands for Voice over Internet Protocol. It is the technology that converts analog voice phone calls into (TCP or UDP) data packets and transmits them over a public (Internet) or private (intranet) IP network.

Further Reading

Bienkowski T (2015) The 5 Misconceptions About the Modern DDoS Attack. Arbor Networks webinar, 25 Feb 2015.https://www.brighttalk.com/webcast/188/144677/the-5-misconceptions-about-the-modern-ddos-attack. Accessed 12 Dec 2020

Felter B (2020) 7 of the Most Famous Recent DDoS Attacks. https://www.vxchnge.com/blog/recent-ddos-attacks-on-companies, Accessed 12 Dec 2020

Kaspersky (2020) Distributed Denial of Service: Anatomy and Impact of DDoS Attacks. https://usa.kaspersky.com/resource-center/preemptive-safety/how-does-ddos-attack-work. Accessed 12 Dec 2020

Lanfear T, Coulter D, et al (2018) Azure DDoS Protection - Designing resilient solutions. https://docs.microsoft.com/en-us/azure/security/fundamentals/ddos-best-practices. Accessed 12 Dec 2020

Newman L (2020) 'DDoS-For-Hire' Is Fueling a New Wave of Attacks. https://www.wired.com/story/ddos-for-hire-fueling-new-wave-attacks/

Nicholson P (2020) Five Most Famous DDoS Attacks and Then Some. https://www.a10networks.com/blog/5-most-famous-ddos-attacks/. Accessed 12 Dec 2020

Porter J (2020) Amazon says it mitigated the largest DDoS attack ever recorded. https://www.theverge.com/2020/6/18/21295337/amazon-aws-biggest-ddos-attack-ever-2-3-tbps-shield-github-netscout-arbor

Part VI
Application and Device Security

Intro to API Security - Issues and Some Solutions!

1 Genesis

The days of one or two major code and functionality releases, developed using waterfall methodology, are over. To stay competitive, today's businesses need to deliver code and functionality at a much faster rate. This has led to the development of the dev-sec-ops paradigm for software development which is built on the tenants of agility, flexibility, automation, (auto) scaling and orchestration to deliver faster, fully tested, smaller functionality releases. Generally, these smaller code releases deliver code with incremental functionality additions and enhancements, sometimes as frequently as every other week.

This new application functionality delivery paradigm has been aided by the concept of micro-services which deliver features and functionality through APIs. The micro-services of today are descendants of the traditional service-oriented architecture (more in use in the early 2000s) which delivered business functionality through large complex and extensive web services – the micro-services deliver something similar but in much smaller chunks (hence the name micro).

The advent of Web Services heightened the need for data security due to the increased risk of unauthorized access and disclosure of sensitive data. The security needs of the SOA enabled Web Services of (e.g. SOAP based JAX/RPC services) were met by security authentication, authorization and trust paradigms enabled by WS-Security, WS-Trust, WS-Federation, WS-Policy, XACML, Liberty and SAML 1.0 etc. in the early 2000s, but the advent of concepts like RESTful APIs and micro-services have changed the authentication and authorization landscape more towards security tokens like OAuth 2.0 tokens, JSON Web tokens (JWT) and API keys (using MAC and HMAC auth). A basic treatment on these tokens and their secure use has been provided in this chapter. Due to the inherent complexity, a detailed treatment is outside the scope of this book.

© The Author(s), under exclusive license to Springer Nature Switzerland AG 2021
R. Badhwar, *The CISO's Next Frontier*,
https://doi.org/10.1007/978-3-030-75354-2_29

2 Introduction

The **Micro-fication** of Web services may have provided the capability to deliver loosely coupled smaller chunks of business capability, but it presents enormous security challenges. As micro-fication brings higher levels of interdependency and complexity to Web services with faster rates of ongoing change, −it is much harder to secure (and monitor) the micro-services and associated APIs from the various external and insider threats.

3 API Security

This chapter is opening the dialogue on API security. It is going to talk about some of the threats faced and some potential mitigations and solutions. Please note that this is a fairly basic treatment and by no means is a comprehensive list of threats and solutions.

3.1 Legacy Web Threats

Micro-services are not immune from current and past threats faced by the web applications, such as encoding and serialization attacks, cross-site scripting (XSS), cross-site request forgery (CSRF), SQL injection, command injection, XML injection, and HTTP verb tampering.

In addition to using the traditional perimeter security stack, these specific threats can also be protected by using combination of inline (a) Web access firewall (WAF) (b) SAST and DAST – providing static and dynamic application security (c) RASP proving runtime application security – where a security agent is "linked" with the application itself and can dynamically mitigate vulnerabilities at runtime within the application or web server as the vulnerability loads into memory (d) Endpoint and network-based traffic pattern monitoring with anomaly detection aided by semi-supervised machine learning algorithms to provide advanced analytics.

3.2 API Key

It is a shared secret and is one of the common techniques used for micro-services authentication. While this theoretically works well for (non-sensitive) data access, the API key is susceptible to common attacks like credential theft and credential compromise. It is also known to be vulnerable to replay, injection and man-in-the-middle attacks and must not be used as an authentication mechanism for APIs that provide access to sensitive data. The use of native API key should be deprecated, given the large number of data breaches that have occurred from its misuse.

Here are some ways of securing the API key:

(a) **API Gateway** - All APIs using an API key to authenticate must be protected within an API gateway or proxy.
(b) **HMAC** - The best way to protect an API key is to verify the integrity, authenticity, and identify of the message sender by using hash-based message authentication code (HMAC) authentication. Although the implementations may vary, this is generally done by creating an HMAC using the API key, a nonce, a local timestamp, and then by making the API invocation with just the HMAC and the Application ID, thereby keeping the API key out of the calling channel.
(c) **SSL/TLS Certificate Pinning** - a technique for preventing man-in-the-middle attacks, associates a host with its certificate or public key, configuring a given app to reject all but a few pre-defined certs or public keys. If the app connects to a server, it compares the server cert to the pinned cert or public key and only if they match does it trust the server and establish the connection. Pinning a certificate to a host prevents an attacker from inserting a self-signed certificate into a trust store for a given app, thereby preventing the decryption of encrypted data traversing through an app or system. (additional details on certificate pinning has been shared within Sect. 4.2 in Chap. 27 in this book).
(d) **Restrictive Controls** - One other way to reduce the risk of using an API key is to shorten the life-span of the key. Also, a separate API key should be issued for each application. Within an application, the use of its API key should be limited by the restrictions enabled for its API sets.
(e) **Conditional Access** - Even though access may have been granted using an authentication token, the token granting service must use modern conditional access paradigms like continuous evaluation to verify if a given token previously granted and used, subsequently needs to be invalidated forcing another authentication event due to change in behavior of the client using it (e.g., the client source IP change).
(f) **Other techniques** - To augment the restrictions just mentioned, conditional access with IP restrictions can also be used. Also, any administrative access to the (IAM) system that either issues the API key or stores the API key must be protected with multi-factor authentication (MFA).

3.3 OAuth 2.0

APIs that provide access to sensitive data or financial transactions should use single use security tokens that have been issued by a secure and authoritative source. OAuth 2.0 enables this via the use of access and refresh tokens. An access token is sent like an API key and provides access to an API. It can fetch any data. Refresh tokens are used to retrieve a new access token if one is expired. Access tokens have risks similar to that of an API Key but have been engineered to provide fine grained access, with restrictions on the type of data they can access and the operations they can perform.

3.4 JWT

These are stateless authentication tokens that can be used to provide access to APIs. The JSON Web Tokens (JWT) can work with OAuth 2.0 tokens (for initial authentication) to obtain a token that encapsulates the user data or access permissions for subsequent API or resource access. JWT is also a secure way to transmit data between two parties.

The following security precautions must be observed while using JWT: (a) the token expiry times should be as short as possible, since they determine the duration of the session, and (b) the token secret key must not be a part of the shared library associated with a micro-service.

Like an API key or OAuth, JWT is susceptible to replay attacks, which can be mitigated by setting a short session time for token use, using one-time password (OTP), and using the inherent capability in the platform (jti field) to blacklist tokens that are suspected of being replayed.

3.5 Dependency and Namespace Confusion

This is an (indirect) API security issue, and talks about the inherent risk that exists within a given application eco system from dependency and namespace-confusion based attacks, which is a technique used by threat actors to push or inject malicious or counterfeit packages to cloud hosted source code repositories.

These attacks are unlike the traditional typo squatting or brandjacking supply-chain attacks of yesteryears. With this new attack technique, a targeted company can automatically receive the malicious package without the developer making any spelling mistakes (in the package get command or the script that resolves build library dependencies), or without falling prey to a social engineering attack.

Dependency confusion is an inherent design flaw in the native installation tool(s) and DevOps workflows [1] that pull dependencies to build an application or service. This flaw exploits the inability of a given development environment to distinguish between a (private) internally created software package within software build and a (malicious) package by the same name available in a public software repository (or in the wild). This problem is further exacerbated by the fact that the npm ecosystem does not follow a standard for namespacing, allowing the threat actors to build time malware injection possibilities.

Security researches have observed over 200 brandjacking packages being used in the wild that we have to be careful about. Microsoft has also released a whitepaper

[2] on the matter and a vulnerability tracked as CVE-2021-24,105 [3] has been opened to track its Azure Artifacts product [1].

4   CISO Take

The threat from unauthorized access and disclosure of sensitive data from APIs that do not have adequate security protection has skyrocketed worldwide in the past 2–5 years. Digital platforms are growing exponentially and need the agility offered by distributed computing and micro-services, but with an unfortunate exponential rise in risks. It is the responsibility of security technologists and evangelists to raise awareness about the need for advanced API security paradigms, help ensure all implementations and usage of JWT and OAuth/2.0 are secure and hardened for common attacks like token replay, ensure the API keys are used securely, and provide for tested and secure implementations of HMAC in commonly used languages such as PHP, Python, Java and JavaScript.

API level integration especially with SaaS applications have also seen an exponential increase, and so have the attacks on these APIs. The threat actors have figured out that if they could breach an API then they could very easily exfiltrate data right through the front door, or use a stolen authentication token to login as the user to gain unauthorized access to a SaaS with sensitive data. It is thus imperative that the CISOs ensure that all API level integrations have been adequately secured (using some of the techniques mentioned in this chapter) and also implement the capability to detect any API level breaches or credential theft.

5   Definitions

DAST – stands for dynamic application security testing. It allows the developers to find vulnerabilities and weaknesses within a running (web) application by using fault injection techniques.

HMAC (authentication) – stands hash-based message authentication code. It is crypto hash function used to verify the authenticity of a message.

XSS – stands for Cross-Site Scripting. It is an attack where an attacker can inject and/or execute malicious code (generally JavaScript) within a user's browser.

CSRF- stands for Cross-Site Request Forgery. It is an attack where a user's session is hijacked using a vulnerability within the application, and is then used to submit forged transactions that the user neither made nor intended to make.

SAML – stands for secure access manipulation language. It is a standardized mechanism that enables an identity provider (IdP) to assert an identity by passing its authentication and authorization credentials to a service provider (SP) to help enable paradigms like SSO.

SAST – stands for static application security testing. It allows developers to find security vulnerabilities in their source code during the development and unit testing phase (i.e., earlier in the SDLC of a product) by using static code analysis techniques.

WAF – stands for web access firewall. It is primarily an application firewall that protects an HTTP/S-based (web) application against advanced attacks like cross-site scripting, cross-site forgery, and sql injection.

References

1. Sharma A (2021). Dependency Hijacking Software Supply Chain Attack Hits More Than 35 Organizations. https://blog.sonatype.com/dependency-hijacking-software-supply-chain-attack-hits-more-than-35-organizations . Accessed Feb 26, 2021.
2. Microsoft (2021). 3 Ways to Mitigate Risk When Using Private Package Feeds https://azure.microsoft.com/mediahandler/files/resourcefiles/3-ways-to-mitigate-risk-using-private-package-feeds/3%20Ways%20to%20Mitigate%20Risk%20When%20Using%20Private%20Package%20Feeds%20-%20v1.0.pdf. Accessed Feb 26, 2021
3. CVE-2021-24105 (2021). Package Managers Configurations Remote Code Execution Vulnerability. https://msrc.microsoft.com/update-guide/vulnerability/CVE-2021-24105 . Accessed Feb 26, 2021.

Further Reading

Chandramouli R (2019). Security Strategies for Microservices-based Application Systems. https://csrc.nist.gov/publications/detail/sp/800-204/final Accessed Dec 24 2020.
Google (2020). Secure APIs - https://cloud.google.com/apigee/api-management/secure-apis Accessed Jan 21 2021.
Lascelles F (2020). API Security: The Definitive Guide. https://www.pingidentity.com/en/company/blog/posts/2020/everything-need-know-api-security-2020.html Accessed Dec 29 2020.
Parecki A (2020). OAuth 2.0 - https://oauth.net/2/ Accessed Dec 24 2020.
Singhal A, Winograd T et al (2007). Guide to Secure Web Services. https://nvlpubs.nist.gov/nistpubs/Legacy/SP/nistspecialpublication800-95.pdf . Accessed on Dec 28 2020.
Staff Writer (2020). Web API Security - https://www.imperva.com/learn/application-security/web-api-security/ . Accessed on Dec 29 2020.

Windows Subsystem for Linux – Security Risk and Mitigation

If some of you are like me, you probably have a machine at home that you dual-boot to use the same machine for Windows 10 and Linux, right? (I do have some Linux boxes, but I like the convenience of having it locally resident on my desktop).

If you're fed up doing dual boot, then look no further, as there is light at the end of this tunnel. (No, you won't be able to do this yourself on your 'managed' work laptop, and even if you can – please don't. But if you like you what read here then make a formal request to your IT department.)

This article introduces Windows subsystem for Linux (WSL) and also provides some commentary and analysis on the security risks to WSL, and some possible mitigations.

1 Introduction

Meet WSL, the windows subsystem for Linux. It lets Linux developers run a Linux environment on windows, including most command line tools, utilities, and applications directly on windows, without any modifications, and without the overhead of a virtual machine (VM).

WSL2 is the new version of the subsystem architecture and changes the way Linux distros interact with windows. It delivers much better file system performance and, by using a virtualization technology and a Linux kernel, adds full system call compatibility (something that was missing in the previous version, WSL1).

Please note that WSL2 is currently only available in Windows 10 version 2004 (build 19,041 or higher). Depending upon when you read this chapter, this version may still only be available to those on the windows insider program [circa pre q4 2020].

WSL2 enables the following actions on a windows platform:

© The Author(s), under exclusive license to Springer Nature Switzerland AG 2021
R. Badhwar, *The CISO's Next Frontier*,
https://doi.org/10.1007/978-3-030-75354-2_30

(a) Selecting a Linux distribution supported by Microsoft and available in their store. (many of the good ones like Ubuntu or openSUSE are in there)
(b) Running all the common command-line utilities (e.g., make, less, find, locate, mv, ln, du, free, top, kill other ELF-64 binaries) that the non-windows Linux systems engineers and developers use on a daily basis.
(c) Executing bash shell scripts and other Linux command line applications including:

  1. Tools: vi, emacs, grep, traceroute, ssh, md5sum, umask, mkpasswd, tar.
  2. Languages: C/C++, C#, Java, Perl etc.
  3. Services: Apache/Tomcat, JDK/JRE, MySql, ActiveMQ, Oracle RDBMS and Weblogic

(d) Installing additional software using the standard Linux distribution package managers like APT or YUM.
(e) Invoking windows applications using a Unix-like command line shell. [1]

2   Installation

Here are basic steps that you can follow to enable the capability to run Linux on Windows–
    Note: Before installing any Linux distributions on Windows, you must enable the "Windows Subsystem for Linux" optional feature.

2.1   Step 1 – Install WSL 1

Open PowerShell as Administrator and run:

```
dism.exe /online /enable-feature /featurename:Microsoft-Windows-
Subsystem-Linux /all /norestart
```

This will install WSL1 (if you restart, or else continue), so now you must install WSL2.

2.2   Step 2 – Install WSL 2

Please remember that you must be on Windows 10 version 2004 or a later version. Also, before you install WSL2, you must enable the optional 'Virtual Machine Platform' feature.
    Open PowerShell as Administrator and run:

```
dism.exe /online /enable-feature /featurename:VirtualMachinePlatf
orm /all /norestart
```

Restart your machine to complete the WSL install, as well as the upgrade to WSL2.

2.3 Step 3 – Set WSL 2 as Your Default Version

To set WSL2 as the default version when installing a new Linux distro, you must do the following:
Open PowerShell as Administrator and run:

```
wsl --set-default-version 2
```

You might see this message after running that command: WSL 2 requires an update to its kernel component. For more information, please visit https://aka.ms/wsl2kernel. Please follow the link and install the MSI from that page to install a Linux kernel on your machine for WSL 2 to use. Once you have the kernel installed, please run the command again and it should complete successfully without showing the message.

2.4 Step 4 – Install Your Linux Distribution of Choice (Available on the Microsoft Store)

Open the Microsoft store and select the distro of your choice and select 'Get'
(Ubuntu 20.04 LTS or openSUSE leap 15.1 are good choices)
Once the installation is complete, an Ubuntu or openSUSE app should appear in your windows start menu.

2.5 Step 5 – Launch Your Distro and Establish Creds

Once you launch your newly installed Linux distro from the app in your start menu, a console window should open for your Linux distro. Follow the instructions to create your username and password and finalize the installation.
You should also check the version of WSL you're running. This can be done by running

```
wsl --list --verbose
```

If the result indicates that it uses WSL1 you can change it to 2 by running

```
wsl --set-version UBUNTU-20.04 2
```

3 Security Evaluation

For security technologists to be highly competent at protecting systems, services, or software against malware and other threat actors, we first have to learn the technology itself so that we can understand its weaknesses and vulnerabilities. Only then can we analyze and design protective schemes.

Now that you know a bit more about WSL, I have provided some very basic security treatment for the threats that it may face and have also talked briefly about some of the mitigations possible.

3.1 Problem Statement

Security researchers have reported that attackers could use the "WSL environment to run Windows malware from a Linux instance and bypass most Windows security products in the process." [4]

While this may technically be true, once an attacker gets in your environment and escalates privilege then all bets are off anyway, for any system. However, there are some fundamental mitigations available for WSL.

3.2 Inherent Platform Security

As most of you may know, Linux already has good fundamental protections built using the principle of least privilege and entitlements, and most of those come with WSL (basically making it more secure than windows itself). Also, WSL is now supported by Windows Defender Firewall, thereby eliminating the need to run iptables within the Linux distro itself (although you can if you really want to run them).

3.3 Security Patching

Having a patched system, windows, Linux or otherwise, provides the best mitigation against known and zero-day exploits. Windows 10 handles the Win10 security updates, including updates to the core WSL/2.

For patching the Linux instance in WSL, you can also do the following:

```
apt update && apt upgrade (from within the Linux console)
```

or

```
%windir%\system32\bash.exe -c "sudo apt update && sudo apt -y
upgrade"
```

3.4 Brute Force Attack Mitigations

One of the items that you would be running in the Linux distro is an SSH server. These could be subjected to brute force attacks. Most attacks should get blocked by windows defender but another simple way to prevent them is to enable Public Key Authentication (and subsequently disable login/password authentication) for your Linux distro. You could also enable Fail2ban, ConfigServer security and firewall and login failure daemon (CSF-LFD), or the SSHGuard utility.

3.5 Use Picoprocess APIs

Microsoft has introduced "Picoprocess" to support WSL [2]. "A picoprocess is a lightweight, secure isolation container which is built from an OS process address space but with all the traditional OS services removed." [3]. "PICO" APIs used by windows to interact with Linux could also be used to monitor the WSL process by Defender ATP or other AV or EDR software, but for the bold and daring, one could write a basic integration between, for example, bitdefender and WSL making PICO calls. The flip side of the coin is that the PICO APIs could also be used in a malicious manner by malware or an attacker, for which we have to be on the lookout.

3.6   Avoid Using WSL as a Server

If you don't have to run and host web servers or other servers on WSL, then don't do it. Harden your configuration and ensure that you are running only the services that you really need.

4   The CISO Take

Windows is the most widely deployed end user operating system but Linux is the most used by developers for system and application development. Making Linux available through Windows is a win-win for everyone.

CISOs must support this endeavor to make Linux available through windows, while ensuring appropriate security measures are in place. They must confirm that WSL is being patched on a monthly basis along with windows, it provides visibility to and has hooks into the windows-based endpoint security tools (like EDR, NGAV, DLP etc.), and ensure that the hackers are not able to use it as a platform to launch attacks on an enterprise.

5   Definitions

API – stands for Application Programming Interface. It is an intermediate layer that enables software applications to talk to other applications, systems, and users.

ELF – stands for Executable and Linkable Format. It is the standard executable binary file format for Unix and Unix-like systems (e.g., Linux) on the x86 family of micro-processors.

DLP – stands for Data Loss Prevention. It is a technology that prevents the unauthorized access to or exfiltration of company and customer sensitive data.

NGAV – stands for next generation Anti-Virus. It is the AV engine with modern ML-enabled AI algorithms to perform behavioral threat detection and remediation and malware sandboxing in conjunction with legacy techniques like malware (static hash based) signatures.

EDR – stands for Endpoint Detection and Response. EDR is the next generation malware detection system. Rather than relying on the legacy static signature provided by/generated by legacy AV detection products, it has the capability to provide visibility into endpoint user, machine and process behavior, and perform dynamic heuristic analysis, which it then uses to detect and block advanced malware.

References

1. Loewen C, Coulter D, et al (2020) Windows subsystem for Linux documentation. https://docs. microsoft.com/en-us/windows/wsl. Accessed 24 Nov 2020
2. Baumann A, Lorch J, et al (2011) Drawbridge: the picoprocess. https://www.microsoft.com/ en-us/research/project/drawbridge
3. Judge N (2016) Pico Process Overview. https://docs.microsoft.com/en-us/archive/blogs/wsl/ pico-process-overview
4. Tung L (2017) Windows 10's subsystem for Linux: here's how hackers could use it to hide malware. Available via ZDNet. https://www.zdnet.com/article/windows-10s-subsystem-for-linux-heres-how-hackers-could-use-it-to-hide-malware/ Accessed 24 Nov 2020

Common Sense Security Measures for Voice-Activated Assistant Devices

1 Introduction

The use of voice-activated assistant devices such as Google Home and Alexa on Amazon Echo and Amazon Dot has skyrocketed in the last couple of years. Having a voice assisted device can be fun and useful. It can tell you the weather, play your favorite music or offer you a music subscription, or remind you about regular orders of home goods. The fledgling Natural Language Processing (NLP) and artificial intelligence in these devices is intriguing to the user. In spite of the "wow" factor for the consumer, the real power of the voice-activated device is in its forthcoming ability to listen to and interpret your conversation(s), or eventually read your email or your text messages, independently making intelligent decisions and taking actions on matters that you did not specifically ask it to perform. While this issue touches on unsupervised machine learning, let's focus back on making sure that when we use these devices, we use them securely and take some common-sense measures to protect our privacy.

Like any other information technology asset or endpoint, these devices are prone to weaknesses and vulnerabilities. They must be patched on a frequent basis just like you patch your iPhone or your browser. Without whipping out the Wayback Machine, let's quickly talk about couple of security issues that two of the most popular platforms for these devices have encountered in the last 12–24 months.

2 Recent Issues

Let's talk about 'Google Home' for a minute:

Without getting into too much detail, in the fall of 2018, security researchers discovered an open and undocumented API in Google Home that was easily exploitable:

© The Author(s), under exclusive license to Springer Nature Switzerland AG 2021
R. Badhwar, *The CISO's Next Frontier*,
https://doi.org/10.1007/978-3-030-75354-2_31

they were able to use simple curl commands to reboot the device remotely, fetch all the device configurations or brick the device by deleting all its configurations.

Anyone intending to exploit Google Home had to be on the same network as the device to do so. As far as I know, those exploits or undocumented features have not yet been resolved or fixed (as of the summer of 2020) by Google – the Android team responded on their behalf, stating that they did not consider it to be an issue, as the API could only be accessed while on the same network. In other words, if someone is able to get on a person's private network (i.e., on their WIFI) then that someone can monkey with their Google Home appliance – do you see a problem with that? The average Google Home user should know that some weaknesses do exist. It is recommended that they do not take these devices and plug them into public networks, nor should they take them to a hotel, a coffee shop, a library, or an airport, or a have an open unprotected WIFI network at home.

Now let's talk about **Amazon Alexa** for another minute:

In the Spring of 2018, security researchers were able to hack Alexa so that it could be remotely activated to stealthily record every conversation it heard in its vicinity, without the knowledge of the owner. There have also been documented instances where Alexa erroneously sent recordings of people to the users who were not the owners of that data (basically, an application bug with a security and privacy implication). Thankfully, both these vulnerabilities were subsequently fixed and resolved, but there is always the potential for more vulnerabilities and weaknesses. There have also been reports in the media that folks at Amazon have access to private user recordings for various training and learning type use-cases – Are you cool with them listening to recordings of your commands and queries – essentially your private data – without your explicit permission?

The intent here is not to bash Google or Amazon, rather is an attempt to highlight security risk that may lurking in some of these devices, something that the consumers should be aware of so that they can take some risk mitigation steps. I think both Google and Amazon are generally very prompt in releasing security patches for vulnerabilities discovered in their platforms.

3 Security Hygiene

I don't want to discourage the use of these devices and if you must use them, then please try to follow these basic security hygiene guidelines:

(a) **Security First** – The Dyn distributed denial of service (DDoS) attack in October of 2016 that took out the internet for a large swath of users in North America and Europe highlighted the risk of comprised internet of things (IOT) systems. Devices and technologies like Alexa and Google Home are very much IOT devices, and must be treated with care, as they are always connected to the internet. If you must use them, then you must ensure that they are always current on their firmware and security patches. The devices can be configured to auto update (like your iPhone or Chrome), but you must enable that capability. Also, since these devices are managed through your Amazon or Google accounts, you must ensure that those account credentials are strong and are properly protected with multi-factor authentication (MFA).

(b) **Mute your device** – if you're not using your Echo or Google Home device, then I recommend that you "mute" it, so that it won't be listening (and thus recording) what you or your family members are saying anymore.

(c) **Account Management** – Be careful which account is connected to your device. I know some of us want these assistants to be artificially intelligent and very soon they will be and will have the capability to order things for you and/or your family based on what it may "hear" and subsequently interpret. Maybe you want this, but if you don't, then you should ensure that you put some restrictions on the amount of money that can be charged to the credit card associated with your account. You must also do this to protect yourself from unauthorized or unintentional purchases.

(d) **Be mindful of your Privacy** – You should know by now that companies like Google, Amazon, and Microsoft (with Cortana) have the capability to collect, store, and mine your data to be used for advertisement and other marketing purposes, among other things. While data mining can be used to bolster your user experience, it can potentially also be shared with other third parties (remember Cambridge Analytica?). If you are not okay with this mining and sharing of your data, then you must be vigilant and take action. Be very careful of what you record on these platforms and how long this recorded data resides there. Frequently visit your recordings and delete those you no longer need.

4   Security Requirements

These are the requirements to achieve a reasonable level of security for home voice assisted devices:

4.1   *Biometric Authentication*

The capability must exist for the voice-enabled assistant devices to perform biometric authentication for a primary user and only perform action once the user has been authenticated.

(a) Each device must create a device or machine identity.

(b) Each device must identify and register a primary user and associated that user with the machine identity.

(c) As part of the registration process, the device must create a biometric profile for the user, which must include voice-based biometric authentication, with a (pin-based) backup authentication capability.

(d) Other secondary users can also be registered to the device (each with their own voice biometric profiles), but they must not have the capability to perform other financial transactions. They should be able to ask Alexa or Siri to play music for them, or give them a weather forecast on-demand, or perform other non-financial transactions.

(e) Each primary user must be (voice) authenticated before any transaction is performed. This is required for security purposes to ensure that an authorized user is performing the said transaction. This can also come in handy for auditing purposes.

(f) The authentication token granted to the device once a primary user has authenticated, must be short lived (say 2 h), after which it must expire and re-authentication must be required for refresh tokens.

(g) The device must be geo-aware and must force another reauthentication event if the device is removed to another location or its source IP address changes.

4.2 Data Security

(a) All structured and unstructured data transmitted, collected or stored by these devices and its backend infrastructure services must be encrypted using NIST-approved cryptographic schemes.

(b) All PI data must be deidentified using one-way hashing mechanisms.

4.3 API Security

(a) The public API calls enabled for the web services (Restful or otherwise) exposed by these voice-enabled assistant devices must be authenticated.

(b) All the API calls must be configured to use a secure protocol (e.g., HTTPS or TLS).

(c) If API keys are used then they must enable HMAC authentication.

(d) Other authentication tokens (e.g., OAuth) used for APIs must either be single use or short lived. An OAuth refresh token's life should be context based, ranging from 2 to 24 h.

4.4   *Right to Privacy*

(a) Any user data collected must comply with privacy regulations like GDPR, CCPA or CPRA, especially around the use of 'sensitive' personal information of users.
(b) Have the capability to limit the use and disclosure of sensitive PI
(c) Have the capability to implement consumer opt-out rights for data mining and for cross-contextual advertising.

5   The CISO Take

Personally, I am a big fan of Google, Amazon, and Microsoft due to the good work they are doing in the AI, ML, and NLP space. Given the fierce competition in the home device segment, most of the product vendors are doing their (product and services) releases using a minimum viable product (MVP) approach and sometimes the security features and capabilities seem to lag behind the product features in the initial releases, leading to security weaknesses and vulnerabilities.

I wouldn't be alone in requesting that product vendors and companies do a lot more due diligence in securing their products from the get go – they should perform thorough penetration testing on their products and devices before they release them and then subsequently test on a periodic basis. Any publicly exposed API must be properly protected. User data and privacy is paramount. Even governments are now stepping in with regulations such as GDPR, NYDFS, and CCPA/CPRA to protect user data and privacy. Companies should go above and beyond to protect this data to establish and maintain the trust of their users and consumers.

6   Definitions

DDoS – stands for distributed denial of Service (attack). It is generally used to bring down critical perimeter security apparatus and other internet-facing high-risk applications, by using a flood of (generally TCP or UDP) traffic.
CCPA – stands for The California Consumer Privacy Act. It is a California state regulation on consumer protection and privacy rights for California residents.
CPRA – stands for California Privacy Rights Act. It will amend and supersede CCPA once it goes in effect on Jan 1st, 2023. It expands consumer privacy rights to align more closely with GDPR.
GDPR – stands for General Data Protection Regulation. It is an EU regulation on data protection and privacy requirements for EU residents.
HMAC (authentication) – stands for Hash-based message authentication code. It is crypto hash function used to verify the authenticity of a message.

IOT – stands for internet of things. It is used to describe a system where ubiquitous sensors and smart devices are continuously connected to the internet.

MFA – stands for multi factor authentication. It is an authentication technique used to grant access to a restricted resource (application, system, website, device etc.) only after the user requesting the access has successfully presented two or more factors of information asserting possession (what a user has) and inherence (who a user is) to an authenticator.

NIST – stands for National Institute of Standards and Technology. It is a non-regulatory US entity with the mission to promote innovation and industrial competitiveness.

NLP – stands for Natural language processing. It is the branch of artificial intelligence that enables a computer to read, understand, and converse in (some) human languages.

Further Reading

Gambin J (2018) Google Home (in)Security. https://jerrygamblin.com/2018/10/29/google-home-insecurity/. Accessed 26 Nov 2020

Gatlan S (2018) Google home hub controllable via undocumented API, no authentication needed. Available via Softpedia News. https://news.softpedia.com/news/google-home-hub-controllable-via-undocumented-api-no-authentication-needed-523513.shtml, Accessed 26 Nov 2020

Joint Task force (2020). NIST Special Publication 800–53 Revision 5 Security and Privacy Controls for Information Systems and Organizations. https://nvlpubs.nist.gov/nistpubs/SpecialPublications/NIST.SP.800-53r5.pdf

Lam B (2020) California Privacy Rights Act passes – dramatically altering the CCPA. Available via The National Law Review. https://www.natlawreview.com/article/california-privacy-rights-act-passes-dramatically-altering-ccpa. Accessed 27 Nov 2020

Murnane K (2018) Amazon's Alexa hacked to surreptitiously record everything it hears. Available via Forbes. https://www.forbes.com/sites/kevinmurnane/2018/04/25/amazons-alexa-hacked-to-surreptitiously-record-everything-it-hears Accessed 26 Nov 2020

Nichols S (2018) Secret API leaves door open for remote commands from other gadgets sharing its Wi-Fi. Available via The Register https://www.theregister.com/2018/10/31/google_home_api/. Accessed 26 Nov 2020

Schwartz EH (2020) Amazon quietly patched an Alexa hacking vulnerability discovered by cyber-security researchers in June. https://voicebot.ai/2020/08/13/amazon-patched-an-alexa-hacking-vulnerability-discovered-by-cybersecurity-researchers-in-june/ Accessed 26 Nov 2020

Vibhu R (2019) Google home Local API https://rithvikvibhu.github.io/GHLocalApi/

The Case for Code Signing and Dynamic White-Listing

1 Genesis

Whether it is open-source software (OSS), commercial off the shelf software (COTS) or even home grown, one of the concerns that is often raised by security minded IT professionals is, "Has this software been tampered with, can it be trusted and/or it is authorized to execute in my environment?" The same can also be asked of any executable or document downloaded from internet.

Gone are the days of the closed system environments when software was developed by specialists for a controlled environment and systems generally used a proprietary CPU architecture and OS (e.g., IBM MVS). In my experience, there is a clear trade-off between ease of use of a universal programming language and system security. After having learned C (programming language) in engineering college and writing code using C for an internship, I had a very different first-hand experience of how difficult it was to program a closed system when I wrote some assembly code for IBM ES/390 (combined with PL/1) for a project almost 25 years ago. I had to get specialized training to understand its register architecture and commands. While the probability of unauthorized personnel tampering with the closed system was very low, the challenge of learning specialized code for every new project was an onerous, inefficient, and cost-heavy task. The software engineer potentially faced the Sisyphean task of becoming fluent in multiple languages for a business model designed like the tower of Babel. This limited engineering careers to specific types of projects. Companies were constantly saddled with a shortage of trained engineers, having to reinvest in training every time they hired a programmer.

As engineering students in the early 1990s, we were all taught x86 family (8085, 8086, 8088, 80,186, 80,286, 80,386 etc.) assembly language, due to its open system architecture – When we became C programmers, we could rely on C-language to create firmware. This programming language is still so relevant in writing device drivers and other low-level code which interacts with the underlying hardware.

With the advent of open systems, internet and the cloud, thousands of companies and millions of developers around the world write software to standardized hardware and software specifications. The open systems model has been a run-away success and has led to the downfall of the IBM closed systems model. It has also given rise to threat actors that can masquerade as "friendlies" while writing malicious code to the same open specifications that can bring tremendous harm to an application, endpoint, server or system.

And then there is our good friend – the web browser (used by ISPs like AOL (my former employer) to bring the internet to the masses). In the 90's, web browsers only served static code, mostly html. Now browsers have pages that involve the dynamic generation of presentation layer code and browser resident (JS) or downloadable web components, such as web plugins and extensions, that (technically) execute locally on the browser and hence, the user's computer. The modern web app can have thousands of lines of (JS) code and makes direct calls (restful and otherwise) to back-end data components, creating nightmare scenarios for security technologists.

In the beginning, there was no way to verify if the plugin or extension code downloaded from the internet running in the browser had been tampered with, either at source or while in transit. To address this opacity, security technologists created a standardized approach called code signing to ensure the CIA (confidentiality, Integrity and authenticity) of any source or executable that runs on workstations or servers. This use of certificate-based Digital Signatures to sign code, executables, scripts and binary files theoretically verifies that the executable is from a reputable and trusted source, and that nothing has tampered with the executable either at source or in transit.

2   Code Signing Basics

A code signing cert provides the capability to sign source code, a binary (executable) or a script with the signing certificate acting as a digital signature. A digital signature is a string of bits that is computed from some data (the data being signed) and the private key of an entity (a person, company, and so on). Upon a request for a signing certificate, a private and public key pair is generated using Public Key Infrastructure (PKI). The private key is retained (generally within an HSM) and the public key is provided with the request for the certificate. Once the provider creates the certificate, then- the act of signing source code will also include the digital signature* along with the (signed) data.

* Similar to a handwritten signature, a digital signature has many useful characteristics:

(a) Its authenticity can be verified by a computation that uses the public key corresponding to the private key used to generate the signature.
(b) It can't be forged, assuming the private key is kept secret.

(c) It is a function of the data signed and thus can't be claimed to be the signature for other data as well.

(d) The signed data can't be changed. If the data is changed, then the signature can't be verified as authentic.

The generated certificate contains information about the signing entity – it is issued by generally an external (but sometimes internal, aka self-signing) certificate authority (CA) after that authority has verified the signing entity's identity. When a code signer signs code with its private key, the code verifier can use the signer's public key to verify its identity.

For the code signing certificate to be trusted it must be signed by a trusted CA (e.g., AOL, DigiCert, Verisign or GoDaddy) authorized to issue certificates. The signing certificates can be verified by following the chain path to the trusted CA. If there is no direct chain, but a certificate is signed by an entity validated by the same CA, this invokes the concept of trusting the executable by proxy.

A verified code or script does *not* guarantee that it can be trusted, but rather that it was indeed signed by the specific entity. An attacker can still get the code signing certificate and sign malware. Therefore, a hardware security module (HSM) must be used to guard the private key. The inability to guard the private key has led to many third party and supply chain attacks.

3 How Does Code Signing Work?

The process of signing of a piece of code, binary or script, follows these steps:

(a) The developer requests a code signing certificate from an authorized code signing certificate authority.

(b) Generally, this CA is internal and a code signing certificate already exists.

(c) But if one does not exist or if there is a specific need to get a certificate from a publicly trusted external source, then once the CA verifies the requester's identity, a code signing certificate is generated and provided to the developer who requested it.

(d) The developer then generates a one-way hash of the software, uses the private key to encrypt this hash, and then bundles the hash and certificate with the executable being signed.

A user receives the signed code and can verify the code by

1. Using the public key in the cert to decrypt the hash
2. Create a new hash of the signed script or code
3. Compare the two hashes and if they match then the user can confirm that the source has not been tampered with since it was signed. This comparison can be done programmatically or by the browser working in conjunction with the OS depending on the usage paradigm.

4   The Future State

Now that we have covered the basics, we can now talk about some future state paradigms. For security technologists to be able to defeat supply chain attacks or malicious unauthorized code, we have to be able to do the same as the micro level so that the authenticity of every executable at runtime (including but not limited to every class that gets loaded in the Java virtual Machine (JVM) or every DLL that executes in the OS), binary and script is verified – both in the browser (client side) or on the backend (server side).

4.1   Continuous Runtime Verification

Dynamic verification of executables loaded in the system memory of the application server for a given application can be conducted in a repeatable (or continuous) basis to compare against known malicious indicators of compromise (IOCs) or signatures (hashes) to highlight items that may be loaded that may not have been caught during application compile time verification.

4.2   Dynamic Class-Loading

Dynamic classloaders can be used in the Java/J2EE world to check the validity of the certificate that signed a given class within a jar file and/or verify that the integrity of the class has not been tampered with before loading the class into the JVM.

A similar construct can be done by windows or other operating systems to verify the integrity of a given DLL on windows or a executable (.a or .so) file in Linux.

4.3   Dynamic White-Listing

The static white listing schemes have worked well in the past. These have primarily relied upon two primary techniques –

(a) Maintaining a white-list of trusted applications and binaries in static configuration files
(b) Using the trust model build upon the signing of applications by trusted partners – i.e., if an application is signed by Microsoft then it must be safe to deploy.

These schemes have worked well but are increasingly being defeated because of –

1. the stealing of the private keys of the code signing certificates by threat actors and subsequently using the same to sign malicious code.

2. The static configuration based white-listing approach is difficult to manage and maintain for hundreds of thousands of applications.
3. the microservices induced application and product development has introduced thousands of (small) product and content creators that are not part of the tradition trust model.
4. The modern white-listing has to be performed at a process level and not at an application level due to multi-process product design and architectures.

The solution is to use dynamic white-listing. It uses a combination of capabilities including but not limited to cloud hosted indicators of compromise to create whitelists, peer-to-peer whitelists and reputation scoring along-with the traditional concepts of application signing augmented by certificate transparency (also see Sect. 3.2 in chapter "The Next Frontier for CA/Certificate Security – DANE and Certificate Transparency"), to deliver a near real-time dynamic white list capability.

5 The CISO Take

Given the advanced threats, man-in-the-middle attacks, and other forms of sophisticated attacks that challenge the security and integrity of the data being transmitted, the CISOs have to ensure that all source code, internally and externally sourced libraries and binaries, feature/functionality updates and security updates, are all signed digitally by appropriate digital certificates, wherever practical and feasible.

They must also ensure that capability exists to implement dynamic whitelisting and continuous runtime (memory) verification to eliminate cyber risk from third party applications and systems.

6 Definitions

CA – stands for certificate authority. Is an entity that issues digital certificates.
DLL – stands for dynamic link library. It is a shared library or executable for windows operating system. It supports modern concepts like runtime linking and class loading, and delayed (library) loading.
HSM – stands for hardware security module. It is a physical or virtual computing device whose primary function is to provide secure storage and management of cryptographic keys and other critical security parameters (CSP).
JVM – stands for java virtual machine. It is a part of the java runtime environment (JRE) and provides the runtime environment for java applications.
MVS – stands for Multiple Virtual Storage. It is/was the operating system on the IBM S/370 and S/390 mainframe computing systems.

Further Reading

Digicert. Signing Java.jar Files with Jarsigner. https://www.digicert.com/code-signing/java-code-signing-guide.htm#jarsigner

Gong L (1998). Secure Java Class Loading. https://pdfs.semanticscholar.org/8e86/5e9eab571f9 5b06f318593c51aea568060ac.pdf accessed 28 Nov 2020.

Korolov M (2017). With new dynamic capabilities, will whitelisting finally catch on? https://www.csoonline.com/article/3198749/with-new-dynamic-capabilities-will-whitelisting-finally-catch-on.html accessed 28 Nov, 2020.

Oracle. Signing Code and Granting It Permissions. https://docs.oracle.com/javase/tutorial/security/toolsign/

Biometrics – Commentary on Data Breach Notification, Threats, and Data Security

1 Genesis

All of you that follow the California Consumer Privacy Act (CCPA[1]) must be aware that there were amendments signed by the California governor in October of 2019, with multiple amendments on the privacy act itself [1]:

(a) AB 25 and AB 1355 on Employee and B2B Exemption
(b) AB 1355 on Clarification of Right to Access
(c) AB 874 on Publicly available information
(d) AB 1146 on Vehicle warranties and recalls
(e) AB 1564 – method of Access/Deletion Requests.

1.1 Data Breach Notification for Biometric Data –

In addition to the CCPA amendments, the governor signed the following **two privacy-related bills** into law that have **cyber security implications**:

(a) AB 1202 regarding Data Broker Registration
(b) AB 1130 on Data breach notification.

The data breach notification is a legal and compliance issue but is also very much a **cybersecurity issue**. Security technologists have to understand any security implications from this new amendment.

I am taking this opportunity not only to talk about the impacts of data breach notification expansion for any unauthorized exposure or breach of biometric data

---

[1] Since the writing of this chapter, CA has passed a new law called CPRA which expands consumer privacy rights to align more closely with GDPR.

© The Author(s), under exclusive license to Springer Nature Switzerland AG 2021
R. Badhwar, *The CISO's Next Frontier*,
https://doi.org/10.1007/978-3-030-75354-2_33

that a California business entity may store, but also to provide an introductory level security briefing about biometrics, the protection paradigms, and some known attacks.

Specifically, this amendment provides instructions on how to notify other entities using the same type of biometric data as an authenticator, to cease relying on such data for authentication purposes. It expands upon the types of data breaches requiring notification, to include unauthorized access, exfiltration, theft or disclosure of unique biometric data generated from measurements or technical analysis of human body characteristics, such as a **fingerprint, retina, or iris image**, used to authenticate a specific individual. Unique biometric data does not include a physical or digital photograph, unless used or stored for facial recognition purposes.

2   Biometrics

Let me give you a quick refresher on biometrics:

Biometric technology provides the capability to measure and perform statistical analysis on the physical and behavioral traits of individuals. Primarily used in biometric authenticators to perform identification, authentication and access management, it reliably, uniquely, and accurately can identify individuals. Generally, a biometric is recognized as a factor (e.g., 2FA), but not recognized as an authenticator by itself. Therefore, when conducting authentication with a biometric, it is unnecessary to use two authenticators because the associated device serves as "something you have," while the biometric serves as "something you are."

A biometric authentication system generally includes:

(a) A biometric reader or scanner to register and record the biometric factor (e.g., fingerprint, retina, face-id) being used for authentication.
(b) A client or server-based application or software to convert the scanned biometric data into a biometric template (e.g., ISO/IEC 19794), which can then subsequently be used for authentication (read and compare) purposes.
(c) A data repository securely storing the biometric data to compare for authentication purposes.
(d) Locally gathered biometric data gathered to perform crypto-graphical hashing to perform authentication or identification,
(e) The biometric systems of the past a decade or so ago stored the *raw* biometric data (e.g., fingerprint images) of all the enrolled users. The modern-day best practice is to convert the raw biometric data into biometric templates (prescribed by ISO/IEC 19794) to provide standardization of use against multiple hardware and firmware providers while only using only a fraction of storage as compared to the raw data. Additionally, the usage of biometric templates avoids

the privacy and security concerns that stem from storing and using the raw data, and the potential for that data to be stolen or compromised.

2.1   ISO/IEC 19794 Template Standard

ISO/IEC 19794 is an international biometric template standard that was created in order to achieve inter-operability between different biometric recognition systems like fingerprint readers, retina scanners, and face-id readers. In other words, it allows biometric templates generated by different vendors to be used in the same system for biometric enrollment and matching.

Some of the associated sub standards are:

(a) ISO/IEC 19794-2:2011 – Finger minutiae data
(b) ISO/IEC 19794-4:2011 – Finger image data
(c) ISO/IEC 19794-5:2011 – Face Image Data
(d) ISO/IEC 19794-6:2011 – Iris (Retina) image data

3   Biometric Template Protection Paradigms

Protection for biometric templates is generally done using two basic techniques: Feature Transformation (FT) and Encryption.

3.1   Feature Transformation

FT = Fn (T, password) – There are two sub techniques, a reversible and a non-reversible transform. In a reversible transform the original biometric template can be obtained, and in a non-reversible transform (just like a one-way hash) the original template cannot be transformed back.

(a) **Bio-hashing** is a form of a reversible transform where the biometric template (T) is transformed using a *password* or a key. It is imperative that this password or key is stored and handled securely for obvious reasons.
(b) **Cancellable biometrics** is a non-reversible transformation. It provides inherent protection against data breaches and compromises and allows for the capability to cancel and re-issue the transformed template by changing transformation parameters.

3.2   Biometric Cryptosystems

The feature transformation techniques are susceptible to password stealing and basic dictionary attacks. The biometric cryptosystems were designed to provide inherent protection against these weaknesses and attacks, and primarily use three basic sub techniques: Key Generation, Key Binding and other new paradigms to account for recent advancements in cryptography.

Key Generation In this scheme, a key is generally generated from the biometric template data itself. There are five known ways of doing this:

(a) **Fuzzy Extractor**, which extracts a linear (encryption and decryption) key from a biometric template, even if a different template is used for the same physical trait (e.g., finger).
(b) **Secure Sketch**, which creates meta-data about the input without disclosing the input itself. This meta-data can then be used to recreate the biometric template.
(c) **Key Binding**: In this scheme, a secret key and a biometric template are bound using a cryptosystem such that it is mathematically infeasible to decode the key or the template. There are two known ways of doing this:
(d) **Fuzzy Vault**, designed primarily to solve the issue around secure key management, using a randomly generated fuzzy meta-data set (instead of a key) to encrypt and decrypt biometric template data.
(e) **Fuzzy Commitment,** which is similar to a fuzzy vault, but with fuzzy meta-data sets represented in the form of binary vectors further divided into multiple segments, each of which is separately secured.

Both Fuzzy Vault and Commitment are compute-intensive and mathematically complex.

4   Other Protection Schemes

There are some other protection schemes available for specific use cases and risk tolerance levels.

(a) **Watermarking**: In this the biometric templates use a hidden digital watermark which must be extracted and verified before the biometric authentication occurs.

(b) **Modern Cryptosystems**: Modern crypto approaches like PKI using Elliptic Cryptographic Curve (ECC), and Rivest Shamir and Adelman (RSA) can also be used to protect the biometric templates.

5 Biometric Attacks

Attacks on biometric authenticators and systems are generally classified into two basic categories: (a) the ones arising from inherent weakness in the systems themselves, and (b) the others from target attacks by threat actors.

5.1 Inherent Weakness

(a) **Malfunction** – The scanner could malfunction and allow unauthorized access due to a false positive. Scanners with high failure rates are an easy target for attackers with rinse and repeat attacks.

(b) **Denial of Service (DOS)** – Many scanners are inherently susceptible to denial-of-service attacks. Once a biometric authentication system crashes then it may be bypassed to gain unauthorized access to the resource it was protecting.

(c) **Insider Threat** – Insiders can defeat the system by registering a false identity for a biometric trait of an individual or by committing enrollment fraud.

5.2 Targeted Attacks

(a) **Biometric Template attack** – The attacker can compromise the integrity of the biometric template by either modifying it or deleting it if they gain access to the database where it is stored or sniff it during transit.

(b) **Fake biometric print** – the attacker uses a fake biometric print (e.g., a fingerprint) to trick the biometric access system.

(c) **Key Breach** – The attacker can perform a brute force attack on a weak cryptographic key.

(d) **Key or Password Stealing** – The attacker can steal a key/password for a reversible feature transformation and use it to get the original biometric template.

(e) **Man-in-the-middle attack** – the attacker can intercept the biometric trait (e.g., fingerprint), replacing it with theirs before it gets processed by a backend server, or acquiring a copy of the print, or compromising the biometric processing module to always send a desired response using a Trojan horse.

(f) **Non-secure Infrastructure** – This can manifest itself in various ways, such as storing biometric prints in native format (e.g., as images), instead of following the best practice of converting them into standardized templates; or, storing biometric templates in a database with poor security, where they are a target for database breach.

6   CPRA – Impact Analysis

On November 3rd 2020, another law called CPRA passed in California. This new law will supersede CCPA when it goes into effect on January 1st 2023.

The CPRA has created new sub-categories of "sensitive" personal information, with one of these new categories being –

(a) the *processing of biometric information* to identify the consumer.

This brings regulatory oversight and the need for additional protections to the consumers regarding the use of their biometric data.

There are four points to note regarding CPRA that are also relevant to this conversation–

1. It extends the scope of the private right to action by adding a cause of action for the unauthorized access and exfiltration, theft, or disclosure of an email address in combination with a password or security questions and answers [2].
2. It clarifies that the implementation and maintenance of reasonable security procedures and practices following the breach doesn't constitute a cure [3].
3. It adds a definition of "proofing" which means that 'any form of automated processing' of PII used to "to analyze or predict aspects of a person's preferences, economic situation, work performance, health, interests, behavior, location, reliability, or movements" [2]. *This profiling may apply to biometric data.*
4. It has significant implications of how AI can be used and explained [4].

7   The CISO Take

Biometric authenticators, very reliable and accurate as secondary authenticators, provide the capability for unique identification and authentication. The usage of biometric data has skyrocketed in the past decade and is only bound to grow as the need for multi-factor authentication grows. Biometric data is classified as personally identifiable information (PII) and must be protected just like we protect other forms of sensitive data (e.g., SSN, DOB, and CC data).

The corporate use of biometric has also gone up exponentially. Microsoft has launched 'Windows Hello' thereby making biometric authentication mainstream by enabling it to be used for authentication into workstations and company networks. In the COVID-19 era a lot of biometric data is being collected by temperature scanners or contact tracing devices and applications. There is a lot of other use of biometrics at the workplace, and in various medical and government facilities. All of this biometric data needs to be adequately protected as this is PII and will be subject to regulatory compliance.

To provide protection to users and consumers against unauthorized access and disclosure of their biometric data, various laws have recently been passed by local, state, and federal regulatory entities, and government agencies around the world (CCPA, GDPR and CPRA). While these are generally classified as legal and compliance matters, these are very much cyber security issues as well and it is a CISO's responsibility to pro-actively ensure that this data is properly protected.

8 Definitions

CCPA – stands for the California Consumer Privacy Act. It is a California state regulation on consumer protection and privacy rights for California residents.

CPRA – stands for the California Privacy Rights Act. It will amend and supersede CCPA once it goes in effect on January 1, 2023. It expands consumer privacy rights to align more closely with GDPR.

ECC – stands for elliptic curve cryptography. It is used to build an PKI cryptosystem that relies on the mathematical structure of discontinuous elliptic curves over finite fields.

PII – stands for Personally Identifiable Information. Any representation of information that permits the identity of an individual to whom the information applies to be reasonably inferred by either direct or indirect means. Further, PII is defined as information: (i) that directly identifies an individual (e.g., name, address, social security number or other identifying number or code, telephone number, or email address) or (ii) by which an agency intends to identify specific individuals in conjunction with other data elements, i.e., indirect identification [5].

PKI – stands for public key infrastructure. It is a methodology used to assign or issue digital identities (certificates) to various entities such as users, applications, devices, and systems, for the purpose of subsequently enabling secure, encrypted communication between them.

RSA – stands for Rivest-Shamir-Adelman. It is a PKI cryptosystem that is used to protect and secure sensitive data in transit.

References

1. California Legislative Information (2018) TITLE 1.81.5. California Consumer Privacy Act of 2018 [1798.100 – 1798.199.100]. http://leginfo.legislature.ca.gov/faces/codes_displayText.xht ml?division=3.&part=4.&lawCode=CIV&title=1.81.5.
2. PROPOSITION 24, THE CALIFORNIA PRIVACY RIGHTS ACT OF 2020, https://vig.cdn.sos.ca.gov/2020/general/pdf/topl-prop24.pdf
3. THE CALIFORNIA PRIVACY RIGHTS ACT OF 2020, Amendments to Version 3. https://www.oag.ca.gov/system/files/initiatives/pdfs/19-0021A1%20%28Consumer%20Privacy%20-%20Version%203%29_1.pdf
4. Eversheds Sutherland (US) LLP, California's new privacy law, the CPRA, was approved: Now what? https://www.jdsupra.com/legalnews/california-s-new-privacy-law-the-crpa-93354/
5. US department of Labor (2020). Guidance on the Protection of Personal Identifiable Information. https://www.dol.gov/general/ppii

Further Reading

California Legislative Information (2019) AB1130 personal information: data breaches. https://leginfo.legislature.ca.gov/faces/billTextClient.xhtml?bill_id=201920200AB1130.

FIDO Alliance (2020) Biometric authenticators. https://fidoalliance.org/product-category/biometric-authenticator/

Grother P, et al (2013) Biometric specifications for personal identity verification. NIST SP800-76-2. https://csrc.nist.gov/publications/detail/sp/800-76/2/final

ISO/IEC 19794-5, Information technology — Biometric data interchange formats — Part 5: Face image data, https://webstore.iec.ch/preview/info_isoiec19794-5%7Bed1.0%7Den.pdf

Jain A, Nandakumar K, et al (2008) Biometric Template Security. EURASIP J Advances Signal Processing. https://doi.org/10.1155/2008/579416.

Security Requirements for RPA Bots

1 Introduction

Robotic Process Automation (aka RPA or RPA bots) provides the capability to perform certain high volume, manual, and repeatable tasks that were previously performed by humans in the security industry, such as call center agents or back office personnel. Over the last 5–7 years, big industry players and startups have funneled investment in RPA bot technology, leading to significant improvements. There are generally two types of RPA bots prevalent in the industry at the current time – attended and unattended bots.

While there is no doubt on the value proposition that this technology brings to the industry for multiple use cases (improving productivity, efficiency, agility and customer service), a little more rigor has to be applied to analyze, identify, remediate and/or mitigate any security risks that may have also evolved with its adoption (just like with any other disruptive and emerging technology).

This chapter provides a description of these bots along with high-level security requirements for the two RPA bot types. It also provides a brief vision into the future paradigm for this technology.

2 Attended RPA Bots

Attended RPA bots are generally designed for a user workstation, using the user's persona or identity context. When configured as an (auto) service, such as a windows service or a Linux daemon, or as a startup app which is capable of starting automatically at a system (or workstation) boot event, or start only as a background task, or one that does not exit during a logoff system event. Attended bots generally augment the tasks or activities performed by users and/or agents for many

© The Author(s), under exclusive license to Springer Nature Switzerland AG 2021
R. Badhwar, *The CISO's Next Frontier*,
https://doi.org/10.1007/978-3-030-75354-2_34

call-center or other front or back office use cases across many industries, such as finance, healthcare, defense, and education.

2.1   High Level Security Requirements

Attended RPA bots can be exploited if the system they are running on is in an auto mode and is compromised or breached by malicious entities. There is also the situation where someone else takes over the workstation while the true owner is either away or inadvertently shares their credentials with another user (behavior sometimes observed in call centers).

(a) It is thus imperative that all the attended RPA bots be configured as an on-demand service started manually, or installed as an application started manually by the user(s). In either case, separate unique credentials must be established and used for the attended bot. The typical credential management standards should apply. Multi-factor authentication (MFA) implementation and integration would greatly lower the risk from unauthorized usage and breaches.

(b) All attended RPA bots must undergo security (code) scanning and architecture evaluation.

(c) All attended RPA bots must follow proper testing and change control paradigms, including security and change advisory board (CAB) approvals.

(d) All attended RPA bots must comply with security logging and monitoring requirements to enable incident response capabilities.

(e) Attended RPA bots must only operate while on the company (or private) network (i.e., while they are domain joined). They must not connect to the internet and capability must be implemented at the user workstation level and within the outbound proxies to prevent such connections from occurring.

(f) All communications between the RPA bot and its primary (controller or orchestrator) must be encrypted.

(g) The master (controller or orchestrator) must follow an implementation guided by the principles of Zero Trust architecture and least privilege.

(h) The RPA attended bots must be hardened so that they are resistant to dynamic (malicious) code injection into the service. Additionally, they must be subjected to a penetration test to detect and mitigate other vulnerabilities and exploits.

(i) A kill switch capability must be established or implemented as a safeguard measure.

3   Unattended RPA Bots

Unattended RPA bots are designed to work on tasks and interact with applications generally without any human engagement, intervention or involvement with capability to handle any runtime issues and errors.

These bots are generally architected to have one primary server and one or many secondary clients or nodes.

These bots are generally scheduled to execute tasks or can be triggered by configured events. For example, unattended RPA bots can be used to remediate file/folder permissions users on file-shares by removing access for users that are either no longer employees or no longer have permission to access a file/folder within a directory structure.

Although somewhat uncommon, attended and unattended bots can work together in certain use cases. For example, customer service reps can rely on attended bots that enter data into a form and then submit that to an unattended bot to perform back office data processing and verification on the input data.

3.1   High Level Security Requirements

(a) The credentials used by unattended RPA bots (clients) must be properly protected. They should not be hard-coded in some configuration file, but could instead be fetched from a LDAP configuration repository or relational database. If creds must be stored in a local file then they must be encrypted.

(b) All administrative and root accounts for the RPA admin servers must be vaulted in a privileged access management (PAM) system.

(c) All unattended RPA bots (clients) must ideally have certificate-based machine identities (preferably issued by an internal CA) established for them that they must use to authenticate to the RPA server.

(d) Any unattended bot nodes or clients exposed to the internet must be hardened, reside in a micro segmented network segregated from other DMZ segments, and use a reverse proxy with MFA enabled.

(e) All communications between the primary and its secondary nodes must be encrypted.

(f) All vulnerabilities in unattended bots must be promptly patched.

(g) All unattended bot code must be scanned for vulnerabilities and weaknesses using static and dynamic code analysis techniques.

(h) Any access privileges or entitlements provided to unattended bots must apply the concept of least privilege.

(i) All unattended bots must have transaction-level logging enabled for transaction auditing purposes.

4 RPA 2.0 – Augmented by NLP and AI

The integration of Natural Language Processing (NLP) with RPA was the first step in making the RPA bots autonomous and enabling use cases like self-service through speech recognition of human communications and semantic analysis.

The second step came with the usage of reinforcement learning (RL) – a Q-learning algorithm which uses the shortest path for a given number of options to arrive at a reward (or conclusion).

The current effort to fully automate RPA is referred to as RPAAI and utilizes Deep learning models a combination of multi-step supervised and unsupervised ML and AI algorithms to enable the capability of task automation without any human intervention whatsoever.

5 The CISO Take

While RPA has helped reduced IT and operational costs by providing agility, speed, and performance enhancements, it is brittle and still needs quite a bit of human intervention to solve complex use cases. This has highlighted to need to adopt the next generational AI based to improve and enhance the current state RPA paradigm.

RPA is also susceptible to vulnerabilities and various security threats and any existing and future RPA implementations need to comply with the security requirements that have been detailed in this chapter.

The implementation of the security requirements becomes even more critical with the incorporation of unsupervised machine learning paradigms.

While IT teams adopt RPA to reduce operational and labor costs, CISOs must have their security teams properly review their company's RPA adoption to ensure compliance with the principle of Zero Trust with least privilege. (See chapter "Cybersecurity Enabled by Zero Trust" for more details on Zero Trust)

6 Definitions

Bot – is a short form for robot. It has the capability to perform certain high volume, manual, and repeatable tasks that were previously performed by humans. Bot perform these tasks much faster than humans.

DMZ – is a "demilitarized zone", when used in the cyber security context it denotes a restricted subnet between the intranet and the internet, generally used to host the external facing sites and services.

LDAP – stands for Lightweight directory access protocol. It is an open and cross platform client/server protocol for interacting with X.500 based directory services (e.g., Active Directory) over a TCP/IP network.

NLP – stands for natural language processing. It is the branch of artificial intelligence that enables a computer to read, understand, and speak human languages.

Q-Learning – stands for quality learning (algorithm). It is a reinforcement learning algorithm. Rather than using an existing policy, it seeks to 'learn' a policy that enables it to take the best possible action or get the best reward.

Zero Trust – is a security architecture and implementation paradigm that reduces enterprise risk by performing secure implementations in compliance with the principal that all assets inside and outside a perimeter firewall are not to be trusted and thus access control for users, devices, systems and services must be provided using least privilege.

Further Reading

Blier N (2019) Text analytics & nlp in robotic process automation https://www.lexalytics.com/lexablog/text-analytics-nlp-rpa-use-cases Accessed 8 Dec 2020

Boulton C (2018) What is RPA? A revolution in business process automation. Available via CIO Digital magazine. https://www.cio.com/article/3236451/what-is-rpa-robotic-process-automation-explained.html. Accessed 8 Dec 2020

Brain D (2016) RPA technical insights, part 3: assisted or unassisted robotic process automation: how to choose the right delivery model for your project. https://blog.symphonyhq.com/rpa-technical-insights-part-3-assisted-or-unassisted-robotic-process-automation-how-to-choose-the-right-delivery-model-for-your-project Accessed 8 Dec 2020

What is RPA. https://www.nice.com/rpa/rpa-guide/, Accessed 8 Dec 2020

Polymorphic and Metamorphic Malware

1 Introduction

With the improvement in malware detection capabilities by the introduction of Next Generation Anti-Virus (NGAV) and Endpoint Detection and Response (EDR), and User and Entity Behavior Analysis (UEBA), malware creators have fought back by developing a new generation of advanced malware to avoid detection.

This chapter discusses some of the advanced malware classes including but not limited to polymorphic and metamorphic malware, and provides some ways of detecting and blocking them.

2 Advanced Malware

Apart from Ransomware (which has been discussed in chapter "The Advanced Malware Prevention Playbook" the advanced malware prevention playbook, in this book), the two other forms of advanced malware that the security technologist really needs to be concerned about are metamorphic and polymorphic malware, due to their inherent ability to change their 'code' as they propagate.

Most advanced malware is either interpreted or hybrid (i.e., uses pre-compilation and interpretation).

Before we go another step further, let's quickly understand the difference between a compiler and an interpreter.

When a compiler 'compiles' a program written in a supported language, it produces an executable that has the instructions of the target machine and thus will only execute or run on a specific operating system with a specific target architecture. This makes the executable perform much better but has the disadvantage of needing to

© The Author(s), under exclusive license to Springer Nature Switzerland AG 2021
R. Badhwar, *The CISO's Next Frontier*,
https://doi.org/10.1007/978-3-030-75354-2_35

compile it again for another targeted machine or architecture (e.g., a C program compiled for an Intel CPU will not run on Apple M1 and vice-versa).

Using a slightly different approach, instead of compiling a program towards a target machine, an intermediate layer called the interpreter 'interprets' the same program differently on different target machines based on its knowledge of the language of the native machine and its architecture. In this case, a program does not directly run on the target machine, but is interpreted instead, giving it the theoretical capability to run on different target architecture and machines. Many modern interpreters pre-compile the code to avoid repeating the 'translation' step.

Although interpreted programs do not perform as well as compiled ones, they have the advantages of inter-platform support, easier implementation, and the theoretical capability to execute 'on the fly.'

Java is an advanced modern language that can technically be considered a *hybrid* – i.e., both compiled and interpreted. A java source code file is first compiled (by javac) into byte-code, and this byte-code runs on an interpreter – the Java virtual machine (JVM).

2.1   Metamorphic Malware

Generally, most metamorphic malware is interpreted. This form of malware has the capability to rewrite itself with each runtime iteration or, to be specific, outputs a different version of machine code every time it is interpreted. In spite of the different machine code, the functionality of the program remains the same.

This makes it possible for the malware to evade detection by the traditional (hash) signature-based AV engines. It also makes it capable of infecting binaries on multiple operating systems irrespective of the target system architecture, which also comes in handy for remote code execution (RCE) where the target system platform is generally unknown.

2.2   Polymorphic Malware

Polymorphic malware can be compiled or interpreted, or it can make use of hybrid techniques.

Polymorphic malware uses two primary techniques – mutation and encryption. It has a mutation engine that mutates the malware executable while keeping its functionality intact. It also uses encryption to hide the main body of its code and has an inbuilt decryption engine it uses to decrypt the code before execution. Once executed, the malware is re-encrypted with a different encryption key, thereby changing its signature.

With metamorphism, each iteration of generated machine code is completely different from the previous version. With polymorphism, mutated code still retains some similarities to its code base and thus also relies on encryption to hide part of the code base. (Because polymorphic malware code is not completely rewritten, it is sometimes slightly easier to detect than metamorphic malware.)

3   Advanced Evasion Techniques (AET)

Threat actors use Advanced Evasion Techniques (AET) in the delivery of malware, known or zero-day exploits, and/or for data exfiltration.

AET, which depends on a variety of stealthy methods, use different network protocols and associated techniques (e.g., DNS tunneling) across OSI layers 3–7 to evade detection by the standard perimeter security stack (IPS, NGFW, etc.).

Security researchers recently developed a combination of supervised and unsupervised (deep learning) capabilities to detect AET, by using training data and indicators of compromise from Intrusion Prevention Systems (IPS) and Next Generation Firewalls (NGFW) as input into deep learning unsupervised machine learning algorithms. Additional details are outside the scope of this book but may be provided in a future publication.

4   Advanced Persistent Threat (APT)

It is used to describe a campaign of attacks by persistent sophisticated threat actors whose intent is to gain long term residence or presence on the network of the target. The list of malicious activities includes but are not limited to stealing intellectual property or company sensitive data, sabotaging key network segments or systems, installing and operating back doors to communicate with CnC servers and conducting complete site takeovers. These attacks are complex, targeted, well-resourced and funded, and are generally conducted by nation states or other criminal organizations that are very well funded.

APT generally uses sophisticated malware like polymorphic, metamorphic malware or AET to gain initial residence or presence on the target network.

5   Detection Techniques

The sophistication of these malware requires the use of advanced detection techniques, some of which are discussed below:

5.1 Static Heuristics Analysis

In this technique, the (polymorphic) malware is decompiled and analysis is performed on its source code by comparing it to the source code of known malware. Any code similarities or any pattern matches are flagged as malicious and are subject to further analysis including but not limited to dynamic heuristics analysis.

5.2 Dynamic Heuristics Analysis or Sandboxing

To perform dynamic heuristics analysis, the malware is sandboxed: it is isolated, loaded into a specialized virtual machine, and subjected to various dynamic analysis techniques to observe any suspicious and malicious behavior exhibited by the malware (e.g., self-replication, decryption, code mutation).

Third-generation sandboxes are generally segmented and secure and have been further augmented with machine learning. Where there is a need to analyze a suspicious unknown item, sandboxes now have the capability to scale up or down within minutes when put inline in the middle of synchronous processes such as email.

5.3 Advanced Behavior Analysis

The next-generation antivirus (NGAV) and endpoint detection and response engines have advanced behavior analysis capabilities to detect security anomalies based on malicious user, application, system, or device behavior. By performing statistical analysis with models that create baselines for behavior, these engines can predict threat vectors and associated risks. As they identify deviations from those baselines, they can flag behavioral outliers as anomalies.

These engines can also enrich, correlate, and add context to existing data, alerts and reports, and work with high-speed real-time and persisted (big) data collected from internal and external endpoint, network and other infrastructural entities, and other threat intel data sources and feeds.

Generally, these engines use an entity risk scoring and visualization model that is compatible with the SIEM and/or other security products or threat intel feeds.

5.4 DNS Sinkholing and Kill Switch

It is a technique that helps with the identification of malware infected hosts on a private (or public) network. It enables the redirection of malicious internet bound traffic by changing the flow of a malicious URL by entering a fake entry into a DNS server. This allows to control any CnC bound traffic and other malicious traffic across a private network.

This can be used to build a list of impacted local/global workstations and servers. This can be further used to also deploy a (malware) kill switch.

5.5 Machine Learning

Data from static analysis and dynamic sandboxing is used to train supervised machine learning algorithms to enable faster detection of sophisticated malware that exhibits polymorphic or metamorphic capabilities, without requiring any data seeding or static signatures, human input, analysis, and/or programming. It can further provide automated real-time threat monitoring and reporting with the ability to conduct proactive investigations, search, and filter live and persisted data, correlate alerts, and create incidents.

5.6 Traditional Forensic Examination

Traditional forensic examination can also be conducted by an eDiscovery agent resident on an infected endpoint or server. Modern eDiscovery agents can perform real-time 'memory forensics' (generally done by creating a raw image and/or a crash dump image of system memory) from live processes to analyze suspicious endpoint, application or process behavior. The images are analyzed by raw image analyzers (RIA) and/or crash dump analyzer (CDA). These analyzers further use one of two approaches - a Tree and List traversal or object fingerprint search.

The Tree and List traversal technique emulates data access performed by the process being examined. It can perform a translation of virtual to physical addresses and a traversal of kernel data pointers using memory address pointers. It is fast and gets the needed info from the memory pointers, but can be unstable and miss unlinked (memory) objects.

The Object fingerprint search technique creates signatures of kernel objects and searches data using those signatures. It is relatively slow and noisy, but can find the unlinked (memory) objects.

The forensics examination is an important tool in determining the malware behavior, and can help in the creation of IOCs or other detection and blocking techniques for the same.

6 The CISO Take

CISOs must ensure that the cyber programs they run and manage can detect and block advanced malware APT and AET. This capability should exist at the endpoint, network, and perimeter security stack and works best when data can be correlated across these three domains within the SIEM and generate targeted events (with a minimum number of false positives) that can be used by incident responders within the SOC and also by automated reactive response orchestration wherever possible.

The CISOs should also enable the bi-direction sharing of threat intelligence on malware that they detect in their networks through information sharing entities like FS-ISAC or intel providers like CrowdStrike, Symantec, Microsoft, Mcafee, Proofpoint and Palo alto networks.

7 Definitions

CnC – stands for command and control (server). Generally, a cloud-hosted server/system often working in tandem with the usage of DGA-generated domains, the CnC is used by threat actors to control and manage infected and breached endpoints and servers (generally resident) on private networks.

EDR – stands for Endpoint Detection and Response. EDR is the next-generation malware detection system. Rather than relying on the legacy static signature generated by legacy AV detection products, it has the capability to provide visibility into endpoint user, machine, and process behavior, and perform dynamic heuristical analysis, which it then uses to detect and block advanced malware.

FS-ISAC – stands for Financial Services Information Sharing and Analysis Center. It is a cyber intelligence sharing community solely focused on financial services.

NGAV – stands for Next-Generation Antivirus. It is the AV engine with modern ML-enabled AI algorithms to perform behavioral threat detection and remediation and malware sandboxing in conjunction with legacy techniques like malware (static hash-based) signatures.

NGFW – stands for Next Generation Firewall. It uses third-generation firewall technology with capabilities such as deep packet inspection, network device filtering, application awareness, threat detection, and intrusion prevention.

OSI – stands for Open Systems Interconnection. It is a reference model that establishes a standard for how a given application, system, or device may communicate and interoperate with others over a network. The OSI layer has seven layers – Application (Layer 7), Presentation (Layer 6), Session (Layer 5), Transport (Layer 4), Network (Layer 3), Data-link (Layer 2), and Physical (Layer 1).

SIEM – stands for Security Incident and Event Management (system). It has the capability to aggregate, correlate, and cross reference security (log) data and events from various systems.

UEBA – stands for User and Entity Behavior Analytics. It uses machine learning algorithms to analyze large datasets collected from user endpoints and/or servers to model and create baselines of typical and atypical behaviors of humans and machines within a network.

Further Reading

Advanced persistent threat (APT), https://www.imperva.com/learn/application-security/apt-advanced-persistent-threat/, Accessed 13 Dec 2020

Fortinet (2019) Third-generation sandboxing delivers AI-based breach prevention. https://www.fortinet.com/resources-campaign/home-stream/third-generation-sandboxing-delivers-ai-based-breach-prevention. Accessed 13 Dec 2020

Google (2020). https://github.com/google/sandboxed-api. Accessed 13 Dec 2020

Haruyama T (2013). Windows memory forensic analysis using Encase. https://www.slideshare.net/takahiroharuyama5/takahiro-haruyama-ceic20110515. Accessed 13 Dec 2020

Lim D (2018) Closing the sandbox generation gap. Available via Fortinet Blog. https://www.fortinet.com/blog/business-and-technology/closing-the-sandbox-generation-gap. Accessed 13 Dec 2020

Miao Y (2015) Understanding heuristic-based scanning vs. sandboxing. Available via OPWAT Blog. https://www.opswat.com/blog/understanding-heuristic-based-scanning-vs-sandboxing Accessed 13 Dec 2020

MtE 0.90b, https://github.com/bnjf/mte. Accessed 13 Dec 2020

Prince B (2012) Stonesoft pen testing tool uses advanced evasion techniques, firm says. Available via Securityweek. https://www.securityweek.com/stonesoft-pen-testing-tool-uses-advanced-evasion-techniques-firm-says.

Wong W, Stamp M (2006) Hunting for metamorphic engines. J Comput Virol (2006) 2:211–229. https://doi.org/10.1007/s11416-006-0028-7 Accessed 13 Dec 2020

Part VII
Cloud Security

Introduction to Cloud Monitoring Security Controls

1 Background

While it is true that many companies have successfully migrated a substantial portion of their IT portfolios to the (public) cloud or have even migrated their entire data centers to cloud-hosted data centers–extracting benefits such as lower cost, high availability, disaster recovery, and auto-scaling—it is also true that many companies have faced very serious security issues and data and network breaches either in the process of migrating or operating in a non-secure cloud environment. I am not going to do any name dropping here as I believe that no one is perfect in this space.

We must take this opportunity to learn from others by identifying avoidable mistakes and correcting them going forward to improve the security of the entire cloud eco-system.

2 Introduction

The fundamentals of performing information security on cloud-hosted systems are the same as on-premises systems. What's different is the priority of security controls. Those security controls for on-premises environments are/were pre-built as part of the waterfall application and code delivery models with existing network and perimeter infrastructure security templates and models, and thus are/were (generally) already in place with go-live. However, to gain the full value of the agility and deployment speed of the cloud, sometimes the IT teams within the CIO orgs do not wait for the full security design, implementation, and operationalization of infrastructure security controls, nor do they have the recommended security practices embedded into their dev-ops CI/CD pipelines. Instead, they start pushing code to production in an incremental manner with only minimal ad-hoc or default security

R. Badhwar, *The CISO's Next Frontier*,
https://doi.org/10.1007/978-3-030-75354-2_36

and access management controls in place and assert that they will include better security controls in subsequent releases. While this is not a good practice and has led to multiple security issues in cloud environments, this has also led to the invention and delivery of the 'security monitoring as code' paradigm to keep up with the incremental delivery of application code. This model applies the most to IaaS but can be used for PaaS and SaaS as well.

What I preach and try very hard to practice is that the security controls required to protect a system or application are the same irrespective of the system or application host environment – i.e., whether securing on-premises private DC, Hybrid Cloud or Public Cloud and apply the principle of Zero Trust (discussed in chapter "Cybersecurity Enabled by Zero Trust").

The tools that implement the controls may change, the controls may be implemented more as code rather than as monolithic tools, the licensing model may change, but the controls are very much needed. Please note that taking sensitive applications hosted in cloud environments live without the proper security control design, implementation, and operationalization is akin to sending a welcome message to the threat actors with the front door open.

This chapter lists the key security domains for providing information security to cloud-hosted systems: Perimeter and Network Security, Monitor and Respond, Identity and Access Management (IAM), Threat Intelligence, Asset and Data Protection, Reduction of Threat Surface, and Training and Awareness. However, I will focus primarily on the monitoring controls for reasons explained below.

3   Monitoring: The First and Most Basic Cloud Security Control

One of the most basic yet fundamental controls that need to be implemented for a cloud-hosted system is monitoring. I am sorry to say that even this most basic capability has been found to be missing in many applications and systems hosted in public cloud environments (e.g., AWS and Azure).

Every firm that has IT applications and/or systems in the cloud MUST have a cloud logging and monitoring strategy. This is required for both public and private cloud-hosted systems and applications to provide visibility into the systems that need protection from both internal and external threat vectors and malicious entities.

If we cannot implement all the (standard) security controls at once, then we must prioritize the monitoring capability over other controls. Assuming the perimeter controls are in place, the implementation of all required data, network, endpoint, and IAM protective security controls can be a second priority to the implementation of the monitoring controls.

3.1 Monitoring Strategy

Here is a simplistic high-level monitoring strategy that may be followed:

1. Enable Cloud-Native Monitoring capability

    (a) Both AWS and Azure have developed API-driven enhanced monitoring services that provide the capability for real-time security monitoring and visibility.
    (b) Utilize pre-canned cloud-native uses cases.

2. Work towards building a hybrid single pane of glass alerting and reporting capability. This is generally done using an on-premises or cloud-hosted (SaaS) Security Incident and Event Management (SIEM).

    (a) Work towards integrating the API-based cloud monitoring capability with standard on-premises SIEM systems. Some industry leaders in this space are QRadar, Splunk, and Logrhythm.
    (b) Enable automation of incident response processes (e.g., by using Lambda functions in AWS).

3.2 Security Monitoring Patterns

Let's review some of the basic monitoring patterns.

3.2.1 Introduction

Let's first introduce what a security pattern and an anti-pattern is:

Security Pattern – provides solutions used to implement good fundamental security design principles for repeatable paradigms or for solving repeatable problems. A security pattern may include but not be limited to step-by-step (security) control implementation instructions and a pictorial representation.

Anti-Security Pattern – indicates the violation of an existing security pattern or of fundamental security design principles. These violations can be used to trigger events that can be used to monitor any misconfigurations, security breaches, or other anomalous activity.

3.2.2 Application Monitoring

Some fairly basic patterns using cloud-native capability to provide security monitoring for applications can be enabled to provide sophisticated and continuous security monitoring for malicious activity and unauthorized behavior. These patterns, often generated by a machine learning-enabled threat detection service that incorporates threat intelligence and anomaly detection, are able to perform at cloud scale.

Here are some examples of some cloud-based monitoring services:

(a) **Guard Duty**, available in AWS, has the capability to analyze billions of events across multiple AWS data sources, such as AWS CloudTrail, Amazon VPC Flow Logs, and DNS logs. Additional information is available at [1, 6].
(b) **Azure Security Center**, available in Azure, has the capability to analyze billions of events and examine the security state of Azure resources, assess workloads and issue threat detection alerts for subscriptions and Azure Active Directory (AAD), perform policy-based monitoring and health checks, and identify security misconfigurations and provide recommendations for prevention and remediation. Additional information is available at [2, 3, 7].

3.2.3 Network Monitoring – Cloud Access Security Broker (CASB)

Some patterns for network-based monitoring can be enabled by using a CASB. This capability (cloud-native and otherwise) can be utilized for monitoring systems hosted in AWS, Azure, other cloud providers, and SaaS, to enable the following:

(a) traffic monitoring capabilities against a set of pre-defined use cases and patterns,
(b) payload quarantine and blocking capabilities against a set of pre-defined use cases, and
(c) enforcement of data loss protection (DLP) controls on outbound transfers of (sensitive) unstructured data.

Multiple commercial CASB implementations (e.g., McAfee (SkyHigh), ZScaler, NetSkope, BitGlass) support integrations with AWS and Azure. Microsoft Azure also has a native CASB implementation available (MCAS).

Apart from its API integrating monitoring capabilities, the CASB can also operate in an inline Forward Proxy mode but discussion of that topic is outside the scope of the current chapter.

3.2.4 Continuous Monitoring and Auditing

Some patterns to provide continuous monitoring and auditing of compute, infrastructure, and application configurations, can do the following:

(a) Automate the evaluation of recorded configurations against desired configurations.

(b) Capture the comprehensive history of cloud (compute) resource configuration changes to enable operational troubleshooting.
(c) Enable enterprise-wide compliance monitoring to identify non-compliant accounts.
(d) Provide scanning support for third-party resources such as GitHub repositories.
(e) Services such as AWS Config are available in AWS. It allows for the review of changes in configurations and relationships between AWS resources, and determines the overall compliance against the configurations specified in any internal guidelines, simplifying compliance auditing, security analysis, change management, and operational troubleshooting. Additional information is available at [4].
(f) Services like Azure Policy are available in Azure. Azure Policy can be used to create, assign, and manage policies. These policies enforce different rules and 'effects' [11] over resources, so those resources stay compliant with your corporate standards and service level agreements. Azure Policy evaluates resources for non-compliance with assigned policies. All data stored by Azure Policy is encrypted at rest. Additional information is available at [5].

3.2.5   SCP (Service Control Policy)

Some patterns for service control can be enabled by SCPs, which offer central access controls for all IAM entities in the accounts for a given cloud environment. These can be used to enforce the required permissions that need to be followed. It provides the developers the freedom to manage their own permissions because they know they can only operate within the boundaries defined by the SCPs.

(a) Services such as AWS SCPs are available in AWS. These SCPs can be used to apply guardrails that will be inherited from the Master Account down. Additional SCPs will be applied for each Account/OU that sits under the master account. SCPs use a similar syntax to that used by IAM permission policies and resource-based policies (such as Amazon S3 bucket policies).
    For more information about IAM policies and their syntax please refer to [12].
    An SCP is a plain-text file structured according to the rules of JSON [9].
    Additional information is available at [10].
(b) Services such as **Azure Policy** are available in Azure [8]. It is a service that can be used to create, assign, and manage policies. These policies enforce different rules and 'effects' [11] over resources, ensuring compliance with your corporate standards and service level agreements. Azure Policy meets this need by evaluating resources for non-compliance with assigned policies. All data stored by Azure Policy is encrypted at rest. It offers several built-in policies that are available by default. For example:

1. Allowed Storage Account SKUs (Deny): It defines the amount of stock keeping unit (SKU) of storage that may be allowed for a given account. All storage accounts that do not meet this policy would be removed.
2. Allowed Resource Type (Deny): It defines the list of resource types that can be deployed. All resources that are not part of this list would be removed
3. Allowed Locations (Deny): It defines the list of available locations for new resources. It is used to enforce the needed geo-compliance requirements.
4. Allowed Virtual Machine SKUs (Deny): It defines a set of VM SKUs that can deployed.
5. Add a tag to resources (Modify): It applies a required tag and its default value to a given resource, if not specified by the deploy request.
6. Enforce tag and its value (Deny): It enforces the application of a required tag and its value to a given resource.
7. Not allowed resource types (Deny): It prevents the deployment of a provided list of resource types.

Note:
The *Deny* effect (in the above policy examples) is used to prevent a request for a resource that does not comply with a given policy definition.

The *Modify* effect (in the above policy example) is used to add, update, or delete a property of a tag on a resource.

3.3   Anti-Patterns

Some of the observed anti-patterns have been mentioned below:

3.3.1   Application and Infrastructure Monitoring

A typical cloud security monitoring anti-pattern is to use an on-premises monitoring system to monitor cloud-hosted applications and infrastructure components.

3.3.2   On-premises SIEM

Hauling all cloud-native application and security log data from a cloud environment to an on-premises SIEM is anti-pattern that must be avoided.

3.3.3   Internet Gateway

Another anti-pattern is to configure the ingress and egress for cloud- hosted services and applications through an on-premises internet gateway.

4 The CISO Take

The industry-wide trend I have observed within the last couple of years is that the migration of the applications to the cloud or the stand up of new applications, systems, or integrations in the cloud, including SaaS, are being spearheaded and managed by the CIO/IT teams without the full engagement of the information security teams, sometimes not following the well-established application onboarding and intake processes that account for information security input and feedback.

While information security teams always adapt to do their best to ensure that all these deployments are secure, CISOs have to make the case to IT leaders that the need for agility and speed to market needs to be balanced with the cyber risk IT leaders assume when they bypass established information security processes.

Also, CISOs need to lead from the front and take an active role in the evangelization and implementation of cloud security controls and be proactive in making them available to the application teams to avoid last-minute fire drills.

As a CISO myself, I treat the cloud environments as extensions to our on-premises datacenters and preach that the security paradigm remains the same irrespective of the hosting solution.

Under the hood, just like the well-established security paradigm for the application and systems hosted on data centers on-premises, the cloud environments need all the security controls to be implemented using a combination of cloud-native and hybrid tools.

5 Definitions

CASB – stands for Cloud Access Security Broker. It is an on-premises or cloud-hosted security policy enforcement point, generally resident between the flow of network or application traffic and cloud-hosted or based services (e.g., SaaS, IaaS, or PaaS). The security policies enforced include Data Loss Prevention (DLP), Secure Sign-on (SSO), Multi-factor Authentication (MFA), logging, and malware detection.

CI/CD – stands for continuous integration and continuous delivery. It is a modern application development paradigm of delivering code (changes) more frequently and more reliably.

Cloud-native – it is the approach of building applications, tools and services specifically for a given cloud environment (e.g., AWS or Azure). Due to their dependency on native technology, services built for one cloud environment may not function as designed on another.

Effects - Each policy definition in Azure Policy has a single effect. That effect determines what happens when the policy rule is evaluated to match. The effects behave differently if they are for a new resource, an updated resource, or an existing resource. [11]

MCAS – it stands for Microsoft Cloud App Security. It's a cloud access security broker (CASB) solution that provides the capability to gain visibility into the applications hosted in Azure and o365.

SIEM – stands for Security Incident and Event Management (system). It has the capability to aggregate, correlate, and cross-reference security (log) data and events from various systems.

Single pane of glass – in the context of cybersecurity, a single pane of glass is a management or reporting console (generally within a SIEM) that cross-references and presents data from multiple log and event sources in a unified display.

VPC – stands for Virtual Private Cloud. It is a virtual network dedicated to a specific cloud account. It has all other infrastructure components needed for a functioning network including but not limited to a subnet, a routing table, an internet gateway, a VPC endpoint, and a classless inter-domain routing (CIDR) block.

References

1. AWS (2020) Amazon Guard Duty. https://aws.amazon.com/guardduty/. Accessed on 2 Jan 2021
2. Microsoft Azure (2020) Azure Security Center. https://azure.microsoft.com/en-us/services/security-center/. Accessed 2 Jan 2021
3. Microsoft 365 (2020) Microsoft Cloud App Security. https://www.microsoft.com/en-us/microsoft-365/enterprise-mobility-security/cloud-app-security. Accessed 2 Jan 2021
4. AWS (2020) AWS Config. https://aws.amazon.com/config/. Accessed 2 Jan 2021
5. Coulter D, Furbush K, Downs J, et al (2021) What is Azure Policy? In: Microsoft Azure Policy documentation. https://docs.microsoft.com/en-us/azure/governance/policy/overview. Accessed 20 Jan 2021
6. AWS (2020) https://aws.amazon.com. Accessed 20 Jan 2021
7. Microsoft Azure (2020) https://azure.microsoft.com. Accessed 20 Jan 2021
8. Coulter D, Furbush K, Downs J, et al (2021) What is Azure Policy? In: Microsoft Azure Policy documentation. https://docs.microsoft.com/en-us/azure/governance/policy/overview. Accessed 20 Jan 2021
9. Introducing JSON (2020) https://www.json.org/json-en.html Accessed 20 Jan 2021
10. Switzer M (2019) How to use service control policies to set permission guardrails across accounts in your AWS Organization. In: AWS Security Blog. https://aws.amazon.com/blogs/security/how-to-use-service-control-policies-to-set-permission-guardrails-across-accounts-in-your-aws-organization / Accessed 20 Jan 2021
11. Azure (2020) Understand Azure policy effects. https://docs.microsoft.com/en-us/azure/governance/policy/concepts/effects. Accessed 20 Jan 2021
12. AWS (2020) Policies and Permissions in IAM. https://docs.aws.amazon.com/IAM/latest/UserGuide/access_policies.html. Accessed 20 Jan 2021

Cloud Monitoring Security Controls for AWS

1 Introduction

As I had mentioned in the previous chapter, full visibility into the cloud-resident applications, network, and infrastructure for your compute instance is one of the most basic yet essential cloud security controls. This can be achieved by implementing cloud-native and easy-to-build monitoring patterns described in this chapter.

These are also very much needed from a security perspective because IT teams often deploy applications in cloud environments without the proper security protections (i.e., without completing the information security design, implementation, and operationalization of infrastructure security and access controls). Detection or monitoring controls give security teams visibility into the new or updated IT stack in cloud environments. I also think this is also very useful for *hybrid cloud or cloud federation* type deployments.

Once monitoring and response patterns have been implemented to attain full visibility into the cloud environment, then the Security and IT teams can work together to implement some of the more complex security controls inherited from the concepts of Zero Trust with least privilege, such as data encryption, identity federation with multi-factor authentication (MFA), network segmentation, key management, guardrails, network traffic analysis, intrusion prevention, and cyber deception.

This current article focuses on the monitoring capabilities that must be enabled in AWS.

2   EC2 and VPC Compute Monitoring Requirements

For any AWS native capability instantiated or invoked, either within or from an EC2 instance, there must be monitoring capability to oversee the items/cloud infrastructure components, as described below. These may include core AWS functionality and services available for public and private invocation from within an AWS virtual private cloud (VPC).

2.1   API Security Monitoring

(a) Should be performed for all internal/external APIs or web-service/microservice calls;
(b) Should be performed at both the (API) Gateway and the Web/Micro service (within the VPC public/private subnets) to detect, alert, and respond to inappropriate behavior;
(c) Must have the capability to detect and prevent (token) replay, man-in-the-middle, and injection attacks; and
(d) Must comply with the below-mentioned cybersecurity logging and monitoring guidelines for all internal and external API or Web-Service or Micro-Service calls.

2.2   Internet Gateway Monitoring

(a) Monitoring capability must exist to detect the addition of an (unauthorized) internet gateway to a VPC. Any addition of an internet gateway must be performed by authorized personnel using proper change and access controls. The addition of gateways through orchestration tools (e.g., CloudFormation or Terraform) must be pre-approved and tested, and still possess the same monitoring capability.

2.3   AWS Services Monitoring

The capability must exist to monitor (and log event data about):

(a) all Lambda invocations, and
(b) other publicly and privately accessible AWS services such as RDS and S3.

2.4   Network Monitoring

(a) The capability to monitor network traffic packets between inter-VPC (peering) or intra-VPC (between subnets) must be enabled.

2.5   Application Monitoring

(a) The capability must exist to log and monitor applications and systems for security events and notable operational metrics within a given VPC.

2.6   Logging

The capability must be enabled to perform logging for:

(a) AWS user account management activity, i.e., account creation and update or deletion events, for all account types, including but not limited to user, admin, and system accounts;
(b) account login and logout activity of privileged users, and account activities that require privileged or administrative access (e.g., using administrator, root, or sudo). The same must also be enabled for any privilege escalation events.

This is what must be logged:

(a) user account information, including but not limited to user ID and IP address;
(b) system (EC2) boot and shutdown timestamps;
(c) system configuration updates; and
(d) all security logging data, which must be sent to a centralized log repository with data analysis and correlation capability generally performed by a security incident and event management (SIEM) or equivalent system using formats including but not limited to syslog, or through http/https handlers or message queues.

2.7   Database Monitoring

Activity monitoring and alerting capabilities must be enabled:

(a) for all data repositories, including but not limited to relational, non-relational, and object-oriented databases, that store in-scope data;
(b) for all privileged and system activity on all in-scope databases and repositories;
(c) for all remote access for all in-scope databases and repositories;

(d) for system administration activities, including but not limited to server creation or provisioning, de-provisioning or decommission, and any other system-level configuration changes; and
(e) for raising alerts locally (in the cloud environment) and for sending alerts to a central server or service (e.g., SIEM), where they can be correlated with other alerts.

2.8 Scanning and Monitoring for Vulnerabilities

(a) Scanning for vulnerabilities is not a primary monitoring control per se. However, given the high number of threat vectors resident in cloud environments, it is essential for all application and infrastructure components within a VPC. Real-time alert events for any vulnerability detected must be sent to a SIEM.

3 AWS Hybrid Monitoring Solutions

An AWS hybrid monitoring solution can be constructed with native AWS services, including CloudWatch, CloudWatch Events, CloudTrail, Config, and GuardDuty, among other services or custom-built applications.

3.1 Basic Hybrid Monitoring Pattern

The diagram below (Fig. 1) provides a high-level hybrid monitoring pattern, using native AWS components:

3.2 AWS GuardDuty

GuardDuty can identify unexpected and potentially unauthorized or malicious activity in your AWS environment. After enabling GuardDuty, the GuardDuty logs need to be sent to a SIEM (generally on-premises). This is generally done by creating an AWS CloudWatch Rule for AWS GuardDuty traffic and then a Lambda Function to stream the GuardDuty logs to have a SIEM (e.g., Splunk) ingest data from AWS services using a SIEM HTTP Event Collector.

AWS – Hybrid Monitoring Pattern

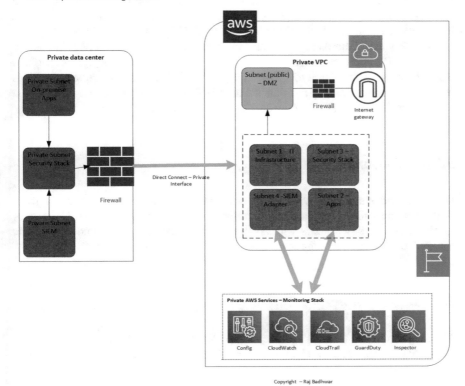

Copyright – Raj Badhwar

Fig. 1 High-level hybrid monitoring pattern

3.3   AWS CloudWatch

CloudWatch can monitor AWS resources and the applications that run on AWS in real time. Additionally, CloudWatch Events can send system events from AWS resources to AWS Lambda functions. This is again done by using AWS Lambda to stream CloudWatch logs to have a SIEM (e.g., Splunk) ingest data from AWS services. Once a Lambda function is configured, events are automatically forwarded in near real-time by Lambda to a SIEM HTTP Event Collector without having to manage a single intermediary server, queuing, or storage.

3.4   AWS CloudTrail

CloudTrail can monitor your AWS deployments in the (public) cloud by getting a history of AWS API calls for an account, including all the API calls made via the AWS Management Console, the AWS SDKs, the command line tools, and higher-level AWS services. It can also identify which users and accounts called AWS APIs for services that support CloudTrail, the source IP address from which the calls were made, and when the calls occurred. CloudTrail can be integrated into applications using the API, automate trail creation for an organization, check the status of trails, and control how administrators turn CloudTrail logging on and off. CloudTrail data can be sent to a SIEM (e.g., Splunk) [1] using the same techniques mentioned above, i.e., configuring a Lambda function to stream event data to a SIEM (e.g., Splunk) HTTP Connector.

3.5 AWS Config

Config provides a detailed view of the configuration of AWS resources for a given AWS account and can capture any configuration changes in real-time. Upon integrating Lambda-based alerts with AWS config, Config can detect and issue alerts for any configuration change to an AWS service or component within a VPC.

3.6 Basic Monitoring Pattern

The diagram below (Fig. 2) provides a high-level hybrid monitoring pattern, using native AWS components and a non-native SIEM:

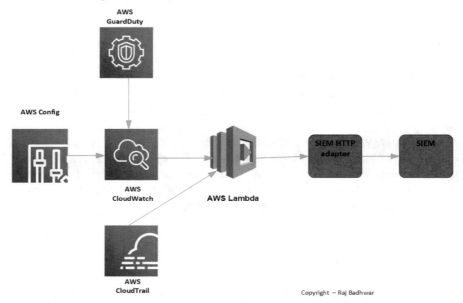

Copyright – Raj Badhwar

Fig. 2 Basic monitoring pattern

3.7   *SIEM App*

Let's use *Splunk* as a specific example of a SIEM App. The Splunk App for AWS has the capability to provide critical real-time alerts on dashboards and reports into the environment for a given AWS account. The Splunk app can meet all the monitoring requirements listed in this article and comes with easy to configure data inputs for AWS Config, Config Rules, CloudWatch, CloudTrail, VPC Flow Log, and AWS Inspector.

The diagram below (Fig. 3) provides a high-level hybrid monitoring pattern, using native AWS components and the SIEM app:

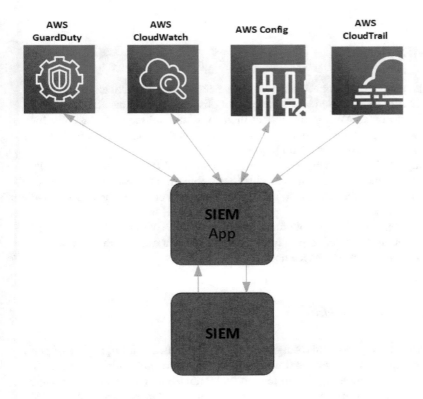

Fig. 3 Hybrid monitoring pattern

4   AWS Native Monitoring

While the previous section focused on a hybrid cloud implementation taking place both on-premises and in the cloud, this section is going to highlight another monitoring pattern that is purely AWS-centric.

CISOs need to ensure that before any application hosted primarily in AWS with no external touch point goes live, the security team enables full native cloud monitoring capability. This pattern may come in handy for those that are either too new at this or aren't aware of cloud native monitoring capabilities.

This pattern builds on existing native AWS services, but I would like to call out two new services that are of special interest here: AWS Detective and AWS Security Hub.

4.1   AWS Detective

Just as the names suggests, Amazon Detective enables the identification and detection of security issues based on its analysis of observed suspicious activities. It can integrate with other AWS tools, collect their logs, and subsequently use machine learning and graph theory to build a dataset that is readily consumable for security investigations and forensics examinations.

Although there are many other complementary AWS security services like GuardDuty, Macie, and Security Hub that can help with any analysis, Detective is the tool of choice if the intent is to get to root cause of a complex incident or suspicious event quickly.

Amazon detective is available for use right from the AWS console.

Please note that Detective was free in early 2020 when it was in preview mode but is a paid subscription service now.

4.2   AWS Security Hub

Just as the name suggests, this tool provides a central hub, i.e., a single pane of glass [4] for a comprehensive view of the various security alerts and events across all the AWS tools, including endpoint protection, vulnerability management and compliance alerts, and multiple other AWS services such as GuardDuty, Macie, AWS Identity and Access Management (IAM) Access Analyzer, Inspector, and AWS Firewall Manager, as well as those from AWS Partner solutions used in the context of an AWS account.

Just like most AWS tools, this tool can be enabled with a couple of clicks in the management console [3].

4.3   AWS Security Hub Integrates with AWS Detective

AWS Security Hub has built-in capability to integrate with Amazon Detective, enabling the user to take the findings from Guard Duty available in Security Hub and load them directly into Amazon Detective for further investigations and evaluations [2].

4.4   AWS Native Monitoring Pattern

The diagram below (Fig. 4) provides a high-level native monitoring pattern, using all native AWS components. This should provide guidance to security technologists and others on how to use cloud native capabilities to establish a good security monitoring eco system.

AWS Native Monitoring Ecosystem

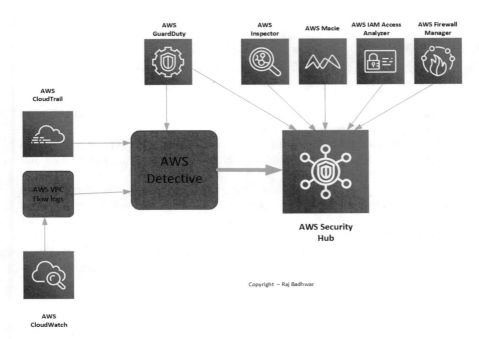

Copyright – Raj Badhwar

Fig. 4   Native monitoring pattern

5 The CISO Take

Although this chapter provides only a basic introduction to cloud security monitoring, I hope that it gets the message across that it is an essential yet relatively easy to implement security control, and that it must be the first thing you do when you move your application(s) to the cloud. These bare-minimum security controls must be present before any internet-facing cloud hosted application is allowed to go live.

This is the recommended cycle of maturity for a cloud environment which also helps set the priority of deployment of these controls:

Perimeter controls -> Basic Monitoring controls -> Advanced detective controls -> Mitigating controls -> Blocking controls -> Zero Trust with Least Privilege controls -> Automated Reactive Response and orchestration controls

Getting even a few of the first steps listed above correct would have prevented major breaches at some of the large financial services firms that are cloud-first with supposedly sophisticated security setups.

It is time that firms learned from the mistakes of others. They need to make sure that they have at the helm the right security leader who understands the fundamentals of cloud security, someone that can get the basics right, rather than someone who merely utters industry buzzwords.

6 Definitions

EC2 – stands for elastic compute cloud. It is a capability provided by Amazon Web Services which enables the delivery of scalable computing capacity in their public cloud. It allows a user to launch virtual servers with the inherent ability to configure security, networking, and storage.

SIEM – stands for Security Incident and Event Management (system). It has the capability to aggregate, correlate, and cross-reference security (log) data and events from various systems.

VPC – stands for Virtual Private Cloud. It is a virtual network dedicated to a specific cloud account. It has all other infrastructure components needed for a functioning network including but not limited to a subnet, a routing table, an internet gateway, a VPC endpoint, and a classless inter-domain routing (CIDR) block.

VPC Peering – It is the capability to establish a networking connection between any two VPCs that enables the private routing of traffic between them.

References

1. Splunk (2020) Configure CloudTrail inputs for the Splunk Add-on for AWS. In: Splunk documentation. https://docs.splunk.com/Documentation/AddOns/released/AWS/CloudTrail. Accessed 24 Dec 2021

2. AWS (2019) AWS Security Hub integrates with Amazon Detective. https://aws.amazon.com/about-aws/whats-new/2019/12/aws-security-hub-integrates-with-amazon-detective/. Accessed 24 Dec 2021
3. AWS (2021) What is AWS Security Hub? https://docs.aws.amazon.com/securityhub/latest/userguide/what-is-securityhub.html. Accessed 24 Dec 2021
4. AWS (2020). Use a single pane of glass for monitoring. https://docs.aws.amazon.com/well-architected/latest/financial-services-industry-lens/use-a-single-pane-of-glass-for-monitoring.html . Accessed 24 Dec 2021

AWS Visio Template Used

AWS (2020). AWS Architecture Icons: AWS-Architecture-Icons_Visio_20191031. https://aws.amazon.com/architecture/icons/, Accessed 4 March, 2020

Cloud Monitoring Security Controls for Azure

1 Introduction

The past two chapters I wrote were primarily based on AWS, but the reality is that most companies generally use multi-cloud environments. CISOs are responsible for ensuring that equal attention is given to other cloud environments as well, to provide appropriate protection to applications and systems against all threat vectors, irrespective of the (cloud) hosting solution.

This article introduces the monitoring capabilities available within Microsoft's Azure, Azure Active Directory (AAD), and o365 (cloud) environments. Enabling the capability to monitor your IaaS applications in the Microsoft cloud environments is critical because of the enterprise workloads that many corporations run there, and the use of many multi-tenant cloud based services by their users, namely: Exchange Online (i.e., email); SharePoint Online; One Drive for business (ODFB) for both internal and external file sharing; AAD with one way or bi-direction sync; Power BI; and Skype for Business (or Teams) and other apps that are part of the Microsoft Office suite. Needless to say, it would cause catastrophic business and reputational losses to a company if any one of their IaaS/PaaS workloads or any of these services were inappropriately accessed or breached.

2 Azure Native Monitoring Solutions

I am elaborating a few security monitoring capabilities that are available in the Azure, AAD, and o365 environments. Although not exhaustive, this list will get the conversation started in the right direction.

© The Author(s), under exclusive license to Springer Nature Switzerland AG 2021
R. Badhwar, *The CISO's Next Frontier*,
https://doi.org/10.1007/978-3-030-75354-2_38

2.1 Secure Score

Microsoft Secure Score enables the capability to measure compliance against configured (security) policies within the various Azure IaaS and PaaS services, Azure Active Directory, and Office 365 (which includes o365, SharePoint Online, OneDrive for Business, and Skype for Business {aka Teams}).

The scores are dynamically calculated at the tenant level by comparing various Azure configured Security, IAM and other policies. The security policies generally include data classification, data encryption, secure port management, vulnerability management, DDoS protection, security configurations, data loss prevention, email security, auditing and logging, and endpoint protection; and the IAM policies generally include Multi-factor authentication (MFA), Access and Permission (Conditional Access) and Adaptive application control capabilities. There are also some other policies for system updates and auditing & logging configured within the various subscriptions or management groups.

Please be aware that: (a) certain policies are at the subscription or tenant level and cannot be individually enabled or disabled, therefore affecting your score; (b) If you use a third-party security product, then Secure Score may not take that into account and thus give you a lower score. Secure Score also provides a historical trend graph of the score per subscription.

Every corporation with subscriptions in Azure, Azure AD, and o365 environments must view their Secure Score and identify all the security remediations that need to be done to reduce cyber risk. Although scores will depend upon the risk tolerance and the (non-Microsoft) third-party security tools installed, a score of 75–85% is highly recommended.

Microsoft Azure product documentation provides detailed treatment of secure score [2, 4].

2.2 Security Center

Azure Security Center [5, 6] enables unified security management and visibility across hybrid cloud workloads. It can be used to apply security policies across workloads, raise alerts on security events in a given tenant or subscription, and determine compliance with security policies and configurations. It also provides visibility on available operations, contract configurations and locations, any proactive tasks required to improve the security of the subscription, and any settings required for the secure storage of data and logs.

Microsoft Azure product documentation provides a detailed treatment of its security center [1, 3].

2.3   Operations Management Suite (OMS) within Azure Portal

The OMS portal, which provided visibility into security-relevant events within o365 and Azure AD environments, has now migrated to the Azure portal to consolidate and streamline monitoring and management. Most of the features of the OMS portal are now part of the Azure portal. The capabilities within Azure portal include:

(a) Traffic Analytics
(b) Dashboard for pinning resources
(c) Advanced search capability to find resources
(d) Consolidated monitoring and management workflow
(e) Azure Process Automation
(f) Azure Configuration Management
(g) Update Management
(h) Recovery Services – Backup

2.4   Azure Log Analytics

It is the primary tool in the Azure portal for writing log queries and interactively analyzing their results. Queries used elsewhere in Azure Monitor are typically first written and tested using Log Analytics. Log Analytics can be used from several places in the Azure portal.

2.5   Azure Network Watcher

Azure Network Watcher provides tools to monitor, diagnose issues, view metrics, and enable or disable logs for resources in an Azure virtual network. Network Watcher is designed to monitor and repair the network health of Infrastructure-as-a-Service (IaaS) products, which include Virtual Machines, Virtual Networks, Application Gateways, and Load balancers.

The Network Watcher is enabled by default on a given subscription in a given region but users can opt out by script.

Note: It is not intended and will not work for PaaS (Platform-as-a-Service) monitoring or Web analytics.

Additional information and tutorials can be found on the Microsoft Azure Network Watcher documentation webpage [7].

2.6   Basic Native Monitoring Pattern

The diagram below (Fig. 1) provides a high-level monitoring pattern, using all native Azure components. This should provide guidance to security technologists and others on how to use cloud native capabilities to establish a good security monitoring eco system.

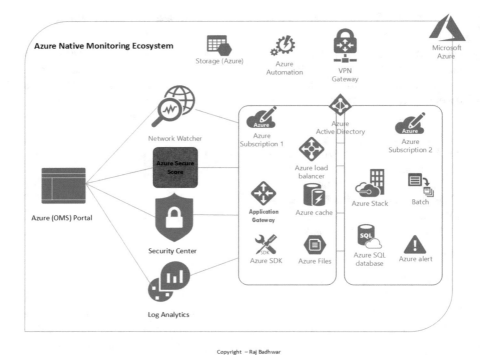

Copyright − Raj Badhwar

Fig. 1 Native monitoring pattern

3 The CISO Take

Establishing basic monitoring is the first thing you must do when you move your application(s) to the cloud. It is imperative that your organization has good visibility and monitoring capability for all that you do in Azure, which means that you host your applications or systems in Azure using their IaaS offerings; use the Azure identity and access management capabilities enabled by Azure Active Directory (AAD) to authenticate users; use Intune and hybrid join your corporate assets to AAD, or (if you have moved some/all your Microsoft services like Exchange or Teams) to office 365 (o365).

These bare minimum (security) controls must be present before any internet-facing cloud-hosted application is allowed to go live.

This is the recommended cycle of maturity for a cloud environment:

Perimeter controls -> Basic Monitoring controls -> Advanced detective controls -> Mitigating controls -> Blocking controls -> Zero Trust with Least Privilege controls -> Automated Reactive Response and orchestration controls

Getting even a few of the first steps listed above (e.g., the basic monitoring controls) correct would have prevented some major breaches at some of the large financial services firms that are cloud-first with supposedly sophisticated security set ups.

4 Definitions

AAD – stands for Azure Active Directory. It is Microsoft's cloud-based Active Directory instance which has the capability to act as an IAM service. It has the capability to synchronize user credentials and other directory attributes with an on-premises AD instance in a bi-directional manner. It lets users access services and systems in Azure by using their regular AD credentials. It also enables the capability to hybrid join a mobile device or corporate asset to the cloud-hosted (AAD) instance.

IaaS – stands for Infrastructure as a Service. It is a cloud computing capability by which a cloud services provider enables access to computing resources such as virtual servers, storage, networking, and many other cloud native security services such as firewalls, Hardware Security Modules (HSM), and Web Access Firewalls (WAF). These can be used by individual users or corporations to host their private applications and systems within a cloud computing provider's infrastructure.

PaaS – stands for Platform as a Service. It is a cloud computing capability by which a cloud services provider enables the users to develop, manage, and deliver applications. In addition to computing resources such as virtual servers, storage, and networking resources, users and corporations are able to use a suite of prebuilt cloud-native tools and systems to develop, customize, and test their own applications.

References

1. Coulter D, et al (2021) FAQ – General Questions about Azure Security Center (Find frequently asked questions about the service and Secure Score) – https://docs.microsoft.com/en-us/azure/security-center/faq-general Accessed 20 Jan 2021
2. Coulter D, Sharkey K, et al (2021) Secure score in Azure Security Center. In: Microsoft Azure product documentation. https://docs.microsoft.com/en-us/azure/security-center/secure-score-security-controls. Accessed 20 Jan 2021
3. Coulter D, Foulds I, Fowler C, et al (2018) Strengthen your security posture with Azure Security Center. In: Microsoft Azure product documentation. https://docs.microsoft.com/en-us/azure/security-center/security-center-monitoring. Accessed 20 Jan 2021
4. Coulter D, Sharkey K, et al (2021) Secure score in Azure Security Center. In: Microsoft Azure product documentation. https://docs.microsoft.com/en-us/azure/security-center/secure-score-security-controls Accessed 20 Jan 2021
5. Microsoft Azure (2021) Azure Security Center documentation. https://docs.microsoft.com/en-us/azure/. Accessed 20 Jan 2021

6. Microsoft Azure (2021) Azure Security Center documentation. https://docs.microsoft.com/en-us/azure/security-center/. Accessed 20 Jan 2021
7. Microsoft Azure (2021) Azure Network Watcher documentation. https://docs.microsoft.com/en-us/azure/network-watcher/. Accessed 20 Jan 2021

Azure Visio Template

Azure (2020). Create Azure diagrams in Visio https://support.microsoft.com/en-us/office/create-azure-diagrams-in-visio-efbb25e7-c80e-42e1-b1ad-7ef630ff01b7, https://docs.microsoft.com/en-us/azure/architecture/icons/. Microsoft_CloudnEnterprise_Symbols_v2.7KP. Accessed on 3 June, 2020.

Further Reading

Microsoft Azure (2021) Azure Active Directory documentation. https://docs.microsoft.com/en-us/azure/active-directory/. Accessed 20 Jan 2021

Burnley A, Myers T, Withee K, et al (2020) What is Azure Active Directory? In: Microsoft Azure product documentation. https://docs.microsoft.com/en-us/azure/active-directory/fundamentals/active-directory-whatis. Accessed 20 Jan 2021

Memildin M, Sharkey K et al (2020) Secure score in Azure Security Center. In: Microsoft Azure product documentation. https://docs.microsoft.com/en-us/azure/security-center/secure-score-security-controls#how-your-secure-score-is-calculated. Accessed 20 Jan 2021

Wren B, Coulter D, et al (2020) Log queries in Azure Monitor. In: Microsoft Azure product documentation. https://docs.microsoft.com/en-us/azure/azure-monitor/log-query/log-query-overview. Assessed 20 Jan 2021

Cloud Policy Enforcement Point

1 Introduction

In the previous chapters, I introduced some of the basic requirements for cloud (AWS and Azure) monitoring and have provided some associated monitoring patterns.

In this chapter, I will introduce the concept of a rudimentary cloud policy enforcement point (CPEP). A CPEP provides a network security and access policy enforcement point between a public data center and an on-premises center or a remote office site or location. The network connectivity could be provided by a Direct Connect (DX) or a MPLS connection. A CPEP is primarily implemented using service control policies. As in the previous (cloud security) chapters, I will try to provide a fairly basic treatment using an AWS ecosystem to this very complex topic.

2 Fundamentals

Let's get some fundamentals out of the way first.

Secure connectivity, the capability to maintain the confidentiality and integrity of sensitive data while it is being transmitted from an on-premises datacenter to the cloud and back, is fundamental to extending (or stretching) one's entire datacenter to the cloud.

Generally, there are two techniques to provide secure connectivity: a site-to-site VPN over the internet, and a dedicated network connection capability enabled by an Amazon service called Direct Connect (DX). For entities that use MPLS (to interconnect sites and their private datacenters etc.), setting up a DX using a MPLS vendor interconnection service can also be accomplished.

© The Author(s), under exclusive license to Springer Nature Switzerland AG 2021   315
R. Badhwar, *The CISO's Next Frontier*,
https://doi.org/10.1007/978-3-030-75354-2_39

This chapter will focus on the *controls that can be enabled for the network connector* responsible for the egress and ingress of network traffic between a public cloud and private datacenter. DX is the recommended and most widely used network connector and this article will use it as the primary connectivity construct.

Please note that this chapter assumes some working knowledge of AWS and concepts such as DX, hierarchical account structure (e.g., organizational unit (OU)), Service Control Policies (SCPs), and IAM policies.

2.1   AWS Direct Connect (DX)

AWS Direct connect is a network service that provides the capability to establish a dedicated one Gbps or ten Gbps dedicated network connection or connections between a customer data center and AWS. The simplest way is to use a DX gateway, which is generally used in conjunction with either a transit gateway or a virtual private gateway.

What are ways to connect to it?

The AWS DX allows for three types of interfaces—public, private and transit.

(a) **Public**: This interface is generally used to connect to AWS resources reachable by a public IP Address (e.g., S3 bucket or RDS) in any AWS region using the public internet. The connected interface additionally provides the capability to create public virtual interfaces in any DX location to receive global IP routes and connect to resources hosted in a Virtual Private Cloud (VPC). This connectivity can be achieved by using the resource's private IP address, which in turn uses a private virtual interface to connect to multiple VPCs within resources such as EC2 in a given AWS region.

(b) **Private**: This interface is generally used to connect private resources within an Amazon VPC using the resource's private IP address within each subnet, providing a safer and more consistent private network experience and throughput than the public interface. This is generally done through a transit gateway by making use of a transit virtual interface, further providing the capability to connect to multiple VPCs within the same or different AWS accounts, associate up to three transit gateways in the same AWS region, and attach VPCs in the same AWS region to the transit gateway.

(c) **Transit**: This interface is generally used within AWS to advertise routes that a customer specifies in the allowed prefixes list in the DX Gateway.

3 Cloud Policy Enforcement Point (CPEP)

An effective cloud policy enforcement point can be implemented using a combination of SCPs, as depicted in Fig. 1.

A SCP is a plain-text file that is structured according to the rules of JSON and offers central access controls for all Identity and Access Management (IAM) entities in the accounts for a given cloud environment, i.e., AWS, in this specific case. SCPs can be used to enforce the required permissions that need to be followed. It provides the developers the freedom to manage their own (sub) permissions because they know they can only operate within the boundaries defined by the SCPs.

These SCPs can be used to apply guardrails that will be inherited from the Master Account down. Additional SCPs can be applied for each Account or OU that sits under the master account. SCPs use a similar syntax to that used by IAM permission

AWS – Monitoring Pattern showing -
1. Direct Connect w/Public and Private interface
2. CPEP v0.1

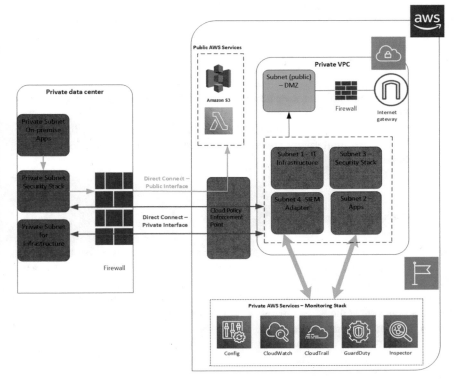

Copyright – Raj Badhwar

Fig. 1 Basic CPEP

policies and resource-based policies (such as Amazon S3 bucket policies). When an SCP is applied to an OU or individual AWS account, you either enable (whitelist) or disable (blacklist) the specified AWS service.

One should note that the SCPs are not effective for an AWS root subscription account. If one were to use an SCP on that (root) account then they would lock themselves out of the account. So, if the SCP is attached to the root of the organization, it will be effective only to the child orgs and the accounts attached to it.

SCPs enable the capability to set permission guardrails by defining the maximum available permissions for IAM entities in an account. If an SCP denies an action for an account, none of the entities in the account can take that action, even if their IAM permissions allow them to do so. The guardrails set in SCPs apply to all IAM entities in the account, which include all users, roles, and the account root user.

Please note that SCPs themselves do not provide the actual IAM permissions and thus cannot replace them: to perform an action, one still needs to grant an appropriate IAM policy permission. SCPs take precedence over IAM policies; thus, even if a principal is allowed to perform a given action via an IAM policy, an attached SCP can override the capability to perform that action.

3.1   Salient Features of CPEP

(a) The system administrator or other privileged account holders cannot override the SCP controls.
(b) It provides protection from misconfigurations and/or from insider threats.
(c) SCPs can be cumulatively added to add to or fine tune any previous controls implemented.

3.2   Basic (Home-Grown) SCP

As depicted in Fig. 2, a home-grown CPEP can be implemented by the resident cyber security or IAM team using SCPs on the "Root level," "OU level," and "AWS account level" to enforce the policies. The SCPs on the top level will be inherited by all the lower levels, including the leaf-level objects. For example, if we set "Deny delete S3 bucket" at the SCP-1 below, it will be inherited by all the OUs and accounts below the root. Admins can create S3 buckets below the root level but cannot delete the S3 buckets. That way, you can have full control, but SCP-1 will not affect the objects in the Root itself. The Root, or the master account, should be used only to manage the billing information. No assets (e.g., S3 and EC2) should be created in the master unless they are needed for billing purposes.

Cloud Policy Enforcement Point

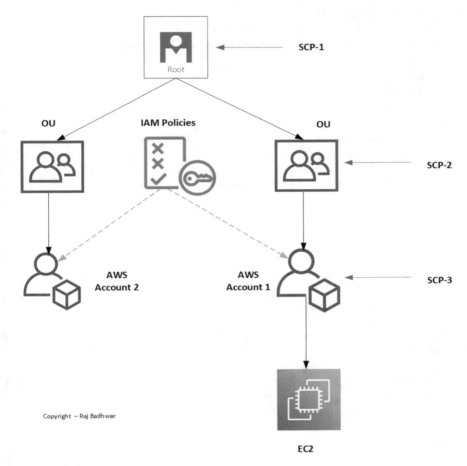

Fig. 2 Basic SCP

3.3 SCP Examples

While a detailed treatment is outside the scope of this chapter, there are three examples of SCPs that I have provided below. These could help implement a basic home grown CPEP discussed in the previous section. These SCPs further enhance some of the samples shared by AWS on their documentation site [1].

3.3.1 Example 1

Prevent the deletion of ConfigRules, Config Recording, Delivery Channel, Organization ConfigRule and Data.

This SCP prevents users that belong to an attached account from deleting ConfigRules, Config Recording, Delivery Channel, Org ConfigRule and data.

```
{
 "Version": "2012-10-17",
 "Statement": [
 {
 "Sid": "DenyDeletingConfigRule4SpecificOrEntireOrg",
 "Action": [
 "config:DeleteConfigRule",
 "config:DeleteOrganizationConfigRule"
 ],
 "Effect": "Deny",
 "Resource": [
 "*"
 ]
 },
 {
 "Sid": "DenyStoppingOrDeletingConfigRecording",
 "Action": [
 "config:DeleteConfigurationRecorder",
 "config:StopConfigurationRecorder"
 ],
 "Effect": "Deny",
 "Resource": [
 "*"
 ]
 },
 {
 "Sid": "DenyDeletingDeliveryChannel",
 "Action": [
 "config:DeleteDeliveryChannel"
 ],
 "Effect": "Deny",
 "Resource": [
 "*"
 ]
 },
 {
 "Sid": "DenyDeletingConformancePackAndDataInIt",
 "Action": [
 "config:DeleteConformancePack"
```

```
        ],
        "Effect": "Deny",
        "Resource": [
        "*"
        ]
        }
    ]
}
```

3.3.2   Example 2

Prevent Users from Deleting VPC Flow Logs, CloudTrail Logs, CloudWatch Log Group and Log Stream
This SCP prevents users that belong to an attached account from deleting VPC flow logs, CloudTrail or CloudWatch log groups or log streams.

```
{
    "Version": "2012-10-17",
    "Statement": [
    {
    "Sid": "DenyDeletingVPCFlowLogs",
    "Action": [
    "ec2:DeleteFlowLogs"
    ],
    "Effect": "Deny",
    "Resource": "*"
    },
    {
    "Sid": "DenyDeletingCloudWatchLogGroupAndLogStream",
    "Action": [
    "logs:DeleteLogGroup",
    "logs:DeleteLogStream"
    ],
    "Effect": "Deny",
    "Resource": "*"
    },
    {
    "Sid": "DenyDeletingCloudTrail",
    "Action": [
    "cloudtrail:DeleteTrail"
    ],
    "Effect": "Deny",
    "Resource": "*"
    }
    ]
}
```

3.3.3 Example 3

Prevent Internet Access for Any Private VPC
This SCP prevents users that belong to an attached account from changing the configuration of an EC2 private VPC to grant them direct access to the internet.

```
{
 "Version": "2012-10-17",
 "Statement": [
 {
 "Sid": "DenyInternetAccessViaInternetGatewayForIPv4andIPv6",
 "Action": [
 "ec2:AttachInternetGateway",
 "ec2:CreateInternetGateway"
 ],
 "Effect": "Deny",
 "Resource": "*"
 },
 {
 "Sid": "DenyInternetAccessViaEgressInternetGatewayForIPv6",
 "Action": [
 "ec2:AttachEgressOnlyInternetGateway"
 ],
 "Effect": "Deny",
 "Resource": "*"
 },
 {
 "Sid": "DenyInternetAccessAccessViaGlobalAccelerator",
 "Action": [
 "globalaccelerator:Create*",
 "globalaccelerator:Update*"
 ],
 "Effect": "Deny",
 "Resource": "*"

 }
 ]
}
```

4 CISO Take

The SCPs that may make up a rudimentary CPEP need to be tested before they are ever enabled in a production capacity. Remember that an SCP affects every user and role and even the root user in every account to which it is attached.

In addition to the cloud native security tools, it is my recommendation that all CISOs consider the implementation of CPEPs for their cloud implementations as a guardrail that would provide them a failsafe last resort of protection.

This concludes the cloud security chapters. A future publication may provide a more detailed treatment of the CPEP and details on the security patterns that can be used to implement the traditional security controls for data, application, network and web security for the various public cloud environments.

5 Definitions

DX – stands for Direct Connect. It links a company network to an AWS Direct Connect location using ethernet and provides direct access to a regional AWS datacenter.

EC2 – stands for elastic compute cloud. It provides scalable computing capacity in the Amazon Web Services (AWS) cloud with preconfigured templates called Amazon Machine Images (AMIs) to create virtual computing environments called instances.

IAM – stands for identity and access management. It is a collection of technologies and techniques used to manage user, system, and machine identities, and their access to IT resources and infrastructure.

MPLS – stands for Multiprotocol Label Switching. It is a label-based data routing technology that enables much faster data transfer and control in a network. It is very scalable and protocol independent i.e., it works with both IP and ATM traffic.

6 Disclaimer

The SCP script examples in this chapter are being provided "as-is" and the author disclaims all warranties or support. If you decide to use them either in their entirety or any part thereof, then you must do so at your own risk.

Reference

1. AWS (2020). Example service control policies. https://docs.aws.amazon.com/organizations/latest/userguide/orgs_manage_policies_example-scps.html. Accessed 24 Dec 2020

AWS Visio Template Used

AWS (2020). AWS Architecture Icons: AWS-Architecture-Icons_Visio_20191031. https://aws. amazon.com/architecture/icons/, Accessed 4 March, 2020.

Further Reading

AWS (2020). Services Documentation. https://docs.aws.amazon.com/ Accessed 24 Dec 2020
Introducing JSON. https://www.json.org/json-en.html. Accessed 24 Dec 2020

Part VIII
Cyber Risk and Privacy

Dynamic Measurement of Cyber Risk

1 Introduction

Cyber Risk can be defined as the probability of one or a series of disruptions or losses due to security breaches. These breaches may either be unintentional or accidental, perhaps stemming from operational systems integrity issues or deliberate and unauthorized attempts to gain access to information systems. Breaches may cause business and network service disruptions, economic or financial loss, sensitive data exfiltration, malware infestation, state or federal regulatory noncompliance fines, or reputational damage.

2 How Can Cyber Insurance Help?

Cyber Insurance transfers the cyber risk that a given entity may be carrying to the insurance carrier. Thus, in the event of a debilitating network breach or malware infestation, the business and the cyber security teams can concentrate on the remediation activity rather than worry about incurring remediation expenses or the current and future financial fallout from lost revenue, litigation or regulatory fines.

Since the inception of the cyber insurance concept, the insurance providers have used a traditional approach of static risk assessment (e.g., using questionnaires with one-type-fits-all questions) to determine the premiums the insured entity needs to pay to the insurer. Both risk levels and policy premiums had been fixed for the period of the policy (generally 1 year). In the past, when the cyber breach risks were lower and the threat was not very sophisticated, this approach worked well for both insurer and insured, as evident from industry data shared by the leading underwriters on the minimal number and number of payouts made for cyber incidents, the low coverage amounts, and low adoption rates of this insurance.

© The Author(s), under exclusive license to Springer Nature Switzerland AG 2021
R. Badhwar, *The CISO's Next Frontier*,
https://doi.org/10.1007/978-3-030-75354-2_40

In the last 5–10 years, cyber risks have dramatically multiplied, due to the evolution of sophisticated malware, data exfiltration and breach tools, monetization of exfiltrated or breached data, publicly known and high profile exploits of internet-facing business applications containing sensitive customer or business data, the emergence of insider threat, Nation states stealing data and IP, the rapid and unfettered migration to the cloud, and the censure, suspension, and massive fines from local, state, or federal enforcement of stricter regulatory guidelines. It is reasonable to assert that the cyber and reputational risk that a given business entity carries today equal to or greater than more traditional notions of risk from inflation, reinvestment, interest rates, business cycles, capital, finance, currency, liquidity, or legislation.

3 Dynamic Risk Assessment and Analysis

It is imperative for the next generation cyber insurance paradigm to rely on *continuous risk assessments* and *dynamic risk analysis* to account for the current scope of elevated risk. This allows underwriters to determine appropriate premiums, and the insured can get appropriate coverage for the dynamic cyber risk they carry and intend to transfer to the insurer.

Obviously, this is easier said than done.

Static analysis was pretty easy and was generally done using a questionnaire with a list of questions answered once every year. The answers were sent to underwriters to help determine the policy and premiums. I have observed in the industry that the questionnaire completed and sent to insurance companies differed from the one used internally by firms, due to the different methodologies for measuring and quantifying the scope of risk. This can lead to divergence in the amount of risk actually transferred from what should be transferred.

I know the insurance companies and their underwriters would like to measure cyber risk dynamically by either having the insured entities send various data points to them on a periodic basis or having it shared through approved third-party providers or vendors that may already have access to that data. While this is an interesting theoretical idea, the risk of sharing this data (anonymized or not) and the inherent risk of the subsequent exposure, breach or misuse of data, **far outweighs the benefits**.

Therefore, any real-time data analysis to calculate dynamic risk must be performed by the insured firm in an environment that is controlled by the insured firm and NOT by the insurance provider or the broker. One such approach CISOs may consider palatable is the use of a dynamically created risk score per identified domain (e.g., endpoint, cloud, network, application, systems, web, regulatory compliance, etc.). This can be achieved by using an **industry standard mechanism or uniformly agreed upon specification** for creating the risk score. While this risk score will help to measure risk, provide dynamic insurance coverage, and determine variable premiums, its primary mission must be for the insured firm to be able to measure its own cyber risk dynamically and take the needed actions to **find the right balance of risk transference, risk mitigation, and risk remediation**.

4   Current Models

So far, we have talked about the need for a uniform industry standard or specification for creating a (dynamic) score for cyber risk. Currently there is no one standardized model per se, but there are a few models to discuss before we cover how to perform dynamic risk assessment.

VaR (Value-at-Risk) This model primarily depends upon the use of these three variables: (a) the amount of potential loss; (b) the probability of that amount of loss; and (c) the time frame. Originally created for determining the risk of financial products such as complex derivative securities, cyber insurance providers have adapted the VaR model by calculating probabilities of likely losses from cyberattacks during a given time frame, i.e., basically using a Monte Carlo simulation – **made popular by the adoption of its use within FAIR** (Factor Analysis of Information Risk) methodology.

FAIR can be used within a firm or investment portfolio to quantify the level of financial risk from cyber events, over a specific time frame. FAIR has been used primarily by financial services institutions but in no way is the industry standard when it comes to calculating cyber risk. It may not create a truly representational risk score for all cyber security scenarios, due to the breadth of the cyber and IT domains and the complexity and variability of associated risks. RiskLens, a company that makes cyber risk management software, has built a platform on top of the FAIR model [2].

Cyber Value-at-Risk This model also calculates the projected annual loss due to cyber-attacks using the value-at-risk (VaR) model, although the implementation is most probably different. CyberPoint has built a platform (CyVaR) on top of this model.

CVSS (Common Vulnerability Scoring System) "It provides a way to capture the principal characteristics of a vulnerability and produce a numerical score reflecting its severity. The numerical score can then be translated into a qualitative representation (such as low, medium, high, and critical) to help organizations properly assess and prioritize their vulnerability management processes" [1].

This universally accepted score generated by CVSS is used in the CVE (common vulnerabilities and exposures), which is a list of entries, each containing an identification number, a description, and at least one public reference, for publicly known cybersecurity vulnerabilities.

CWSS (Common Weakness Scoring System) "It provides a quantitative measurement of the unfixed weaknesses that are present within a software application. The CWSS scores can be automatically calculated, e.g., by a code analysis tool, or they can be manually calculated by a software security consultant or developer" [4].

All CVSS data is taken from CVE vulnerability data published by the National Vulnerability Database, NVD [3].

Proprietary Models These are models which use proprietary logic to calculate a risk score. Currently there are various proprietary models in the industry used primarily by the financial consulting services providers, i.e., the big five auditing firms (EY, Deloitte, KPMG, PWC etc.) or other firms like Willis Towers and Watson (now part of AON). These models may be proprietary variations of open models optimized by these providers based on knowledge gained from large sample datasets available to them over the years, or they may be privately developed models.

Hybrid Models These are the models that may use concepts from the various VaR models, combined with the usage of CVSS and CWSS.

Other Notable Model PCI DSS (to calculate risk for a sub segment).

As you can see, there are various models, many of which were developed to solve specific security reporting and business problems and later adapted to suit other use cases as well.

5   Risk Assessment and Analysis

Generally, each model uses two basic steps to create the risk score: (1) collect data, and then use it for the dynamic calculation of the cyber risk score, and (2) repeat the process continuously or periodically. The risk score calculation includes but is not limited to the mapping of the score to the model elements, whether it be the open models discussed above or a proprietary or hybrid risk calculation algorithm. The models should be able to score custom data based on unique use cases or requirements and then subsequently be able to map them to its elements.

Apart from the models (e.g., VaR, CVSS etc.) and the tools based on those models (e.g., RiskLens, CyVaR etc.), there also some **third-party companies** and agencies (e.g., FICO, BitSight, SecurityScorecard) that (most probably) have created their own (proprietary) models to calculate the risk. Many security endpoint or network-based tools also create risk scores using their own proprietary models when they detect malware or malicious events and use internal risk scoring methods to rate their severity as critical, high, medium, or low. A hybrid model could use all of the above to create a holistic risk score.

1. **Basic Dynamic Risk Assessment and Analysis** – is exclusively based on externally available information – whatever can be gauged by **publicly available**

information generally facilitated by non-profit entities (e.g., securityfocus.org, incident.org, packetstormsecurity.org, https://haveibeenpwned.com/) or commercial for-profit entities (e.g., BitSight, SecurityScorecard). The types of information include annual and quarterly financial results data, state and federal regulatory filings, correlated information obtained from third-party public breach information (if any) and publicly known vulnerabilities, along with any data deemed relevant and thereby provided by the firm getting scored.

This data should be obtained on a continuous monthly or quarterly basis and a risk score should be generated from a public or proprietary algorithm using the all identified sources of data to quantify and determine the risk. This type of activity can be easily outsourced to a third party, which can use a scoring algorithm or model agreed upon with the client. The risk scores calculated using this approach are only directional vectors and are generally not very accurate, but may highlight the need for a more comprehensive assessment.

2. **Intermediate Dynamic Risk Assessment and Analysis** – These build upon the basic dynamic risk assessment and analysis. This data can potentially be collected by using the capability to perform **dynamic scans** performed by an internal or external entity (preferred), from an external vantage point. Most of the data can be sourced from third-party providers using web crawling capability or by using open-source scanning tools (e.g., Shodan.io, censys.io, reputationauthority.org, haveibeenpwned.com, phishtank.com, openbugbounty.org) and the ethical usage of penetration testing tools such as nmap and Metasploit. The risk scores using this approach can provide a decent score and a good representation of the true cyber risk that a given entity may be carrying. Intermediate-level assessment and analysis is generally the sweet spot and **what most companies are willing to undertake**. Companies can use the calculated risk scores for cyber insurance, identifying remediation targets, and board and executive reporting.

Some of the data elements used in performing this level of risk analysis are defined below:

(a) Externally known digital and network footprint
(b) Brand hijacks or domain squatting
(c) Business interruption incidents
(d) Internet-facing compromised systems or systems using compromised or deprecated technologies (e.g., Struts), open ports/protocols (e.g., HTTP, SMTP, RDP, IRC, Telnet)
(e) Dark web scans
(f) Publicly known DNS leaks or hijacks
(g) Publicly known SPF and DKIM mis-configuration
(h) DMARC compliance
(i) Website performance
(j) Social media presence and chatter
(k) Web popularity
(l) Company stature and publicity

(m) Regulatory exposure

> **NOTE**: The client should either perform this assessment and analysis itself by using internal resources or an authorized third party with an NDA (nondisclosure agreement) to gather this data. Please also note that the usage of the above-mentioned (scanning) tools in an unauthorized manner can lead to litigation, fines, penalties, or the pursuance of other legal or disciplinary actions.

3. **Advanced Dynamic Risk Assessment and Analysis** – This approach builds upon the basic and intermediate levels, and requires sophisticated and diverse data collection capability. This is not for everybody and should only be used by entities with mature security programs, with well-documented implementation of security controls, including strict data and network security and fine-grained access management. Most of this data can be collected by gauging live traffic off a SPAN or TAP port off the core datacenter network switches, accessing CMDB, having visibility into the corporate SIEM, and other active or passive data sources. This data, only visible internally, is extremely confidential and sensitive. Care must be taken to protect it in an appropriate manner. Also, creating a risk score from this type of data will most certainly require a hybrid model customized to the type of data that can be collected and then mapped back to data elements within a standard or hybrid model.

Please be advised that this activity should only be undertaken by the cyber security teams using internal resources. Using an external (third-party) entity or an IT department to perform this data collection and this level of assessment and analysis is not recommended due to the sensitive nature of this data, exposure of which could lead to a security or privacy incident.

PS: The intent here is not to reveal the data, but instead to create a trustworthy standardized risk score from the data that is truly representational of the cyber risk the entity may be carrying.

Some of the data elements used in performing this level of risk analysis are defined below:

(a) Malicious or Anomalous indicators
(b) Tor activity
(c) Unauthorized VPN connections
(d) Email spam, spoofing, and phishing
(e) Unencrypted sensitive structured and unstructured data
(f) Unencrypted data in transit (north-south, east-west)
(g) DRM adoption
(h) Open files share and SharePoint sites
(i) Key management
(j) End-of-life software and applications
(k) Unlicensed software or applications
(l) Unsecured printers
(m) DMARC compliance
(n) Network complexity

(o)   Data breaches and exposures
(p)   Lack of Multi-Factor Authentication (MFA) for external-facing high-risk sites
(q)   Unsecured or unprotected mobile apps
(r)   Proliferation of authentication and authorization technologies
(s)   Lack of secure coding practices

Note: There are various third-party network, endpoint, and cloud-based tools that can help a firm tailor the collection and analysis of some of this data to the needs of the company. Some examples of these tools are crowdstrike, cybereason, cylance, exabeam, darktrace, zeek, bro, and securonix. Although there are tools available to generate risk scores, currently there are no insurance industry standards or specifications to measure, report, and cross-reference the risk scores across the insurance carriers, underwriters, and brokers. This lack of standards and specifications is especially true in cyber risk measurement and reporting for both internal consumption and also for comparison with peer firms. Having an industry standard may be beneficial for all parties involved – the underwriters and the insured entities and may lead to better measurement of risk and reduction of insurance premiums.

Note: It is recommended that the reader write security requirements specific to their needs and a conduct proof-of-concept (POC) with some of the above-mentioned providers. The author has provided the above-mentioned products list in no specific order and is not making any assertions on their performance, capability or maturity. Also, since this is a fast-evolving space, there are other interesting products in the market that have emerged recently. I also recommend that the readers look at the Gartner Magic quadrant for this space before they make a selection.

Currently, I believe the risk scores calculated from this endeavor are best used for internal consumption (by first and second line of defense personnel) to get an honest assessment of the cyber risk that an entity may be carrying to take proactive measures for risk mitigation and remediation. These may also be used to justify to regulatory entities and external auditors increased or decreased cyber security spending.

6   The CISO Take

Given the advanced state of threats and the exponential increase in the amount of cyber risk for almost every company in the world, dynamic risk measurement is a must for a firm to get the appropriate visibility into the amount of cyber risk they carry at any given time, and to take the needed actions to achieve the right balance of transference, mitigation, and remediation of risk.

With the SolarWinds attack, and increased risk of cyber breaches stemming from third party attacks, dynamic measurement of risk is going to be the new industry norm.

CISOs must also lobby for the standardization of risk scoring, if not universally, then at least across business domains (e.g., insurance, banking, entertainment, defense, pharma, healthcare). This will lead to better peer-to-peer comparisons, standardization of the scoring models, lower cost of risk audits, eventual reduction of insurance premiums, and last but not least, the lowering of cyber risk across a given business or risk domain.

7 Definitions

Monte Carlo Simulation – is a technique of estimating risk using a large number of variable and random inputs. These simulations use a repetitive technique of sampling a large number of random inputs to create a distribution of expected results.

FAIR – stands for Factor Analysis of Information Risk. It is a standard quantitative risk analysis model for information and operational risk used by cybersecurity professionals to quantify and measure risk.

PCI DSS – stands for Payment Card Industry Data Security Standard. It is an information security standard for entities that handle credit cards and associated data.

References

1. Forum of Incident Response and Security Teams, Inc. (FIRST) Common Vulnerability Scoring System SIG. https://www.first.org/cvss/. Accessed 5 Dec 2020
2. RiskLens (2020) The RiskLens FAIR Enterprise Model™ (RF-EM™). https://www.risklens.com/risklens-fair-enterprise-model. Accessed 5 Dec 2020
3. US Department of Commerce National Institute of Standards and Technology (2020) National Vulnerability Database https://nvd.nist.gov/. Accessed 5 Dec 2020
4. Common Weakness Enumeration (CWE) (2014) Common Weakness Scoring System (CWSS™). https://cwe.mitre.org/cwss/cwss_v1.0.1.html. Accessed 5 Dec 2020

Further Reading

FAIR Institute (2020) https://www.fairinstitute.org/. Accessed 5 Dec 2020
Forum of Incident Response and Security Teams, Inc. (FIRST) (2019) Common Vulnerability Scoring System version 3.1: Specification Document. https://www.first.org/cvss/specification-document Accessed 5 Dec 2020
PCI Security Standards Council (2020) https://www.pcisecuritystandards.org/pci_security/maintaining_payment_security Accessed 5 Dec 2020
US Department of Homeland Security Cybersecurity and Infrastructure Security Agency (2020) Common Vulnerabilities and Exposures. https://cve.mitre.org/cve/. Accessed 5 Dec 2020

OEM and Third-Party Sourced Application and Services Risk

1 Introduction

The average corporate-owned or personal endpoint devices – laptops, desktops, mobile devices and tablets, have generally proven to be the weakest links in the security chain. They have unfettered access to the internet, they frequently enter, leave, and re-enter the corporate or personal walled garden, with commercial and consumer users exposed to all things risky and malicious. Information security professionals make a special effort to harden and protect (corporate) endpoints. We deploy a plethora of security software and tools – namely, AV, DLP, eDiscovery, EDR, VPN, host IPS, and FW. These tools and software have 'detect and respond' capabilities to protect these corporate endpoints, but third parties, supply chain vendors, and services that provide software and firmware updates to these endpoint devices, remain a significant weakness.

2 The Genesis for High Risk

The risk is high for those who consume these (third party provided) services directly in real time from their laptops, desktops or mobile devices at home. They have no way to verify if a patch or an update is malicious, or if an OEM installed service is fully patched or not. They put their full faith in the provider(s) sufficiently securing their products and services. For consumers who are aware of what is involved in securing endpoints, they hope that the vendor has performed all due diligence, such as compatibility testing, performance testing, and vulnerability detection and mitigation. I bet a majority of the users are not even aware that apart from the operating system (e.g., Microsoft Windows), there are other (mostly unnecessary) services installed by the hardware manufacturer (e.g., Dell, HP, Lenovo) running on their

R. Badhwar, *The CISO's Next Frontier*,
https://doi.org/10.1007/978-3-030-75354-2_41

335

devices. Hardware manufacturers (e.g., Dell, HP, Lenovo) have really dropped the ball here by allowing "too many cooks into the kitchen." For the potential to offset costs, they have installed services from other third parties hawking their free six-month service or whatever else. Another reason for an OEM's reliance on other third parties (generally referred to as fourth party) is to outsource the creation and maintenance of support type services and documentation. Again, those additional parties also expect either to up-sell some service to you, or to mine and use your data to advertise or sell some other product or service. Users may not know what data third parties can access, or to which mother ship their data is being sent, or what drivers, software, or services have been automatically installed on their devices. Some of the blame also has to fall on users themselves, who are constantly looking to buy the cheapest possible device with the best possible configuration and hardware. Something's gotta give here, and generally what gives is the security and maintenance capability of these devices. So far, Apple products have been the exception to this problem.

By contrast, these risks are mitigated quite a bit in corporate environments, as most of the bloatware and optional services are disabled, and most of the third-party updates, (such as the software and security patches from Microsoft or firmware updates from PC manufacturers like Dell, HP, Lenovo, ASUS, or Apple), are tested in a test and non-production environment before they are pushed to production machines. Corporations can rely on a trust chain, with a lower-level environment to test new updates, along with a verifiable signed private key issued by the vendor.

Corporations clearly have a better risk management system than individual consumers; unfortunately, even corporate entities must contend with the issue of broken trust, sometimes due to their unacknowledged and unmanaged relationships with other third parties. If a vendor-issued or managed private key used to sign the firmware updates is compromised, breached, or stolen or exfiltrated by threat actors, then all bets are off. These threat actors can then sign malware with the same trusted key and embed that into the updates being made available for download by thousands or millions of users worldwide. The onus is then really on the recipient firms and corporations to verify there is nothing malicious or vulnerable in the third-party feeds, patches, and/or services.

We also need to be worried about the false sense of security that security tools may give to home users. If they have anti-virus (AV) and a local (host) firewall (FW), they think they have all the security tools required to protect them from malware but are unaware or unsuspecting that the hardware manufacturer may have installed vulnerable third-party services not patched by the OS or application providers. I have also noticed that these third-party services have a tendency to become corrupted and stop working altogether, or, if they talk on custom ports (other than 443), then they may get blocked by the default firewall rules of windows defender or the vanilla home router-based firewalls, and are thus unable to ping the mother ship to obtain a patch.

So far, this section has focused on endpoint machines because the risk to them is the highest, but the same risk also holds true for other backend systems and applications that host and run third party software.

3 Making the Case – Some Recent Incidents

To make my case, I am going to put special emphasis on a couple of weaknesses in the past couple of years, exhibited by support services (e.g., Dell's SupportAssist), OEM software, or third-party tools by the world's three most popular desktop and laptop manufacturers. Most of the custom support services or software installed on almost every laptop and desktop shipped by these manufacturers is not written by them. They source it as OEM software from other providers (e.g., Dell uses and re-brands PC Doctor) and many times, without performing proper due diligence and continuous vulnerability assessment and testing, exposing millions of users to various vulnerabilities.

3.1 Dell

Around mid-June 2019, Dell released a security advisory to address a Dell SupportAssist software vulnerability. In a nutshell, an attacker can load onto a service a DLL (Dynamic Link Library), either unsigned of signed by an unauthorized certificate, which runs with SYSTEM privileges, thereby allowing it to perform privilege escalation and. Using this exploit, an attacker could bypass established security controls – namely, signed execution, white-listing and driver signature enforcement. For the user, it's game over – hasta la vista!

Additional details have been provided in a blog post by SafeBreach – the security researchers who found this vulnerability, and have been made available in the reference section [3].

3.1.1 Tactical Recommendation

If you are still running the vulnerable version of Dell SupportAssist software, then I would suggest you immediately upgrade it or apply the recommended patch. Uninstalling the offending service should also be an option for savvy users who know what to do and directly where to go to obtain the updates for Dell drivers and support services going forward.

3.2 HP

On June 26, 2019, two critical vulnerabilities were discovered by the McAfee advanced threat research team: the HP Support Assistant 8.7.50 and earlier versions allow a user to gain system privilege and then further allow unauthorized modification of directories or files. (These are being tracked through CVE-2019-6328 and CVE-2019-6329).

Additional details have been provided in the post by HP [2].

3.2.1   Tactical Recommendation

I would immediately upgrade the software (i.e., HP Support Assistant) or apply the recommended patch. Uninstalling the offending service should also be an option for savvy users who know what to do and where to go to get the updates for HP drivers and services.

3.3   ASUS

Many of you may have heard the report of attackers hijacking ASUS automatic software update tool and pushing malware to hundreds of thousands of unsuspecting customers around the world in 2018. This was a unique attack, as the attackers seem to have compromised the ASUS private keys, and thus were able to use legitimate ASUS digital certs to send malicious trojanized updates.

Additional details have been provided by Symantec [1].

3.3.1   Tactical Recommendations

(a) All the impacted endpoints should be taken off network, or at least their egress to the internet should be blocked.
(b) All impacted endpoints should be scanned for the malware and remediated and sanitized.
(c) All the known indicators of compromise (IOCs) must be loaded into the EDR tool running on the endpoints and servers to detect any ongoing malicious CnC communications or data transfers from the impacted servers or any other assets on your network.

3.4   Solarwinds

Perhaps the most egregious and famous incident stemming from a third-party breach is that of Solarwinds, a provider of network monitoring and management software. This incident did not impact endpoint machines but rather a monitoring service.

In this case, upon breaching Solarwinds, the attackers – injected a malware called 'Sunburst', a trojanized digitally signed component of the Solarwind's Orion software framework which contains a backdoor. After an initial period of dormancy, the malware makes an HTTP connection through the backdoor to domain generation algorithm (DGA)-generated sub-domain(s) for a set command and control (CnC) server. Once a communication is established with a CnC server, the backdoor can execute any system command it receives and also send data to the CnC server.

The malware was found to be capable of evading detection by the traditional AV tools by using evasive techniques like obfuscated blocklists, although some EDR and UEBA tools have been established to flag some of the activities as anomalous.

Multiple well-established and sophisticated companies like FireEye and Microsoft, federal government agencies, and many other organizations were found to be impacted, highlighting the seriousness of this and other breaches using this same technique.

3.4.1   Tactical Recommendations

(a) If you are running the impacted version of the Solarwinds software, then you must immediately shut down any servers hosting Solarwinds and get them off your network.

(b) If you're not running the impacted version of the Solarwinds software or are not sure, then you should immediately isolate the Solarwind servers, and prevent them from accessing the internet by implementing an egress block.

(c) You should scan the servers for all malware, including Sunburst.

(d) Subsequently you should load the indicators of compromise (IOC) hashes (for Sunburst trojanized binaries and CnC domains) obtained from FireEye, Microsoft, and others, into your EDR (or NGAV) tool to enable the detection and alerting of the malware and its activity through your entire network (since the malware may have spread or may have installed other malware on other parts of your network). Over 250 signatures/hashes have been created and made available for use by the threat intel providers.

(e) All infected servers and binaries should be sanitized and remediated before they're allowed back on the network.

(f) Deploy the kill-switch released by security vendors to stop the execution of the backdoor in your environment. A kill-switch was also implemented in conjunction with the DNS Sinkhole implemented by FireEye and Microsoft.

(g) If you are/were impacted, you must report this to the regulatory entity (e.g., NYDFS, Finra, SEC, OCC, DSS) that has oversight over your business. If any customer data was exfiltrated or exposed, then you must also get into compliance with privacy regulations like CCPA/CPRA or GDPR.

(h) Specific indicators are mentioned below. These should help you with your forensic examination:

- Processes:

1. SolarWinds.Orion.Core.BusinessLayer.dll (this contains the Sunburst malware)
2. Netsetupsvc.dll (teardrop memory dropper)

- Domains: (these can be used to build a list of impacted entities using DNS sinkholing and also to deploy a kill switch)

1. *avsvmcloud[.]com (CnC but acquired by Microsoft)
2. Deftsecurity[.]com (CnC)
3. Freescanonline[.]com (CnC)
4. Thedoccloud[.]com (CnC)
5. Other DGA-generated domains

- String (to search):

1. OrionImprovementBusinessLayer
2. solarwinds.businesslayerhost

- Named Pipe (to search):

1. 583da945-62af-10e8-4902-a8f205c72b2e

- Microsoft (Defender) antivirus detections:

1. Trojan:MSIL/Solorigate.B!dha
2. Trojan:MSIL/Solorigate.BR!dha

- Authentication token (SAML) abuse (aka Golden SAML)

1. Token time-to-live (TTL) altered to extend life of tokens
2. Token 'create time' made identical to subsequent token 'accessed time'.

4   Strategic Remedies and Recommendations

One question we really need to ask is, do we really need all these third-party OEM software suites and services running on our Dell, HP, Lenovo, Acer or ASUS machines? On our servers?

It has become abundantly clear that hardware OEMs are not proactive: they do not do their due diligence to test the software provided by these third parties and supply chain vendors. Instead, they are reactive: only after these types of issues are discovered, do they limit their response to patching. If they ship an OEM software or service, then they should shoulder the responsibility in the same manner as OS vendors, ensuring that it is continuously assessed for vulnerabilities and weaknesses and patched promptly.

1. My recommendation is that we consider uninstalling most of these endpoint (bloatware) services altogether. There are a couple of options listed below that should also be considered:

   (a) All firmware and OEM application or driver updates for every hardware configuration should be sent along with all the OS-level security updates and patches provided by the creator of the OS (e.g., Microsoft, Apple, RedHat).

Yes, this will add to complexity, will be expensive and difficult to achieve, but if this is done, then there is a higher possibility that these will be tested and verified by the OS vendors themselves, rather than relying on the OEM vendors.

(b) One other cheaper and less complex way to deal with this problem would be to handle these updates asynchronously through a basic notification service rather than a local service with admin privileges that could become corrupted or vulnerable. While this is not for everyone, in this case, the onus would be on the user to get the updates from the hardware vendor or manufacturer and install them once they are notified. Savvy users should be able to perform some manual and basic signature (hash) validations to ensure that nothing has tampered with the update.

2. For other key services that cannot be uninstalled or removed (e.g., network monitoring, or feature/functionality patches), the only solution is **Zero Trust**. We have to stop trusting the feature functionality updates and patches, even if they are signed with a trusted digital certificate or come from Microsoft, Oracle, HP, or Dell. Every update must be scanned, tested, and sandboxed in a lower-level environment before they are allowed to be brought into a production environment. Yes, this is going to be expensive, and take a lot longer, but the outcome of not doing this is going to create the potential for more Solarwinds-style attacks.

3. The software build and distribution infrastructure used by vendor/partners and all software and product creators, needs to be hardened. Some recommendations on the how-to are mentioned below –

(a) Use Secure Frameworks – There are many secure frameworks that have mature software development and hardening processes built it. While the specifics depend on the workstream and business domains, the use of NIST 800-53 (rev5) and 800-161, CMMI v2 and ISO 27001:2013 should be evaluated and considered for incorporation into the product creation and distribution.

(b) Penetrating Testing – The continued use of penetration testing paradigms needs to be followed. This can be done by the use of dynamic application security testing (DAST), and purple (red and blue) teaming exercises.

(c) Zero Trust – Although already mentioned in previous item (2), the core concepts of zero trust including but not limited to network micro segmentation and application segmentation – with least privilege, must be followed.

4. The active use of Threat Intel to know about the adversaries and threat actors should be undertaken.

(a) Active Intelligence – Using the threat intel platform the capability must exist to use Indicators or compromise (IOCs) and Tactics, techniques and procedures (TTPs) to detect patterns of malicious activities or methods associated with threat actors.

(b) Advanced Monitoring – Capability must exist to perform advanced monitoring and analytics. This can be done by getting visibility into north-south and east-west lateral movement activities by insiders. This can also be used to detect malicious activity or other anomalous activity within the corporate network. Modern analysis engines use semi-supervised machine learning capabilities to perform this analysis very close to real-time by looking at live traffic taken off a span or tap port.

5 The CISO Take

Desperate times call for desperate measures. The risk to our endpoint and server assets is immense. We have to reduce the bloatware on our devices. We have to create better ways to detect malware on our devices and prevent privilege escalation, optimize our ML capabilities to detect and defeat malware signed by valid certificates, and drastically reduce the number of services running on our devices with privileged access. We must be vocal in demanding that device OEMs not sell our data or install unnecessary services as part of marketing and advertising deals to save a couple of dollars. We should also be ready to pay a little bit more for our devices – trust me, it is money well spent. OS and OEM vendors must win back our trust by ensuring that all the software they write and ship to us and subsequently patch and maintain is free from malware and vulnerabilities.

An incident of the magnitude of SolarWinds subjects a company to a tremendous amount of reputational and regulatory risk. If consumers lose trust in a given business from repeat incidents, then it will be very difficult for that company to survive.

It is imperative that CISOs be given the authority and resources to ensure that all third-party application and infrastructure software updates and patches are thoroughly tested and sandboxed before they are deployed in production. Ideally, all network and endpoint infrastructure should be under the direct supervision of the CISO to ensure that they remain secure through the various software installations and updates. Yes, some of these changes may need larger change windows, more testing, and more sandboxing environments, but without adopting such measures, we risk paying millions of dollars of regulatory fines and losing our customers to other more secure entities.

6 Definitions

CCPA – stands for California Consumer Privacy Act. It is a California state regulation on consumer protection and privacy rights for California residents.

CnC – stands for command and control (server). It is generally a cloud-hosted server/system using DGA-generated domains that are used by threat actors to control and manage infected and breached endpoints and servers (generally resident) on private networks.

CPRA – stands for the California Privacy Rights Act. It will amend and supersede CCPA once it goes into effect on Jan 1st, 2023. It expands consumer privacy rights to align more closely with those outlined in the EU's GDPR.

DNS Sinkhole – stands for Domain Name Service Sinkhole. It is a technique that helps with the identification of malware infected hosts on a private network. It enables the redirection of malicious internet-bound traffic by entering a fake entry into a DNS server to change the traffic flow of a malicious URL. The sinkhole allows to control any CnC bound traffic and other malicious traffic across a private network. These can also be used to deploy kill switches against malware.

EDR – stands for Endpoint Detection and Response. This is the next-generation malware detection system. Rather than relying on the static signature-based schemes of legacy AV detection products, it has the capability to provide visibility into endpoint user, machine and process behavior, perform dynamic heuristical analysis, and use that to detect and block advanced malware.

GDPR – stands for General Data Protection Regulation. It is an EU regulation on data protection and privacy requirements for EU residents.

IOC – stands for Indicator of Compromise. It is either a unique signature, log entry, or an event that indicates that a network or system breach has occurred. These can be used as a forensics evidence, either individually, or in combination with other IOCs.

OEM – stands for Original Equipment Manufacturer. In the context of software, this is the entity that creates the original version of the large and complex software (e.g., Microsoft is the OEM for Windows OS, and Oracle for its relational database) and sells licenses for private and business use.

References

1. Symantec Security Response Team (2019) ASUS software updates used for supply chain attacks. Available via Broadcom Symantec Enterprise Blogs/Threat Intelligence. https://www.symantec.com/blogs/threat-intelligence/asus-supply-chain-attack
2. HP Product Security Response Team (2019) HPSBGN03620 rev. 4 – HP Support Assistant Escalation of Privilege Vulnerability. Support Communication Security Bulletin. https://support.hp.com/us-en/document/c06388027
3. Hadar P (2019) OEM software puts multiple laptops at risk. Available via SafeBreach blog. https://safebreach.com/Post/OEM-Software-Puts-Multiple-Laptops-At-Risk

Further Reading

Cimpanu C (2020) Microsoft and industry partners seize key domain used in SolarWinds hack. Available via ZDNet. https://www.zdnet.com/article/microsoft-and-industry-partners-seize-key-domain-used-in-solarwinds-hack/
FireEye (2020) Highly Evasive Attacker Leverages SolarWinds Supply Chain to Compromise Multiple Global Victims with SUNBURST Backdoor. Available via FireEye Blogs: Threat

Research.   https://www.fireeye.com/blog/threat-research/2020/12/evasive-attacker-leverages-solarwinds-supply-chain-compromises-with-sunburst-backdoor.html.

FireEye   (2021)   Sunburst   Information   https://www.fireeye.com/current-threats/sunburst-malware.html

Joint Task force (2020). NIST Special Publication 800-53 Revision 5 Security and Privacy Controls for Information Systems and Organizations. https://nvlpubs.nist.gov/nistpubs/SpecialPublications/NIST.SP.800-53r5.pdf

Jon Boyens, Rama Moorthy et al (2015). NIST Special Publication 800-161, Supply Chain Risk Management Practices for Federal Information Systems and Organizations. https://nvlpubs.nist.gov/nistpubs/SpecialPublications/NIST.SP.800-161.pdf

Krebs   B   (2020)   Malicious   Domain   in   SolarWinds   Hack   Turned   into 'Killswitch.' Available   via   Krebsonsecurity.   https://krebsonsecurity.com/2020/12/malicious-domain-in-solarwinds-hack-turned-into-killswitch/

Microsoft   365   Defender   Team   (2020)   Using   Microsoft   365   Defender   to   pro-tect   against   Solorigate.   https://www.microsoft.com/security/blog/2020/12/28/using-microsoft-365-defender-to-coordinate-protection-against-solorigate/

Rashid FY (2020) Stopping Solarwinds backdoor with a killswitch. Available via Decipher. https://duo.com/decipher/stopping-solarwinds-backdoor-with-a-killswitch

Reiner S (2020) Golden SAML Revisited: The Solorigate Connection. Available via Cyberark Threat   Research   Blog.   https://www.cyberark.com/resources/threat-research-blog/golden-saml-revisited-the-solorigate-connection

Commentary on Insider Threat

1 Introduction

In the cyber security world, the term "insider threat" is generally used to define the (cyber) threat to the security of an organization that comes from within – similar to the concept of a Trojan horse. This threat is generally attributed to the risk of data exfiltration and/or network breach by current or former employees, or by other vendors, contractors, suppliers or partners that may have physical access to company premises and/or remote access to company networks or systems.

2 Threat Types

These threats can be generally classified into five broad categories – criminal, hacktivism, extortion, process, and accidental, and can lead to a variety of risks, such as network or system breaches resulting in unauthorized exposure and/or disclosure of company-sensitive data and business secrets, reputational risk, regulatory risk, or business loss from fraud.

(a) A **hacktivist** could be a current or former employee either disgruntled or motivated by a political or social agenda trying to embarrass the company by hacking into its systems. A hacktivist might cause system/network disruption, access or disclose sensitive company data, or even knowingly install malware on company systems.

(b) Generally, most insider threat activity that is classified as **criminal** is financially motivated. Data exfiltration falls under this category. Business competitors or even state-sponsored entities often get their agents or infiltrators hired as target company employees or contractors to steal intellectual property, company-sensitive or personally identifiable information.

© The Author(s), under exclusive license to Springer Nature Switzerland AG 2021
R. Badhwar, *The CISO's Next Frontier*,
https://doi.org/10.1007/978-3-030-75354-2_42

(c) There have been reported instances of **extortion** in the industry where current or former employees have been blackmailed into stealing company data for a variety of reasons.

(d) Security teams in the industry frequently also see cases where insiders (employees or contractors) violate security policies because they either don't understand what the correct **process** is to do something, or they don't want to take the time to follow it.

(e) **Accidental** insider threat activity is generally attributed to accidental deletion or destruction of data, falling victim to a credential phishing event, or ignorance about company policy on how to handle company data (e.g., emailing company data to personal email accounts, or even other external accounts, for a variety of non-malicious reasons).

Note: Taking part in an activity that is classified as insider threat can lead to termination of employment and/or fines and/or criminal prosecution by a local, state, or federal government entity.

3 Detection and Prevention

There are two primary ways to detect and prevent insider threats: technological and human.

3.1 Technological Solution

(a) The technological solution comprises the usage and cross referencing of alerts and events from the existing security stack generally already deployed in most organizations. This stack generally comprises of various tools providing security coverage across endpoint, network, perimeter, cloud, application and mobile devices.

(b) The use of cyber deception technologies like Honeypots, Honeynets and the modern (AI enabled) cyber deception systems to act as decoys and lure the insider's threat in exposing their identity and their intentions.

(c) The use of security principles like Zero Trust, Defense in Depth, and Least Privilege in the configuration, implementation, and administration of the above-mentioned security stack. This makes it possible to detect and prevent external threats and data exfiltration from insiders.

(d) Also, technological solutions like Digital Rights Management, User Behavior Analysis aided by Artificial Intelligence and Machine Learning have provided additional capabilities to detect, mitigate, and prevent this threat.

3.2   Human Solution

(a) However, the most effective defense, however, is achieved by raising human awareness of these threats through frequent training and communications, so that these activities can be detected and reported by other employees using the very basic yet effective principle of "see something, say something."

The combination and collaboration of these two elements can make it hard for threat actors to be successful and that is what security technologists' practice and preach in the industry on an ongoing basis. Security of customer and company data and systems is everyone's collective responsibility.

4   Using ML or AI Algorithms

All the technological options and the commercial tooling mentioned above in Sect. 3 can be made better, faster, and more effective by using Machine Learning (ML) and Artificially Intelligent (AI) algorithms.

While AI and ML capabilities and their use in cybersecurity have been treated in much greater detail in chapter "The Case for AI/ML in Cybersecurity" in this book, a brief list of capabilities to detect scanning activity by insiders that have been augmented and enhanced by AI and ML algorithms has been provided below, and have been further mapped to the (four) modified Northrup Grumman cyber kill-chain phases [1].

Although this book has chosen to use the Lockheed Martin kill-chain, further enhancements can be done using the popular and more sophisticated MITRE ATT&CK framework, using mapping already established between the two.

4.1   Reconnaissance

In this phase, the insider threat (actor) conducts reconnaissance activities, i.e., scans or scouts the target host or system to identify known vulnerabilities, or exposed ports or services, or other weaknesses that could be remotely exploited.

The detection/prevention techniques are –

(a) Internal IP Scan Detector
(b) Internal Port Scan detector
(c) UEBA (user and entity behavior analysis) for insider threat type use cases among many other data exfil use cases, with the capability to detect IP/Port scans by both by known and unknown entities, as well UEBA on trusted users.

4.2 Breach (Weaponization + Delivery)

In this phase, the insider threat (actor) weaponizes, customizes, or creates a malicious package (malware) designed to exploit one or many known vulnerabilities or known backdoors, and delivers it to the target host or system.

The detection/prevention techniques are –

(a) Detection of Privilege Escalation (user-to-root attacks)
(b) Detection of unauthorized/non-compliant network nodes
(c) Detection of malicious activity using network deception technology and sophisticated honeypots further augmented by supervised machine learning algorithms like Decision Trees and Support Vector Machine (SVM)

4.3 Infection (Installation, Privilege Escalation, Remote Command and Control, and Code Execution)

In this phase, the insider threat (actor) installs and subsequently executes a malicious package (malware) designed to exploit one or many known vulnerabilities, on a target host or system.

The detection/prevention techniques are –

(a) Anomaly detection using Markov-chain model and EVT (extreme value theorem) based anomaly detection
(b) Beaconing (periodic or random)
(c) Lateral movement detection (Malicious use of psexec, powershell and remote desktop; token stealing and pass-the-hash, pass-the-ticket, golden ticket, silver ticket, kerberoasting attacks; network sniffing, ARP spoofing and other Active Directory attacks)
(d) Network protocol anomaly detection

4.4 Mission Goals/Malicious Actions (Data Exfiltration, DATA Destruction)

In this final phase of the cyber kill-chain, the insider threat (actor) performs various activities such as data exfiltration, data encryption (ransomware), and data destruction (virus/worm).

The detection/prevention techniques are –

(a) DNS tunneling detection (HTTP, HTTPS, FTP, and POP3 tunnels)
(b) Unauthorized data encryption detection
(c) Unauthorized data destruction or corruption activities detection
(d) Unauthorized Data access and manipulation (alteration) detection

4.5   *Commercial Implementations*

While a lot of these algorithms can be implemented in-house, these implementations are not for the faint-hearted, as these supervised or reinforced machine learning algorithms require constant optimizations and updated (training) datasets.

There are also a variety of commercial security tools that make use of equivalent algorithms or variations or the optimizations listed above. These commercial tools can be primarily classified into endpoint-based, network-based and cloud access security broker (CASB) implementations. These commercial entities include but are definitely not limited to the names mentioned below.

(a) Exabeam, Securonix, FireEye, Splunk UBA (formerly Caspida), Dark Trace, and Vectra are examples of *network-based* tools that primarily use UEBA capabilities.
(b) Carbon Black, CrowdStrike, Cybereason, Cylance, Rapid7, SentinelOne, and Mcafee are examples of *endpoint-based* tools that primarily rely on endpoint detection and response (EDR) capabilities.
(c) Bitglass, Mcafee (Skyhigh), Microsoft (MCAS), Palo Alto (Aperture), ZScaler and Netskope are examples of *CASB* implementations.

Many of these tools support API level integrations with each other, with some other tools, or with industry standard SIEM platforms (e.g., Splunk or QRadar).

Note: It is recommended that the reader write security requirements specific to their needs and a conduct proof-of-concept (POC) with some of the above-mentioned providers. The author has provided the above-mentioned products list in no specific order and is not making any assertions on their performance, capability or maturity. Also, since this is a fast-evolving space, there are other interesting products in the market that have emerged recently. I also recommend that the readers look at the Gartner Magic quadrant for this space before they make a selection.

5   The CISO Take

Insider threat detection and mitigation is a team sport. Currently there isn't one tool or a magic bullet than can help detect and mitigate the threat, but the combination of the above-mentioned tools, the full traffic packet capture and analysis to account for any north-south and east-west traffic, and the real-time and passive correlation of logs within a SIEM can get the job done right at the current time (until the advent of a fully unsupervised machine learning paradigm in the not-so-distant future).

The security teams should continue to perform their training and awareness exercises on how to recognize insider threat, and continue to push the fundamental security theme that has worked very well to thwart insider threat – 'See something, Say something!'.

It is the responsibility of CISOs to ensure that suitable insider threat detection capabilities are implemented. I have highlighted some additional specialized insider threat detection capabilities such as cyber deception systems and honey pots within a separate chapter ("Cyber Deception Systems") in this book.

6 Definitions

MCAS – stands for Microsoft Cloud App Security. It is a cloud access security broker (CASB) solution that provides the capability to gain visibility into the applications hosted in Azure and o365.

ARP – stands for Address Resolution Protocol. It is a protocol that translates IP addresses to a MAC address, and vice-versa. It is generally used to locate a device on an ethernet network.

ARP command – it is a command used to view and modify the local ARP cache (on windows), which contains a list of all the recently resolved MAC addresses of IP hosts on the network.

Pass-the-ticket – it is an Active Directory (AD) attack where an attacker impersonates a valid user by stealing their Kerberos token from a compromised system and re-uses that stolen token to authenticate as that user.

Pass-the-hash – it is a common AD exploit where an attacker impersonates a user by stealing the cryptographic hash of their password and uses it to authenticate as the user.

Zero Trust – is a security architecture and implementation paradigm that reduces enterprise risk by performing secure implementations in compliance with the principal that all assets inside and outside a perimeter firewall are not to be trusted and thus access control for users, devices, systems and services must be provided using least privilege with risk-based access reviews.

Defense in Depth – it refers to a multi layered approach of defense in cyber security. A threat actor would have to breach multiple layers before they can achieve their (malicious) mission goal.

Least Privilege – it generally refers to a cybersecurity practice that ensures that users and/or processes be granted the least amount of privilege required for them to successfully accomplish their tasks.

Reference

1. Lockheed Martin (2015) Gaining the Advantage: Applying Cyber Kill Chain® Methodology to Network Defense. https://www.lockheedmartin.com/content/dam/lockheed-martin/rms/documents/cyber/Gaining_the_Advantage_Cyber_Kill_Chain.pdf. Accessed 20 Nov 2020

Further Reading

Cybersecurity & Infrastructure Security Agency (2020) Insider Threat Mitigation. https://www.
cisa.gov/insider-threat-mitigation. Accessed 6 Dec 2020
Green A (2020) What is DNS tunneling? A Detection Guide. Available via Varonis. https://www.
varonis.com/blog/dns-tunneling/. Accessed 6 Dec 2020
National Vulnerability Database. NIST Special Publication 800-53 (Rev. 4), Insider threat pro-
gram. National Institute of Standards and Technology, Gaithersburg. https://nvd.nist.gov/800-
53/Rev4/control/PM-12. Accessed 7 Dec 2020
Yuan SH, Wu XT (2020) Deep Learning for Insider Threat Detection: Review, Challenges and
Opportunities. https://arxiv.org/pdf/2005.12433.pdf. Accessed 7 Dec 2020
Zhang E (2020) The early indicators of an insider threat. In: Data Insider: Digital Guardian's Blog.
Available via Digital Guardian. https://digitalguardian.com/blog/early-indicators-insider-
threat Accessed 6 Dec 2020

Simplified Approach to Calculate the Probability of a Cyber Event

1 Introduction

Given the current cyber threat landscape, it would not be far-fetched to assert that the cyber and reputational risk a given business entity carries these days is equal to or greater than other more traditional market risks, such as inflation, reinvestment, interest rates or risks involving capital, business, finance, currency, or liquidity, or risks associated with regulation and legislation.

2 Cyber Risk

Cyber risk has the potential to materialize or manifest into a 'cyber event'. In their effort to provide cyber protection to the firms where they work and to the overall cyber ecosystem, security professionals deploy countermeasures to detect, mitigate, remediate, and transfer cyber risk to reduce the probability of being subjected to a cyber-breach.

There are some well-established paradigms on how to calculate and quantify the cyber risk that a given entity may be carrying on its books. Quantifying risk is required to determine which IT area for a given business needs more cyber investment and rigor to remediate or mitigate its cyber risk. This is also required to determine the cyber insurance that one entity needs to acquire to transfer that risk.

The accepted industry-wide approach to determine cyber risk is generally cited as:

$$\textbf{Cyber Risk} = \textbf{Cyber Event Probability} * \textbf{Business Impact}$$

There are various options to help quantify the cyber risk. One of them is to hire a big four consulting firms (i.e., PWC, Deloitte, EY and KPMG) or equivalent firm to help quantify the risk. Alternatively, the firm (with the assistance from the inhouse cybersecurity and risk teams) could self-quantify and assess the cyber risk by calculating the cyber event probability and business impact from a potential breach.

In either case, calculating the cyber event probability and the business impact is not an easy task for a firm and requires extremely good self-visibility into:

(a) Its technology debt (i.e., how current the technology stack is), including but not limited to all the vulnerabilities and weaknesses that may exist in its high-risk, external-facing and internal applications and systems;
(b) Maturity of its (cyber) security stack and its incident response capability;
(c) Data security, including but not limited to encryption and masking of its sensitive data;
(d) The impact a cyber-event may cause to the processes and procedures used to conduct business for a given line of business (LOB);
(e) Its disaster recovery and business resilience capability;
(f) Its reputational risk (depending upon the nature of the business and past track record);
(g) Third-party and supply chain risk;
(h) Its cyber adversaries or threat vectors including but not limited to insider threats.

One of the more important aspects of determining the cyber risk is to calculate the probability of a cyber-event. This chapter tries to provide a high-level and introductory treatment of that need, introducing this basic equation:

Cyber Event Probability = Risk Score * Threat Score * Defensive Score

Putting all the complexity aside for starters, given a scale of 0–1, the probability that a given application or system may encounter a cyber-event is not a binary number (0 or 1) but is somewhere between 0 and 1 depending upon its cumulative cyber risk, its threat score, and its defensive capability.

Also, the equation that determines the overall probability of a cyber-event for a given firm is not linear, and thus requires complex mathematical and statistical analysis to provide an accurate estimate. As previously stated, that level of detailed analysis is outside the scope of this book, and only a high-level introductory treatment is being provided at the current time.

The treatment below can be used to provide a high-level view to *self-assess* the cyber breach probability of an entity using internal resources with medium level of accuracy (at best).

2.1 Risk Score (rs)

This score is assigned to each application or system. It encompasses the risk from vulnerabilities, currency (N-?), exploitability and occurrence of vulnerabilities, and other security issues such as data and network security that increase the risk of application, system, or network breaches. The risk score accounts for internet-facing high risk and internal low risk applications and systems. It also accounts for the maturity (or not) of the work force and their ability to recognize phishing emails and other cyber threats.

The simplistic risk scoring used for this chapter uses a scale of 0–1 and has been calculated by using this equation:

$$rs = \textbf{Function 1}(x);$$

where Function 1 is a hypothetical non-linear equation based on observed data that signifies the cumulative risk score stemming from vulnerabilities, currency, and other issues, such as data security, for a given application (x). It has been used to create a simplified scoring scheme based on an average of observed scores for the various risk variables discussed above, which exhibit non-linear behavior. Detailed mathematical treatment of the equation is outside the scope of this book.

Critical – 1.0
High – 0.7
Medium – 0.4
Low – 0.1

2.2 Defensive Score (ds)

This score, assigned to each application and system, measures a range of defense-related capabilities: countermeasures deployment against malware and other advanced threats, as well as insider threat; monitoring and mitigating controls deployment; the hiring of educated and well-trained cyber security professionals; and the maturity level of the security stack, which includes perimeter, network and endpoint security tools and the implementation of good security hygiene and practices like zero trust with least privilege with full network segmentation. The defensive score generally comprises of an application score and a system score. The system score is based on the inherent perimeter, network and endpoint security implementations, and maturity for a given entity. The app defensive score is based on the security built into the application itself (e.g., secure coding and good design).

The defensive scoring described in this chapter uses a scale of 0.5–0.9 and has been calculated with this equation:

$$ds = \textbf{Function 2}(x);$$

where Function 2 is a hypothetical non-linear equation based on observed data that signifies the cumulative defensive score for each app, taking into consideration the defensive capabilities of an app(x) and/or system(x). It has been used to create the simplified scoring scheme (below) that is based on an average of observed scores for the various defensive variables discussed above, which exhibit non-linear behavior. Detailed mathematical treatment of the equation is outside the scope of this book.

Excellent – 0.5
Good – 0.6
Medium – 0.7
Poor – 0.8
None – 0.9

2.3   Threat Score (ts)

This score is assigned to each application or system. It measures the risk from advanced malware, sophisticated threat actors, or malicious entities (e.g., criminals, nation states), and other forms of advanced persistent threat, and insider threat.

The threat scoring used for this paper uses a scale of 0–1 and has been calculated by using this equation:

$$ts = \textbf{Function } 3(x);$$

where Function 3 is a hypothetical non-linear equation based on observed data that signifies the cumulative threat score stemming from advanced malware, sophisticated threat actors, or malicious entities for a given application (x). It has been used to create the simplified scoring scheme that is based on an average of observed scores for the various threat variables discussed above, which exhibit non-linear behavior. Detailed mathematical treatment of the equation is outside the scope of this book.

Advanced – 1.0
High – 0.7
Medium – 0.5
Low – 0.2

2.4   Cyber Event Probability

Cyber Event Probability (CEP) for a given entity is the summation of products of the average Risk Scores (rs), Threat Scores (ts) and the defensive scores (ds) for a given ecosystem being assessed.

$$CEP = \sum_{x=1}^{x=n} \frac{rs(x)}{x} * \sum_{x=1}^{x=n} \frac{ds(x)}{x} * \sum_{x=1}^{x=n} \frac{ts(x)}{x}$$

While the CEP is itself a score that needs to be calculated and tracked, as previously established, it is also further used to calculate the cyber risk.

The Cyber risk can also be used to determine the amount of cyber insurance an entity needs to purchase to transfer cyber risk that has either not been or cannot be mitigated.

2.5 A Basic Case Study

Let's do some very basic and simplistic modelling, with a hypothetical case of a small financial startup.

Let's assume:

(a) The company has a total of 10 applications. For the sake of simplicity let's assume

  - Two applications are considered to have critical risk
  - Three applications are considered to have high risk
  - Three applications are considered to have medium risk
  - Two applications are considered to have low risk

(b) The net investment of the company at risk from a cyber event is $25M.
(c) The reputation risk has been estimated to be another $10M.
(d) If we wanted to calculate the CEP for this ecosystem then we can calculate the rs, ds, and ts scores using the equations previously discussed:

$$rs = (2*1.0 + 3*0.7 + 3*0.4 + 2*0.1)/10 = 0.55$$

$$ds = (2*0.8 + 3*0.8 + 3*0.7 + 2*0.7)/10 = \left(\begin{array}{c} \text{assuming good and medium} \\ \text{level of defensive posture} \end{array}\right) = 0.75$$

$$ts = (2*0.7 + 3*0.7 + 3*0.5 + 2*0.5)/10 = \left(\begin{array}{c} \text{assuming high and medium} \\ \text{level of threats} \end{array}\right) = 0.60$$

$$CEP = rs * ds * ts$$
$$= 0.248$$

(e) Thus, using the CEP, the total amount of Cyber Risk (i.e., worst-case financial loss) can be estimated to be 0.248 * $35M = $8.9M
(f) Thus, the company should either transfer $8.9M worth of risk by buying cyber insurance, or by investing a portion of that money in the IT and Security programs to reduce the inherent risk level by fixing vulnerabilities, thereby reducing their total exposure from a CEP.

3   The CISO Take

Given the sophisticated adversaries, the advanced persistent threat, the spread of ransomware, and the number of breaches that occur almost on a daily basis in the industry, the cyber risk is one of the biggest risks that an enterprise faces at the current time, regardless of their size or the maturity of their cyber security programs. Generally, the firm's enterprise risk management (ERM) teams do a pretty good job of modelling and managing financial and associated risks (like credit or market risk), but generally may not have a good handle on the large amount of cyber risk that their firms may be carrying.

To do their job of protecting the enterprise and remediating or mitigating all known cyber risk, CISOs need to be able to quantify the cyber risk and subsequently have the capability to calculate the probability of an (adverse) cyber event on a continuous basis. This work is generally best performed by the (first line of defense) security risk assessment team under the leadership of the CISO. This data would also come in handy while determining the amount of cyber insurance a firm needs to purchase to transfer some of the cyber risk.

This chapter provides a hypothetical approach of using a basic self-service technique to calculate the cyber risk and the cyber event probability. While engaging a professional services company (like Deloitte, PWC or EY) would provide more accurate results, this could definitely be a good starting point for small to medium-sized firms. This would also build in the needed hygiene to continuously assess the cyber risk and make sure it remains within risk tolerance limits.

4   Disclaimer

The cyber risk and cyber event probability calculation technique(s) provided in the chapter is hypothetical. If you choose to follow this technique or approach, then you must do so at your own risk.

5   Definitions

Currency – is a term used to define the lifecycle of a given product, where N is used to denote the current version. Anything older than N-2 is generally considered out of currency. Product vendors generally stop issuing security patches and updates for out of currency items.

Linear Equation – is an equation that has a degree no higher than 1. When graphed, a linear equation is always a (straight) line.

Non-Linear Equation – is an equation that has a degree higher than 1. When graphed, a non-linear equation is always a curve, a degree 2 is a parabola, a degree 3 is generally a curvy x-shape or other curvy variations thereof.

Further Reading

Sobers R (2020) The Likelihood of a Cyber Attack Compared. Varonis Inside Out Security Blog. https://www.varonis.com/blog/likelihood-of-a-cyber-attack/. Accessed 06 Jan, 2021

General Electric (2017) Cyber Security and the Probability Challenge. https://www.ge.com/digital/sites/default/files/download_assets/Cyber-Security-and-the-Probability-Challenge.pdf. Accessed

Liu Q, Xing L, Zhou C (2019) Probabilistic modeling and analysis of sequential cyber-attacks. Engineering Reports. 2019;1: e12065. https://doi.org/10.1002/eng2.12065.

Wikipedia (2020) Cyber risk quantification, https://en.wikipedia.org/wiki/Cyber_risk_quantification. Accessed 19 Jan, 2021.

Privacy Concerns from Publicly Available Meta-data

1 Introduction

Data privacy is at the top of everyone's mind, and it should be, given the high profile unauthorized personally identifiable information (PII) disclosures and breaches that have recently hit the average unsuspecting consumer (e.g., Facebook, Marriott). Apart from these unauthorized disclosures and breaches that are deliberate and mostly malicious, there are various other non-deliberate avenues for potential exposure or disclosure of sensitive data of many unsuspecting users, some of which are disclosed below.

2 Concerns

The numerous applications and systems that we use in our daily lives collect significant amounts of PII. The GPS in our phones and in our cars, and the pictures we take and post on social media, among many other apps, all have geotagging and PII storage capabilities. Geotagging refers to latitude and longitude coordinates, giving a precise location. When one takes a picture with a digital camera or a smart phone these days, its logs the global positioning satellite (GPS) coordinates (i.e., latitude and longitude coordinates also known as geotagging) and embeds it in the image meta data stored in a structured format known as exchangeable image file format (EXIF). The EXIF data travels with the photograph (or video) and can be viewed by anyone that has access to the picture to determine with great accuracy the time, the location where it was taken and even the unique identifier of the device used. The EXIF data format is also used to store meta-data on audio (wav) files as well and enables tracking capabilities similar to those for the image files.

R. Badhwar, *The CISO's Next Frontier*,
https://doi.org/10.1007/978-3-030-75354-2_44

3 Recommendations

Although storing meta-data like this enables the capability to arrange pictures, it can also be used to review and even edit and/or fix the images. Privacy concerns outweigh the usefulness. Now that there is a bit more awareness about this 'feature,' lingering privacy and unauthorized data exposure concerns can be addressed by disabling the gathering and storing of this data. Some recommendations are below:

1. The geotagging capability on your devices can be turned off. This is applicable to mobile phones, cameras, and most of the apps on your mobile phone or your tablet that have the capability to geotag you or store and report this data to Apple, Samsung, Google or the app manufacturer (e.g., Facebook).
2. All the EXIF data (or other meta-data) can be manually deleted before the images or audio files are published on a social media platform or otherwise.

I am also providing here what social media platforms do with this meta-data before they load the images and audio/video files. Obviously, if you send these images or files through email then the meta-data is not deleted by the email carriers or the ISPs that transport it.

(a) Facebook, Instagram, Twitter, eBay and Craigslist seem to delete the metadata as part of pre-processing before they load the data to their online platforms.
(b) Flickr, Google Photo, Tumblr and Google+ (now defunct) do not seem to delete the metadata.

Please note that whether this data is deleted or not before posting online, there is a high probability that these platforms may save and mine this data for targeted advertising campaigns. Although this data may not be available to the folks that may view or download your images, it is still susceptible to leak through third parties (e.g., Cambridge Analytica) that these platforms may share the data with, or if it is stolen through frequent network and data breaches.

4 CISO Take

If this worries you, then the best way to protect yourself from the risk of disclosure is to either delete this metadata yourself (some of which is as simple has viewing the document properties and deleting the offending data elements), configure your camera and other applications not to store this data before posting to social media (although sometimes the settings are refreshed when the apps or software is updated), or if possible, not sharing the data itself on a publicly available platform.

The CISOs must impress upon the electronics manufacturers and the social media platform providers to ensure that all meta data in their respective platforms and systems containing personal data elements is de-identified using a one-way hash so that it cannot be traced back to violate the privacy of the persons involved.

It must also be encrypted while at rest using NIST approved algorithms, to protect it from any data breaches. They can also propose tactical compromises by getting agreements from the social media providers to make it easy for the said data to be deleted by the owners themselves or the aggressive aging-out of that meta-data while universal de-identification type capability can be built and made generally available.

5 Definitions

De-identification – is the process used to prevent the exposure of sensitive or personal data. This is generally achieved by masking the data using hashing cryptographic functions.

EXIF – stands for exchangeable image file format. It is a standard that specifies the information that maybe stored for digital media recorded by equipment like digital cameras and video recorders. The information stored includes but it not limited to date/time the media was captured, GPS location etc.

PII – stands for Personally Identifiable Information. Any representation of information that permits the identity of an individual to whom the information applies to be reasonably inferred by either direct or indirect means. Further, PII is defined as information: (i) that directly identifies an individual (e.g., name, address, social security number or other identifying number or code, telephone number, or email address) or (ii) by which an agency intends to identify specific individuals in conjunction with other data elements, i.e., indirect identification [1].

GPS – stands for global positioning satellite. It is a global navigation system based on satellites that works free of cost $24 \times 7 \times 365$ under any weather conditions. The satellites used were originally put into orbit by the DOD for military use, but then were made available for (global) civilian use in the 1980s.

Reference

1. US department of Labor (2020). Guidance on the Protection of Personal Identifiable Information. https://www.dol.gov/general/ppii

Further Reading

Ghazinour K, Ponchak J (2017), Hidden Privacy Risks in Sharing Pictures on Social Media, https://www.sciencedirect.com/science/article/pii/S1877050917317775, Accessed Dec 5, 2020

Nair R, Ahern S et al (2007). Over-Exposed? Privacy Patterns and Considerations in Online and Mobile Photo Sharing – http://infolab.stanford.edu/~mor/research/chi241-ahern-mediaprivacy.pdf, Accessed Dec 5, 2020

Roulo C (2018), What on Earth is the Global Positioning System? https://www.defense.gov/Explore/Features/story/Article/1674004/what-on-earth-is-the-global-positioning-system/. Accessed Dec 24, 2020

Dark Web & Dark Net

1 Genesis

There is a lot of chatter about the Dark Web today. The Dark Web is generally presumed to be associated solely with the Internet's hotbed of malicious and anomalous activities. This is presumed to be a hotbed for the sale of everything from user credentials, email addresses, and passwords; to ransomware kits and advanced malware and DDoS attack as a Service to target unsuspecting victims. This is presumed to be the place where hackers have been enabled by various data breaches of sites such as Marriott, Equifax, Yahoo, Home Depot, Target, or JP Morgan Chase to engage in illicit trade and outright theft of personally identifiable information (PII) and other sensitive information; where stolen private keys or client or server certificates could be obtained; or where people can buy illegal drugs or controlled substances and medication without prescriptions.

Do you know what? All this is true, but rather than focusing just on the negative, we security technologists have to look at both sides of the coin. The technology that powers the dark web and Dark net was originally created by security engineers and technologists to anonymize internet traffic for the protection of journalists, human rights professionals, whistle-blowers, victims of (domestic) abuse and other activists. Anonymizing the internet traffic of these groups prevents them from being targeted online and allows them to bypass (regional) censorship.

2   Introduction

Rather than only bemoaning the threats, let's talk about and understand the technology and associated terminology.

(a) **Internet 1** – The internet is nothing more than a network of interconnected computers over public or private networks - it is also called the commodity internet (aka Internet1) with average data download speeds of 4 mbps.

(b) **Internet 2** – provides a secure high-speed network with gigabit speeds connected via the Abilene network to provide cloud solutions, research support, and services tailored for research and educational institutions. It is thus at least 100 times faster than regular internet.

(c) **Surface Web** (aka the World Wide Web) – The surface web is that part of the internet that is publicly available to anyone and everyone on the planet that has an internet connection. It is indexed and searchable with the standard search engines (e.g., Google, Bing, Yahoo). Contrary to popular belief, the surface web only forms a fraction of the total content available on the internet.

(d) **The Deep Web** is that part of the *commodity internet* that is either not accessible to the general public or not searchable by them using the standard search engines. Most of the (web) content on the deep web is confidential or private and is only available via direct links. The deep web is by far the largest component of the internet.

(e) **The Dark Web** is that part of the deep web that is only accessible by using a web anonymizer (Dark Net). The websites on the dark web run on hidden services and are identified with Onion addresses – where the clients and onion sites negotiate rendezvous points to establish a connection. The IP addresses of the servers that host the websites on the dark web are hidden (masked) and also transient (short-lived) in nature. The dark web is generally used for illegal activities or criminal enterprises but could also be used by reporters, whistle-blowers and dissidents in authoritarian countries.

(f) **Dark Net** – Is the anonymous network (e.g., Tor, I2P, and Freenet) that enables access to the websites on the dark web and have the inherent capability to avoid surveillance and tracking.

3   Tor

Tor was developed and is now maintained by the Tor project (https://www.torproject.org/), a nonprofit organization. The patent for the onion network for securely moving data through communication networks is held by the United States Government (USG). Generally, there is a browser that is installed on a client machine that connects to a Tor network entry node which encrypts or layers requests to ensure that nodes trace only to the previous node, not back to the source. The client negotiates a separate set of encryption keys for each hop on circuit; each hop can't trace these connections as they pass through, thereby providing the capability to do the following:

(a) Anonymize internet traffic and browsing
(b) Protect journalists, human rights professionals, whistle-blowers, victims of (domestic) abuse and other activists from being targeted online
(c) Bypass (regional) censorship

3.1   Using Tor in Combination with Virtual Private Network (VPN)

It is highly recommended that Tor be used in conjunction with a VPN service, for the following capabilities:

(a) Maintain the confidentiality of the user's IP address by making it anonymous to the Tor entry node
(b) Encrypt some of network traffic that Tor does not natively support (e.g., ICMP)
(c) Protect against DNS leaks
(d) Maintain the confidentiality of the user from his/her own ISP or carrier (i.e., obscuring the fact that they are connecting to Tor)

3.2   Using Tor in Combination with Pretty Good Privacy (PGP)

It is highly recommended that Tor be used in conjunction with PGP to enhance the confidentiality of email traffic.

3.3   Using Tor in Corporate Environments

Due to its purported use for malicious activities, traffic anonymization or other cyber hacking type activities, it is my recommendation that Tor not be used in corporate settings unless its use is necessitated for whistleblower type use cases. Most modern corporate security environments generally block the download of the Tor browser and any off-network acquisition and subsequent usage of the same on a corporate network or asset may trip endpoint or network security based monitoring alerts leading to the traffic or connection being blocked by corporate proxies. The usage of Tor (from home) may also be monitored by ISPs and other governmental entities, and thus if it must be used for ethical and legally justified use cases then its best to use it in conjunction with VPN to maintain the anonymity of the user.

4   The CISO Take

The dark web and dark net bring tremendous risk to business entities, individual consumers and users worldwide. The risk can potentially be mitigated by doing periodic or targeted searches and scanning to identify any impacted businesses, consumers and users whose data may have been found to be exposed. The companies should also consider investing in Threat Intel platforms that can get real-time intelligence for company user or customer data found to be resident on the dark web or being discussed in internet chatter.

There are some remedial actions available including but not limited to engaging law enforcement agencies. (although this is easier said than done due to the global aspect of the dark web).

However, using Dark web and dark net capabilities also raises ethical concerns – e.g., should the security teams purchase credentials or other sensitive data on the dark web marketplaces in order to learn what company information may have leaked? If customer or partner data is found, should they proactively inform the users although the data may be stale or even a false positive. The disclosure laws for this specific example reside in a gray area. Security technologists must face such ethical dilemmas by identifying which use-cases are justified and which are not by close consultation with their legal and compliance teams.

5   Definitions

DNS – stands for Domain Name System. It is a global naming system which enables the mapping and the subsequent syncing of a website or other internet/intranet-hosted resource name, to an IP address.

ICMP – stands for Internet Control Message Protocol. It is a protocol within the internet protocol suite and is generally used by network devices like routers to diagnose network communication issues.

PGP – stands for pretty good privacy. It is an open-source data encryption technology that can be used to encrypt and decrypt unstructured data (i.e., files) and emails.

VPN – stands for virtual private network. It provides the capability to extend a private (corporate) network across a public network (e.g., the internet) assigning a remote user a private IP address and enabling a remote user or employee to send and receive data as if he/she were onsite at a corporate facility.

Further Reading

Feigenbaum J, Johnson A et al (2007), A Model of Onion Routing with Provable Anonymity, https://www.researchgate.net/publication/220796974_A_Model_of_Onion_Routing_with_Provable_Anonymity. Accessed 12 Dec 2020.

Internet2. https://internet2.edu/community/about-us/, Accessed Dec 8, 2020.

Onion Routing. https://www.onion-router.net/, Accessed Dec 8, 2020.

Øverlier L, Syverson P (2007), Improving efficiency and simplicity of Tor circuit establishment and hidden services. https://www.petsymposium.org/2007/papers/PET2007_preproc_Improving_efficiency.pdf, Accessed 12 Dec 2020.

Reed M, Syverson P et al (2001), US Patent – Onion Routing network for securely moving data through communication networks, https://patentimages.storage.googleapis.com/05/26/89/e2080c39d938c4/US6266704.pdf, Accessed 12 Dec 2020.

Tor. https://www.torproject.org/, Accessed Dec 8, 2020.

Risk-Based Vulnerability Management

1 Introduction

Vulnerability Management, one of the most important functions within any cyber program, is the best way to provide for the security of a given organization by ensuring that all known vulnerabilities have been patched and any new vulnerabilities get patched as soon as they are discovered or disclosed.

2 Risk Treatment

Practically speaking, for a medium to large organization housing large amounts of sensitive data with hundreds or even thousands of applications, tens of thousands of servers and user endpoints, and network appliances, it is not feasible to patch all vulnerabilities upon disclosure or discovery.

Generally, these vulnerabilities are patched based on the level of severity or criticality of the weakness commensurate with the amount of risk that they may pose to the security posture and state of an enterprise.

2.1 Risk Rating

As a de facto industry standard, vulnerabilities are risk rated by level of severity, along with the general time period by which they need to be patched.

2.2 Risk Scoring

The risk rating scheme (critical, high, medium, low) discussed above in Table 1 is determined using risk scores. These risk scores are standardized across the industry using the **Common Vulnerability Scoring System** (CVSS) which "provides a way to capture the principal characteristics of a vulnerability and produce a numerical score reflecting its severity. The numerical score can then be translated into a qualitative representation (such as low, medium, high, and critical) to help organizations properly assess and prioritize their vulnerability management processes" [1].

This universally accepted score generated by CVSS is also used in the common vulnerabilities and exposures (CVE) which is a list of entries of publicly known cybersecurity vulnerabilities, each containing an identification number, a description, and at least one public reference.

The risk rating is driven by the CVSS score range and is provided below in Table 2.

3 Risk Optimization and Re-rating

As discussed in the previous section, under ideal conditions for cyber risk management, all the vulnerabilities would be fixed according to their severity rating in the time allocated. However, the reality is that the number of vulnerabilities for any medium-sized or large corporation with sensitive data and a relatively large portfolio of diverse apps is so large, that the cost to remediate all known critical, high, medium, and low vulnerabilities in the time period recommended by the de facto industry standard is not only cost prohibitive but also very time consuming.

These impediments often lead to several bad behaviors:

(a) IT teams generally prioritize vulnerability remediation without consulting information security teams or taking cyber risk into account.

Table 1 Risk scoring

Rating	Patch period	Comment
Critical	Must be patched immediately.	Can be catastrophic if exploited. These issues include zero-days.
High	Patched in 30 days.	Issues that still pose a significant risk and need to be patched as soon as possible but need thorough testing to avoid any app downtime or outages if a patch is rushed to production.
Medium	Patched in 90 days.	Issue poses medium level risk but can cumulatively become high risk if multiple medium issues go unfixed for a given application or system.
Low	Patched in 365 days.	Lowest risk, but must neither be ignored nor risk accepted for prolonged periods. Many firms tend to risk accept these items.

Table 2 Risk rating

Risk rating	CVSS score range
Critical	9.0–10.0
High	7.0–8.9
Medium	4.0–6.9
Low	0.1–3.9

(b) IT teams may defer vulnerability remediations, citing lack of financial resources or availability of test environments or unavailability of slots for production deployments.

(c) IT teams may decide to risk accept some of the high or medium vulnerabilities and assume risk on behalf of the corporation.

(d) The above three approaches lead to a large cumulative backlog of some high, many medium, and a large number of low-risk unpatched vulnerabilities.

In balancing enterprise IT software and product release deadlines with the urgency of patching of security vulnerabilities, CISOs need to devise ways to walk a tightrope of ensuring that high-risk vulnerabilities posing a real threat to the enterprise are remediated within the patch period, without impacting weekly, monthly, or quarterly releases on the one hand, and without adding to a large backlog of high and medium-risk vulnerabilities on the other. CISOs must at the same time devise ways for security and IT teams to be aware of risks with lower probability of exploitation or occurrence.

This is possible if the vulnerabilities ratings and scores can be optimized and potentially changed (reduced) from the universal scores by also accounting for the local security controls in place for a given enterprise.

3.1   Universal Risk Score

The Universal Risk Score is the CVSS risk score provided for a vulnerability rating (see Table 2).

3.2   Local Risk Rating

The local risk rating in accordance with the local risk score is calculated as an optimization. (equivalent to the rating/score in Table 2).

3.3   Local Defensive Factor

This factor is representative of a defensive posture of a firm's cyberinfrastructure ecosystem or a specific datacenter or cloud environment. It can be applied at a micro- or macro-level. It encompasses several capabilities: to deploy counter measures against malware and other advanced threats, or against insider threats; to deploy monitoring and mitigating controls; to hire educated and well-trained cyber security professionals; to develop a mature security stack, including but not limited to perimeter, network, and endpoint security tools; and to implement good security hygiene and practices like Zero Trust with least privilege and full network (micro) segmentation.

The defensive factor accounts for the exploitability and occurrence of the vulnerabilities as applied to the local environment, and the local security controls, and defense-in-depth implementation that can reduce the severity of one or more high vulnerabilities.

The defensive factor is generally calculated as an average of maturity scores of multiple security domains – endpoint security, network/web/cloud security, perimeter security, and currency posture.

The currency posture reflects the extent to which the application and security stack is current (i.e., N or N-1), the extent to which network infrastructure and application deployments are based on Zero Trust, and the maturity of human capital.

The cumulative local defensive factor (*ldf*) used for this book has a scale of 0.85–1.0. It is a hypothesis based on observed data. It uses a simplified scoring scheme derived from an average of observed scores for the various defensive variables discussed above, which exhibit non-linear behavior (see Fig. 1).

The lower the numerical value of the *ldf*, the higher the risk reduction.

- Excellent – 0.85
- Good – 0.90
- Medium – 0.99
- Poor – 1.0
- None – 1.0

3.4   Local Threat Factor

This factor is representative of a local threat posture of a firm's cyberinfrastructure ecosystem. It is inclusive of but not limited to the risk and susceptibility from advanced malware, sophisticated threat actors, or malicious entities (e.g., criminals, nation states) and other forms of advanced persistent threat, and insider threat. This score tracks other unhygienic conditions such as a lack of network micro-segmentation, lack of data at rest and transit encryption, lack of monitoring and visibility of application and network stack, and a large backlog of vulnerabilities.

Fig.1 Risk based Patching

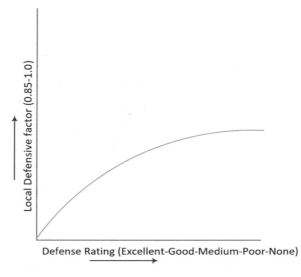

Copyright 2020 – Raj Badhwar

The local threat factor (*ltf*) used for this book has a scale of 1.0–0.85. It is a hypothesis based on observed data. It uses a simplified scoring scheme that is based on an average of observed scores for the various threat variables discussed above, which exhibit non-linear behavior (see Fig. 2).

The higher the numerical value of *ltf*, the lower the risk reduction.

- Critical – 1.0
- High – 1.0
- Medium – 0.99
- Low – 0.90
- None – 0.85

3.5 Local Risk Score

The local risk score accounts for the local security controls and defensive posture. It uses a scale of 0.1–10, which is the same as the universal risk score (Table 2).

$$\textbf{Local Risk } Score\left(lrs\right) = \textbf{Universal Risk Score}\left(urs\right)*$$
$$\textbf{Local Defensive Factor}\left(ldf\right)*\textbf{Local Threat Factor}\left(ltf\right)$$

Thus, $lsr(x) = urs(x) * ldf(x) * ltf(x)$
Where x is the vulnerability being examined for optimization.

Fig. 2

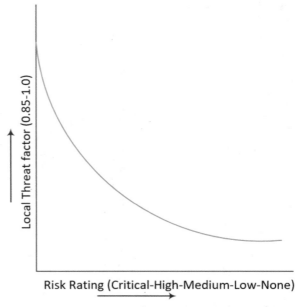

Copyright 2020 – Raj Badhwar

4   Simple Case Study

Let's assume the following about a firm's on-premises subnet (DMZ):

- There are three high-risk vulnerabilities with universal risk scores of 10, 9.5, 9.1; and a cloud environment VPC with three high-risk vulnerabilities with universal risk scores of 10, 9.6, 9.2.
- The on-premises defensive factor is good (0.9), and the local threat factor is medium (0.99).
- The cloud defensive factor is medium (0.99), and the local threat factor is high (1.0).

Using the equation from above, these are the new local risk scores:

10*0.9*0.99 = 8.91
9.5*0.9*0.99 = 8.5
9.1*0.9*0.99 = 8.1

10*0.99*1.0 = 9.9
9.6*0.99*1.0 = 9.5
9.2*0.99*1.0 = 9.1

Conversely, if another on-premises subnet had:

- Two medium vulnerabilities with scores of 8.8 and 7.5, and another cloud VPC had two medium vulnerabilities with scores of 8.6 and 7.0;
- An on-premises defensive factor of medium (0.99) and a local threat factor of medium (0.99);
- A cloud defensive factor of medium (0.99) and a high local threat factor (1.0);

then the new local risk scores would be:

$8.8*0.99*0.99 = 8.6$
$7.5*0.99*0.99 = 7.35$

$8.6*0.99*1.0 = 8.5$
$7.0*0.99*1.0 = 6.93$

To summarize, the hypothesis asserts that the universal risk score assigned for a vulnerability by an OEM or product owner can be optimized based on the defensive and threat scores for a given environment.

5   The CISO Take

It is the responsibility of CISOs to ensure that all the vulnerabilities within the application, infrastructure, and network stack are patched in accordance with their risk rating.

Practically speaking, a lot of corporations in the financial, defense, and medical services sectors have built quite a bit of technology debt running many legacy applications with a large number of vulnerabilities, which have not been patched or cannot be patched because the applications running on the legacy technology stack are in need of rewrites. While CISOs have made inroads and are getting these vulnerabilities patched by making the case to CIOs, sometimes the large backlog, in addition to the large number of new vulnerabilities discovered on a monthly basis (e.g., monthly patch Tuesday for Windows), makes it very difficult to patch all known vulnerabilities within the agreed upon remediation terms of SLAs.

If all known vulnerabilities cannot be patched, due to either financial or technical constraints, then CISOs must prioritize the patching of the vulnerabilities posing the highest risk to the environment, depending upon vulnerability occurrence or exploitability. The other option also available to CISOs is to re-assess the vulnerability risk rating to ensure that the universal risk rating assigned by the OEMs is appropriate for their environment, since the actual level of risk from a vulnerability tagged as high risk may vary, depending on whether the overall environment is mature and secure, or not so secure.

This chapter provides a hypothetical approach of using a basic self-service technique to perform the vulnerability risk re-assessment. While engaging a professional services company specializing in this arena (e.g., FireEye/Mandiant, Microsoft, or PWC) would provide more accurate results, this could definitely be a good starting point for small to medium-sized firms. This would also build in the needed hygiene for continuous cyber risk re-assessment for legacy and new vulnerabilities and make sure any risk accepted due to non-patching or delayed patching remains within risk tolerance limits.

6 Disclaimer

The vulnerability risk and score re-assessment technique provided in the chapter is hypothetical. If you choose to follow this technique or approach, then you must do so at your own risk.

7 Definitions

DMZ – is a "demilitarized zone," a restricted subnet between the intranet and the internet, generally used to host external-facing sites and services.

Reference

1. Forum of Incident Response and Security Teams (FIRST) (2020) Common Vulnerability Scoring System SIG. https://www.first.org/cvss/. Accessed 05 December 2020

Index

© The Author(s), under exclusive license to Springer Nature Switzerland AG 2021   379
R. Badhwar, *The CISO's Next Frontier*, https://doi.org/10.1007/978-3-030-75354-2

Printed in the United States
by Baker & Taylor Publisher Services